Walst

2009

VOICES
FROM THE
DARK YEARS

VOICES
FROM THE
DARK YEARS

THE TRUTH ABOUT
OCCUPIED FRANCE 1940–1945

DOUGLAS BOYD

SUTTON PUBLISHING

First published in the United Kingdom in 2007 by
Sutton Publishing, an imprint of NPI Media Group Limited
Cirencester Road · Chalford · Stroud · Gloucestershire · GL6 8PE

British Library Cataloguing in Publication Data
A catalogue record for this book is available from the British Library.

Hardback ISBN 978-0-7509-4116-7
Paperback ISBN 978-0-7509-4117-4

Typesetting and origination by
NPI Media Group Limited.
Printed and bound in England.

*'Having no literary pretensions, I never intended to publish my notes.
Yet now, when so many want to forget it all happened,
we must go on record.'*
Pierre Mignon, farmer, patriot and survivor of the
extermination camps

'History tends not to repeat itself exactly. Next time, it could be worse.'
Renée De Monbrison, who wore a yellow star in the Occupied Zone

'If I could not be your sword, at least I have been your shield.'
Marshal Philippe Pétain, in his last message to the nation before being
abducted to Germany by the SS in August 1944

'Everything I did was for France and the cause of peace.'
Pierre Laval, shortly before he was executed for high treason at Fresnes
prison on 15 October 1945

CONTENTS

List of Abbreviations		ix
List of Illustrations		xi
Acknowledgements		xv
Introduction		xvii

PART 1: DEFEAT AND OCCUPATION

1	From Sitzkrieg to Blitzkrieg	3
2	Pétain Quells the Panic	11
3	An End to the Killing	23
4	'Trust the German Soldier!'	33
5	Behold the Man!	41
6	The Lie that was True	47
7	The Number of the Beast	57

PART 2: LIFE, LOOT AND LOVE UNDER PÉTAIN'S NEW ORDER

8	Clearing up the Mess	67
9	Of Cheese, Plays and Books	79
10	Of Bread and Circuses	91
11	Courage of a Quiet Kind	103
12	Of Culture and Crops	117
13	Saving the Children	129
14	The Women's Ordeal	145
15	'We have Learned of the Scenes of Horror . . .'	157
16	The Protests Gather Strength	165

PART 3: 1944 – THE BEGINNING OF THE END

17	Soap and Sabotage	175
18	Casualties in the Great Game	185
19	Happy New Year!	199
20	Dancing in the Dark	211

PART 4: THE PRICE OF LIBERATION

21 Atrocities on Both Sides   221
22 Murderous Midsummer   233
23 'Hell is the Others'   243
24 A Carpet of Women's Hair   253
25 Death of a Town   261
26 After the War was Over . . .   267

    Notes and Sources   275
    Further Reading in English   289
    Index   291

LIST OF ABBREVIATIONS

BCRA	Bureau Central de Renseignements et d'Action – eventual title of the London-based coordinating centre of Gaullist intelligence networks
BEF	British Expeditionary Force
CGQJ	Commissariat Générale aux Questions Juives – main body charged with enforcing anti-Semitic laws
CNR	Conseil National de la Résistance
EIF	Eclaireurs Israélites de France – the Jewish Scout movement
ERR	Einsatzstab Reichsleiter Rosenberg – Nazi Cultural Agency
FFI	Forces Françaises de l'Intérieur – Free French forces inside France
FFO	Forces Françaises de l'Ouest
FTP	Francs-Tireurs et Partisans – left-wing Resistance movement
GFP	Geheime Feldpolizei – German Military Police investigation branch
GP	Groupe de Protection – Pétain's bodyguard
LVF	Légion de Volontaires Français – French volunteers fighting in German uniform
MSR	Mouvement Social Revolutionnaire
NSKK	Nationalsozialistiche KraftfahrKorps – the armed and uniformed corps of volunteer drivers working for the Wehrmacht
OKW	Oberkommandantur der Wehrmacht – German Army High Command
PCF	Parti Communiste Français – French Communist Party
PPF	Parti Populaire Français – Doriot's extreme right-wing party
PQJ	Police aux Questions Juives – special anti-Jewish police force
RG	Renseignements Généraux – French equivalent of Special Branch
RHSA	Reichshauptsicherheitsampt – Himmler's umbrella organisation running SS and SD
RMVE	Régiment de Marche de Volontaires Etrangers
RNP	Rassemblement National Populaire – Déat's extreme right-wing party
SD	Sicherheitsdienst – Amt VI of RHSA covering external security
SIS	British Secret Intelligence Service
SNCF	Société des Chemins de Fer Français – French state railway system

SOL   Service d'Ordre Légionnaire – forerunner of the Milice

SPAC   Service de Police Anti-Communiste – anti-Communist police units

STO   Service de Travail Obligatoire – organisation of compulsory labour in the Reich

UGIF   Union Générale des Israélites de France – umbrella organisation by which the Germans organised the fate of the Jewish community

LIST OF ILLUSTRATIONS

PLATES

1. Propaganda photograph of General Charles De Gaulle
2. Official portrait of Marshal Philippe Pétain
3. Marshal Pétain and Prime Minister Laval
4. Louis De La Bardonnie and wife after his release from concentration camp[1]
5. The Bardonnie children[1]
6. One of Louis De La Bardonnie's false ID cards[1]
7. Identity photograph from another of the false ID cards[1]
8. Château La Roque
9. Type 3 Mk 2 transceiver
10. Charles De Gaulle as head of government visiting Château La Roque post-war[1]
11. Certificate of appreciation signed by General Montgomery[1]
12. Wedding of Cathérine Bouchou and Robert Hestin[3]
13. Marius Bouchou in naval reservist's uniform[3]
14. Identity card photograph of Georges Chabrier[2]
15. Sten guns, Lee-Enfield .303 rifles and MAS 36 rifle from cache discovered in 1998
16. 9 mm ammunition from the cache
17. Browning pistol and ammunition from cache
18. Former Gestapo HQ in Castillon-la-Bataille
19. Joseph Darnand
20. Eugène Deloncle
21. Occupation street scene: *gendarme* working with Wehrmacht soldier
22. French police chief René Bousquet with SS General Oberg
23. Victor Faynsylber and his children
24. Jewish detainees leaving Vélodrome d'Hiver for Drancy camp
25. General Delestraint
26. Official portrait of Jean Moulin as Prefect
27. Jean Moulin in his undercover identity as 'Max'
28. Klaus Barbie
29. Renée De Monbrison[4]
30. Captain Frenay

31. Colonel Pommiès
32. Kriegsmarine Feldwebel Stahlschmidt
33. General Von Choltitz
34. German military band near Place Vendôme, Paris
35. Official portrait of Prefect François Martin
36. Commemorative plaque at La Maison de Moissac
37. La Maison de Moissac
38. Shatta Simon and son[5]
39. French Chief Scouts on solidarity visit with Shatta Simon at Maison de Moissac[5]
40. Some of Shatta Simon's girls camping[5]
41. Group of the Moissac EIF scouts singing[5]
42. Young recorder class at La Maison de Moissac[5]
43. Older boys learning metalwork at La Maison de Moissac[5]
44. Major Helmut Kampfe, assassinated by *maquisards* near Oradour-sur-Glane
45. Major Adolf Diekmann, who commanded the SS at Oradour
46. Colonel Stadler of SS Division Das Reich
47. Main street in Oradour after the fires
48. Butcher's shop at Oradour after fire
49. Oradour church where the women and children died
50. Class picture of some of the children murdered at Oradour
51. Altar showing window through which Madame Rouffanche escaped
52. SS bullet holes in memorial plaque
53. Marguerite Rouffanche, the sole survivor from the church
54. Human-powered road-roller, Natzwiller-Struthof
55. The main gate of Natzwiller-Struthof concentration camp
56. Natzwiller-Struthof in the 1930s
57. The gas chamber, Natzwiller-Struthof
58. The camp gallows, Natzwiller-Struthof
59. Detail of Edwardian poster for the casino at Royan
60. Royan casino after the Allied bombing raids
61. Aerial view of Royan after the raids
62. Two Sikhs in German uniform on the Atlantic Wall
63. Wehrmacht soldiers surrendering in the Royan pocket
64. Three *maquisards* with parachuted Stens
65. General De Gaulle pinning medal on General De Larminat

All photographs are from the author's personal collection except: 1. reproduced by permission of Jacques De La Bardonnie; 2. reproduced by permission of Christian Chabrier; 3. reproduced by permission of Cathérine and Robert Hestin; 4. reproduced by permission of Françoise De Monbrison-Blanchard; and 5. reproduced by permission of Jean-Claude Simon.

MAPS AND ILLUSTRATIONS

De Gaulle's broadcast, 18 June 1940	26
Map of France divided by the Armistice	30
Bread tickets	39
Georges Chabrier's permission to cross the Demarcation Line	104
Map of Castillon area	106
School holiday pass	122
Hostage ordinance	126
Anti-sabotage poster	127
Sippenhaft ordinance	152
Map of concentration and deportation camps, August 1942	155
Charles Wajsfelner's last postcard from Drancy	160
Map of occupied France after 11 November 1942	176
Award of Légion d'honneur to Marie-Jeanne Bouchou	188
Award of Légion d'honneur to Marius Bouchou	189
Letter informing Kramer of his Christmas bonus	195
Map of the German pockets of resistance after June 1944	263
Teletype of Royan bombing mission order	265

ACKNOWLEDGEMENTS

Many people contributed to the research for this book by re-living with me their experiences during the dark years of the German occupation of France. They recalled moments of anguish and joy, of triumph and shame, of fear and hope. They unearthed personal papers, showed me treasured mementoes and lent precious documents, manuscripts, photographs and books on trust. Many said at the end of our meeting, 'I haven't helped you much,' but research is like an iceberg: it is the nine-tenths below the water-line that gives balance and perspective.

From Bordeaux in the south-west of France to Schirmeck in Alsace, survivors asked to remain anonymous after telling me things they had never divulged to anyone else. To them goes my greatest gratitude. Among those I can thank, in Tarn-et-Garonne Andrée Fourcassié, née Giraud, was my unassuming guide to the misty timescape of the past, opening doors I should never otherwise have known existed; Chantal Fraïsse welcomed me to the Archives Municipales of Moissac; Joseph and Paulette Gouzi offered hospitality, shared memories and lent precious unpublished documentation, while Jean-Claude Simon made available photographs of the Maison de Moissac rescue operation and Françoise Blanchard, née De Monbrison, unlocked the rich resource of her family's published and unpublished records of the Occupation.

In Paris, Naomi Wilson shared her research for a PhD thesis on women's experience of the Occupation. In Gironde, Christian Chabrier, Jacques De La Bardonnie, Cathérine and Robert Hestin and many other neighbours and friends dug into their personal memories; Major Len Chaganis unearthed material on Operation Cockade; and the wife of dying hero Henri Salmide (formerly Heinz Stahlschmidt) put aside her grief to talk to me. In Lot-et-Garonne, Guy De La Bardonnie generously shared both published and unpublished resources. In Charentes, Philippe Delaurain gave me the benefit of his encyclopedic knowledge of the Occupation, as well as access to his unsubsidised museum, Le Musée de la Poche, which tells so well the story of the Royan pocket of resistance. And fellow BBC-pensioners Don Craven and Brian Johnson helped me track down the Morse Vee-sign used for so many broadcasts to occupied Europe.

With good reason, historical writers thank the spouses or partners who tolerate the solitude imposed by their craft and their spending more time with the dead than the living. For a person as sociable as Atarah, this is doubly hard; her enthusiasm and active support is more valued than she imagines. Among my predecessors on the research trail, the American historian Robert Paxton deserves acclaim for first shining the light of enquiry on the dark years at a time when nobody in France wanted to talk about them.

On a professional plane, my thanks go to my agent Mandy Little for introducing me to Sutton Publishing, where Senior Commissioning Editor Jonathan Falconer went fishing for a book that did not yet exist in the author's mind – and hooked this one. It is always a pleasure for an author to work with a team that has done him more than proud on previous books. Calmly presiding over the production again was Jane Hutchings, surely among the world's most flexible and least flappable project editors; Elizabeth Stone pulled the book into shape as copy-editor; and for the third time Martin Latham magicked the right cover for a book of mine. To them all, my thanks.

INTRODUCTION

The seed of this book was sown at a diplomatic reception in Bordeaux by an elderly Englishman who confided to me, out of earshot of the French guests, that he first saw the city through the bomb-sight of an RAF Lancaster during the Second World War. When I asked whether he had been targeting the immense bombproof shelters constructed by the Todt Organisation for the long-range German submarines that wrought havoc among the Atlantic convoys, he laughed: 'With all that Jerry flak coming up at us, all I cared about was dropping my load and getting back home in time for breakfast.'

Since befriending a French *assistant* from Normandy while at school, I had known that RAF strategic bombing raids killed thousands of innocent French civilians during the war and destroyed entire towns, but it was not until several years after meeting the bomb-aimer that this book took shape over lunch in a Gloucestershire pub with my editor Jonathan Falconer: an account of the Occupation of France, not as seen from London and Washington, but as *lived* by the French people.

President John F. Kennedy observed that the great enemy of the truth is very often 'not the lie . . . but the myth, persistent, persuasive and unrealistic'. Because of the way the media were used for propaganda purposes in wartime, two contradictory myths became the accepted bases for the history of the Occupation. In France, people said that Lord Gort's British Expeditionary Force had fought 'to the last drop of French blood' before running away in 1940. Conversely, standing alone against German-dominated Europe, Britain fortified itself with the counter-myth that the French Army had cracked and run because our erstwhile allies lacked moral fibre. 'It would never happen here,' people boasted, forgetting how Britain's cleverest and most privileged sons voted by 275 to 153 at the Oxford Union in 1933 that 'this House would not fight for King and Country'. So it could well have 'happened here', but for the 20 miles of water between a largely unprepared Britain and her abandoned continental allies.

Similarly, it is easy to pretend that the British would never have collaborated if conquered, yet London in the thirties saw street fighting between Fascists and Communists and window-smashing of Jewish-owned shops. Long into the Second World War many Britons of all social strata were both anti-Semitic and either supported Hitler or wanted an accommodation with him.

On screen and in print, the German Occupation of France is polarised as a period when the French people united against its alien occupiers and a handful of traitors working for them. The truth is that about 1 per cent of the population was actively pro-German and about the same proportion was committed to resistance before 1944. Finding work, food and heating, tilling one's fields or running a business, or simply trying to keep a family together, were so time-consuming in that era of shortages, fear and repression that most French people could do little about the Occupation except take François Mauriac's advice: 'Have eyes that see nothing.'

The largest single organised faction of the essentially urban Resistance was the French Communist Party (PCF). Controlled from Moscow by the Comintern, it hampered the French war effort for the first twenty months of the war in line with the non-aggression pact signed between the USSR and Germany in August 1939 as a prelude to the two signatories carving up Poland. Similarly, in Britain the Communist *Daily Worker* was banned for its defeatist stance.

When Hitler ignored the pact and invaded the USSR in June 1941, the PCF leadership was instructed by Moscow to launch a campaign of assassination of German personnel and thereby provoke retaliation by the taking and shooting of hostages. On 13 August two Communist activists hacked a German soldier to death with bayonet and chopper. Eight days later, 22-year-old Pierre Georges, who styled himself 'Colonel Fabien', gunned down in a Metro station an inoffensive Kriegsmarine sub-lieutenant on his way to work in a naval clothing store.

The deathly round of assassination and reprisal was launched. This had nothing to do with French interests. Moscow's aim was to tie down in a restive France many thousands of German troops who could otherwise have been sent to the eastern front. The Comintern always played a long game, and the second aim of its strategy was to divide and confuse the French people, leading to a power vacuum at the end of the war, in which the tightly disciplined PCF could take over the government by political means or armed uprising.

The Maquis was altogether different, being initially composed of autonomous bands of young Frenchmen who took to the hills and forests to escape conscription for labour service in Germany. As a neighbour of mine recalled, 'What could we do when young men with guns knocked on the door at night, demanding clothes and food against handwritten receipts they said would be redeemed by General De Gaulle after the Liberation?'

Despite lengthy negotiations and extensive bribery by De Gaulle's emissary Jean Moulin, who was charged with uniting the mutually hostile factions of the Resistance and Maquis into one integrated command structure, internecine conflict between the various political groups continued. Only after

the Liberation were the myths of concerted heroic resistance to the invader
invented to unify a divided nation.

Charles De Gaulle has rightly become the symbol of resistance to the
German occupation of his country, but when it began he was just a
substantive colonel, stranded with a handful of companions in a country
whose language he did not speak very well and whose policies he often rightly
mistrusted. To most of his compatriots, he was a runaway correctly
condemned *in absentia* by a court martial to a traitor's death.

Thousands of French servicemen in Britain after Dunkirk rejected De
Gaulle's appeal and chose to return home even when this lay in the Occupied
Zone. Their legitimate head of state, Marshal Philippe Pétain, was a First
World War hero and a popular and respected political figure of the inter-war
years. Many of his original policies were laudable, if naive – and yet the
cruelty of his regime has become legendary. 'I hate lies,' he said just after the
Armistice to a population disillusioned with its leaders. And, 'I think of those
who are suffering, of those who do not know where tomorrow's food is to
come from, of the children who will not hear this year the church bell of
their own village.'

How could the man who said that go on to cause the death of so many of
his citizens, including men who had lost their sight and limbs to win the
same medals that decorated his uniform? The Marshal was old and too tired
to stay on course when manipulated by more devious colleagues. Yet what
perverted his policies above all else was the absolute power with which his
fellow-politicians voted to invest him. When the National Assembly killed the
Third Republic at Vichy, making Pétain a dictator, one solitary voice cried out,
'*Vive la République, quand même!*'

Politics makes strange bedfellows, but no pair more disparate than Pétain
and Pierre Laval have been harnessed together by its exigencies. Prime
Minister Laval seems to epitomise the schemer avid for power who cares not
whence it comes. A Socialist MP, or *député*, and lawyer who made his
reputation successfully defending left-wing activists against the interests of
the 200 families said to own France, he avoided military service in 1914–18
and slipped around the semi-circular Chamber of Deputies to sit with the
Conservatives, causing one enemy to comment that such a 180-degree turn
was to be expected from a man whose name read the same from left or right.
The energy with which Laval promoted the worst excesses of the Vichy
regime earned him death by firing squad. Few mourned his passing, yet he
argued to the last that he had acted throughout the Occupation as a pacifist
and patriot.

The term 'collaborator' came after the Liberation to mean a particular form
of treason exemplified by Pétain and Laval. If French citizens actively pro-
German from political conviction, anti-Semitism, or because they thought
Hitler was bound to win the war were definitely *collabos*, what of the
companies that made vast profits from the Occupation and the great wine

châteaux who slaked the German thirst for claret, burgundy and champagne? In Paris and other big cities luxury commerce thrived and huge untaxed fortunes were made on the black market while the aged and poor suffered hypothermia and malnutrition, yet many profiteers bought protection from one Resistance group or another and were never accused of any crime.

It was undoubtedly collaboration of the most shameful kind when uniformed Paris policemen rounded up 12,884 people in the summer of 1942, including 4,051 children who were brutally separated from their mothers and left terrified in a huge sports stadium with no food, water or usable toilets – as a prelude to being herded into cattle trucks, destination Auschwitz. But did Louis Renault, who avoided a probable death sentence after the Liberation by dying from injuries sustained in prison while awaiting trial, have any choice about making vehicles for the Wehrmacht? The alternative was to see his factories dismantled and his workmen sent to Germany.

Lower down the social scale, if the only work available in coastal villages of the Occupied Zone was labouring on the Atlantic Wall, why *should* a man with wife and children to feed have refused it, even had he been given the choice? In the Free Zone, if the only job a woman could find was as a shorthand-typist or telephone switchboard operator in a Vichy government department, did that make her a collaborator? And what about all the men who wore the many uniforms of Pétain's regime in the police, gendarmerie, the Army of the Armistice and as members of the Milice?[1]

At least 105,000 alleged *collabos* were murdered without trial during the Liberation and the Purge afterwards. Yet Vichy civil servant François Mitterrand accepted the post of editor of Oréal-owned magazine *Votre Beauté* as first step up the ladder that led to presidency of the Republic from 1981 to 1995, when he is said to have actively impeded the investigation of collaborators like the wartime Interior Minister René Bousquet and Maurice Papon, who signed the arrest warrants that sent the Jews of Bordeaux to die in cattle trucks and gas chambers.[2]

What can one say of the role played by the Catholic Church? Some priests were active in the German cause, blessing French volunteers to fight for the Reich; others gave their lives gladly in fighting the Occupation while the Church hierarchy long turned a blind eye to the excesses of Vichy's anti-Semitism in keeping with the Vatican line that Nazi Germany was a bulwark for Christianity against the godless hordes in the East.

Researching this book has been the more difficult because military defeat and occupation are regarded as shameful, and fighting a powerful oppressor always seems heroic. Yet, was it heroic for Communist Maquis chief 'Kléber' Chapou to defy the orders of his Résistance superiors on the day after D-Day and order his private army of 400 *maquisards* to massacre forty German soldiers in Tulle – and then run away to let SS Division Das Reich hang ninety-nine uninvolved local men the next day and despatch another hundred to concentration and extermination camps where most of them died?

It was undoubtedly heroic for French men and women to risk their lives by helping downed Allied airmen, because the price they paid if caught was imprisonment, torture and death – not only for themselves but also for spouses and children. Was all their suffering militarily justifiable, when ✓ weighed against the fact that only *nineteen* of those airmen ever flew again in combat? And what about the many thousands of memorials all over France commemorating young men who died after the Normandy landings in 1944 fighting armoured cars and tanks with Sten guns and ammunition parachuted from RAF aircraft? Did their deaths serve any militarily justifiable purpose, or were they pawns in a cynical deception operation by Britain's Secret Intelligence Service (SIS)?

Well over 60 per cent of the French nation then lived in rural areas, so hitherto unpublished accounts of the lives of my neighbours and acquaintances living in the small towns and countryside of south-western France are as valid as better-documented incidents in Paris, Bordeaux and Lyons. Against all the odds, Pierre Mignon – a patriotic farmer from a village 10 kilometres from my home – returned from the dead to write a memorial to the comrades whose emaciated corpses he left stacked like firewood in the camps, or who were shot by the roadside during the final lunatic death marches. In the preface to his account of betrayal and torture that took his courageous friends to agonised deaths in Germany, he wrote modestly: 'I made some notes afterwards, so that my children would know what happened to us.'[3]

Contrary to what the reader might think, those who shared memories with me and lent souvenirs and precious keepsakes for my research were not boasting. Imprisonment, torture and starvation leave a lifelong burden of shame on their victims that makes talking about their suffering extremely difficult. In the sixty years since her public humiliation during the Liberation, I was the first person to whom Marie-Rose Dupont spoke of that awful Sunday when her head was shaved for the 'crime' of falling in love with a German.

The four years of the Occupation are called 'the dark years' literally because of the shortages of fuel and frequent power cuts and figuratively because few people talk about them, even six decades later. Yet recording the experience of the Occupation is vitally important at a time when encyclopedias and schoolbooks are being rewritten to present a sanitised view of recent history for students in the currently united Europe. Memorials to those who died during the Occupation are sometimes reworded during refurbishment. A bald statement like '*fusillés par les Allemands*' (shot by the Germans) might offend today's political partners and thus becomes ambiguously '*tués par les Hitlériens*' or even more anonymously '*tués par l'Occupant*'. So when the survivors die in silence, old myths become new truth.

This is the survivors' story.

I began this work in a spirit of scepticism not improper in a historian, yet as it progressed I was frequently humbled by the courage of ordinary French men and women who followed their consciences at a time when doing so invited torture and death for oneself, one's friends and loved ones. Their memories are harrowing, but we owe them a hearing before those memories are lost forever.

Douglas Boyd,
Gironde, France,
Easter 2007

 PART ONE

DEFEAT AND OCCUPATION

TRAVAIL PATRIE

FAMILLE

Chapter 1

FROM SITZKRIEG TO BLITZKRIEG

T he Berliner Sportpalast was as near as one could get in 1939 to the ambiance of a twenty-first-century rock concert. Spotlights played on the thousands of upraised arms giving the Hitler salute and the red-white-black banners and the Nazi aristocracy on the platform. The hall was packed with the uniformed Party faithful and a sprinkling of soldiers, airmen and sailors on leave. The PA system was cranked up as high as it could go. After several underlings, top-of-the-bill speaker Adolf Hitler thumped the rostrum on the dais to wind his audience up to the usual fever pitch. The text of his sermon was fear – the fear of the Blitzkrieg machine that had destroyed Poland and was about to be unleashed on the Western Allies.

Hamming it up, the Führer posed the question in so many Dutch, Belgian, French and British minds: '"When is he coming?" they ask.' The audience was silent as he paused and scanned the hall as though seeking the answer among his followers. Then, with his impeccably theatrical sense of timing, he said, 'I tell them, don't worry. He's coming all right!'

'*Sieg heil! Sieg heil! Sieg heil!*' The chanting and roars of applause rang out over radios throughout Europe – yet another exercise in the war of nerves in the autumn and winter of 1939–40. The waiting period before the bloodshed was deprecatingly called 'the phoney war', but was also christened the 'bore war' by the soldiers in Lord Gort's British Expeditionary Force on the western flank of the Allied line in France, because nothing much seemed to be happening on the ground. With similar humour, the men in field-grey on the other bank of the Rhine called it *der Sitzkrieg* in contrast with their Blitzkrieg conquest of Poland the previous September.

Reporting to HQ of 2nd French North African Division at Toul in Lorraine, reservist Captain Barlone found the lack of clothing, arms, ammunition and vehicles 'disastrous and scandalous'. There was a general assumption in the officers' mess that if it came to a shooting war, France would somehow muddle through. The main problem, as he saw it, was that the General Staff was everywhere preparing for the static war of 1914–18 and thus had no defence in depth against fast-moving modern mechanised columns. Even rations were inadequate, the army being supposed to live off the land by slaughtering animals belonging to the evacuated civilian population and looting their crops and fruit. When temperatures in Lorraine dropped below

−36°C that winter, his men were sleeping in barns, where their horses' bodies were the only source of warmth.[1]

One astute observer of the Parisian scene as the shooting war drew nearer was American publisher Thomas Kernan, managing editor of the French edition of *Vogue*. Well connected and welcome in all the best places, he watched the final rounds in the game of musical beds that had been a feature of French political life under the two empires and three republics that had succeeded each other since the Revolution. When in March 1940 Prime Minister Edouard Daladier – Chamberlain's co-signatory to the disastrous Munich Agreement that had given Hitler the green light to invade Czechoslovakia in 1938 – resigned the premiership, Kernan knew that Daladier's hand had been forced by the Comtesse de Portes, Paul Reynaud's intelligent and ambitious mistress.

Daughter of a rich merchant in Marseilles, Hélène Rebuffel had married Count Jean de Portes for the title and social standing that went with it, enabling her to set up her own *salon* in Paris. There in 1929 she met Paul Reynaud, a lawyer making his way up the political ladder. Short, poorly dressed, nervous in speech and uncomfortable in manner, Reynaud was not her type – until he was made Minister of Finance the following year after predicting the Wall Street Crash well ahead of the event. His second great political success was as Minister for the Colonies, after which gossip said that Hélène de Portes intended to make Reynaud the ruler of France so that she could rule through him. Pre-war France, where women did not have the vote and were debarred from political office, was nevertheless a country where ambitious and intelligent women exercised considerable political power in the traditional way.

Daladier's own mistress was the coolly attractive daughter of a rich sardine packer who had married the Marquis of Crussol for his title, to the dismay of the aristocratic Crussol family. It was at her *salon* that Daladier fell victim to her charms. André Tardieu, founder of the Republican Centre movement, was bedding Mary Marquet, a star of the Comédie Française – which is where Yvon Delbos, Foreign Minister in the Popular Front government, found his stately brunette mistress Germaine Rouer; Georges Mandel, who had been *chef de cabinet* to Clemenceau, found his blonde, buxom mistress Béatrice Bretty there too. At the time he was French delegate to the League of Nations, Paul Boncour wrote to his mistress Magda Fontanges, 'When I think of your lovely body, I don't give a damn about Central Europe.' Rather embarrassingly, the letter was read out in evidence when she was on trial for shooting Count Charles Chambrun.[2]

Watching all the moves, Kernan saw the Comtesse de Portes increasingly worried as Reynaud became more and more reliant in the developing crisis on his astute friend and *chef de cabinet* Gaston Palewski. Her best hope of regaining control over him was to marry her lover. Reynaud was 52 – exactly twice her age. Father of one child and separated from his wife, he was unable to get a quick divorce under the existing law, which could only be changed by the Minister of Justice. Paul Reynaud was that minister, but for him to upset the Church by altering the law for his own benefit was too near the knuckle, even in the Third Republic.

So the Countess had a little *tête-à-tête* with her rival, the Marquise de Crussol. After a little fencing between these two powerful women, Portes proposed to Crussol that it would solve both their problems if Reynaud were moved down to his old post as Minister of Finance, where he would present less of a threat to Daladier. Georges Bonnet, a member of the pals' club whose disastrous pro-Munich policy had cost him the Foreign Ministry, could then be made Minister of Justice – in gratitude for which Bonnet could sort out the divorce law, enabling the countess to marry Reynaud. *Voilà!*

Bonnet's law of 29 November 1939 reduced the waiting period for divorce from three years to one but, with Reynaud gathering support from both the Left and the Right, the Marquise de Crussol complained to the Comtesse de Portes that she was not keeping to the deal they had agreed. When Hélène de Portes explained that the problem was Palewski's influence over Reynaud, against which she was powerless, Palewski's time was up because the marquise instructed her lover Daladier to pressure Reynaud into replacing him with two less savvy advisers named Lecca and Devau. Both countess and marquise heaved sighs of relief, but when Daladier's hold on power slipped in March 1940, Reynaud became prime minister anyway. Enjoying their success and their rivals' discomfiture, both he and his mistress were unaware that on the stage set for the comedy of musical beds, a *folie à deux* tragedy was about to be played with her in the principal role.[3] Demonstrating his ability to sniff the wind of change, Palewski wrote off the lot of them and later slipped across the Channel to become a crucial figure in the Gaullist movement, both during and after the war.

Not every foreigner in the French capital was interested in the political scene. In the spring of 1940, a dilettante Englishman named Denis Freeman returned to his beloved Parisian home after wintering in Switzerland. His diary is full of more mundane things: the gardeners setting out bedding plants behind the cathedral of Notre Dame and in the courtyard of the Louvre; magnolias blooming in the Avenue Gabriel and the leaves on the chestnut trees that had never looked greener and fresher. Less overcrowded and emptier of motor traffic than in previous years, the capital exuded a peculiar air of nostalgic beauty, with smartly dressed women on the Champs Elysées wearing colourful flowered dresses and pretty hats, as though thumbing their delicate noses at the men in field-grey lurking across the Rhine.

'A new and trivial comedy by Cocteau made its appearance at the (Théâtre) Bouffes,' Freeman wrote.

Médée by Milhaud, with *décor* by André Masson, was produced at the Opéra on the stage which a few days earlier had been filled by Maurice Chevalier and Gracie Fields. People still went to the theatres and music halls. The Parisians dined out as usual – the Germans, we were constantly told, would sooner or later starve. At least three-quarters of the night clubs had closed, but the few remaining open were full. The *guignol* puppet theatre in the Luxembourg with new (villains) Messrs Hitler and Goering, was a big draw. There were even races at Longchamps and the Entente Cordiale was weekly cemented by some inter-allied sporting event.[4]

If that does not sound like a capital preparing for war, Freeman complained that on three days a week no meat could be bought, except for sucking lamb which was classed as fish for some reason. Coffee and sugar, when they could be found, cost far more than the previous year. With no hard liquor to be had on Monday, Wednesday and Saturday and no pastry or confectionery on Tuesday, Thursday and Friday, those addicted to rum babas could enjoy them only on Sunday. Restaurants were permitted to serve only one meat dish of 100 grams per person, and the clients got butter only with cheese or sardines.

By the end of the cool spring of 1940 coal and wood were almost unobtainable in Paris. A law had been passed limiting the period during which central heating might be used. Only government monopoly cigarettes were available in the *tabacs*. World-famous luxury goods stores in the main thoroughfares had shut down, and many Metro stations were closed. With only a reduced service of buses, taxis were scarce and at night practically unobtainable. Several times a week Freeman heard anti-aircraft guns in action, by night and by day.[5]

Five hundred kilometres to the south, spring came a little earlier than to Paris. The town of Moissac, on the River Tarn near its confluence with the mighty Garonne, was not a place where people worried much about perfume, jewellery and fancy cakes. Known throughout France as the centre of production of Chasselas dessert grapes, the town had its normal population of 8,000 already swollen by an influx of refugees from the Spanish Civil War, welcomed by its left-of-centre mayor Roger Delthil, who intoned the '*Internationale*' as often as the '*Marseillaise*' at public events. He was also senator for the *département* of Tarn-et-Garonne – in France it is still quite usual for one man to hold several public offices simultaneously. After war was declared in September 1939, Delthil reminded his fellow-citizens that when disastrous floods had swept homes away and caused many deaths in 1930, the country had been generous in its financial support for reconstruction. On all the hoardings, a notice read:

We have been asked to welcome 1,500 compatriots, women, children and men above military age who have been obliged to flee the atrocities of a war that has been thrust upon us. These unfortunate people of all classes have had to leave their homes with nothing. They will arrive in Moissac completely unprovided for. The municipality will find or requisition the necessary accommodation. . .

I am counting on the patriotism of the people of Moissac, whose sons are doing their duty on the frontier. I am counting on them also because when misfortune struck our town in 1930 all France in an admirable groundswell of solidarity sent us many millions. We have a debt to pay. We shall pay it.

Roger Delthil, Mayor of Moissac, Senator of Tarn-et-Garonne

By 12 September 1939 municipal employees had requisitioned 1,910 blankets, 400 stoves, 400 oil lamps and all the basic necessities to see the expected flood of refugees through the winter. An eighteenth-century town house at 18 Quai du Vieux Port was opened as a reception centre for them. Known as La Maison de Moissac, it initially housed eleven refugees from Germany, Austria and the Saarland.

The 1,500 refugees predicted by Delthil for the first wave from the north and east of the country turned out to be 2,000, increasing the population of Moissac by 25 per cent. Despite this, local people carried on with their lives. In 1870 and 1914 German guns had shelled Paris, but Moissagais families, except those with a man in uniform, showed little interest in a war to be fought hundreds of kilometres to the north. As he would many times in the next four years, the Prefect of the *département* decried the insular attitude of these peasants concerned only with their land and with selling their produce at the best price.

The bubble burst on 10 May 1940 when Hitler launched a three-pronged attack on Holland, Belgium and France. The French had a very efficient intelligence network all along the front, which reported troop movements across the Rhine: signals from their agents in neutral Luxembourg the previous day had warned of the arrival there of storm troopers disguised as tourists. Woken at 1 a.m. to hear the latest reports, the French Commander-in-Chief, General Maurice Gamelin, muttered, 'Take no action,' and went back to sleep.

Each side had used the eight months of bluff and counter-bluff to build up front-line strength. A major reason for Hitler prolonging the phoney war was that Polish heroism had shot down or severely damaged 30 per cent of the Luftwaffe's aircraft, and Goering needed time to replace pilots and aircraft before launching a new aggression in the west.[6] By the beginning of May, with the eastern front secured politically for the moment by the Ribbentrop–Molotov non-aggression pact, Hitler was able to deploy 135 divisions along Germany's western front, including twelve Panzer divisions with 2,439 tanks and a total of 3,369 warplanes.[7]

Facing them were the 104 French and fifteen British divisions of the British Expeditionary Force, which should have been more than enough to fight a defensive battle in prepared positions, without counting the Dutch and

Belgian armies and fortifications that would absorb the first German thrusts. The British government had promised its French allies to build the BEF up to thirty-two divisions and eventually forty-five, but not before 1941 at the earliest.[8] Although French tanks outnumbered the German armour by four to three, less than one-third of these were in mobile armoured units, because of the failure of the general staff to re-think this tool of modern warfare along the lines argued for more than a decade by a cavalry colonel named Charles De Gaulle.

Ninety per cent of French artillery pieces dated back to the First World War. The 55th Infantry Division, defending the key city of Sedan, had not a single anti-tank gun capable of stopping a Panzer.[9] Thanks to the Depression and the pacifist stance of inter-war governments, particularly Leon Blum's left-wing Popular Front, the French Air Force was also poorly equipped. Flying off grass fields with their outdated motors fuelled by 70 or 87 octane fuel, its pilots went up against Messerschmitts and Stukas of the Blitzkrieg-tested Luftwaffe with little on their side but courage and willingness to die for their country.

It is not true that the French General Staff placed *all* its faith in the supposed impregnability of the Maginot Line fortifications running along the Franco-German frontier from Switzerland in the east as far as Belgium in the west, but that is perversely where its best troops were stationed – and not in the unfortified stretch at the western end of the line.

When Hitler had invaded Poland the previous September, the British journalist Nicholas Bodington had been with the French armies on the Alsace–Lorraine frontier with Germany. Taking advantage of the inevitable thinning of the forces ranged against them, the French General Staff had 'straightened the line' by ironing out a few kinks, in the process annexing thirty-six German villages which became briefly French after only a few salvoes of artillery from the retreating defenders. It seems that this early success engendered a false sense of superiority in Paris.

In the summer of 1940, with the left flank of the Allied line anchored on the Channel coast and entrusted to Lord Gort's BEF, the space between it and the Maginot Line was filled by some very second-rate French units, rotated so often that their officers did not know which units were on their flanks, while the men they commanded were less acquainted with their weapons than the picks and shovels they were using to construct blockhouses and trenches in a too-little, too-late attempt to extend the Maginot Line westwards on the cheap.

It was to this stretch of the front between Longwy at the north-west end of the line and Sedan that General Franz Halder had pointed on a map at OKW (the German Army High Command) six months earlier. 'Here is the weak point,' he said. 'Here we have to go through!'[10] Launched on 10 May, the northern thrust of the German attack sliced through the Dutch army, while the central drive took the Panzers deep into Belgium and the southern prong of Hitler's trident drove through the Ardennes forest of southern Belgium and Luxembourg like an arrow pointing straight at Sedan.

General Erich von Manstein's *Fall Sichel*, or Operation Sickle, was a classic, fast-moving, massive Panzer offensive with close air cover – that essential feature of successful Blitzkrieg which the chiefs of both the RAF and the French Air Force thought a misapplication of air-power. By coming through the theoretically impassable Ardennes forests, Manstein wrong-footed the Allied defence so brilliantly that, three days after the start of the offensive, his advance units were in France.[11] Holland surrendered to the inevitable on 15 May. Hearing the news, Premier Paul Reynaud took one look at the war map and telephoned the new British Prime Minister Winston Churchill to say, 'The battle is lost.'

Far from the sound of the guns, on 18 May Mayor Delthil warned the stunned inhabitants of Moissac to expect a new wave of refugees from the north and east. It was almost a relief for him to have something so mundane to worry about after the weeks of rumours about parachutes dropping on remote areas, of women seen struggling along country roads carrying cases so heavy they *must* have contained weapons – obviously storm troopers disguised as nuns – and of mysterious aircraft engines heard at night. At least the refugees were real.

On 28 May, Belgium also surrendered, to avoid further useless loss of life. What else could King Leopold's government have done? One unique political gesture of the little-respected Belgian politicians was to rush through a law authorising the destructions of *état civil* records of Jewish children to give them the names of non-Jewish adoptive parents. No count exists of how many young lives this saved.

After the Panzers of the northern and central thrusts regrouped and swung southwards, they poured through the weakest point in the centre of the Allied line. Judging the Battle of France lost, Lord Gort began withdrawing the BEF to the coast in preparation for evacuation by sea before the line of retreat was cut. They nearly missed the boat literally after General Heinz Guderian's tank columns reached the Channel coast near Abbeville on 20 May and swung north to cut off the British from the ports of Calais and Dunkirk. However, on 24 May Hitler ordered Guderian to halt on the canal line just outside Dunkirk and let the Luftwaffe wipe out the men on the beaches, which it failed to do. By the end of the seaborne evacuation 198,000 British and 140,000 French and Belgian soldiers, sailors and airmen had crossed the Channel to safety. Such was the elation in Britain that Churchill had to warn his people 'not to ascribe to this deliverance the character of a victory'.

Chapter 2

PÉTAIN QUELLS THE PANIC

T he Germans did not have it all their own way. Among commanders who bloodied their nose more than once was Colonel Charles De Gaulle, France's premier advocate of tank warfare. The success with which he practised what he had preached in books between the wars earned a citation from his commander-in-chief, General Maxime Weygand: 'An admirable leader, daring and energetic, on 30 and 31 May he attacked an enemy bridgehead, penetrating more than five kilometres into the enemy lines and capturing several hundred prisoners and valuable *matériel*.'[1] However, in the chaos of the German breakthrough not even officers like De Gaulle could do much at the front, so he was recalled to Paris by Reynaud and appointed Under-Secretary for War in a government that was numbed at being abandoned by its only ally.

Reynaud still had two million men under arms in the area of conflict, but, having taken losses of 92,000 dead and over 200,000 wounded in the brief campaign against German losses roughly half as severe, his Cabinet was irrevocably divided over the course of action to pursue. A minority of six ministers supported his plan to fight on and eventually withdraw to French North Africa and continue the war from there, but Reynaud's political credit was all but spent. Exactly two months earlier, on 28 March 1940, he had signed an agreement in London under which both British and French governments undertook not to negotiate peace terms unilaterally. Reynaud had signed without first seeking the approval of his Cabinet, which made his signature unconstitutional and not binding on the French government. In any case, as President Lebrun argued after the war at Pétain's trial, Britain had unilaterally vitiated the agreement on two counts: she had never committed her air force to the common cause and she had withdrawn her ground troops from the conflict without consultation.

In Paris hardly anyone of consequence, inside the Cabinet or elsewhere, believed it was still possible to stop the German advance. The great hero of 1914–18, Marshal Henri-Philippe Pétain, told the American Ambassador on 4 June that he firmly believed the British would shortly sign a pact with Germany.[2] Although Charles De Gaulle was despatched to London on 5 June with the acting rank of brigadier, there was little he could do there at this stage.

The majority of thirteen ministers in Reynaud's Cabinet wanted to sue for terms immediately, never mind what pieces of paper had been signed with the British, who in their consideration had deserted France in her hour of need. Their position was strengthened by Marshal Pétain as Vice-President of the Council of Ministers and General Weygand, who had replaced Gamelin as Commander-in-Chief of the Army after the disastrous first week of the invasion. France's two senior soldiers, they saw no alternative to an armistice, providing it 'did not stain French honour'[3] or involve handing over the intact French Navy, built up and modernised by Admiral of the Fleet Xavier-François Darlan despite the pacifist policies of inter-war governments.

With the army in full flight and no prepared positions to fall back on, there was nowhere the French Army could stand and fight with any reasonable chance of holding a line against so fast-moving an enemy. There was also the question of morale. In the First World War, France and the British Empire each mobilised between eight and nine million men against the Central Powers, but the total French casualties had been twice as high as those for the whole empire. From a population of forty million, France lost 1,357,800 men killed, with 4,266,000 wounded and another 537,000 taken prisoner or missing in action. At the other end of the scale, the decisive but late entry of the USA into the war cost only a total of 323,018 American casualties, including 116,516 dead.[4]

So, by November 1918, one out of ten French citizens of all age-groups and both sexes was a casualty in one way or another, without counting the hundreds of thousands made homeless by the fighting and the concomitant disruption to family life. Coming as it did after the Revolutionary wars, the wars of the two empires and the Franco-Prussian War of 1870–71, the First World War traumatised the whole nation. Long lists of names on war memorials in small villages all over France testify to the slaughter of all the adult males in many families. In the southern *départements*, telephone directories show as many Italian and Spanish surnames as French ones, thanks to the flood of landless younger sons who came from Italy and Spain between the two world wars to replace the dead youth of France by marrying local girls otherwise condemned to lifelong spinsterhood.

In addition to the demoralising scale of French casualties, there was another factor in the war-weariness of French soldiers by 1917 and 1918 that caused extensive and brutally repressed mutinies. For the British, Empire and American forces fighting on their flanks, the war was destroying a foreign land they would forget soon after returning home, whereas the *poilus* were fighting in a wasteland where formerly their farms, villages and cities had stood – but which was so torn and cratered by the bombardments that it seemed impossible for street lines to be traced with certainty, let alone homes rebuilt or fields poisoned with chemicals ever made fertile again.

It would have been surprising if, after only three decades, the survivors of that carnage and their sons had wished to repeat the experience after being abandoned by their allies and with totally justified lack of faith in their divided leaders, a disrupted command structure, virtually no working communications, outdated weapons and grossly inadequate air cover.

Paradoxically, to defend the country they loved, many foreign residents volunteered to fight for France. Accepted as combatants only in the Foreign Legion, they were formed into Régiments de Marche de Volontaires Etrangers (RMVE, with numbering upwards of 20), to distinguish them from the 'old' Legion, shipped over from North Africa in this hour of need. 22 RMVE listed men of forty-seven nationalities, but 25 per cent of them were Republican refugees from the Spanish Civil War. Both they and the East Europeans in these temporary regiments included a high percentage of Communists, which made their officers consider them politically unreliable. Issued inadequate kit and weapons or none at all, they were held in reserve until after the invasion and then thrown into the line to sink or swim, poorly trained and ill-equipped. Yet their combat record was no worse than that of many regular regiments.[5]

In Alsace, behind the Maginot Line, the eminent Parisian surgeon and army reservist Joseph Gouzi worked day and night in a well-organised mobile surgical unit, moving from one pre-planned position to the next; but things were not like that in the centre of the line. Denis Freeman and his friend Douglas Cooper enlisted in the French Army as ambulance drivers and found themselves in the headlong rout, driving badly wounded men to improvised hospitals where doctors and patients were on the point of being re-evacuated as the enemy pressed closer. On 7 June at Oigny, Freeman noted:

The villagers could not have left so very long before, for the little gardens looked well tended and there was an air of orderliness and well-being about the place. It was difficult to reconcile the ceaseless thunder of the distant guns and the busy movement of the doctors, *infirmiers* and stretcher-bearers with the rural scene. Cottages had been transformed into dressing-stations. The simpler operations were performed in the forge.[6]

From time to time, the two English volunteers crossed paths with compatriots. On 8 June near Troyes, Cooper noted:

Outside in the street I found several English soldiers (from) the Pioneer Corps, whose duty it was to follow the RAF around, making landing-grounds for them, and digging reservoirs for petrol. Now that most of the English airmen had left, they themselves were expecting to be moved any day.

The Germans had reached Forges-les-Eaux and were pressing on towards Rouen and the Seine. They seemed to be advancing everywhere. Weygand had issued a proclamation: '*Nous sommes en dernier quart d'heure*' [meaning, a quarter of an hour to go, with victory in sight], but the roads were horribly congested. The stream of refugees had swollen to considerable proportions in the space of an afternoon and there were not only lines of people on foot and in cars, but in addition a large assortment of barking dogs of all sizes, goats, cattle and poultry they were taking with them. Heavy military vehicles too were on the move and when I looked closer I saw petrol (tankers), radio cars and the ground staff of airfields going south. It was an alarming sight.[7]

On 9 June Charles De Gaulle returned to his office in Paris after a meeting with Churchill in London in time to hear General Héring as military governor of the capital declare that the city would be defended street by street. The following day, Italy declared war on France and moved troops across the border, with Mussolini intent on occupying as much of the country as possible before the inevitable armistice. Hearing the news in London, Churchill is said to have remarked maliciously, 'It's only fair. We had them on our side in the last war.'[8]

From Paris, the government fled south-west – away from both Germans and Italians – over roads choked with refugees. General Héring, ordered not to defend the capital after all, requested to be relieved of his redundant post and given a combat command. The art treasures of the Louvre Museum and the bullion reserves of the Banque de France had gone during the phoney war – the former to various châteaux in the Loire Valley and the latter spread far and wide in North America, Martinique and French West Africa. As it had during the German invasions of 1870 and 1914, the government continued its flight from Tours towards Bordeaux, with politicians and civil servants sleeping in their official cars by the side of roads lined with abandoned horse-drawn and motor vehicles. During the brief halt in Tours, Reynaud made a desperate appeal for air support from the United States, which fell on deaf ears.

On the night of 13 June the Parisian suburban hospital at Orsay was staffed by seven desperate nurses caring for eighty sick and elderly patients, plus refugee casualties. With no proper meal for days and only a few hours' sleep, they asked a passing army major what to do about the patients who could not be moved when the time came to evacuate the others. 'Give them a last injection,' he replied. 'Morphine or strychnine is best.' Too exhausted to think any further, four of the nurses prepared the fatal doses and administered them, rather than leave seven aged patients behind. The intended act of mercy cost them between one and five years' imprisonment when they were sentenced in May 1942.

North of Paris, Freeman and Cooper in their ambulances were stopped in Sens by a general trying to rally some troops, who asked whether they had any maps he could borrow. A general without a map! It was unreal – as was their experience of driving into Sens with a naked, screaming, delirious wounded man being tended by a wounded African soldier, to find

. . . the café at the big crossroads full of people leisurely sipping their aperitif. Busy housewives laden with their baskets were completing their weekend shopping and in the courtyard of the Hôtel de Paris opposite the cathedral the tables with their chequered cloths and gay umbrellas were already laid for the evening meal.

The vast courtyard (of the hospital) presented an extraordinary spectacle. Hundreds of ambulances, parked without any attempt at order, were being loaded and unloaded at the greatest possible speed. Nurses, doctors, medics and stretcher-bearers . . . looked tired and bewildered by the unmanageable influx of new cases that had suddenly been flung upon them. Some drivers who had been waiting to unload for some time . . . had just been told that they were to go on to Auxerre [60 kilometres distant].[9]

Arriving there in the blackout and a power cut, with no lifts working, they had to carry their stretchers upstairs and along corridors, picking their way between other wounded lying on stretchers all over the floors. From every corner came groaning as a few nuns carrying torches did their best without drugs to calm the wounded with prayers and a drink of water. The doors of the operating theatre opened for one man to be carried out and another immediately carried in.

The German advance was so rapid that, no sooner had a hospital been staffed and started to work, than it had to be evacuated. Ordered back to Sens, Freeman and Cooper drove through the night without lights against the press of military and civilian traffic fighting its way southwards. The two Britons found what had been a calm provincial town the previous evening transformed:

Every available inch of space was occupied by some kind of vehicle . . . being loaded ready to leave. The food shops were besieged; everyone was scrambling to purchase as much as possible. One sensed a feeling among the people that they might not see food again for many days. There were no newspapers to calm their fears, no garages to attend to repairs, no petrol to help them on their way, and no police to control them. Desperate, they seemed unable to decide whether to fight for the food they needed now, or take a risk and escape before the arrival of the Germans. In the space of one hour, Sens had become a *ville en panique*.[10]

It was not alone. While the driver of the van taking all the municipal records of the Paris suburb of Boulogne-Billancourt was desperately searching for petrol, two soldiers hijacked the vehicle and disappeared with the registers of births, marriages and deaths.

Heading back the way they had come, Freeman and Cooper passed columns of African and Vietnamese troops, the latter carrying their kit on sticks over their shoulders. Unable to find a refuelling dump, they took the risk of filling up their tanks from a pump at a service station that was already blazing from a bomb. From time to time they met up with comrades from the same unit and a group of English women volunteers driving ambulances financed by a large American acting as their commandant.

On 14 June at 5.30 a.m. the first German units drove through the Porte de la Villette and into the heart of Paris beneath clouds of black smoke from fuel dumps set on fire by the retreating French Army. The previous afternoon two French officers with a trumpeter had met the Germans at Sarcelles and confirmed that the city would not be defended. With most of the capital's food supplies coming from the north, where the disruption to road and rail traffic was total, the 700,000 Parisians who had not fled watched the enemy from behind closed shutters and drawn curtains, venturing out only when the sparkling clean mobile kitchens of the German Winterhilfe organisation began dispensing hot soup and bread for the asking. It would be well into the autumn before all the other 2,100,000 residents returned, less the more prudent Jewish ones.

The inhabitants of Orleans who had defied orders to flee found it impossible to replace lost documents after the municipal records and Joan of Arc's house went up in smoke during German air raids on 14 and 15 June. The telephone system was destroyed. Had it been working, there was no one in local government offices to deal with the problems of the 3,000 families whose homes had been destroyed. The various departments were dispersed in Nontron, Tulle, Guéret, Millau, Bordeaux, Toulouse, Tonneins and Marmande – and would stay there until 17 July.

With water and gas mains ruptured, fires smouldered everywhere for the next two weeks, causing more destruction. Streets were blocked by collapsed buildings. There was no electricity and no food. The French Army had blown up the Joffre and Georges V road bridges, which did not prevent the incoming Wehrmacht from using the intact Vierzon railway bridge to cross the River Loire, but the disruption for normal traffic was so great that clearing up by French prisoners of war and unemployed Parisians was to last eight months. In nearby Neuville-aux-Bois the only medical care for refugees streaming in was provided by the wives of Generals Ecot, Berre and Velle, whose ambulance had run out of petrol there, with Madame Ecot literally taking a hat round each morning to beg money for food.

That month, a record 1,212,000,000 francs were withdrawn before the savings banks put up their shutters. The Finance Ministry, finding itself stuck at Avoine near Saumur with the Germans approaching, paid a street-cleaner to burn banknotes to the value of 25,000,000 francs. When the Prefect of the Nord *département* demanded several million francs for the immediate needs of his population cut off from the rest of France by the German advance, the government loaded the money aboard two Glenn-Martin aircraft that were shot down as unidentified by a British ack-ack battery near Lille. Of the six crewmen, only one managed to parachute to safety in a sky filled with whirling banknotes. Millions were lost: the Prefect eventually signed a receipt for only 240,000 francs.[11]

South of Orleans, the remaining inhabitants of Poitiers dismantled the makeshift barricades erected by men of 274th Infantry Regiment and sent the mayor out with a white flag to inform the approaching Germans that the town would not be defended. A few miles away at Le Blanc, veterans from the First World War beat up the sappers trying to destroy the bridge over the River Creuse and stamped out the sputtering fuses before the charges blew. At St-Benoît-sur-Loire, the 54-year-old surrealist poet Max Jacob refused to flee because St-Benoît had neither bridges nor factories meriting German bombardment. The decision to stay put was to cost this long-term friend of Picasso his life.

In Paris, apart from an ordinance prohibiting listening to non-German radio stations in public places, there seemed nothing to fear, just the curious sight of a swastika flag atop the Arc de Triomphe. On 15 June, as the government straggled into Bordeaux, the cinema Pigalle in Paris reopened its doors. The following day, being a Sunday, the faithful in many northern parishes, whose priests had fled, had the bizarre experience of hearing Mass read for them by Wehrmacht chaplains.[12] With the litany in Latin, only the celebrants' accents were different.

Also in the north, near Abbeville, British POW Terence Prettie managed to escape from a column of prisoners being marched from Dunkirk towards captivity in Germany. In the several days while he was on the run before recapture, he experienced the gamut of civilian attitudes. One Belgian refugee told him to give himself up because the Germans would treat him well; other homeless Belgian refugees insisted on sharing their precious last chocolate bars with the escapers; a French farmer fed and sheltered Prettie and his companions despite a foraging party of Wehrmacht men politely but insistently requisitioning supplies at the same time; a priest procured for them charts and tide tables in the hope they could find a seaworthy boat that had not been confiscated by the Germans.[13]

The Académie Française met by tradition every Wednesday, but on 12 June the only *académicien* who turned up was the aged Cardinal Baudrillart, who sat alone beneath the cupola working on the great dictionary. To him, as to many right-wing Catholics, the incoming Germans were welcome as an alternative to the godless Communists of Stalin's USSR. It was on this day that Churchill had his last meeting, before flying back to Britain, with Admiral of the Fleet François-Xavier Darlan. When the British bulldog growled at the man who controlled the fourth largest navy in the world, 'Darlan, you must never let them get the French fleet,' Darlan promised he would not.[14]

Bordeaux, the government's temporary home 700 kilometres to the south-west, had its peacetime population swollen by half a million refugees. In every restaurant and on the café terraces were to be seen famous faces from the world of politics, literature, entertainment, journalism. Every lapel seemed to sport a button or ribbon of the Légion d'honneur. Politicians went through the motions of governing the country by meetings held in hotel corridors and on street corners. High functionaries were reduced to sleeping in corridors or in their cars. Even so august a figure as Marshal Pétain could at first not find a bedroom until offered one in a private home, whose concierge raided her 'bottom drawer' to find a set of linen for the Marshal's bed. In the corridors of their temporary accommodation ministers discussed mobilising all male school-leavers and throwing them into the battle against the Panzer spearheads advancing at a rate of 50 kilometres and more a day. The only thing that stopped such lunacy was the non-availability of uniforms and weapons with which they would have got themselves killed.

All over France, in churches and before war memorials, the mothers, wives and fiancées of soldiers prayed and wept, holding the hands of young sons and daughters terrified by the bodies of men, women, children and animals by the roadside after Stuka attacks. Other planes emblazoned with the swastika bombarded the half-empty cities and the military units still fighting with leaflets reading, 'The English warmongers want the war to last another three or five years. People everywhere, however, want peace. EACH OF YOU WILL BEST SERVE HIMSELF AND THE INTERESTS OF HIS COUNTRY IN LIVING FOR FRANCE, RATHER THAN DYING FOR ENGLAND!'

Never mind dying *for* anything, the young and old were dying of exhaustion en route. Children, and even babies, had become separated from their parents in the panic of being machine-gunned by Stuka dive-bombers swooping on the columns of refugees with sirens screaming. Pathetic advertisements in shop windows and those newspapers that still appeared asked for information about a lost child or infant last seen hundreds of kilometres away, or appealed for whoever had stolen a car, a wallet or a handbag to contact the advertiser for a reward. Outside the *mairies* and town halls, crowds gathered for news about food distribution or a roof over their heads, and scanned the boards used for election posters, on which were pinned thousands of requests for news of loved ones. By the end of 1942 the French Red Cross had managed to return nearly 90,000 children lost during the panic of the defeat.

One of the few positive forces in the maelstrom was made up of the courageous women volunteers of the Service Sanitaire Automobile. Using their own vehicles when no official ones were available, they rescued infant orphans found by the bullet- and shrapnel-torn corpses of their parents. They moved with and against the flood of terrified civilians, convoying bandages, dressings, plasma and blood to hospitals overflowing with injured and sick people, before returning to the dangerous highways and byways to transport the exhausted, the dying and the newly wounded to those hospitals still manned. Often without food for themselves and sleepless for nights on end, they stacked up mileages all the more incredible when one considers the impassable state of many roads and the hundreds of bridges that had been pointlessly blown up by retreating engineer units.

Other women led to safety through the lines the elderly, the infirm and the insane. Others still did what they could for the dead also. Medically trained women pilots of the Infirmières Pilotes, Secouristes de l'Air flew badly wounded soldiers to safety almost from the front line. One of them, Germaine L'Herbier Montagnon, logged all sightings of downed aircraft, and spent months afterwards defying the transport chaos, the heat of summer and the snows of winter to trace 500 crash sites on the ground and arrange burial for what remained of the crews.

On 16 June in Bordeaux Reynaud was persuaded by the Comtesse de Portes to resign and seek appointment as ambassador to the US – whether to escape or in an attempt to enlist help from Washington is unclear. His aides Lecca and Devau had been named financial attaché in Washington and Head of the French Purchasing Commission to enable them to travel with a diplomatic bag, whose contents were known to few. Confronted with Reynaud's resignation, Albert Lebrun, the debonair moustachioed *polytechnicien* President of the Republic, called the leaders of the Senate and the Chamber of Deputies to a consultation. All three men were personally in favour of continuing the fight, but Lebrun resisted the house leaders' urging that Reynaud be invited to form another Cabinet, because there was nothing to be gained by it and further indecision would only cost more lives.

In accordance with French tradition, whereby outgoing prime ministers suggested likely successors, a few days earlier Reynaud had tentatively put forward the name of Pétain. Lebrun therefore summoned the 84-year-old Marshal, who arrived in civilian clothes looking like a stern but benign grandfather. Accustomed during his eight-year term as president to lengthy negotiations in such situations, Lebrun was enormously relieved when Pétain opened his wallet after a couple of minutes and took out the handwritten list of names he proposed including in his Cabinet – all men with whom he had worked in previous administrations because the Marshal had a horror of new faces.

After two hours and with a minimum of wheeling and dealing – in which the 57-year-old wheeler-dealer Pierre Laval was at first in, then out of, the government – all was agreed. At twenty minutes before midnight, Pétain's Cabinet included all thirteen of Reynaud's ministers who were in favour of an armistice. Among those out of favour was Georges Mandel, who had been arrested while dining in a restaurant with his mistress. Released, he confronted Pétain and received a written apology, which he still had in his pocket when murdered in July 1944 by the Marshal's Milice.

When Pétain called the first meeting of his Cabinet, although the short notice and general confusion meant that many were absent, it was agreed in minutes to ask the Germans for an end to the conflict. The urbane and imperturbable Spanish ambassador to France, Señor José-Maria de Lequerica, made the ideal neutral channel to relay the Cabinet's decision to the German government. Over an open telephone line, he passed it to St-Jean de Luz, where two of his staff forwarded it to the Foreign Ministry in Madrid via Irun, and thence to Berlin.

At 1 a.m. on 17 June, Pétain retired to bed exhausted. An hour later, his Foreign Minister Paul Baudouin personally conveyed the decision to British Ambassador Sir Ronald Campbell and Mr Biddle, the US chargé d'affaires – in the absence of Ambassador Bullitt, who had remained in post at the Paris Embassy, where the Germans had by now been settling in for three days.

While the Marshal slept, in the depopulated cathedral city of Chartres 41-year-old Prefect Jean Moulin was agonising over the best way to kill himself after refusing to sign a document blaming on a unit of French Moroccan infantry civilian casualties in St-Georges-sur-Eure resulting from German action.[15] If he signed, innocent men would be shot for the crime and the guilty would go free. If he refused, he would have to pay the price. Moulin was a handsome debonair divorcee, an accomplished sportsman and talented cartoonist, whose playboy lifestyle disguised a rare breed of courage. Despite being in German custody, he managed to slash his throat with a broken glass, but was resuscitated by his guards.

Sporadic fighting under conditions of total confusion had now reached within 300 kilometres of Bordeaux. The German spearheads were at Le Mans, Cherbourg, Rennes and Angers. Near Saumur, the whole *promotion* of cadets from a military academy were pointlessly killed as they attempted to halt a Panzer column in their parade uniforms. In the east of the country an entire army of 400,000 men was encircled and cut off from resupply.

Just after noon on 17 June, Pétain sat down at a microphone hastily rigged in the Préfecture building in Bordeaux, pince-nez perched on his nose, and read a prepared speech to the nation in the voice of a tired old man:

Français![16] At the request of the President of the Republic, I have taken over as from today the government of France. Confident of the support of our wonderful army, which is fighting with a heroism worthy of its long traditions against an enemy superior in numbers and equipment, I can say with certainty that its magnificent resistance has acquitted all obligations towards our allies. Confident also of the support of the ex-servicemen I have had the honour to command and of the trust of the entire nation, I dedicate myself to the task of resolving France's misfortunes.

At this painful hour, I send my compassion and my caring to all the unhappy and destitute refugees thronging our roads. It is with a heavy heart that I say to you today that the fighting must stop. Last night, I contacted the enemy to ask soldier-to-soldier whether he can find an honourable way to put an end to the hostilities. May all Frenchmen rally to my government in these testing times, forgetting their anguish and placing all their faith in the destiny of the Fatherland.

When he heard the news that France was surrendering, King George VI remarked to his mother that it was a great relief not to have to be polite to his foreign allies any longer. She had been born German as Princess Mary of

Teck, and the House of Windsor had only changed its family name from Saxe-Coburg-Gotha after three long years of the First World War. Was that really all Britain's king-emperor felt about the suffering of his Czech, Polish, Belgian, Dutch and French allies?

At that moment four German officers were in the crypt of Les Invalides, recovering the German regimental banners captured during the 1914–18 war, and Parisians were looking at notices warning that they were now forbidden to drive a motor vehicle in the capital. These, however, were minor drawbacks. Virtually 100 per cent of the listening population heaved a sigh of relief that the Saviour of Verdun was now in charge. For them, the war was over – or so they thought.

On that same confusing day in Bordeaux Charles De Gaulle, the 49-year-old acting brigadier who had paid two visits to London pleading for help, made several appointments for the afternoon to conceal his movements before accompanying his British opposite number, Major-General Sir Edward Louis Spears, to the military side of Bordeaux-Mérignac airport. As head of the now redundant British military mission to Reynaud's government, Spears was on his way home in an RAF aircraft. With his agreement, De Gaulle had had several heavy cases of confidential files secretly placed on board, but the pilot would not take off until they had been secured, in case he had to take evading action during the flight. Lieutenant Geoffroy De Courcel, the tall, gangling reservist cavalry officer serving as De Gaulle's aide-de-camp, departed to hunt for a ball of twine, leaving his master and Spears increasingly tense as the minutes ticked by. Had De Gaulle's plan become known, or the contents of his cases been suspected, he would have been arrested on the spot and the course of the war and shape of postwar Europe all changed, for want of a piece of string.

Spears recalled:

At last Courcel appeared, his stilt-like legs carrying him fast although he appeared to be moving in slow motion. In his hand, a ball of string. I hope that never again will this commonplace article be so important to me. Our troubles were over. We had begun to move when, with hooked hands, I hoisted De Gaulle on board. Courcel, more nimble, was in in a trice. The door slammed. I had just time to see the gaping face of my chauffeur and one or two more beside him.[17]

Their flight path lay directly over the sinking French liner *Champlain*, going down with 2,000 British troops aboard after hitting a mine. The plane refuelled at Jersey and landed at Heston before noon, at which moment one of the main actors in the Second World War placed himself on the board with immaculate timing. Although Madame De Gaulle managed to take ship to Britain the following day, among those of his family who paid a price for this was his brother Pierre, deported to Germany in 1943. His sister and her husband were imprisoned and sent to Buchenwald and a niece was deported to Ravensbrück.

TRAVAIL PATRIE
FAMILLE

Chapter 3

AN END TO THE KILLING

Heard over the radio by millions, the ill-considered phrase 'the fighting must stop' was the last straw for the French soldier and his officers because the Marshal's actual words, '*Il faut cesser le combat*', could be taken to mean, 'You must stop fighting!' After French-speaking Wehrmacht radio monitors picked up this ambiguity, all along the shifting front German officers approached French units under a flag of truce with the message, 'What are you waiting for? Pétain said to stop fighting.'

France's second most senior serving soldier, Major-General Doumenc, hastily signalled the armies and military regions from GHQ as follows: 'No armistice has been signed. The enemy has used the white flag to approach defended positions. I remind you that the white flag covers only (unarmed) parleys and not armed troops. We must continue to defend our territory everywhere with our last reserves of energy.'[1]

Cleaving a path through the panic and terror, on 18 June the Germans reached the great naval port of Brest in Brittany, its magazines and fuel storage tanks blazing beneath a pall of smoke just after the French Atlantic battle fleet put to sea, leaving behind one torpedo boat and four submarines. Too dismantled to move, they had been reduced to scrap metal. The largest and most heavily armed submarine in the world, the 3,300-ton *Le Surcouf* had been in dry dock, its diesel engines removed for overhaul. Unable to dive, it was heading slowly on its two 1,700-horsepower electric motors towards the English coast.

Admiral Darlan, the short, balding, pipe-smoking Minister of the Navy in Pétain's Cabinet, had graduated first in his *promotion* from the naval gunnery school, but, like Gilbert and Sullivan's 'admiral in the Queen's Navee', spent little time at sea. With the army and air force beaten, he was the only commander whose forces were intact. On his orders, a total of seventy-four warships and seventy-six merchant vessels were now steaming away from Brest, some heading for French North African ports and others to a nearer haven in England.[2] What else could Darlan do, when ordering his warships to bombard the incoming Germans would have destroyed not only the port, but the town with its thousands of inhabitants and homeless refugees? From Fécamp, St Nazaire and Bordeaux also, every naval vessel remotely seaworthy steamed away from the enemy at its best speed, some under fire from German field artillery until safely over the horizon.

On the morning of 18 June Darlan received from President Roosevelt a cable suggesting that the French Mediterranean fleet should similarly put to sea, and head for American ports. Coming from the head of a state that refused to become engaged in the conflict, this understandably enraged Darlan, whose proper office on the Place de la Concorde in Paris was now the Kommandantur von Gross-Paris, from the windows of which the new occupants had a grandstand view of the daily parade down the Champs Elysées of a Wehrmacht band and goose-stepping storm troopers. On an even shorter fuse than usual, Darlan dictated a barely diplomatic reply to Roosevelt's démarche: 'The head of the French Navy has no need of advice from other people as to the decisions he should take to defend the honour of the flag which has been entrusted to him alone.'[3]

To his deputy, Admiral Auphan, Darlan confessed that it was 'not only the Americans who are pissing me off'. Anglophobic since Britain signed a naval pact in 1935 sanctioning the rearmament and expansion of the German fleet without consulting France,[4] Darlan had received that afternoon First Lord of the Admiralty A.V. Alexander and the First Sea Lord, Admiral of the Fleet Sir Dudley Pound, who had flown by seaplane to the naval air base on Biscarosse Lake to ask for similar assurances. In a signal to the Fleet dated 28 May Darlan had already given instructions that no return to French or other German-controlled ports should be made unless over his signature and counter-signed 'from Xavier-François'. A letter from Darlan to his wife the next day likened the British envoys to 'heirs come to the deathbed in order to be sure the will has been made in their favour'.[5]

Thanks to Darlan's foresight, the bulk of the world-class navy he had created was out of Hitler's reach in ports of North Africa, the Far East or Britain – with the exception of Admiral Duplat's Mediterranean Fleet, moored 400 kilometres away from the Demarcation Line in Toulon harbour after its latest raid on Genoa. Should the Germans or Italians try to take over Duplat's vessels, there would be plenty of time to see them coming.

In London, Churchill was in a mood to grasp at any straw. He took little persuading to use De Gaulle for his propaganda value and agreed that, as the highest ranking French serving officer in Britain, he should broadcast a rallying call to his fellow-countrymen over the BBC's French service that evening. So little importance was attached by BBC staff to this broadcast by the tall, arrogant, aloof French officer that no recording was made of this historic event. To listeners in France, De Gaulle promised that 'the flame of French resistance must not and will not go out'.[6] To the many thousands of French servicemen evacuated from Norway and Dunkirk, and those elsewhere who could make their way to Britain with or without their weapons, and to French civilians trapped by the German attack in Britain, he offered the possibility of continuing the war by enlisting in his personal army. This army was at the time devoid of any legal status and consisted of himself and Lt De Courcel with their secretary, 24-year-old shorthand-typist Elisabeth

De Miribel, working in a private house put at De Gaulle's disposal by its owner in London's West End, from where the voice of Free France was a lone cry in the wilderness.

François Mauriac, later a supporter, remarked at the time: 'Purely symbolic, his obstinacy. Very fine, but ineffective.'[7] The reaction of most of his audience to the radioed call to arms, or its clandestinely printed copies, was bafflement. They reasoned that France's two most famous soldiers, Philippe Pétain and Maurice Weygand, must know the situation better than this unknown in London. There was also the worrying thought that, should De Gaulle lose his solitary gamble – which seemed only too likely at the time – his supporters could legally be shot for high treason by the French government.

In his elegant château above the sleepy Dordogne village of Le Breuilh, gentleman farmer Louis De La Bardonnie agreed with every word. He had belonged to the right-wing Action Française party, whose members were pro-Pétain, but regarded the defeat as wholly the result of poor leadership and a matter of national shame. Perhaps there was an element of bloody-mindedness in his decision to rally to De Gaulle, for the Bardonnie family was Catholic whereas most of their neighbours were Protestant. Whatever his reasoning, De La Bardonnie's actions followed swiftly and resulted in a handful of friends he trusted getting together to assemble intelligence for London. With two of them working as pilots for the port of Bordeaux, there was a lot of useful information. The problem was how to transmit it; and, when that was solved, it was never acted upon because London thought it too good to be true.

North of the Channel, the rally De Gaulle expected was no flood, but a mere trickle. Coming ashore from one of the French warships moored in Portsmouth harbour, the reservist Marcel Verliat was undecided whether to stay or go home until confronted with his first meal on English soil. In civilian life a garage mechanic from the Dordogne, he warily tasted the sausage and chips served up by Royal Navy cooks before deciding with most of his shipmates 'to go home, where at least the grub was better'.[8] In addition, most of the married servicemen marooned by the tide of war in Britain wanted to get back to France and make sure their wives and families were alive and well. Typically, from the 8,000 men of Division Béthouart, only 1,500 chose to remain in Britain.

In France, newspapers in those parts of the country not already occupied by German forces reprinted De Gaulle's radio speech in whole or in part, inspiring a small number of patriots to hitch a lift to England on aircraft, ships and even small boats – only to find on tracking down De Gaulle in London that he had no headquarters, no staff, and no uniforms, weapons or work for them. They were told to keep in touch with De Courcel and await orders. Shortly after those newspaper reports had appeared, a government announcement from Bordeaux was relayed over the radio stations still under French control to the effect that De Gaulle was 'no longer a member of the

The abbreviated version of De Gaulle's first broadcast, 18 June 1940, used as a poster.

Translation: To all the French people / France has lost a battle! / But France has not lost the war! / Unworthy leaders have capitulated through panic and delivered the country into servitude. However, nothing is lost! Nothing is lost because this war is a world war. The immense forces of the free world have not yet come into play. One day, they will crush the enemy. On that day, France must share in the victory to recover her liberty and her prestige. That is my sole aim, and the reason why I invite all Frenchmen, wherever they may be, to join me in action, in sacrifice and hope. Our fatherland is in danger of dying. Let us all fight to save it. Vive la France!

government and has no authority to make public announcements. He has been recalled from London and ordered to place himself at the disposal of his superiors. His statements must be regarded as null and void.'[9]

That night was a night of storm on land and tempest at sea. The requisitioned 16,000-ton three-funnelled SS *Massilia* that had been transporting troops from North Africa was anchored 90 kilometres north of Bordeaux, at Le Verdon on the tip of the Médoc peninsula, because the captain regarded docking in the port of Bordeaux as impossible because of magnetic mines dropped by the Luftwaffe in the Gironde estuary.

The *Massilia* was the best transport Adm Darlan could arrange to convey to French North Africa those senators and *deputés* who wished to continue the war from there, of whom Edouard Daladier was the doyen. Jewish parliamentarians who had good reason not to await the German arrival included Pierre Mendès-France, Georges Lévy-Alphandéry, Saloman Grumbach and Georges Mandel, who had found time to marry his blonde lady friend in Bordeaux. Even the captain had no idea how many passengers to anticipate. Estimates varied from forty to 600. In the event, at about 9 p.m. in the teeth of the gale, the car ferry from Royan drew alongside *Massilia* with twenty-six *deputés* and one senator aboard, plus their families and personal vehicles, which they fully expected to take with them. Since the captain of *Massilia* refused to load cars as deck cargo in such weather conditions, they were abandoned on the quayside, whence they disappeared without trace.

That night the Luftwaffe bombed the military/civilian airfield at Bordeaux-Mérignac. From a hayloft on the opposite bank of the Garonne the future Duchess of St Albans, then an adolescent, watched what her younger sisters were told by their mother was a firework display. Ordered by the mayor of Royan to leave next morning, because he did not want the incoming Germans to find any British citizens on his commune, the family was given enough petrol to reach Bordeaux and set out crammed into their car, soon to suffer heat exhaustion. On their mother's instructions, all the children were wearing several layers of clothing, in case they should never find any more shops open. When the car broke down on the road, they stripped off the unnecessary layers and joined the stream of refugees on foot heading for Bordeaux, where there was a British Consulate.[10] At Le Verdon, the crew of *Massilia* mutinied, refusing to sail to Morocco and leave behind their families, many of whom lived in Bordeaux and could have died in the air raid. Disbelieving the intention of their VIP passengers, especially the five Jewish *deputés*, to set up an emergency government in North Africa and continue the war from there, they yelled at them, 'Why should we risk our lives to save you runaways?' The mutiny was swiftly suppressed by a detachment of armed marines and the captain was handed sealed orders from Adm Darlan commanding him to set sail for Morocco. Rapidly filled with army and navy personnel and their families, *Massilia* slipped her moorings at 2.30 p.m., negotiated the tip of Médoc and set course westwards across the Bay of Biscay. Unfortunately for Mendès-France and the others, they were interned on arrival in Morocco, those with military rank being treated as traitors.

Admitting in his memoirs that he felt like a solitary swimmer setting out to cross an ocean, De Gaulle wrote to Gen Weygand via the French military attaché in London on 20 June that his sole wish was to serve his country. He diplomatically pleaded an inability to return due to lack of any aircraft in which to travel. The letter was returned to him in September bearing a typewritten note: 'If Colonel (retired) De Gaulle wishes to contact General Weygand, he should use the proper channels.'

Also on 20 June, the German Military Governor in France issued a proclamation which included a ruling that all businesses must open as normal or risk being placed under an administrator appointed by the Germans. The best news for the general population was that no prices might be increased above the levels on the day of the invasion – not that there was much to buy in the shops. All firearms were to be handed in. Any acts of sabotage would be severely punished, as would any insult to the German Army or its leaders. Hoarding was a punishable offence. All public employees were to continue at their posts and would be paid as usual.

Sounding like a blessed restoration of law and order, the proclamation was welcomed by most civilians, who were relieved to hear on 22 June that Hitler had signed the Armistice agreement in Rethondes near Compiègne. In despair, Adm Darlan dined that night in Bordeaux gourmet restaurant, Le Chapon Fin, drowning and deadening his sorrows with the best of its cellar and cuisine.[11]

Hitler had insisted that the ceremony should take place in the Compagnie Internationale des Wagon-Lits dining-car No. 2419. This had been used by General Foch as his mobile office in the First World War and was where the defeated Germans had signed the surrender in November 1918. Arriving at Rethondes at 3.30 p.m. that day, the French team under General Huntziger asked for an immediate cessation of hostilities. Across the table, neither Hitler nor Goering uttered a word. General Keitel, as German spokesman, refused Huntziger's request because Hitler had laid down that no concession was to be made to the defeated French before they had signed. Afterwards, why bother? After three hours of attempted clarification of the *Diktat* with which he was confronted, Huntziger signed at 6.50 p.m. – forty minutes before Keitel's ultimatum ran out.

The Führer had written in *Mein Kampf* as long ago as 1925, 'The mortal enemy of the German people is and remains France,' so the terms could have been worse. However, destroying what remained of the French state and replacing Pétain's fragile government by a puppet government, as in Poland and Czechoslovakia, risked provoking France's extensive overseas territories – in North Africa alone there were 250,000 men under arms – into siding with Germany's enemies on the grounds that their once-proud fatherland had been reduced to the status of a Nazi-controlled province. Secondly, there was the wild card of the French Navy, out of German reach thanks to Darlan's foresight, but still under his personal command.

To preserve the appearance of French independence, conditions were therefore considerably softened from Hitler's original intentions. To relieve him of the burden of garrisoning the entire country, Pétain was to remain the legal ruler of the whole of France after certain border adjustments. Two of the three *départements* making up the provinces of Alsace and Lorraine were to be annexed into the Reich under their ancient title of Elsass und Lotharingen. West of them was a Zone Réservée. The *départements* of Nord and Pas-de-Calais were for strategic reasons to be governed by the German military administration of Belgium. South of this lay la Zone Interdite, or the forbidden zone.

The northern and western three-fifths of the country, including its financial centres, most of its industry, oil and mineral reserves and the strategically vital Channel and Atlantic littoral, would be occupied by German forces for the duration of the continuing war against Britain. There, the French government would wield authority subject to the Wehrmacht and other German organisations. In the Free Zone, comprising the south-eastern two-fifths, it was to have sovereign powers. Should Pétain's government wish to re-install itself in Paris, that would be considered later. Fifty-two *départements* were thus occupied in whole or in part, with Vichy's theoretically unfettered writ to run in thirty-four *départements* and parts of seventeen others.

French Army and Air Force units not already captured were to withdraw to the Free Zone for disarming and demobilisation, but all surrendered and captured troops would be held as POWs. This particular clause of the *Diktat* sentenced 1,600,000 men, including 4,000 priests serving as chaplains, to four or five years of incarceration in fifty-six Stalags and fourteen Oflags[12] spread out all the way from north-eastern France to Poland. For the most part, officers were not required to work, but the men and NCOs left their camps without escort each morning and marched themselves to work in factories, on farms and as road-building gangs. Their daily rations were ersatz coffee made from acorns, a thin soup in which small pieces of unidentifiable meat floated and 250 grams of bread per man per day. The best-off were those working on farms, where extra food could be had. Supplementary food parcels from home were allowed, but limited to one 5kg parcel or two 2kg parcels per man per month.

No mention was made of occupying the French North African territories, for fear of prompting their secession. The French fleet was to be neutralised, but not delivered to the Germans. The bitterest pill Huntziger had to swallow was Article 23, which made the Armistice subject to Italian confirmation. Dictator Benito Mussolini had only attacked France in order to suffer a token few thousand casualties that would permit him to attend the anticipated

France divided by the Armistice, 22 June 1940.

peace conference and make territorial demands on France after its defeat by German arms. On the Alpine front in the south-east of the country, he had massed thirty-four divisions totalling 550,000 men against 80,500 French soldiers with a few outdated planes and hardly any anti-aircraft defences against the Italian Air Force. Yet, Mussolini's invasion gained little ground against an intelligently led and flexible defence that contrasted sadly with the disastrous inflexibility in the north.[13]

Two amendments to Article 9 passed unnoticed by the general population. In the first, Admiral Canaris of the Abwehr[14] required the immediate liberation of German citizens imprisoned by the French authorities 'for espionage and defeatism'. In the second, aimed at Jewish and political refugees, Heinrich Himmler required *all* German refugees in France to be handed over to his Gestapo.

While the fate of France was being thus settled, 800 kilometres to the south on the Spanish border, the Comtesse de Portes' final gamble had come unstuck. In defiance of customary diplomatic dispensation, Franco's border guards insisted on opening the diplomatic pouch in the car of Lecca and Devau. Inside, they found the Countess' personal jewellery as well as bonds and currency. They also found $2,000,000 in gold. Confiscating the contents, they informed the new French government.

It could all have been quite innocent. After all, what could a French Purchasing Commission do without money to buy things with? However, the Countess panicked Reynaud into meeting her clandestinely at a remote country inn to discuss their situation. After some time spent in visibly anxious conversation, they left with Reynaud at the wheel of their car. There were no witnesses when he drove into a telegraph pole, killing the Countess and sustaining head injuries himself so grave that for several days he hovered between life and death after being transported by ambulance to his villa at St-Maxime.[15]

The first German troops to arrive at the Spanish border in Hendaye shook hands with the jubilant Spanish customs men in their tricorne hats and were toasted with local brandy. They had arrived in a motley collection of patched-up German vehicles and commandeered French trucks, the mobile field workshops having been left far behind in their unopposed dash over hundreds of kilometres since the ceasefire. Captain Barlone had noted in his diary the impeccable organisation of the Germans, with each column having several French-speaking interpreters and a reserve of drivers to take over French Army transport, to augment their own.[16]

Heading for the beach to strip off and bathe nude in the Atlantic surf, the Germans were approached by a number of French soldiers carrying their rifles. When they attempted to hand their weapons over, the laughing bathers told them to go away and give them to the nearest gendarme. All Military *matériel* in the Occupied Zone was declared legitimate booty; in the Free Zone it was to be stockpiled under German control.

The Armistice terms came into force on 25 June. That day, the Marshal warned his people by radio, 'The conditions are severe, but at least our honour is safe. The government is free. France will be administered only by Frenchmen. I hate the lies that have done so much harm.'

Did he really think that was not a lie? His country was divided by an internal frontier of more than 1,000 kilometres running from the Spanish border north to the level of Tours and then in an irregular zigzag north-east and east to reach the Swiss border near Geneva. The annexation of the oil reserves, potassium mines and metallurgical industry of Alsace and the coal mines and steel industry of Lorraine meant that they did not contribute to the heavy taxes payable to cover occupation costs. Dismantled machinery of factories north of the line disappeared eastwards on French rolling stock that never returned, and industry's needs for 49,500,000 tons of coal per year could not be met from the 3,000,000 tons left after German requisitions. The better part of two million men of working age were POWs in Germany sending back no money, unlike most countries' emigrants, and even after the return home of all the refugees, unemployment would stand at one million. Few governments have faced worse problems.

The following day, Mussolini imposed his terms for an armistice, which included occupation by Italian forces of seven pockets in the south-east that would become a haven for thousands of Jewish refugees, safe there from the Gestapo's writ.

Chapter 4

'TRUST THE GERMAN SOLDIER!'

Early on the Sunday morning after the Armistice, Hitler made a lightning tour of deserted Paris, to be photographed for propaganda magazines against the Eiffel tower, before feasting his amateur painter's eye on the Trocadero. His vision of parading like a Roman emperor in triumph at the head of his legions down the Champs Elysées had to be foregone for security reasons, which were cloaked in pretended concern for French pride. Pretended, because he had prophesied seven years earlier to Hermann Rauschning, '[The French] do not want any more to do with war and greatness . . . We shall find plenty of allies on the spot. We shall not even need to buy them. They will come to us of their own accord, driven by ambition, blindness, partisan discord and pride.'[1]

With his obsession for racial unity, how could the Führer respect a nation of forty million, of whom 1,700,000 spoke a Germanic dialect and another 10,500,000 did not have French as their first language?[2] However, the achievements of France's glorious past were something else. Architect Charles Garnier's Second Empire opera house was high on his must-see list. Shown around the resplendent red and gold interior by a concierge, in the absence of any other staff, he discussed the statuary with his guide, the sculptor Arno Breker. As the party was leaving, one of the escorting officers proffered a tip to the concierge, who refused it politely, to the surprise of the Germans.

Breker, who would spend much of the war in Paris, had the distinction of being the first German civilian to enter the capital, having been invited by his Führer because he spoke French and knew the capital intimately, having lived there until 1934. He afterwards recalled Hitler being most moved at the tomb of Napoleon in Les Invalides, where he decided to return the remains of Napoleon's son the Duke of Reichstadt, interred at Shönbrunn Palace outside Vienna, as a gesture to France's past greatness.

By this time Freeman and Cooper were ignoring orders and counter-orders, and using the priority accorded their ambulance bells to part the flood of refugees in hope of reaching Bordeaux before the consulate staff had left. As they drove across the elegant Pont de Pierre over the Garonne into the crowded city, the weather was sultry. Crowds thronged outside the Grand Théâtre where the Chamber of Deputies was in session, as well as every other place where news might replace gossip. Along the chic rue de l'Intendance and rue Ste-Catherine in the city centre, piles of uncollected garbage stank in the sun between the intermittent showers. On the Place des Quinconces, where the temple to the tutelary gods of the Roman city had stood, motor vehicles with empty tanks and registration plates from all over France were jammed bumper-to-bumper.

It was not only the French authorities that had abandoned their citizens. The British Consulate staff had fled, although the Dutch, the Poles and the Belgians still had diplomatic representatives in Bordeaux.[3] Rumour had it that passage could be procured for England in fishing boats from Bayonne, Biarritz, St Jean de Luz or Hendaye on the Spanish border. By any transport they could find, hundreds of stragglers from the sizeable British community in south-west France were heading south, indulging in their favourite game of complaining about the way the French had let them down.

More calmly, the elderly but still majestic 'Baboushka' Cahen d'Anvers was trying to get her English grandchildren, Madeleine and Nelly, safely home to their parents after curtailing their summer holiday at the family's seaside villa near Arcachon. Her friend, British Ambassador Campbell, declared himself unable to help before departing precipitately, but she hoped for better luck on receiving a telegram telling her to hurry to the Hôtel Splendide in Bordeaux. Driven there by the chauffeur of her neighbour Robert De Rothschild, Baboushka met his employer 'looking distraught, nervous and terribly worried'. He asked whether she needed money, which was thoughtful because it was next to impossible to withdraw money from a bank. Also in the Hôtel Splendide was the famous pianist-conductor Alfred Cortot, hoping to follow in the footsteps of Vladimir Horowitz and Arturo Toscanini, to whom Baboushka had bidden farewell there not long before as they were leaving for New York.

The Cahen d'Anvers family was well connected, to put it mildly. Among Baboushka's other friends in the hotel was ex-Queen Amelia of Portugal, who could not help either. Learning that the only port where a ship for England might be found was Bayonne, Baboushka had herself and the children driven there in De Rothschild's car, against the advice of her daughter Renée, who was afraid their ship might be torpedoed. As the British consul had fled, a surly underling stamped the children's travel documents while an elderly Englishwoman announced grandly that 'Mr Churchill will never let us down'. Churchill had other preoccupations, but when Robert De Rothschild's daughter-in-law commandeered the car for her own escape to neutral Portugal, Baboushka and her granddaughters were stranded until the Dutch-owned SS *Queen Emma* entered port. Hurrying to the quayside, they had to step over hundreds of exhausted people sleeping on the pavements.

The *Queen Emma* was full of celebrities as it pulled away from the quay with the two children waving to their relieved grandmother. She could not afterwards recall how she made her way back to the family's villa along 120 kilometres of roads choked with refugees, to find that her son-in-law, Captain Hubert De Monbrison, had briefly called in to see his wife and children when his unit passed nearby during the rout. On being taunted by his 14-year-old daughter Françoise that the Germans would be there before her fifteenth birthday on 18 June, he had given her a stinging slap across the face. But he had now departed and Baboushka found instead another anxious relative relying on her to get him away to safety: the anti-fascist author Ignace Legrand had no illusions how the Germans would treat him. On the morning of Saturday 22 June, his wife ran to the villa with the news that a Royal Navy pinnace was waiting at the Moulleau jetty, less than a kilometre distant, to shuttle the last British officials to a destroyer waiting just over the horizon. Hurrying to the jetty, Baboushka's tall and beautiful auburn-haired daughter Renée begged transport for the Legrand couple.

'And who would be responsible for them in Britain?' asked the RN commander sarcastically.

'My sister lives in England,' Renée replied. 'She is married to an Englishman, Anthony De Rothschild.'

'Good Lord,' said Commander Ian Fleming (later to achieve fame as the creator of James Bond), 'Tony Rothschild's a chum of mine. I'll take all your family on board, if you like.'[4]

Some people have all the luck! Hungry and exhausted by three weeks of driving on the lethally dangerous roads, Freeman and Cooper headed for the docks on arriving in Bordeaux. Finding a single White Ensign flapping damply in the breeze, they were not alone in wondering what a British destroyer was doing there at this late stage. After explaining away their French uniforms, they were allowed to board, largely on account of their native diffidence in protesting that they did not want to be a bother to anyone if there was no room on the ship.

The captain of the destroyer was a lieutenant-commander, but there was also an RN commander on board, a high-ranking army officer and an admiral, which made Freeman and Cooper surmise that the ship was in Bordeaux on some important intelligence or diplomatic mission. Their 400 last-minute fellow-passengers on a vessel designed to carry no passengers at all included three autocratic betrousered Englishwomen, who were given the captain's cabin as the only suitable accommodation. In a gesture of positive discrimination typical of the all-male Navy, they were also allotted half the officers' 'heads' or toilet facilities for their exclusive use on the crowded journey.

Understandably, Freeman and Cooper were hazy about exact dates by this time in their odyssey, so this destroyer may have been the same one that rescued the Legrands from Moulleau, in which case the supernumerary commander was Ian Fleming. After casting off, the White Ensign was hailed with loud cheers of 'Vive l'Angleterre!' from the crews of French warships at their moorings. Then followed a nail-biting few hours' being piloted between the shifting sandbanks of the Gironde estuary on constant lookout for magnetic mines. Passing at dusk the Le Verdon memorial on the tip of the

Médoc peninsula to the first 'doughboys' who landed there in 1917, Freeman thought it looked like a beacon whose flame had gone out, for he had seen no evidence of the 'resistance' of which De Gaulle had spoken on 18 June.

In the darkness of German-occupied Royan on their starboard bow, Pablo Picasso was preparing to leave his top-floor studio in a typical turn-of-the-century seaside villa built there by the city-dwelling middle classes when the railway arrived at the end of the nineteenth century. A refugee from civil war in Spain, he had been painting at Antibes in September 1939 and fled from there to Paris. The German advance had panicked him and his mistress-model Dora Maar into heading with his secretary Jaíme Sabartés and dog Kasbec for the south-western resort, where his daughter Maïa and her mother were already staying, in the belief that they would be safe there. Now that the Wehrmacht had caught up with him, he decided to take his complicated *ménage* back to Paris, where life was more amusing.

Taking refuge with friends in the Loire Valley after fleeing the capital, Simone De Beauvoir wrote of the German arrival there, 'To our general surprise, there was no violence. They paid for their drinks and the eggs they bought at farms. They spoke politely. All the shopkeepers smiled at them.'[5] Further north, General Erwin Rommel was writing to his wife, 'The war is turning into a peaceful occupation of the whole of France. The population is calm and in some places even friendly' – as they were in the British Channel Islands, where the Wehrmacht landed on 30 June without opposition, the islands having been demilitarised a week earlier as impossible to defend.

Casualties of the German advance included one of the first tax exiles. P.G. Wodehouse, creator of Jeeves and Bertie Wooster, had arranged for himself and his wife to be warned of the German advance by British troops near their home in Le Touquet but were caught out by its speed, having refused to return to Britain earlier because their Pekinese dog would have been put in quarantine for six months. Like all male citizens of enemy powers less than 60 years old, Wodehouse was taken hostage, being confined in a former mental hospital at Tost in Upper Silesia to await his 60th birthday.

One of the most bizarre jobs handed out by Pétain's government at this time landed on the desk of General De La Porte du Theil, whose 7th Army Corps had fought well in Alsace and retreated in good order successively to the Marne, the Seine and the Loire, before withdrawing for re-grouping at Bourganeuf, near Limoges, safely inside the Free Zone. This unknown general is very much a man of his time, to evaluate whom is difficult today. On 2 July he was Commanding Officer of 13th Military Division, based in Clermont-Ferrand. Summoned to nearby Royat, where Gen Weygand's War Ministry was in temporary accommodation, De La Porte du Theil was informed of his new posting. While all else failed in the debacle, the bureaucracy of conscription had continued to run impeccably: 70,000 20-year-old men had been called up for military service on 8 and 10 June, since when they had been without uniforms, weapons, NCOs or training. Since, under the

Armistice agreement, it would have been illegal to issue them with uniforms or weapons, De La Porte du Theil asked Weygand what exactly he was supposed to do with so many useless mouths. The answer: anything that would occupy these bored and rightly angry young men.

'And where do I get the officers to train them?' he asked.

'You can have the pick of the cadet schools,' was Weygand's reply.

He had chosen the right man for a near-impossible job. In 1928, aged 44, De La Porte du Theil had grown bored with peacetime soldiering and had since alternated between his chair at the War Academy and being a sort of Baden-Powell for the French Scout movement. Brought up as the son of a forestry inspector, he was a great outdoorsman, first-rate hunter and good horseman. Two days later he was back in Weygand's office, having acquired a small staff and core of NCOs, to explain his plan for dividing the unemployed conscripts of the Free Zone into regiment-sized formations of 2,000 and sending them into remote areas where they could perform useful work like logging, road-making and reafforestation. In lieu of the obligatory military service traditional in France, each conscript on reaching the age of 18 was to serve eight months of a healthy back-to-nature life, living under canvas until the work-teams had constructed themselves more permanent accommodation.

When Weygand told Pétain, the Marshal thought it was a wonderful way of stiffening the moral fibre of the nation's dissolute youth by removing them from the temptations of city life and inculcating a respect for manual labour and a sense of patriotic duty against the day when military conscription was resumed. On 30 July he announced the inauguration of the Chantiers de Jeunesse, or youth work camps, placed under the aegis of the Ministry of Youth and the Family, so that the Germans would not be alarmed by thinking it a clandestine army, although privately when appointing De La Porte Du Theil Commissioner-General of the Chantiers, he said unequivocally, 'Make me an army.' Whatever the two men took that to mean at the time, it is unlikely that either foresaw the mission ending with the Commissioner-General's arrest and deportation by the Germans, while his enemies accused him of supplying a ready-made source of manpower for the German compulsory labour programme, despite evidence that men from the Chantiers made up less than 2.4 per cent of the total, partly because they had learned self-reliance and were prepared to risk the alternatives.

Modelled on the army that the Commissioner-General knew well, the Chantiers were organised into six regiments, five in the Free Zone and the other in French North Africa. In each, approximately 2,000 men were to be deployed on public works, divided into companies and platoons. To avoid military nomenclature, the largest units were called *groupements* and each was divided into ten *groupes* of 200 men each – roughly equal to a company – with each *groupe* divided into *équipes* or light platoons of fifteen men.

The first intake eventually numbered 87,000 conscripts issued with green and khaki military-style uniforms, in which they served until February 1941.

Their duties were decided by unit commanders, with the proviso that they be kept busy. The day began with a salute to the colours, followed by a pep talk and a morning devoted to work, with the afternoon for physical training and technical instruction. In practice, the unwilling conscripts found pay of 1 franc 50 per day and campfire sing-songs in the evening a poor compensation for money in their pockets, girls, bars and billiard halls. They made this plain by stealing, fighting, drinking when they could and sabotaging state property most of the time. The propaganda posters likening them in battledress and beret to the warlike ancient Gauls were treated with due derision, and they showed little enthusiasm for planting trees, making roads and digging ditches under quasi-military discipline. In the Occupied Zone, young men were offered a different adventure: to go and work in the Reich. Figures are unreliable, but between 40,000 and 72,000 volunteered and joined the one and a half million foreign workers already replacing German manpower in factories and on farms.

On 6 July all foreigners' visas were cancelled and non-residents were made subject to travel restrictions. That month, acts of open hostility to the Occupation forces were swiftly punished to serve as lessons to the general population. In Rouen, Epinal and Royenne, lone protesters cut German telephone lines and were executed by firing squad. The only violence in Bordeaux came when a distraught Polish refugee shook his fist at a military band, for which he too was shot on 27 August.

By then, Baboushka's family had filled their villa with refugees to avoid it being requisitioned when the first troops arrived at Le Pyla, watched by silent crowds wondering what was going to happen next. Renée and her mother told the children not to look at the Germans, but just pretend they were not there. It was all rather English. François Mauriac put it more poetically. 'Have eyes that see nothing,' he advised his compatriots. However, it was very hard for a Frenchwoman not to thank a polite, smiling soldier who lifted her heavy suitcase onto a train, as it was for Renée to refuse a seat on a bus when a German politely stood up for her.

The empty Rothschild villa next door to the De Monbrisons' was requisitioned for a German general and his staff. Renée's sons were fascinated by the two armed sentries goose-stepping at the bottom of their driveway, day and night. A thirsty sentry who asked them to sneak him a bottle of lemonade from a nearby shop rewarded the boys with cigarettes. When their mother found out, they were sent to bed without supper.

They watched an anti-submarine net being strung from the beach below their villa to Cap Ferret on the far side of the entrance to Arcachon lagoon. Thus protected, the Wehrmacht rehearsed Fall Seelöwe or Operation Sealion, its planned landing in Britain. Soldiers were pushed overboard from landing barges to test how well they could swim with full pack and weapons and trucks were driven ashore towing a dozen bicycle-soldiers on a rope, most of whom fell off in the soft sand. Forbidden to have anything to do with the unwelcome neighbours, the boys took a potentially lethal pleasure in hiding by the roadside and pelting the last trucks of German convoys with pine cones.[6]

As motor fuel became unobtainable for civilians, bicycles came into their own. Like many others, Renée rarely went out without her trailer – not that there was very much to buy, apart from locally caught fish, artichokes, root vegetables and horse meat once a month. Bread rationing was already in force. Coupons for 100 grams per person were usable only on the date printed on them, to prevent stockpiling.

People spent hours every day in the long queues outside the few bakeries and food stores still open. The problem at this early date was not so much shortage of food as disruption to food production and distribution caused by eight million refugees far from home, butchers, bakers and other shopkeepers among them. In many areas that were under no military threat, the population had been *ordered* to leave their homes, taking only three days' provisions with them. In their deserted villages and towns it was often the German army that replaced the French infrastructure by setting up a soup kitchen for stay-at-homes and returnees or by distributing bread. German railwaymen were already driving trains, which enabled some refugees to return home. On the bandstands in public parks, Wehrmacht musicians played afternoon concerts to calm the population. On the hoardings, the tattered general mobilisation notices from the previous September covered by later posters warning of a mythical Fifth Column stabbing the army in the back were swiftly covered by new ones showing a valiant Wehrmacht soldier holding a grateful small child in his arms above the message 'Abandoned by your leaders, put your trust in the German soldier!'[7]

That there were rapes and some armed robberies was inevitable with over a million armed men in areas populated by a few old men, women and

The vital bread tickets.

children. In some places, soldiers in uniform demanded food and drink at the point of a gun when their own supplies had run out, but this tended to occur in the country and small villages. In the towns policed by the Feldgendarmerie they were on their best behaviour and insisted on paying for what they wanted. True, they used German money, but from 20 June onwards that was declared legal tender at the very favourable rate of exchange imposed by Berlin: one Reichsmark equalled 20 francs. Indeed, the Wehrmacht was mostly so well behaved that many bewildered French refugees wondered why they had been ordered by the authorities to flee their distant homes.

A rigid curfew was imposed between 10 p.m. and 5 a.m. – the start being put back on 7 July to 11 p.m. and midnight in November as a reward for the population's good behaviour. It was decreed that householders were now responsible for cleaning the space in front of their houses, as in Germany. Similarly, peasants must clear weeds and tidy up their farms. Clocks must be put forward an hour, to Berlin time. The French *tricolore* flag must be removed from town halls and war memorials. The first wave of German orders seemed to a population fed up with the vacillations and ineptitude of their own authorities and elected representatives a small price to pay for the end of the bloodshed. And Marshal Pétain was the hero of the hour, for it was he who had achieved this miracle.

Chapter 5

BEHOLD THE MAN!

W hat kind of man was Philippe Pétain, whose name has become a synonym for cruelty and collaboration in the worst degree? A career soldier who never expected to become a general, let alone head of state, he was born in April 1856 into a family of farmers a few kilometres from Béthune in northern France. Admitted to the military academy of St-Cyr after attending the village school and a religious secondary school, he was an outstanding cadet. Commissioned second-lieutenant in an Alpine regiment, he was popular with his men but not his superiors because of an inability to keep his mouth shut when disagreeing with them – a trait that has blighted the career of many a peacetime soldier. While an instructor at St-Cyr, Pétain opposed the nineteenth-century obsession with offensive operations at any cost, arguing that a commander must possess superior fire-power before launching an attack and that a well-organised defence to wear the enemy down was often a better course.

Thus, advancement came his way slowly. In 1914 he was a handsome blue-eyed unmarried 58-year-old colonel stationed in Arras with a record that even his hagiographical biography by General Laure described as distinctly below average. On the point of resigning his commission from sheer frustration when war broke out, Pétain was promoted to general on the strength of commanding at Guise in 1914 one of the few successful operations against the invading armies of Kaiser Wilhelm II. Given command of 6th Division and then 33rd Corps, he distinguished himself again at Artois by the use of massive artillery barrages to reduce the horrific scale of casualties that his fellow-generals thought acceptable. Promoted to command the Second Army for the 'big push' in Champagne during September 1915, he failed to break the German line, but was called on six months later to stem the attack under Crown Prince Wilhelm on the crucial fortress-city of Verdun. On his appointment, the situation was regarded as hopeless, but he reorganised the front, the transport system and the disposition of artillery, inspiring his demoralised troops. Unashamed to show his grief at the sight of the casualties, he earned at Verdun a reputation for humane and far-sighted generalship.

In June 1917, after the widespread mutinies following the ill-considered offensives of General Nivelle that cost hundreds of thousands of lives to no purpose, Pétain's success at Verdun and his popularity with the troops resulted in his replacing Nivelle as Commander-in-Chief of all French armies. His first problem was not the enemy, but the low morale of the men under his command. A brutal series of executions intended to break the mutineers' spirits had succeeded only in reducing morale even further. Pétain's revolutionarily modern method was to reduce punishments and reward good conduct and bravery, even allowing men in the ranks to make recommendations for their own comrades who merited the Croix de Guerre.

Conscripts who had been fighting for three years in the trenches without seeing their families were astonished to be given leave passes. They enjoyed regular rest periods out of the line – and better food. The latter he achieved by random visits to other ranks' canteens, where he startled his aides-de-camp by sampling the fare personally and commenting on it frankly. In August and October 1917 at Verdun and Malmaison Pétain again made a name for himself by using enormous bombardments to save his men's lives, and finished the war as France's most respected soldier since Napoleon. It had taken him forty years to rise from second-lieutenant to colonel; from there to Marshal of France took only four. His rise was all the more spectacular because the majority of his fellow generals were discredited and it seemed to the nation that he was the only one who had never been wrong since 1914.

At the age of 62, he was popular enough to enter politics, but chose to do what great Roman generals had done, retiring to a farm to occupy himself with husbandry while awaiting his country's call. It came in 1926 when he was sent to Morocco to suppress the revolt against French colonial domination led by Abd el-Krim. Inheriting the chair of his deceased rival Marshal Foch at the Académie Française on 22 January 1931, he was hailed by the poet Paul Valéry as the man who had gone to war in 1914 at the head of 6,000 men and had three million under his command by 1918. However, outside the ivory tower of the Academy lay the smokeless factory chimneys and the hunger marches of the Depression years. After nationwide strikes and riots in 1934, it was Pétain's presence in the unstable government of Gaston Doumergue that was largely responsible for the re-establishment of public order: people trusted the Saviour of Verdun to bring in the reforms they wanted.

His last public office in the thirties was as ambassador to Spain. Aged 81 on appointment, the old soldier charged with opening diplomatic relations with Franco's government was so widely respected that even the *caudillo*[1] wept with emotion on hearing of his appointment. However, Pétain did not have the political sense it takes to be a diplomat and was easily duped into allowing himself to be photographed with German members of the Condor Legion or warmly shaking the hand of Hitler's ambassador, Von Stohrer. Even after the declaration of war with Germany in 1939, Pétain was again photographed apparently reviewing swastika-badged German flagbearers at the re-interment of Falange[2] founder José Antonio Primo de Rivera in the Escurial. Goebbels' propaganda machine naturally made the most of these photo opportunities before the Marshal was recalled by Reynaud on 16 May 1940.

If that was the public Pétain, what was the private man?

All the world loves a lover, and France more so than most countries. Pétain had a great love affair, which endeared him to many women who admired him for saving the lives of their menfolk at Verdun. The long affair began in 1881 at Menton. Aged 25, 2/Lt Pétain dandled 4-year-old Eugénie Hardon on his knee – and fell in love with her. In the guise of family friend, he consoled young Ninie on the loss of her mother and then her father. On his regular visits to the bereaved Hardon household, he watched her grow from an enchanting child into a beautiful, elfin-faced young woman, looking uncommonly like Leslie Caron in the film version of Colette's *Gigi*. The perfect gentleman, Philippe Pétain bided his time, waiting until 1901 when she was 24 and he 45. Such age-gaps were neither uncommon at the time, nor disapproved of. Yet when the nervous suitor proposed marriage, he was rejected by Eugénie's guardians because of his poor military prospects. Two years later, she married and had a son.

Her marriage failing, Eugénie became aware of Pétain's *amour de loin* expressed in passionate love letters. Despite his enormous responsibilities, Pétain wrote to her every single day throughout the First World War, his letters revealing a tortured, jealous admirer. On the threshold of the greatest carnage the world had known, he wrote to her on a ruled signal pad dated 21 August 1914: 'I face a great battle without regret or apprehension for I have already offered my life to my country, but the physical suffering ahead is as nothing compared with the spiritual torture you cause me.'[3] In April 1916 he wrote to her, not of guns and glory but of a lovers' fantasy tryst: the two of them alone 'with just some books for company and a few good friends, who do not include your old sweethearts or mine'.[4]

As the war progressed it was Eugénie's turn to be jealous of the many beautiful women pursuing France's great hero. Jealous of each other, now bitter, now loving, they were together when Joffre called Pétain to command the army at Verdun. Reluctantly he tore himself away from Ninie to fulfil his destiny. It was not until 1920 that the lovers could get married: he now 64 and she 43, a fashionable woman of beauty, poise and presence. Not in the high society of Paris, but in the bucolic setting of Villeneuve-Loubet in the Alpes Maritimes between Nice and Antibes, Pétain returned to his roots – becoming expert in raising chickens and rabbits, growing vegetables and pruning vines.

The rural idyll, interrupted by his suppression of the Abd el-Krim revolt in Morocco, ended for good when Pétain was sent to Madrid. When he was recalled by Reynaud in May 1940 to serve in the Cabinet, Eugénie did not accompany him to Paris, having no place in his political life. However, she came to take up her duties at his side when the government moved from Bordeaux to Clermont-Ferrand and then to Vichy. She stayed loyally with him from then on, and accompanied him by choice on 20 August 1944 when the SS drove the ageing Marshal into exile on the other side of the Rhine. She was still with him on his return via Switzerland in 1945 to face trial and a sentence of death. Briefly imprisoned with him, she was released, but showed both dignity and courage in standing by one of the two most vilified men in France – Laval was the other. After the commutation of Pétain's death sentence immediately after its pronouncement in August 1945, she moved to the bleak Ile d'Yeu in the Bay of Biscay, where he was imprisoned, and stayed there near the prison until his death in July 1951 at the age of 95.

That, then, was Philippe Pétain, the soldier and the man. How did it all go so wrong?

Stimulated by the crisis of June 1940 and his unique ability to resolve it, Pétain aimed to rebuild the French people's shattered morale by promising them the birth of a new intellectual and moral order after the signature of the Armistice. A brand-new France, he promised the people, would surge forth from the ashes of the old.[5] It was a beautiful dream and at a time when reality is intolerable most people can be seduced by the right dream. A measure of his popularity is the speed with which his personality cult grew in this pre-television era when portraits of Stalin, Hitler, Mussolini, Franco and Salazar were in millions of homes and every public building in their respective countries. Post offices in the Free Zone sold within the space of two weeks 1,368,420 portraits of the man who had saved Verdun and now France itself. They were hung on office walls, in homes and factories and especially on the radio sets that then occupied a focal point in living rooms, bars and hotel dining rooms.

Men sported Pétain handkerchiefs and propelling pencils bearing his picture. Children carried proudly to school souvenir pencil boxes in the shape of the Marshal's baton. In the classroom a new national hymn, 'Maréchal, nous voilà!' replaced 'La Marseillaise' and competition was fierce to be the child chosen to write a letter to the Marshal, whose prompt reply came complete with a portrait of him looking noble on horseback. His fan mail averaged 1,200 letters per day. In every town and village, streets and squares were renamed in his honour – to be renamed again at the Liberation.

Although the Third Republic had no established religion, the vast majority of the population was Catholic. To them, the Marshal's sacrificial phrase in the broadcast of 17 June, 'Je fais à la France le don de ma personne' ('I offer myself to France') had almost Christ-like connotations, as though Pétain had been sent by God to redeem the nation.[6] An entire iconography was to be created on the theme: Behold the man . . . The state-owned Imagerie du Maréchal recruited artists to produce icons in two and three dimensions. A colouring book for children showed twelve significant events from his life, after the manner of the Stations of the Cross. Fairy stories were written about his life, some beginning, 'Once upon a time, there was a Marshal of France . . .'

Philippe Pétain was 84 when he became prime minister and subsequently head of state. His clothes were always immaculate and his bearing upright, but if at times his step was still sprightly and his wit razor-sharp, at others he was absent-minded, forgetful and unable to concentrate as his brain slowed down. He could easily be worn down by persistence and would doze off in afternoon meetings, losing the track of an argument and tending to cover the inattention by agreeing with the last person to speak, even when doing so contradicted himself. Unfortunately, circumstances obliged him to work in partnership with a man adept at taking advantage of these failings: the cunning and devious lawyer-politician and self-made millionaire Pierre Laval.

TRAVAIL PATRIE

FAMILLE

Chapter 6

THE LIE THAT WAS TRUE

With France's politicians dispossessed of their temporary capital in Bordeaux by the Germans requisitioning all the public buildings, on 29 June the impromptu convoy of private and official vehicles headed north-east for Clermont-Ferrand, in the centre of France. While its geographical position guaranteed good communications, this major manufacturing town was home to the giant Michelin rubber company and not equipped to accommodate the government and civil service with all their hangers-on and camp-followers. Ministers and their staffs were spread out in surrounding towns, without even a working telephone system to communicate with each other. It was a recipe for chaos, had one been needed.

With eight million displaced people, the country was in turmoil. Lack of motor fuel caused havoc with food distribution. Public transport for those who wanted to return home was non-existent. Even the police and gendarmerie had no clear idea who was in charge of what. The postal service, where it existed at all, was reduced to a few cyclists carrying official communications. Shops of all kinds had been broken into and pillaged, mostly by refugees desperate for food. Abandoned French Army horses and farm animals roamed loose in the fields and ownerless dogs scavenged the streets. Everywhere there were queues for food, shelter, news and vital papers that had been lost in the panic.

As so often, a single-minded and ambitious man took advantage of everyone else's confusion. On 16 June in Bordeaux, when the Marshal presented his handwritten list of Cabinet ministers to President Lebrun, the name of Pierre Laval had not been on it because he had been offered, and refused, the Ministry of Justice. It was as Foreign Minister that Laval saw his role in Pétain's government because that brief would embrace relations with Germany, whose leaders he already knew personally. Informed by the Marshal that Foreign Affairs had been given to Paul Baudouin, Laval's unbridled fury was such that he stormed out of the Marshal's borrowed office, slamming the door.

France's diplomats heaved a collective sigh of relief, the Ministry's Secretary-General having indicated to Pétain that making Foreign Minister a man with Laval's anti-British reputation would destroy the tattered remnants of the Entente Cordiale. Despite Britain's unilateral withdrawal at Dunkirk, a surprising number of influential French people were still anglophile at this stage. Having drawn a line in the sand by stipulating that he wanted the Quai d'Orsay or nothing, Laval therefore played no part in the negotiations for the Armistice – a fact that was often subsequently overlooked by his denigrators. Nevertheless, Pétain knew Laval too well to leave him out of the new government, knowing that he could foment trouble, and therefore brought him in as one of two vice-presidents of the Council of Ministers, or Cabinet.

Pierre Laval's solution to his country's woes was simple: he proposed the abolition of the Third Republic on the grounds that it was responsible for the defeat. On the morning of 30 June a poorly attended Cabinet meeting in Clermont debated his proposition. Not every minister was in favour, some arguing that the best way to put the country back on its feet was to give Pétain six months to govern without parliamentary oversight. Using a battery of courtroom lawyer's tricks that would have worn down the resistance of men far stronger than the senescent Marshal, Laval returned to the attack in the afternoon Cabinet meeting. When Pétain argued that such a radical step should await their return to a free Paris after the conclusion of a definitive peace treaty, Laval riposted that only a strong France could negotiate on equal terms with Germany the treaty to replace the Armistice agreement.

Back in March he had said to the British politician Robert Boothby, 'If we had come to terms with Mussolini, as I wanted to do, we might have held Hitler. . . . That is no longer possible. Let us try to hold on to what we have left. I am a peasant from the Auvergne. I want to keep my farm, and I want to keep France. Nothing else matters now.'[1] Weakening in the face of Laval's sustained arguments, Pétain protested that only a National Assembly of both the Senate and the Chamber of Deputies had the power to alter the Constitution. Calling that assembly required the assent of the President of the Republic. It was the moment for which Laval had been waiting. Scattering cigarette ash – he was a chain-smoker – over his trademark white tie, he leapt up from the conference table and drove to the nearby town of Royat, where President Lebrun was quartered. An hour later he returned with Lebrun's assent to the National Assembly. Overwhelmed by Laval's fait accompli, Pétain gave way.

As to where the assembly could meet, the nearest suitable place lay 50 kilometres to the north-east of Clermont. Some guessed that Vichy was chosen because it suited Laval, whose home was only 20 kilometres distant; others more poetic averred that it was because its famous Celestins spring was the only one in the world that gushed water tasting exactly like tears. The true reason was that Foreign Minister Paul Baudouin suggested Vichy to the Marshal because the prosperous spa resort had 15,000 hotel rooms, a modern telephone exchange and a direct railway link with Paris.[2] Thus it was to Vichy that the ministers, senators and deputies made their way on the afternoon of 1 July.

Its unsought role as capital of the divided country was to cost the town dearly. Such is the stigma of having been the capital of collaboration that half a century later few people want to be seen taking the cure there, and many hotels never reopened after the war. As the many bedrooms barely sufficed to accommodate and afford office space for a government that historian Robert Aron described as 'a comic opera government adrift in a cataclysm',[3] many top civil servants had to use their bedrooms as offices. The secretary of Xavier Vallat, Minister for Ex-servicemen, took dictation sitting on his bidet. Files were stacked in open drawers between Monsieur's underpants and Madame's lingerie. The chairman of a meeting would get up from time to time to check the vegetables boiling on a camping stove on top of the dressing table. Nobody worried at first that most of the hotels habitually closed for the winter season and had no heating because Article 3 of the Armistice agreement could be read to mean that the government would soon be returning to Paris.

The phoney war had been a period of exceptional prosperity for Vichy, filling its hotels with middle-class families displaced by the armies in the north-east, but the brief hot war in June saw them in turn displaced by trainloads and road convoys of wounded soldiers. The Germans installed themselves briefly and left again, apart from a few liaison personnel. When the government moved in on the first day of July, the last *curistes* and tourists who had been turned out of their rooms at a few minutes' notice were left gaping at cars and trucks of all sizes and conditions disgorging ministers, their staffs, wives and secretaries, filing cabinets and trunks of documents – all the paraphernalia of state.

Weygand's Ministry of Defence moved into the Thermal Hotel; Darlan's Navy into the Helder with the Army taking the Hotel des Bains; Justice and Finance requisitioned the Carlton; the diplomatic corps took the aptly-named Ambassadors Hotel, with each mission being allocated a nearby farm for food supplies. Baudouin's Foreign Ministry moved into the Hotel du Parc with Pétain and Laval staked his territory there after arriving in a muck sweat, his official car having broken down with clutch trouble some way out of town.

President Lebrun was allotted the elegant Pavillon Sévigné at the far end of the central park and the Ministry of Education was lodged in the prestigious Casino itself. The Majestic Hôtel, which shared a common entrance with the Parc, swiftly filled with senators and deputies, who continued to arrive long after the blackout, searching by the light of pocket torches for a bed in the overcrowded rooms and corridors. Only 200 of them had made it to Bordeaux, yet a week after the Marshal's arrival three times as many had reached Vichy.

French and foreign journalists and broadcasters, businessmen in search of government contracts or fearing to lose them, and gamblers like the Egyptian Khedive who sought the throne of Damascus, which was then in the French giving . . . They all came to Vichy in that first week of July. Well, not quite all. Among the foreign journalists who did not come was a correspondent of the London *News Chronicle*. While reporting the Spanish Civil War, Arthur

Koestler had narrowly missed being executed by Franco's forces and had no intention of being handed over to the Germans. On 17 June he walked into a Foreign Legion recruiting office that in the general chaos had received no instructions to cease operations and there reinvented himself as Albert Dubert, a Swiss taxi driver. Persuading the recruiting sergeant to issue him with papers as a *volontaire étranger* in that name, he used them to find food and lodging in military barracks right across France. Reaching Marseilles after six weeks of meanderings, he eventually escaped from there to Britain.[4]

The town of Vichy, enclosed in a circle of low hills, sweltered moistly in the stifling midsummer heat as people fought for a bed, for status and recognition. Among the politicians scrambling for advantage, only Pétain preserved the appearance of authority. On his morning promenades through the town, accompanied by his aide Dr Ménétrel, and at the salute to the flag on Sunday morning the Marshal moved with dignity among the people, gravely acknowledging their salutations or hushed respect and always finding time to greet children in their Sunday best on his way to Mass at the church of St Louis.

With normal communications almost non-existent, news travelled mostly by word of mouth in the traumatic summer of 1940. And news there was, all of it bad. The border *départements* of Alsace and Lorraine were not merely occupied by the Wehrmacht, but on 7 August annexed directly into the Reich as an integral part of German territory. In the schools of the two former *départements* the curriculum changed overnight, and all textbooks and exercise books were collected and burned. At the start of the new term, schoolchildren learned in their first geography lesson that they now lived in Elsass, not Alsace. Although German propaganda was trying to make all Alsatians conscious that they spoke the Germanic dialect Alsässisch and were therefore German, speaking the dialect was discouraged in school, while French was totally forbidden. Lessons were all in German from then on, with the biggest surprise for the pupils in history lessons to learn the Nazi version of European history.[5] However, the pull of home is strong and two-thirds of the 420,000 Alsatian refugees decided to return after months of living on handouts in temporary accommodation, although the thought of becoming German citizens if they returned home made others decide to stay in the south-west, somehow surviving on daily handouts of 10 francs per adult and 6 francs for a child.

In rural Moissac the first Belgian refugees had been welcomed by the townsfolk until some young Flemings got into fights with local youths after expressing pro-German sentiments. The massive influx that followed threatened to swamp the town altogether: by 1 July an additional 16,000 refugees[6] had arrived needing lodging and food and clothing and, at times, as many as 40,000 people, including 15,000 military, were also passing through. For most of June, Moissac was among the most important *villes-refuges* in all France. Only at the end of July did life return to something like normal.

At Ponthivy, in Brittany, a German-sponsored puppet Breton separatist government briefly surfaced before foundering for lack of support. Later Corsican and Basque separatists would be encouraged by the Germans as a way of fragmenting national sentiment, but Goebbels' main priority was to drive an unbridgeable rift between France and Britain. On the evening of 3 July came news from Mers el-Kebir that fulfilled his wildest dreams.

Back on 23 June, with the Armistice already signed, a Royal Navy vessel – probably the same one on which Freeman and Cooper escaped, with the supernumerary commander and admiral on board – had brought to Admiral Darlan in Bordeaux a message from A.V. Alexander and Admiral Pound which did not refer to their recent meeting but 'reminded' Darlan that the 'condition imposed' by Great Britain for an armistice was that the French Navy should previously have steamed to English ports in order to 'continue the struggle' against Germany.[7] At the time – and until 28 June – French vessels that had taken refuge in British ports were permitted to steam away unhindered as belonging to a neutral nation. So there was no reason for Darlan or anyone else on the French side to suspect that the British Admiralty was about to implement an operation planned months before: it was code-named Catapult, although later dubbed 'Operation Boomerang' by Admiral Cunningham, the British Commander-in-Chief in Alexandria, because of its predictably disastrous consequences.

It was the greatest gift Churchill could have given to Goebbels. Like all great propaganda coups, it was so simple that anyone could understand it. On 3 July 1940 a British battle fleet appeared without warning off the great natural harbour of Mers el-Kebir in the Bay of Oran, in Algeria. Without giving any warning, the British vessels shelled the French fleet moored there, before the French had time to get steam up. With no power to rotate their gun turrets, ships were sunk and thousands of sailors killed.

It wasn't *quite* like that, but the differences were only of detail.

On 24 June Admiral Sir Dudley North, based in Gibraltar, had paid a visit on HMS *Douglas* to the French naval base at Mers el-Kebir outside Oran. His object was to convince Admiral Marcel Gensoul, commanding the base, to throw in his lot with the Royal Navy. Although a great anglophile, Gensoul reminded North that he took his orders from Darlan and Pétain, who had already given him and the other fleet commanders orders on 28 May to scuttle their ships, were there any danger of them falling into the hands of the Germans or Italians. At 1500 hours on 2 July, still wary of the Axis powers getting their hands on the French battle fleet moored at Mers el-Kebir, the British Admiralty ordered Admiral Somerville in Gibraltar to implement Operation Catapult. Under his command Force H arrived off Mers el-Kebir in the pre-dawn mist next day. For the first time since Waterloo, British weapons were then trained upon French servicemen.

In the harbour, Gensoul's staff was carrying on with the demilitarisation of all vessels in compliance with the Armistice agreement. Ships' boilers were cold. Reservists with homes in North Africa had already been demobilised. Naval planes had mostly been disarmed. In the coastal batteries, all shells had been sent back to the magazines and breech-blocks removed and locked away. The day was going to be hot, so the remainder of the French crews on board the ships in the harbour – reservists and regulars from metropolitan France – were looking forward to a day of sports and recreation.

At 0600 the destroyer HMS *Foxhound* was sighted offshore through the mist. At 0615 it signalled, 'British Admiralty is sending Captain Holland to confer with you. Stop. Permission to enter, please.' Now commanding the aircraft carrier *Ark Royal*, Holland had been naval attaché in the Paris Embassy. Until 8 April he had been a liaison officer with the French Admiralty. However, it was Adm Gensoul's duty not to compromise French neutrality. Despite his personal liking for Holland, he had to be as wary of British naval vessels and personnel as he would have been of Italian or German ones.

He decided therefore to send aboard *Foxhound* his aide-de-camp Lieutenant Dufay, who was both a fluent English-speaker and a close friend of Holland. At 0715 the launch from *Dunkerque* pulled alongside the gangway of the British destroyer. When Holland attempted to board it, briefcase in hand, Dufay informed him that Gensoul refused to receive him.

Back on board *Dunkerque* at 0745, Dufay found his admiral reading a signal received from *Foxhound* which read, 'The Admiralty is sending Capt Holland to confer with you in the hope that his proposals will permit the gallant and glorious French navy to remain on our side. In this case, your vessels will remain under your control and you need have no care for the future. A British squadron is standing out to sea to bid you welcome.'

With the mist clearing, it was at that moment the lookouts aboard *Dunkerque* made out the silhouettes of the cruiser *Hood*, the battleships *Resolution* and *Valiant* and *Ark Royal*, whose torpedo-carrying Swordfish were already in the air. From *Hood* came the flashing of an Aldis signal lamp: 'We hope that our proposals are acceptable and that you will be on our side.'

Enough men in the French crews could read Morse for them to be aware what the British were up to. Reservists packed their kitbags and demanded to be let ashore, rather than be press-ganged into the Royal Navy, while officers attempted to calm them with assurances that there was no question of this.

Fretting at the loss of time, Holland authorised *Foxhound* to rejoin station and headed for *Dunkerque* in the destroyer's launch, determined to find some compromise. Intercepted by Dufay in the admiral's barge between the anti-torpedo net and the jetty with the news that Gensoul still refused to receive him, he handed to his friend the sealed letter whose contents he had hoped to soften orally.

At 0830 Adm Gensoul was reading the ultimatum from the War Cabinet in London that gave him the choice between three impossible courses of action:

(1) to sail with the British ships and fight until victory over the Germans and Italians;
(2) to sail with skeleton crews to a British port, the crews to be repatriated as soon as possible;
(3) if he believed himself obliged to stipulate that his vessels might not be used against the Germans and Italians because that would compromise France's neutrality, to sail under escort with skeleton crews to a French port in the Antilles such as Martinique where the ships could be demilitarised or handed over to the (neutral) USA and the crews repatriated.

The sting was in the tail. Should Gensoul reject all three courses of action, he was given six hours to scuttle all the vessels under his command. Failing this, Adm Somerville was charged 'to take all necessary measures to see that your ships do not fall into German or Italian hands'.[8]

At 0900 Gensoul ordered all ships to make steam and prepare for action. Ashore, crews of the coastal batteries began feverishly to rearm their weapons and ground crews started checking and rearming aircraft. Aboard his launch at the torpedo net, Holland watched all these preparations with mounting concern, which Gensoul's reply brought to him by Dufay did nothing to allay.

It was short and to the point:

(1) the assurances given by Adm Gensoul to Adm Sir Dudley North will be respected. In no circumstances will French vessels fall intact into the hands of the Germans or Italians;
(2) in view of the form and content of the ultimatum that has been given to Adm Gensoul, the French vessels will defend themselves with force.

Holland admitted that the ultimatum was a clumsy attempt at bullying a neutral force. The War Cabinet should have expressed the *hope* that the French would come over to the British side. When he argued that disarmed ships left in port with maintenance crews aboard could be taken by surprise by the Germans or Italians before they could be scuttled, Dufay assured him that the sea-cocks were manned night and day and scuttling entailed no delay awaiting further orders from the French Admiralty.

Aware that his cause was lost, Holland wrote a note to Adm Gensoul setting out his point of view. Thirty minutes later, Captain Danbé brought him Gensoul's second reply. It contained the words: 'The first shot fired against us will result in the whole fleet turning against Great Britain – a result diametrically opposed to that sought by British Admiralty.'[9]

Thanking Danbé, Holland said that his reply in the circumstances would have been no different. A few minutes later, at 0950, *Foxhound* signalled the French: 'Regret to inform you that I have orders not to allow you to leave the port unless the terms of His Majesty's government are accepted.'

The confrontation was by now inevitable. In the full light of a day already so hot that touching metal was painful, Somerville could see black smoke pumping out of the funnels of the French fleet. He gave orders for Swordfish from *Ark Royal* to mine the harbour entrance. Although in compliance with his orders from London, the step meant that the first three suggested courses of action in his ultimatum were now impossible – a point that was not lost on Adm Gensoul.

Aboard the British ships at action stations, men sweated under a brazen sky without the slightest breeze, waiting to fire on fellow sailors. During the past winter, many of them had sailed in convoy across the Atlantic with *Dunkerque* and other vessels in the harbour. Aboard *Hood*, Adm Somerville signalled London that he was ready to commence firing. Disgusted with the whole operation imposed on him, he also asked Holland whether there was anything else that could be done and, at his suggestion, ordered *Foxhound* back within visual signalling range. From its bridge flashed the message to *Dunkerque*: 'If you accept the proposals, hoist a square flag on the main mast. If not, I open fire at 1300 hours. Your port is mined.'

Gensoul acknowledged that he would be prepared to parley. At 1315, with still no shot fired on either side, he signalled back that he was in communication with his government, had no intention of leaving harbour and was prepared to receive a spokesman to seek an honourable solution. 'Do not,' he said, 'take the irreparable step.'

At 1515 Holland, wearing no decorations other than the Légion d'honneur, stepped aboard *Dunkerque* with two other RN officers. The French now had steam up and all gun turrets were pointing in the direction of Force H. Shown Darlan's message to all ships dated 28 May, Holland murmured, 'If only we had known about this.'

Softening on his side also, Gensoul seemed prepared to consider disarming and sailing to the Antilles or the USA, but freely, without Royal Navy personnel on board or under armed escort. Holland signalled this apparent breakthrough to Somerville, who replied that this was unacceptable.

Although neither side knew it at the time, the local negotiations had been pre-empted. Gensoul's signals to the French Admiralty had gone to its temporary HQ at Nérac in Gironde, just to the east of the Demarcation Line. There, Admiral Leluc attempted to contact Darlan, who was in Clermont-Ferrand and could not be reached. But Leluc was not idle. Gensoul was now instructed to inform the British that *all* French warships in the Mediterranean were steaming to his rescue. Intercepted in London, where the Prime Minister and former First Lord of the Admiralty was determined to do things his way, the result was an instruction to Somerville to end the business rapidly or face French reinforcements.

At sea, sailors traditionally saved the lives of fellow-mariners. To fire on an enemy, whether or not he had opened fire, was one thing. But to fire on vessels of a country with which Britain had been allied until shortly before, and with which she was not at war, was a breach of international law. Despite his strong disapproval of the action, Somerville signalled *Dunkerque*, 'If none of the proposals is accepted by 1730 BST – I repeat by 1730 – I shall have to sink your ships.'

At 1625 local time – five minutes before the deadline – the three Royal Navy officers were shown off *Dunkerque* with all the usual honours. Not until they had passed the exit in the net was the first shot fired by *Hood*. Although the French warships had steam up and could return fire until their limited stock of shells ran out, little manoeuvring was possible in the confines of the harbour. They were thus sitting ducks for the Royal Navy's bombardment, which killed a total of 1,297 French sailors, with several hundred wounded. While shrouding the corpses, many aid workers were killed when three flights of Swordfish from *Ark Royal* flew in at deck level, machine-gunning them to add to the casualties.

As Gensoul had prophesied, the political result was the opposite of what Churchill may have hoped. François Mauriac summed it up: 'Mr Winston Churchill had united France against England – perhaps for many years.'[10] One ancient cruiser was sunk and the admiral's flagship put out of action for months, but the rest of the damaged fleet steamed at battle readiness to Toulon, where they were nearer by far to the Germans. There, sixteen months later, on 27 November 1942, they were scuttled by their crews after the Wehrmacht crossed the Demarcation Line, in compliance with Darlan's instruction of 28 May 1940 to stop them falling into German hands.

Churchill had no regrets, seeing the action as strategically justified and showing his subjects and the world that Britain would stop at nothing, however repugnant, to win the war. That was arguable, but as far as France was concerned, Mers el-Kebir was the final straw that killed any sympathy for the British cause. It made of the furious and grieving Adm Darlan an implacable enemy for Britain and provided a heaven-sent opportunity for Nazi propaganda to claim that France's true enemy was perfidious Albion and not the Reich.

Even De Gaulle, whose only hope was to side with the British, called it 'an odious tragedy'. In London, he deplored the British action. Obliged to submit the text of his broadcast for prior approval by Downing Street, he consented with the rider that, if asked to change a single word, he would never broadcast again. Privately, he admitted that the irregular trickle of volunteers to his banner dwindled to nothing after Mers el-Kebir.

Behind the major tragedy were several others that rarely make it into the history books. The previous night, Royal Navy prize crews had seized forty or so French warships in Portsmouth, Plymouth, Falmouth and Cowes harbours to forestall the natural reaction to the news from Mers el-Kebir among the thousands of armed French soldiers in Britain and the 500 armed marines and battalion of infantry under the command of a French admiral in Portsmouth, with double that number in Plymouth and Falmouth.

On board the submarine *Surcouf* perfidy changed to tragedy. Moored alongside the submarine HMS *Thames*, her captain and crew had been entertained both aboard their neighbour and ashore. In the confusion of the midnight seizure by men they knew, three British sailors and one French serviceman were killed. In Alexandria, where the squadron of French naval vessels that had thought themselves safe were demilitarised without bloodshed by Adm Cunningham's more subtle approach, it was he who remarked that Catapult had been executed 'with perfect perfidiousness'.[11] In Dakar, French West Africa, Royal Navy frogmen placed mines that immobilised the battleship *Richelieu*.

Marcel Gensoul retired two years later, refusing for the rest of his life to discuss the tragedy of Mers el-Kebir. After returning to Gibraltar, Captain Holland showed his disgust at the illegal action in which he had been obliged to take part by resigning his commission, to spend the rest of the war in the Home Guard.

Chapter 7

THE NUMBER OF THE BEAST

Pierre Laval had not always been anti-British. While prime minister on 19 September 1931, he had been awakened at 1 a.m. by His Britannic Majesty's chargé d'affaires in Paris, in the absence of the ambassador, with a request that the Banque de France support the Bank of England after a catastrophic run on its gold reserves that the US Federal Reserve Bank could not cover. Both for speed and to avoid consulting his Cabinet – a member of which might leak news of this potentially disastrous situation for Britain – Laval personally granted London a credit of 3,000,000,000 gold francs.[1]

As Foreign Minister of the short-lived Doumergue administration in February 1935 he had agreed with the Foreign Office in London that neither country would make unilateral deals with Hitler's Germany. It is hardly surprising that Britain's signature four months later of the Anglo-German agreement to rearm and expand the German fleet triggered in Laval a deep and abiding mistrust of British policies.[2]

Physically, a greater contrast with the silver-haired Marshal's elegant and grandfatherly manner would be hard to find. Laval's stocky build, swarthy complexion and heavy dark moustache made him look like Josef Stalin's suntanned brother. Vincent Auriol, who emerged at the Liberation from three years of imprisonment for resisting Vichy's collaborationist policies and went on to become first president of the Fourth Republic, knew Laval from long acquaintance and described him thus: 'A cigarette permanently between his lips, slightly hunched posture and awkward manner . . . He approaches a group and stops, pretending to listen to one colleague while surveying everyone else. Of his piggy little Mongolian eyes, imprisoned in the folds of their heavy lids, one sees only two black dots.'[3]

Born on 28 June 1883 in the Auvergne village of Châteldon, near Vichy, to a hard-working butcher and café-owner who doubled as the village carter conveying merchandise and passengers to the local railway station, Pierre Laval left school at 11, like his father. Studying in his spare time with the help of the priest, the mayor and the local teacher, the boy prepared himself for his *baccalauréat* so well that his stubborn father was eventually persuaded to let him go back to school. As a boarder at the *lycée* in far distant Bayonne, where his older sister lived, Laval obtained his *bac* only a year later than middle-class coevals who had never interrupted their studies.

Earning a paltry salary as a *pion*, or assistant master, looking after boarders in a *lycée*, he next studied for and gained a degree in natural sciences, which entitled him to apply for a teaching post. This was only a step, for already Laval's sights were set, not on the classroom, but the courtroom. A law student of 20, he joined the Socialist Party and was called to the bar in 1909 at the age of 26. That same year he married the daughter of Châteldon's mayor. Among the contradictions of the man so many came to hate are that he was a fond husband to her and a loving father to their daughter José, who published an impassioned defence of him when he was on trial for his life after the war.

José grew up in Paris, where her parents set up home soon after the wedding. For eighteen years Laval worked in the Palais de Justice with the same application he had devoted to his studies, all the while sniffing the political winds and awaiting his moment. Most of his clients were union officials. Hailed in the left-wing press after gaining an acquittal for one of them accused of sabotage, Laval realised the power of the media – and never forgot it. Successfully campaigning for election with the same energy he had put into his legal work, he was in 1914 welcomed by *L'Humanité*, then the official organ of the Socialist Party, as the youngest *député* of the Left.

During the First World War, while Pétain was at the centre of the war effort, Laval managed to be get himself exempted from conscription on the grounds of varicose veins. As a Socialist and pacifist, he made no secret of the fact that he deplored the war with Germany, and was for a time under police surveillance on this account. The exiled Leon Trotsky was among his friends until expelled from Paris in September 1916.

Despite these question marks against him, Laval's intellectual qualities were such that he was offered an under-secretariat of state in 1917, which he had to turn down on instructions of the Party. To free himself from its discipline, he distanced himself from left-wing friends, making the final break at the 1920 annual Congress in Tours when the Party split into Communists and Socialists. Accepting neither party machine, Laval stood as an independent Socialist candidate in the elections of 1924, while in the process of building an empire of printing, press and broadcasting interests that made him a millionaire.

Elected senator with a large majority, he became Minister of Public Works within twelve months and soon afterwards Under-Secretary for Foreign Affairs. Of this stage of his career the ageing statesman Aristide Briand said, 'Once he's got teeth into something, that Auvergnat never lets go of it.'[4] A Nobel laureate known as 'the poet of peace', Briand advocated a federal Europe as early as 1930. With a similar background in the law before taking up politics he exercised a great influence over his much younger colleague. Seeing himself also being called to Stockholm one day to receive a Nobel, Laval pursued Briand's unrelenting search for peace through various appointments in France's troubled governments of the thirties. In 1935 he strengthened the Entente Cordiale with Britain; at the Stresa Conference of First World War allies he spoke out against German rearmament in defiance of the Versailles

Treaty; in Moscow he signed a treaty of mutual assistance in an endeavour to encircle Hitler's infant Reich by alliances. He once declared, 'In the whole world, there are five or six men on whom peace depends. I am one.'[5]

By 'peace' he meant peace for France. Thus, the Hoare-Laval pact of 1935, which he concerted with British Foreign Secretary Sir Samuel Hoare, carved up Ethiopia, despite its being a member of the League of Nations. A vast swathe of the country was awarded to the Italian invader in a vain endeavour to entice Mussolini into the Franco-British camp. Details of the pact leaked to the press on 10 December 1935 caused Hoare's resignation, while Laval's penalty was to be deprived of further ministerial responsibilities until 1940 – a period during which he spoke out whenever his successors undid agreements he had set up as guarantees of peace.

After the Munich settlement in September 1938, he condemned Daladier's and Chamberlain's appeasement of Hitler on the grounds that one did not avoid war by humiliating oneself, but rather by dominating one's adversary. And yet, almost exactly a year later, Laval was the only speaker at the Senate Foreign Affairs Committee to come out openly *against* French support for Poland after the German invasion, telling Premier Daladier to look at a map and see who were France's allies and what they could do for her before taking a step that would cost millions of her citizens' lives. He never lets go, Aristide Briand had said. Six months later, Laval was still offering his services to Daladier, believing he could restrain Mussolini from taking the German side in the coming war. Daladier turned a deaf ear, as did his successor Paul Reynaud when Laval repeated his offer at the beginning of June 1940, with the Italian army already massed on the border with France.

This, then, was the tenacious millionaire lawyer-politician who walked always a few paces behind the Marshal as together they led France into the dark years ahead. The last civilian refugees in Vichy – men in linen suits and panama hats, the ladies in floral-patterned summer dresses, open sandals and pretty hats – watched as the dark-suited politicians in collar and tie wearing trilby or homburg hats emerged from their cars and set about the first business of the day: finding a bed. Not all succeeded in having a roof over their head the first night, although the situation was eased by the reduction in their numbers due to the expulsion of the Communists at the beginning of the year and a prohibition from returning to metropolitan France to attend the National Assembly for all those who travelled on the *Massilia* to North Africa in the belief that they were going to form a last-ditch government there.

On 4 July, when everyone else was still grappling with the news from Mers el-Kebir, Laval read out at the morning Cabinet meeting a text he had drafted with Minister of Justice Raphaël Alibert for the National Assembly's approval. It was nothing less than an abdication of parliament that placed all power in the hands of Pétain. The Marshal said nothing, but when seven members of the Cabinet raised objections, Laval cut them short by pretending he had no time to listen because an important group of senators was waiting for him.

Like all spa towns, Vichy had been run by its doctors. In the meeting hall of the medical societies, sixty senators awaited his arrival. If they were seeking clarification of their role, it was quick in coming. Laval informed them that the Constitution had to be drastically reformed if France were to continue to exist in a German-dominated Europe. If parliament did not agree to do this, Berlin would impose it by force and occupy the rest of France. This was a blatant fabrication. With less than a year to run before the launch of Operation Barbarossa, it suited Hitler that Pétain should govern the two-fifths of the country with no immediate strategic importance and thus reduce the number of German divisions tied up in the west.

The assembled senators were hardly reassured by Laval's proposals, but they were without leaders capable of restraining Pétain's deputy with the bit between his teeth. Reynaud, with his head bandaged from the accident that had cost the life of the Countess of Portes, was discredited by the scandal. The whereabouts of Herriot and Blum were uncertain. Daladier and Mandel were in custody in North Africa where, as in other overseas possessions, the administrators were nearly all loyal to Vichy, fearing that they would lose their pension rights if they opted for De Gaulle.

But there was more to it than that. Most of the deputies and senators had been elected under the Popular Front and knew – although they would never have admitted it – that they were *responsible* for France's downfall. Driving to Vichy along roads littered with the human and material debris of the exodus from towns and cities, through throngs of bewildered and unhappy people making their way back to homes that had been destroyed, they had been all too aware that the electorate trusted only one man. Laval – whom few trusted except the voters in Aubervilliers, a working-class district of Paris which had elected him mayor in March 1923 and stayed loyal to him all the way until 1944 – claimed to be speaking for that man.

Next day, Jean Taurines, leader of twenty-five senators who believed that Pétain would listen to them because they were ex-servicemen, tabled a motion expressing complete confidence in the Marshal within normal parliamentary constraints. That afternoon, Laval faced eighty deputies in the great hall of the Casino. To their leaders defending parliamentary democracy, he retorted that the time for speeches was past. The rebuilding of France could only be achieved by destroying what had caused her problems. Either the deputies accepted his way of solving the problems, or Hitler would impose his own solution. With his years of courtroom experience, Laval knew he was on thin ice as he spent the next hours lobbying small groups everywhere, promising anything and playing on everyone's fears of German intervention.

That evening Taurines' ex-servicemen senators took to Pétain a counter-proposal: that the Constitution be not abolished but *suspended* for the duration of the war, with government by decree until then. They had the impression that Pétain was in favour. Was he going to dump Laval? That was the question.

The answer next morning was Laval's speech as the Marshal's spokesman before the National Assembly, in which he informed the deputies and senators that, although parliament had no place in post-Armistice France, they would be allowed to keep all their prerogatives of office, including salaries. Taurines returned to the Marshal, who said that he had not changed his mind, but nothing could be done without Laval. Wheeling into the attack, Laval gave a furious ultimatum. Should the counter-proposal be voted, he would resign his office and they could resign themselves to a *coup d'état* led by Weygand or General De Lattre de Tassigny, military commander of the region – neither of which had any foundation in fact.

With the death knell of the Republic that Laval was so vigorously sounding ringing in their ears, the lower house had another idea: to get rid of Lebrun, making Pétain both head of government and head of state. There was nothing in the Constitution of 1875 to prevent it. Failing to grasp that the ploy was directed against Laval and not himself, President Lebrun refused to resign.

Laval pressed on, his next legal weapon Article 8 of the Constitution, which required both houses to vote separately on whether or not to amend the Constitution and then meet in joint assembly within forty-eight hours to pass the amendment. If that was legal, his use of lies, promises and threats to divide the many deputies and senators who were against him smacked more of sharp practice in the courtroom than parliamentary democracy.

The largest hall in Vichy was the theatre of the Casino, where on 9 July – the day the Parisian publisher Mercure de France rushed into production a cheap French edition of *Mein Kampf* [6] – 398 deputies in the morning and 230 senators in the afternoon voted to amend the Constitution. Of the deputies only three voted against; of the senators, only one. After sixty-five years, the Third Republic was being laid to rest, complete with eulogy from one senator, acknowledging that it was the Constitution that had made France a free country. It was, he said, not the Constitution that had failed, but rather its guardians who had not done their duty.

On 10 July, beneath a cloudless sky and a burning sun, 666 soberly dressed deputies and senators, including Herriot, Blum and other late arrivals, passed through the massive police cordon holding off a crowd of the curious and into the 1,450-seater opera house for their joint secret session. There were no women present. Not until 1944 would women gain the right to vote or stand for public office in France. Did anyone there remember the text of the Book of Revelation 13:18? 'Here is wisdom. Let him that hath understanding count the number of the beast: for it is the number of a man; and his number is six hundred threescore and six.'

One man may have done. Léon Blum, France's first Socialist and first Jewish premier, whose Popular Front coalition of 1936–7 had contributed so much to the fatal unpreparedness for war, looked around at his fellow parliamentarians and watched 'all the courage and integrity one knew certain men possessed disappear before my eyes, corroded and dissolved in a human swamp'.[7] He was perhaps projecting his own guilt, for courage was shown by Taurines' group insisting on their counter-proposal being debated after the bill had been read. However, Laval outflanked any opposition by inserting into the bill a clause that the new Constitution must be ratified by the nation – and then carried the day by reading a letter from the absent Marshal in which Pétain declared the bill necessary for the safety of the country. Out of respect for him, the veteran's group withdrew their counter-proposal.

Having won the day, Laval launched into one of the most extraordinary speeches ever delivered to any parliament. Mixing histrionics and history, he accused Blum and the Popular Front of bringing France to this terrible pass; he accused De Gaulle in London; he accused the parliamentarians in North Africa. 'We cannot save France by running away from her,' was his gist. The occasional interruption was overridden roughshod. Winding himself and his audience up to a climax, Laval ended, 'Make no mistake about it. We are now living under a dictatorship. The functions of parliament will be restricted. We shall accept no amendment. This evening, I know, not a single vote will be cast against the bill, for it is to France that you give your vote!'[8]

Carried away by his rhetoric and by his unquestioning belief in his vision of what was best for the country, the assembly burst into applause. The eloquence that had won so many courtoom victories had cut the ground from underneath his opponents' feet.

Proving Blum wrong about other people's courage, a few voices were raised in defiance of Laval's statement that the Vichy government would set up labour camps on the model of the Russian and German totalitarian states. Sixty-nine senators signed a declaration of reservation, but it was not permitted a reading. Another group of twenty-seven refused to vote for a bill that would inevitably lead to the disappearance of the republican regime. Their spokesman was forcibly removed from the rostrum by the ushers when he tried to read their signed protest. As the joint houses rose, to return that afternoon in public session for the vote, Laval could not resist having the last word. The government, he said, had drafted the bill as the way to give France the least evil peace. It was a curious phrase: '*la paix la moins mauvaise possible.*' But by then he was almost feverish with triumph.

At 2.30 p.m. the public session opened with no sign of Pétain. The President of the Senate read the obituary notice of the Third Republic: 'The National Assembly gives complete powers to the government of the Republic under the authority and with the signature of Marshal Pétain for the purpose of promulgating, by one or more laws, a new Constitution for the French state. This Constitution is to guarantee the rights to work, of the family and the country. It will be ratified by the nation and applied by the assemblies it will create.'

The necessary majority being defined as half those present plus one, Laval was at his most charming while the formalities for the vote were being conducted, assuring everyone that, until new assemblies were set up under the new Constitution, the two houses would not be dissolved, but merely suspended. As a sop to those deputies and senators who feared that Pétain might be coerced into going to war on the German side, he also guaranteed that the head of state had no power to declare war without the consent of the suspended legislative assemblies.

When the vote was counted, the majority in favour exceeded by far the minimum required: 569 votes for and only eighty against, with seventeen abstentions.[9] After the result was announced, among the cries of 'Vive la France!' and 'Vive le maréchal!' one lone voice was heard to call, 'Vive la République, quand-même!'

The briefly glorious Second Empire of Napoleon III had been extinguished by France's defeat in the Franco-Prussian War; its successor state died of the same disease on that torrid afternoon in July 1940 and was buried in the Casino at Vichy with a mere ninety-seven mourners at the graveside. Of these brave men, fifteen were to be arrested for having the courage of their convictions, five of them dying in German camps; two others were murdered in France.

One who survived was député Jules Moch, who had returned clandestinely from North Africa in order to attend the assembly. After the vote, he changed back into his officer's uniform and was driven to the railway station to take the first train out of Vichy, no matter what its destination. Alighting from a taxi in the closely guarded station forecourt, he expected to be arrested on hearing the guard called out – only to find that Pétain had found time on that fateful morning to reinstate the honours due to officers in peacetime. Moch was required not merely to return the salute of a single sentry but to inspect the whole guard as a mark of respect to the uniform he was wearing.[10]

The following day, the Théâtre de l'Oeuvre, last theatre in Paris to close its doors on 10 June, was the first to reopen – with a frothy comedy. Next came Les Ambassadeurs with a show whose posters promised 'three hours of non-stop laughter'. Why not? Lest any single person in France doubted that the country was a military dictatorship on both sides of the Line, Pétain's three decrees of 11 July were regal declarations beginning: 'We, Philippe Pétain, Marshal of France . . .' In the first, he declared himself head of state. In the second, he enumerated the powers with which he was invested – total powers, excepting only the right to declare war. In the third, he adjourned sine die both houses of parliament, which could reassemble only if he summoned them. Equally alarming was that France was officially no longer a republic, its title having been changed by the Marshal from 'République Française' to 'Etat Français' – the French state.

As when Hitler became Reichskanzler quite legally in 1933, so all the constitutional forms had been duly observed by the National Assembly. The new French state was accordingly recognised by most foreign powers with the exception of the United Kingdom. France was a dictatorship, as Laval had been saying for days it must be in order to survive in Hitler's New Europe – and he more than any other man had made it so.

PART TWO

Life, Loot and Love under Pétain's New Order

Chapter 8

CLEARING UP THE MESS

Calculated ambiguity about the long-term future was a psychological device used repeatedly by the Nazis. 'Do this to our satisfaction,' they told their victims, 'and you'll get the best possible treatment afterwards.' It worked even with lawyer-politician Laval, who decided on no evidence at all that the Armistice agreement would soon be replaced by a definitive Franco-German peace treaty and devoted himself to achieving the most favourable bargaining position at the coming peace conference – which never came.

To carry through the intrigues necessary for this, he needed Pétain as a figurehead or, as he put it in one unguarded moment, 'He's the vase on the mantelpiece.' As to why the Marshal needed Laval, there is a widely believed exchange between the two men that may be apocryphal. Laval is reported to have said at one time when Pétain was reluctant to tie the knot of their alliance more tightly, *'Monsieur le maréchal, nous sommes dans la merde. Laissez-moi être votre vidangeur.'* ('Marshal, we are in the shit – let me do the shovelling.')

In Pétain's view, France had tried feudalism, monarchy and three democratic republics – in the last of which the changing governments of the thirties had schemed themselves to death – so it was now time for a Platonic benevolent dictatorship because no other form of government could weld together a people rent by political and religious differences, demoralised by crushing military defeat, deserted by its allies and allowed a semblance of national identity only so long as that suited the traditional enemy now occupying three-fifths of its territory.

The Marshal, as he himself once remarked, had been invested with more power than even Louis XIV. But a dictator must have a policy. What was Pétain's? Whether not to alarm Berlin and/or the French people by declaring himself in one fell swoop, or because it was actually evolved piecemeal, this was never enshrined in any formal constitution of the new French state, but proclaimed in a sporadic series of *Paroles aux Français* – printed tracts, broadcasts and publicly delivered homilies addressed to the people in the tone of a stern but caring paterfamilias.

Major General Doumenc wrote a brilliant analysis of the military mistakes that led to the collapse of the French armies, which few people ever read because it was easier to blame everything on a few scapegoats – this despite Pétain telling his subjects as early as 20 June that the defeat was due to the mistakes of their former leaders 'and to the moral corruption of the nation'.

By this, he meant the grab-all-you-can mentality encouraged by the Popular Front. While Germans had been labouring fifty or sixty hours a week east of the Rhine, French workers had enjoyed paid holidays and a forty-hour week. The Marshal saw the pursuit of pleasure and material comfort as the cause of France's moral decline, which had to be eradicated from the national psyche, so back-to-the-land honest toil was a recurrent theme of his speeches, with the peasant-farmer epitomising the masculine ideal. On 23 June he likened the defeated nation to a hard-working farmer whose fields had been devastated by a freak hailstorm, but who did not despair. Instead, he reploughed and replanted to ensure a good harvest.

Already on 25 June, as the last shooting died away except on stretches of the Maginot Line where local commanders fought on pointlessly for several days, the Marshal was talking of the New Order then beginning, and which would bring about a healthier moral climate. 'I hate the lies that have done us so much harm,' he said. 'Yet the earth does not lie.' Repeating often that the worst immorality was to hide the truth, he avoided acknowledging the awful cost of the Occupation: France was paying 400,000,000 francs a day and suffering widespread spoliation.

On 11 July he announced a plan to rebuild France's destroyed infrastructure, bypassing the mistakes of both socialism and capitalism under a slogan that replaced the Republic's *Liberté, Egalité, Fraternité*. 'Work, family and country,' Pétain declared, 'are the eternal verities, so from now on our slogan is *Travail, Famille, Patrie!*' To a population fed up with being deceived by its politicians, the home-spun philosophy came like a breath of fresh air.

The following day, Pierre Laval was officially appointed his successor – the *dauphin* to France's uncrowned king – after which triumph he divided his time between Vichy and the official residence of French prime ministers, the Hôtel Matignon in Paris. There he lived in style, fostering personal relationships with the blond, blue-eyed German Ambassador Otto Abetz – a former biology teacher turned art historian from Karlsruhe – and other leading German military and political figures whom he courted as being important for France's future. The only outward difference between his lunch parties and those of profiteers[1] and black marketeers entertaining their cronies in the same restaurants was a respect for form: at one lunch in the Café de Paris, Laval insisted that all his bemused guests hand over that day's bread coupons.

The great secular holiday of the year in France is the anniversary of the storming of the Bastille in 1789, but that 14 July was a glum travesty. Everyone knew that within a few days a million men would be demobilised in the Free Zone and thrown onto a job market in chaos with a gratuity of 1,000 francs, which would not go far. The Armistice provided for Vichy to keep an emasculated symbolic army of eight divisions comprising 100,000 regular soldiers. For transport they had bicycles, with the exception of eight Bren-carriers per cavalry regiment. No tanks, no heavy artillery, a few anti-aircraft batteries. To reduce the officer corps to the 3,768 allowed, a special *congé d'armistice* was granted, an open-ended leave of absence for all who applied.[2] Minister of War General Colson penned a personal letter to the commander of each military region, suggesting that he actively camouflage *matériel* and stores against the day when . . .

The results were sometimes surprising. By the following spring, 65,000 rifles, 9,500 machine guns and automatic rifles, 200 mortars, fifty-five 75mm cannons and anti-tank guns had been administratively 'lost'. Several thousand trucks were 'leased' to civilian transport contractors who agreed to maintain them ready for return to the army at six hours' notice. The MD of one small trucking company thus saw his fleet rise from five vehicles to 687! Sadly, when the Wehrmacht invaded the Free Zone in November 1942, all the hidden arms were useless to stop it.

In the Marseilles garrison, escaped POW Captain Henri Frenay, known for his anti-Nazi sentiments before the war, pretended to have clandestine links with London when recruiting a number of like-minded friends to his own underground group named Combat. Among its activities was *Le Bulletin*, a weekly digest of news from the BBC and Swiss press reports published under a quotation from Napoleon, 'To live defeated is to die every day.'[3] However, by July 1940 your average Jacques Dupont had had enough of life in uniform. If lucky enough not to be stuck in a German POW camp for the foreseeable future, he was as unlikely to 'continue the fight underground' as to be seduced by the time-worn inducements used in appeals for volunteers to serve in the Army of the Armistice: 'Continue the glorious traditions of the . . . regiment. An interesting career with regular pay rising for privates from 3,600 to 5,700 francs. More ample rations than for the civilian population'.[4]

The Marshal's *Paroles aux Français* became progressively more specific, with decrees reforming education, social security and regional government. One subsequently much criticised aspect of this reorganisation was inaugurated by a statute of association deposited on 25 July at the Sous-Préfecture of Lapalisse, 20 kilometres north-east of Vichy. Although ostensibly a private initiative, the Compagnons de France movement was the result of an interview Gen Weygand had been asked to grant earlier that month by Paul Baudoin to the crippled French Chief Scout, Henry Dhavernas.

Moved by the plight of homeless children and youths separated from their families during the retreat, Dhavernas wanted to do something for them. Weygand immediately had telegrams sent to a number of suitable officers, recalling them to participate in this initiative. Together with André Cruiziat, another top scouting figure, the diplomat Etienne De Croy and others, Dhavernas aimed to form a youth movement that would embrace all male adolescents of whatever class, whether or not they were church-goers, Scouts or members of any political party. It would therefore have to be acceptable to all existing youth organisations, in order to enlist their cooperation, and not replace them, lest Vichy be tempted to take over a monolithic youth movement on the model of the Hitler Youth.

From 1–4 August a conference was held in the forest of Randan, near Vichy, where thirty men and eight women representing both religious and lay youth movements agreed with Dhavernas on a structure like the Boy Scout movement, which was divided into troops and patrols to encourage *esprit de corps*. Compagnons were therefore organised in teams of ten boys each, five teams making a company and every three to six companies forming a *commanderie*.

As few French families were prepared to allow their adolescent daughters to escape parental supervision, only boys could become Compagnons. The congress was swiftly followed by a training camp for the leaders of the new movement targeting male adolescents between the ages of 14 and 19, before they became eligible for the Chantiers. The uniform was a cross between Scouts and Hitler Youth: a navy blue shirt bulging with useful pockets, shorts, stout boots and a floppy alpine beret. On the right shoulder, a French cockerel; on the left, a regional badge. The leaders also wore shorts because 'they had to be as cold as the boys to show they could take it'. Everyone used the familiar *tu* form when talking to each other, with leaders being called *chef* (or 'boss') and saluted with a relaxed gesture, palm to the front level with the face.

To launch the movement, Paul Baudouin somehow scrounged 2,000,000 francs from his Foreign Affairs budget – with the approval of the Marshal, Weygand and others. Boys entered as 'apprentice' – or 'tenderfoot' in scouting terms. They took an oath to be kind to other Compagnons and loyal to their leaders, and to work hard for the new France. Their day started with a bugler blowing Reveille at 6.30 a.m., followed by physical training, personal hygiene, breakfast and a salute to the flag drawn up in square formation. '*Compagnons à l'aise,*' was 'Stand at ease.' '*A moi, compagnons,*' was 'Attention!' From 8.30 to 4 p.m. work was interrupted only by a brief lunch-break. Evening activities after an early dinner included campfire singsongs and moral guidance.

After one to three months, the apprentice won his uniform if judged worthy of it, and was then solemnly sworn in. Ahead lay, not knots and lashings and cross-country paper-chases, but real work. Since a majority of the 1,600,000 POWs were farm-workers, it was up to the Compagnons to replace them in the fields, getting in the harvest. Within three months, 10,000 boys had been recruited, mostly refugees who had nowhere else to go. The majority were employed as cheap labour, but some were given genuine apprenticeships in skilled trades. To create jobs for men, women in the public service were employed only as secretaries and switchboard operators. To enable women to stay at home and bring up children, on 7 July a circular from Vichy instructed heads of large companies to 'return to the home' all women except war widows, single women, women supporting families and those in traditionally female jobs.[5]

The small ads in *La Petite Gironde*, a regional daily published in Bordeaux, make curious reading. Those interested in getting away from it all were advised that American Export Lines operated weekly departures from Lisbon to New York! For smaller budgets, another ad ran, 'Looking for small cutter or similar boat. Contact Havas agency in Bordeaux quoting 2799.' North of the Channel, De Gaulle's navy under the unpopular, ambitious Admiral Emile Muselier numbered 120 officers and 1,746 ratings – almost as large as his army, which comprised on 10 August a mere 140 officers and 2,109 men![6]

On 26 September, in case any readers had not yet learned the art of barter, *La Petite Gironde* printed the story of a lady who had realised the twenty litres of petrol in her car could be siphoned out and traded a litre at a time for butter, noodles, even coffee and salt. But beware, the paper warned, there are no fixed exchange rates, so buy what's cheap and, if you don't want it, pass it on later when the price has risen. Buying on a colossal scale was the business of the Deutsche Beschaffungsamt or Procurement Office, comfortably installed in the Hôtel Wagram in Paris. Its brief was wide, but there were many other procurement agencies. Starting in 1941, the Bureau Otto used funds from the Occupation taxes paid by Vichy to buy for the German war effort metals, leather, foodstuffs and other goods. Employing over 200 people at its peak and with warehouses in St-Ouen covering three hectares, it greased the wheels of every deal by an absence of paperwork and no awkward questions as to provenance of the goods.

Everywhere along the interface between French producers and stockholders and the German purchasing organisation, racketeers flourished. The price of leather was fixed by Vichy at 9 francs a kilo. Dealers offered 15 francs, but sold their purchases on at 30, while the Bureau Otto paid as much as 70 francs a kilo. The parallel mark-up on a kilo of copper was from 15 francs to 85 and on lead from 6 to 27 francs a kilo.[7]

So many fortunes were made in this area that no action was ever taken after the war, although gangland turf wars claimed some lives much sooner.[8] Mandel Szkolnikoff, a lawyer from Latvia who had arrived in 1933 and acquired an Argentine passport, ignored the anti-Jewish laws and drove around Paris in his personal Rolls-Royce, amassing a fortune of 2,000,000 francs in three years by acquiring for the SS textiles of all kinds. The money was invested in hotels and other property before he was killed by a rival. A fellow-immigrant was scrap-metal dealer Joseph Joanovici, known as 'Monsieur Joseph', who sold millions of tons of metal to the SS purchasing commission, in return for which his fortune was estimated even higher than Szkolnikoff's. Joanovici escaped justice after the Liberation by large payments to the Honneur et Police Resistance group.

The little men involved in the procurement business were often enrolled as auxiliary *gestapistes* to prise hidden stocks away from their reluctant owners, thus becoming prone to blackmail by the SD and other intelligence agencies, at first controlled by Sturmbannführer Karl Boemelburg and his deputy Untersturmführer Josef Kieffer. Boemelburg, considered 'not very bright' by his underlings, delighted in being driven around Paris to expensive restaurants in an armour-plated Cadillac, whose previous owner PCF chief Maurice Thorez had deserted from the French Army, slipped across the border into Belgium and from there been spirited away to the USSR, to sit out the war in Moscow preparing for the planned Communist takeover of France when the Germans were driven out.

Although Pétain banned freemasons from public office in August – ostensibly as enemies of the state, but really because of their republican sentiments – it was not until 3 October that Jews were similarly excluded from public life in both zones of France by the first Statut des Juifs, whose wording defined a Jew as being 'a person with three Jewish grandparents or two if married to another Jew'. This was in fact less prejudicial than Talmudic law, which considers that any child of a Jewish mother is Jewish.

On 9 November all trade unions and employers' associations were banned. In the general rush to identify with Pétain's New Order, a dissenting voice came from the town of Auch in the south-west. At the monthly meeting of the chamber of commerce, the businessman Fernand Mauroux refused to add his name to a sycophantic joint letter to the Marshal. Together with two friends who had also belonged to the Democratic Popular Party, he founded the Liberty resistance network that rapidly spread throughout the *département* of Midi-Pyrénées. In the same town but independently, soldiers of the 2nd Dragoons under Lieutenant-Colonel Schlesser, the strongly anti-German former head of French counter-espionage, were secretly 'losing' weapons and ammunition to hide them from the Armistice Commission.

When the Marshal had taken his seat in the Académie Française in 1929, Paul Valéry's welcoming speech had praised Pétain's ability to adapt to changed realities and his dislike of rigid theories. So there was a certain consistency in the Marshal's *Paroles* adding up to a constitution evolved in reaction to the changing realities of post-Armistice France. His new state promised the working classes freedom and dignity in a society no longer dominated by financial greed. In future, work was to be regarded not as an unpleasant necessity, but as the only honourable way of getting money. Embodying something of the disenchantment of Kierkegaard, Bergson, Heidegger, Marx and Sartre, much of Pétain's national socialism could be read as proto-Christian. Although his civil marriage to a divorcee was not recognised by the Church, Pétain started attending Mass to make himself more acceptable to the predominantly Catholic population. He also reintroduced school prayers, which had been prohibited under the Third Republic, and abolished the prestigious state colleges that had traditionally provided the elite of France's administrators, politicians and businessmen.

To sum up in his own words, the New Order was *nationalistic* in its foreign policy, *authoritarian* in internal politics, economically *coordinated and controlled* – and above all *social* in spirit.[9] Most importantly, it was not a slavish copy of the German or any other national revolution, but specifically French. Fortunately, the Marshal's vision of France as primarily an agricultural country coincided with Hitler's requirement that the conquered territories produce all the primary materials including food needed by an increasingly industrialised Reich. One German general admitted privately to a French friend that Berlin's unspoken plan was to make France part kitchen garden and part brothel.

Anti-Semitic French people of all classes traditionally voiced their feelings as freely as their British counterparts. Lunching during October with Fernand De Brinon, soon to be appointed Vichy's ambassador to the German authorities in Paris, Captain Ernst Jünger noted in his diary how his host used the word *Youpin* (equivalent to 'Yid') despite having a Jewish wife, who spent most of her time at their country home to avoid embarrassing him. Jünger's war diary was the draft of a literary work. A former foreign legionnaire, he spoke fluent French and charmed his way into what passed for high society, both German and French. At another society luncheon he met the fashion designer Coco Chanel, who had made trouser suits fashionable for women and suntanned skin acceptable in a world that had despised it as indicative of manual labour. Convinced she had been cheated out of control of a perfumery company by Jewish competitors, Chanel launched into a vicious anti-Semitic tirade turning to plain bitchiness when 'everyone agreed that Cathérine d'Erlanger's emeralds were nothing but bits of green bottle glass'.[10]

The artistic world was far from hostile to the Occupation forces: the pianist Lucienne Delforge envisaged a more appreciative audience for her recitals because their presence meant that the spirit of Mozart had come to Paris! Guests invited to the winter collections of Chanel, Nina Ricci, Jean Lanvin and the other haute couture houses included numerous high-ranking German officers who did not share Goering's opinion that French women were grossly overdressed. The faithful came to buy for their wives, who had not seen haute couture for several years. The unfaithful and fancy-free came with the companions of their leisure hours in Paris hoping shortly to wear the clothes paraded on the catwalk. As the newspaper *La Gerbe* commented acidly, 'for certain people the principal charms of Paris reside in nicely rounded backsides'.[11] But there was also money in some French purses. Szkolnikoff's wife Hélène Samson had three cars of her own in which to flit from one collection to the next, and reputedly bought fifty original dresses that season.

For ladies compelled to cycle in the absence of motor fuel, the house of Paquin showed split skirts and an audacious short skirt with a detachable lower half that the wearer press-studded on after dismounting on arrival at her hostess' house. However, for fashion-conscious Parisiennes with smaller budgets, 'my wonderful little dressmaker just around the corner' was reduced to going through Madame's wardrobe and transforming an old dress into a skirt, to be sported with a blouse made of black-market material, or converting the evening wear of an absent husband, who would not need it in his POW camp, into an elegant tailored jacket and a pair of cocktail trousers.

Paris was heavy with Occupation forces. The Supreme Commander in France, or Militärbefehlshaber Frankreich, General Otto Von Stülpnagel had his headquarters in the Hôtel Majestic on the Place de l'Opéra. The Hôtel Meurice on the rue de Rivoli was the seat of the Kommandant von Gross-Paris – responsible for Paris and the neighbouring *départements* of Seine, Seine-et-Marne and Seine-et-Oise. The Chambre des Députés, festooned with swastika banners, was requisitioned as offices for his twin staffs, both commanders having a military and a civilian staff, or Verwaltungsstab. The confusion of demarcations was infinite, Parisian prisons such as La Santé and Fresnes being divided into separately governed French and German wings, while the Germans took other jails over for their exclusive use, together with the forts at Vincennes and Mont Valérien – where so many *résistants* were to die in front of firing squads. Filling the cell blocks was no problem because the joint headquarters of the German security services at 11 rue des Saussaies had previously been the home of the Sûreté Nationale or national police headquarters, whose archives had been handed over to the Germans largely intact.

By contrast with Laval's ostentatious lifestyle, Pétain lived abstemiously in Vichy's Hôtel du Parc because it was more convenient for meetings than his official residence in the luxury mini-palace of that prolific letter-writer the Marquise de Sévigné. Gravely acknowledging the acclamation of the public on his morning constitutionals, he was always guarded by the sinister Dr Bernard Ménétrel, whose three young daughters were pressed into service for photo-calls showing the Marshal smiling at them with grandfatherly benevolence – which may be more than a simile, for rumour had it that Ménétral was Pétain's illegitimate son by the wife of Dr Louis Ménétrel, who had been his personal physician until dying in 1936.

Bernard Ménétrel had been called up as a reservist captain in May 1940, but on his return from Madrid Pétain arranged for him to remain a civilian, ostensibly in order to look after his uncertain health: he needed daily injections from the man whose powers extended far beyond those of physician and private secretary. In the course of time, one in ten of all recipients of the Vichy regime's medal called the Francisque would owe their awards directly to Ménétrel.

On his travels and even when making speeches on the balconies of public buildings, Pétain always kept his faithful retainer near him. The 400 men of the Gendarmerie Nationale in the Marshal's personal bodyguard were ordered by Ménétrel to allow no one near their charge unless approved by the doctor personally. Even Pétain had to circumvent his vigilant watchdog from time to time, once bending down to peer through the keyhole of his office door to make sure he was not outside before talking off-the-record to a man he knew to be in the Resistance. After appointing the one-legged and one-eyed First World War veteran Xavier Vallat as Minister for Jewish Questions *because* he was a lawyer known for his anti-Semitism, Pétain on one occasion sought to restrain him, but used an intermediary to pass on his instructions because he knew Ménétrel would be furious if he found out.

With one exception, introduced to give the illusion that the new government was drawn from all parties, Pétain's entourage was of the political Right. But even this small group of men he had known for years was rarely taken into the Marshal's confidence. He mistrusted everyone around him, reasoning that they and the top civil servants had been collectively responsible for weakening the army he loved and bringing the country to misery and shame. As a career officer, the Marshal was accustomed to changing one aide-de-camp for another without any personal feelings for any of them. On meeting his newly appointed *chef de cabinet* Henri Du Moulin de Labarthéte, he said, 'I don't trust anyone, Du Moulin – not even you. But at least I can put a name to your face.'[12]

As with all totalitarian states, paranoia reigned from the outset in Vichy, with even humble secretaries in government office being followed by plainclothes detectives. In the Occupied Zone, arrests were soon taking place of people who refused orders from their new masters. One strange case was of Rudier, the brass founder who had cast all Rodin's statues and now refused to make armaments in his workshop. From Fresnes prison he smuggled out a note on a scrap of paper, which an unknown friend took to Berlin and handed to Arno Breker.

After acting as the Führer's guide on the lightning tour of Paris, Breker had already refused an invitation to return to France from Jacques Benoist-Machin, who was to become Minister of State charged with Franco-German relations. At the time Rudier's plea arrived, the pro-German intellectual Pierre-Eugène Drieu la Rochelle was in Berlin trying to persuade Breker to mount an exhibition in Paris. To help the old craftsman, Breker accepted Drieu la Rochelle's invitation and told Albert Speer that he could not cast his work in Germany because all the foundries had been diverted into war work. Could Speer help? In the usual way of the Third Reich, strings were pulled, Rudier was released, his team of ninety skilled workmen exempted from war work, and Speer allocated thirty tons of precious bronze to the casting of Breker's statues for the exhibition.

Hitler's favourite sculptor moved into a large requisitioned suite in the Paris Ritz, enjoying the hospitality of 37-year-old Ambassador Abetz and his French wife née Suzanne De Bruycker, as well as haute cuisine at restaurants recommended by Rudier. He became a lifeline for French artists in trouble. When fellow-sculptor Aristide Maillol's Jewish mistress was arrested, Breker went straight to Müller, the head of the Gestapo, to get her released. And when in 1943 Pablo Picasso was finally caught red-handed by SS-Hauptsturmführer Theo Danneker feathering a bolt-hole in Russia, it was Breker who intervened and saved his skin too – which did not stop Picasso from financing his son's studies in Switzerland by giving his ex-wife, Olga Koklova, a sketchbook for her to sell in Geneva for hard cash.

But all this lay in the future. More urgent than the wellbeing of a few artists in the summer of 1940 was the restoration of normal life in those parts of France that had been devastated by the fighting. With 2,500 bridges destroyed and 1,300 railway stations rendered unusable by German action and demolition by the retreating French Army, even evacuated Parisian railway workers, urgently needed to get trains running again in the capital and suburbs, had trouble getting home. It took eight days for men who knew the railway network intimately to accomplish what should have been a journey of only 385 kilometres. They left Clermont-Ferrand at midday on 28 June and eventually arrived in Paris at midday on 5 July after a zigzag journey avoiding demolished bridges and German-occupied stations, with the blackout regulations making night travel difficult. In the general chaos, they had difficulty finding anything to eat after their provisions ran out.

Things were better on 18 July, when a train left Bordeaux for Paris carrying 1,700 railway workers, 728 employees of the Peugeot car factory and 450 employees of the aircraft industry, whose journey took only eighteen hours instead of the usual five. Travel priority was also given to civil servants, factory workers and farmers needed back on their land to bring in the harvest. Not until the end of July could the general population return home by train. With a million people then travelling north, the congestion and discomfort in the summer heat can be imagined.

Paris' pre-war population of five million had shrunk to less than two million. Between 27 July and 8 August by one means or another half a million refugees returned, unaware that for two weeks their cardinal had been under house arrest, forbidden both food and the spiritual comfort of the Mass[13] as a way of teaching him who was master. That Cardinal Suhard learned the lesson well and performed the balancing act familiar to many churchmen entrusted both with the spiritual welfare of their flock and the properties of the Church, was to earn him Pétain's support and De Gaulle's enmity.

For those with anything to sell the Germans, business was better than usual. After years of living under Goering's don't-do-what-I-do, do-what-I-say dictum that guns were better than butter, off-duty soldiers flocked to street markets and the Paris flea market, buying anything that could be sent home as 'a present from France', edible or not. Intellectuals of all ranks discovered the joys of browsing in the boxes of the *bouquinistes* along the embankment of the Seine and finding books in many languages long banned in Germany.

Amateur painters in field-grey set up their easels in the streets of Montmartre. Military bands gave open-air concerts of German music with an extract of Bizet's *Carmen* as a sop to the natives. At the upper end of the musical scale, the Paris Opera indulged those with a taste for Wagner so richly in the next four years that his works would be excluded from the repertoire for half a century after the war. The Berlin Philharmonic under Wilhelm Fürtwangler was among the first of the German orchestras to play in the conquered former capital of France and Walter Gieseking was acclaimed by Parisian critics for his playing of Debussy and Ravel.

The accountants were also literally having a field day. From the Banque de France down, every financial establishment was required to draw up statements of all balances in gold, paper money, foreign exchange and jewellery held on behalf of clients. Even neutral foreigners were unable to open their own safe deposit boxes to remove documents or riches secreted there. Before the end of July, property of Jews and the absent, including prisoners of war, was seized against paper receipts stamped with Gothic script.

A major attraction of war has always been loot. Yet, in the villages of eastern France, the invaders of 1940 were considered less prone to pilfering than their fathers in 1914 and their grandfathers who in 1870 had looted all the clocks and watches. However, in the now German areas of Alsace and Lorraine *all* industrial premises belonged to the Reich. June, July and August saw the beginning of organised looting throughout France, with the 7th Army 'liberating' from warehouses in the port of Bordeaux 5,718 tons of coffee plus 2,315 tons of cocoa, 450 tons of rice and 4,544 hectolitres – equivalent to six million bottles – of wine.

The evacuation of German troops from Lyons, which lay in the Free Zone, was scheduled for 25 June under the Armistice agreement but delayed by five days to permit the seizure and removal to the Reich of 162 locomotives and 2,800 railway trucks and carriages, 2,500 tonnes of various foodstuffs, 2,000 tonnes of fuel, 310 tonnes of chemicals and 9,600 tonnes of variegated metals. Altogether, one-third of all French rolling stock headed east and never came back.[14] Before the end of the month entire oil refineries and rolling mills had been dismantled and were rolling eastwards to enhance the Reich's manufacturing capacity, along with 22,000 machines from state factories and 3,000 from private enterprise.

If all this was in the tradition of conquering armies, it was also in flagrant contravention of the Hague Conventions forbidding confiscation of civilian property except in conditions of military necessity.

Chapter 9

OF CHEESE, PLAYS AND BOOKS

Posted to Paris as Kriegsverwaltungsabteilungschef, or department head of General Otto von Stülpnagel's administrative staff, Helmut Rademacher later recalled his boss returning from shopping trips incognito to ask awkward questions like, 'Why is the cost of cheese so high?' Since his multifarious duties embraced the live theatre, Rademacher once ordered Sacha Guitry to remove patriotic speeches from his production of *Pasteur*, opening at the Madeleine theatre on 31 July as an antidote to all the comedies playing elsewhere. Guitry had a tantrum, but got away with it because he was being courted as an example of *französiche Kultur*, but it would be one of the things for which he was called to account after the Liberation.

Rademacher's spicier duties included the inspection and licensing of forces' brothels, which could only employ girls holding a permit from his office. There were forty-five establishments in Paris where *collaboration horizontale* was officially available – forty for German rank-and-file, four for officers below general rank and one for the generals. Rules for the inmates were strict: no Jewesses or Blacks allowed, condoms obligatory and medical checks regular. Off the premises, the girls were watched to ensure they did not work 'on the side'. Business boomed, with German regulations taxing brothels at the same rate as boxing matches – a loophole that was slammed shut by *fisc* inspectors after the Liberation, when they demanded four years' arrears with interest.[1]

Although One-Two-Two, the capital's most expensive *maison de tolérance* never ran short of caviar or champagne, it was out of bounds for German military personnel. Any officer found there or in any other unauthorised brothel was immediately transferred from France for having ignored the obligatory notice outside the entrance: '*Das Betreten dieses Lokales ist deutschen Soldaten und Zivilpersonen strengst verboten.*' All ranks, on leaving a brothel, were given a card bearing the name of the establishment, the date and the girl's working name, for medical follow-up if necessary. It was forbidden for military personnel to have any relationships with the whores, to divulge personal details or give them photographs or other keepsakes.

Between 5,000 and 6,000 street- and bar-girls also had bilingual ID cards declaring them reserved for German use, but the Kriegsverwaltung estimated that in addition to 1,600–1,800 licensed whores in the *maisons closes* and the registered street-walkers there were at least another 80,000 unauthorised female sex-workers in greater Paris alone, constituting a permanent source of venereal infection.[2] Nevertheless, the Wehrmacht's unhypocritical policy paid off: there was no epidemic of gonorrhoea and syphilis such as followed the GIs' arrival after the Liberation.

So many officers managed to wangle a posting to France that some wag invented the apocryphal JEIP travel agency, the initials standing for '*Jeder Einmal in Paris*', meaning 'everyone gets to Paris once'. For newcomers, *Pariser Zeitung* listed places to avoid and hints on 'what to do if . . .' In Montmartre, nightclub settlements between the Corsican Mafia and the *carlingue* (thieves' slang for the Gestapo's hired gangsters) were so frequent that officers were advised to draw their sidearms at the start of a fight and form a human fence around the dancefloor, weapons pointed outwards at the clientele until the police arrived. With SD identity cards in their pockets, the *carlingue* risked nothing in these fracas.

Pariser Zeitung also carried paid publicity for nightclubs, restaurants and brothels where German money was welcome, but not all officers came for *les girls*: during the four years of Occupation German opera-lovers purchased tickets to the value of 6,500,000 francs. For them, the Opera Garnier reopened on 24 August. Its first production, selected to celebrate the marriage of French and German culture, was Gounod's *Damnation of Faust* inspired by Goethe's *Faust*. Bookings were ten times better than for the last performance on 5 June.

The White Russian ballet-master Serge Lifar had taken refuge during the German entry into the capital with a part-Jewish patroness of the arts, Marie-Laure De Noailles, who had remained in her town house to defend her collection of Goyas by waving at any approaching German a letter from US Ambassador Bullit stating that her house and contents were American property. Emerging when he thought it safe, Lifar directed the Opera ballet company in an anodyne choice: *Coppélia* opened on 28 August. Later, he would even invite Baldur von Schirach, head of the Hitler Youth, to open an exhibition.

Within days of the German arrival, gourmet restaurants like Fouquet's and La Tour d'Argent saw takings soar through the roof. Maxim's was quietly taken over by the Berlin restaurateur Otto Horcher, whose colleague Walterspiel also 'administered' forty or so bistros requisitioned from racially unacceptable owners. Another function of Rademacher's office was approving their orders for champagne and fine wines, although everyone was aware that monthly consumption was systematically overestimated so that the surplus purchased at the regulated price of 5 marks per bottle could be sold off on the black market at 20 marks a bottle.[3]

Over a succulent Châteaubriand steak at his table in Le Catalan restaurant, Pablo Picasso held court for writers and artists such as Simone De Beauvoir and Jean-Paul Sartre, Georges Braque and Albert Camus. Throughout the Occupation, he was left alone by the Gestapo despite a Jewish mother and known Communist sympathies. Abetz even sent a lackey offering a supplementary coal allocation, which was refused by the man who had exposed worldwide the Condor Legion's bombing of civilians in his painting *Guernica*. There is a story that one German officer looking at a copy of the painting asked the artist, 'Did you do that?' Picasso is said to have replied, 'No, you did.' Yet, those who look for any evidence of the Second World War in his work during the Occupation look in vain. Expressing contempt for the critics, he said afterwards, 'Perhaps an art historian will demonstrate how my painting was influenced by the war. I don't know.'[4]

The English bookshop on the rue de Rivoli had an enormous sign reading '*Frontbuchhandlung*' tacked in front of 'W.H. Smith' and everywhere *Man spricht deutsch* replaced *English spoken*. At Longchamp and Auteuil the racing set in all its furs and finery, now swollen by Germans in and out of uniform, watched the horse races and placed its bets. The Jockey Club welcomed back its elite members and if the president's box was now reserved for the Kommandant von Gross-Paris and his high-ranking compatriots, the shift troubled no one.

For officers preferring the other kind of horseflesh, the Folies Bergères reopened on 1 August with a new review of scantily clad dancers, which was featured in the French-language edition of the propaganda magazine *Signal* to show how normal life was now in France. The revue was to become less erotic as the autumn drew into a coal-less winter and goose-pimples on the girls' shivering bodies were hard to disguise beneath sequins glued on strategic places. Nightclubs such as Don Juan, Chez Elle, Le Tabarin and the Lido were doing a roaring trade, and the management of one Montmartre dive stuck up a large notice outside, 'The staff and performers in this establishment are all Aryan.' Outside Le Moulin Rouge soldiers queued to see the high-kicking dancers expose their frilly knickers, unaware that the Cancan music had been composed by a Jewish composer.

With 'Paris by Night' now '*Paris bei Nacht*,' Sacha Guitry and Maurice Chevalier had no qualms about performing for the occupying forces. Nor did Edith Piaf spurn their money. Like Chevalier and Charles Trenet, she also accepted tours in Germany. Life was harder for the *chansonniers* in cabarets, who had to word their satirical ditties carefully. Stand-up comedians with no wish to offend either the Occupation authorities or their own humourless government targeted poor performance by Mussolini's troops during the invasion. Everyone appreciated the joke about the Italian airborne attack when a Forza Aerea plane invaded French airspace carrying twelve strong men, all highly trained to throw the single reluctant parachutist out when over the drop-zone! More risky was the story of Mussolini asking the Führer what the German eagle signified. Hitler replied, 'The head of the eagle with its piercing eyes, is me – the brains of the Third Reich. The heart is Goebbels, who guides the soul of the great German nation. The two wings represent Reichsmarschal Goering, master of the Luftwaffe. The belly is Dr Funk, in charge of food production.' At this point Italian Foreign Minister Count Galeazzo Ciano clutches the Duce's sleeve: 'Let's leave now, before he reaches the arse-hole. That'll be us!'[5]

If theatres and the opera had to advance the start of performances by an hour or more to ensure the curtain came down in time for the last Metro train, with priority at the cloakroom for those with a connection to make, in nightclubs many clients were deliberately distracted by the hostesses until they had no choice but to continue drinking and paying for the ladies' drinks until 5 a.m., when they could depart with lightened wallets. Typically Parisian *système D* – the initial being for *débrouiller* (or 'wangle') – saw curfew-exempt post office vans taking routes that enabled the drivers to collect patrons from nightclubs and drop them off at home for cash.

Guitry, in between buzzing around town sometimes in a little electric car to get around the shortage of petrol, said in his film *Donne-moi tes yeux*, 'Before these marvels [of Impressionist art and music created despite the Occupation of France by Germany in 1870] we have the . . . right to consider that such creations are equal to a victory.' Intended as a justification for business-as-usual in the arts and entertainment industry, this and other indiscretions were to cost him two months in prison after the Liberation.[6] Maurice Chevalier tried to play it both ways, photographed in *Signal* singing for POWs at the same camp where he had been imprisoned in the First World War but also protesting a blind obedience of the Marshal that got him into trouble after the Liberation.[7]

At the top end of the cultural scale were the senior officers, whose personal interest in Paris lay in her artistic riches. The Hague Conventions imposed on the victor in war the duty of safeguarding works of art. This enabled General Keitel at OKW to order the first military commander of Paris, General von Vollard-Bockelberg, to take possession of all works of art belonging to the French state and those of émigré Jews and other runaways. Using the logic that all the paintings, statues and smaller valuables were being taken under the protection of the Wehrmacht, the fight began despite an ordinance of 15 July signed by the Militärbefehlshaber in Frankreich:

1. No work of art may be removed from its present place nor modified in any manner without the written authority of the military administration;
2. Removal of any work of art must be authorised by me in advance;
3. Works of art whose value exceeds 100,000 francs must be registered in writing by their owners or present holders before 15 August 1940.

There were always conflicting chains of command emanating from the Führer. Thus, Ambassador Abetz acted on instructions from Ribbentrop when informing Gen Vollard-Bockelberg on 6 July that the responsibility of looking after the works of art fell to the embassy. Accordingly, Gruppe 540 of the

Geheime Feldpolizei was charged with entering private homes and art galleries belonging to Jewish runaways and placing everything valuable under Abetz's care. Within hours the Paris home of Baron Edward De Rothschild was a shell, empty frames hanging on all the walls, furniture, tapestries and even curtains disappearing into the 'protective' maw of the Reich. Army trucks pulled up in front of the art galleries with famous names – Seligman, Bernheim, Rosenberg – while they too were emptied of their treasures.

Before the afternoon was out, Abetz had been overruled. Lieutenant-Colonel Hans Speidel, acting directly for OKW, invoked the Hague Conventions, under which the Kunstschutz or Wehrmacht art protection service was to take charge of all works of art in the conquered territory. Museum curator Count Franz Wolff Metternich was placed in charge of the operation and carried it out so conscientiously that he was dismissed in the summer of 1942, and was later the only German of the Occupation administration to be awarded a French decoration.

On 17 July a counsellor at the Legation, SS-Sturmbannführer Baron von Kunsberg, arrived with a team of Foreign Ministry 'experts' to re-start the official looting. He was soon replaced in the game by Dr Carl-Theo Zeitschel, also an SS-Sturmbannführer and an officer in the GFP, who outranked Abetz both in age and seniority as member of the Nazi Party.

Dr Kummel, whose authority as director-general of the Berlin museums stemmed from Reichsminister Josef Goebbels, next appeared at the head of a commission charged with 'recovering' the works of German artists. If Dürer and Cranach were among them, so also were Rubens, Van Dyck and many others who had not previously been German. While this was ongoing, a Dr Posse from Dresden made his entrance, charged directly by the Führer to seize the best pieces for the greatest art collection in the world at his planned European capital of Linz.

By now the embassy was out of storage space, with canvases and statues and furniture stacked all over. So the Jeu de Paume museum in the Tuileries gardens was requisitioned to serve as a holding area where works could be assembled and sorted. Yet another agency, the Einsatzstab Reichsleiter Rosenberg, was later estimated to have looted 21,903 major works of art.[8] Rosenberg, the Nazi ideologue and author of *The Myth of the 20th Century* – a fictitious elaboration of the origins of the German race – had been placed in charge of the nascent Party by Hitler when in prison after the Munich beer-hall *Putsch* because he was too stupid to be of any danger. The ERR representative in Paris was Dr von Behr, formerly head of the German Red Cross. He was now supposed to be collecting 'cultural property' for an institute where all the intellectual works of Jews and others would be kept and analysed, but was able to stretch the definition to include, for example, a Vermeer looted from a Rothschild residence.

No one, however, outdid arch-collector Hermann Goering. In civilian clothes, the head of the Luftwaffe – then supposedly destroying the RAF prior to a seaborne invasion of Britain – spent whole days in the Jeu de Paume, looking like a mobile tent in his ankle-length overcoat as he ambled among the works of art. With a shopping list including ten Renoirs, ten Degas, two Monets, three Sisleys, four Cézannes and five Van Goghs,[9] he returned nine times, chalking on the works that took his fancy a large *G* if he wanted them for his personal collection at his private palace named Karinhall in memory of his first wife or an *H* if he decided they should go to the Führer, no matter who else might have selected them. He also bought on the open market, endearing himself to dealers by spending 100,000,000 francs in cash from his apparently bottomless briefcase stuffed with untraceable notes.[10]

To support Metternich's Kunstschutz, the Wehrmacht sought to prevent exportation of works of art by making no transport available, a measure that Goering circumvented by commandeering Luftwaffe trucks to convey his loot to his personal train named *Kanada*, in which it travelled eastwards. When a courageous Luftwaffe officer explained that exporting works of art was contrary to military law, Goering simply retorted that he was the ultimate authority on the law[11] and as such empowered to grab pictures by Goya, Rembrandt, Rubens, Franz Hals, Degas, Renoir, Manet, Sisley, Cézanne, Van Gogh and others.

One courageous woman was quietly observing all the pillagers. The sentries at the Jeu de Paume took no notice of the bespectacled, plain-faced and humbly dressed Rose Valland, a young curator at the Louvre who had taken the risk of hiding certain works of art there behind false walls. Each day, she crossed the gravelled courtyard between her office and the Jeu de Paume, surreptitiously compiling an inventory of the looted works of art with details of who had seized them, when and whither they had been despatched. Her log was the principal tool used in recovering thousands of state- and privately-owned works after the war, a labour for which she received several decorations.

Vichy was also doing its best to limit the looting. Many private collectors had donated their favourite pieces to the new French state in the hope of protecting them. Pétain's government now declared that all works of art belonging to runaways, whether Jewish or not, automatically became state property. However, where the original owners were Jewish, the German ruling was that they were German property because transfer of ownership was due to Wehrmacht force of arms. As to the provisions of the Hague Conventions, these did not apply because Jews and their property were not protected by any laws . . . .

What the Nazis called *entartete Kunst*, or degenerate art, presented a different problem. Berlin had sold off works of despised 'un-Germanic' artists during the thirties through Swiss galleries for foreign currency. Similarly, pictures by Picasso, Braque, Pissarro and other modern artists were now sold off at a fraction of their true value to French intermediaries while five or six hundred others were simply taken outside the Jeu de Paume and burned on the terrace. Works of Klee, Miró, Susanne Valadon, Max Ernst and Picasso were reduced to a pile of ashes, as so many books had been in Germany. Typically, Goering obtained works of Jewish or other 'degenerate' artists by arrogating to himself the decision of who was Jewish and what was degenerate. The looting continued until the last train of thirty-seven trucks, whose contents included a Van Dyck, a Rubens and several Renoirs, was immobilised just outside Paris by the Resistance in August 1944.

The German expression *wie Gott in Frankreich* means more or less 'as good as it can get'. Certainly the rear-echelon military, the administrators, the Gestapo and other functionaries who arrived in Paris in the wake of the Wehrmacht were delighted to be on the west bank of the Rhine where, to begin with, shop windows were filled with so many things unavailable in Germany. Many were genuine francophiles, like Ribbentrop's ambassador Otto Abetz, whose elegant French wife immediately drew up lists of the great and good to invite to her lunch parties. The smooth-talking, rather Scandinavian-looking career diplomat Ernst Achenbach, who had been *en poste* in Paris before the war, estimated that most of those invited were patriotic French people trying to accommodate the occupiers, yet they included far-right activists such as Eugène Deloncle. With financial backing from Eugène Schueller, owner of the Oréal cosmetic empire, he formed Mouvement Social Revolutionnaire in September. MSR, pronounced *aime-et-sert* (meaning 'loves and serves'), was to end the Occupation with much blood on its hands.

Abetz, a reluctant Nazi who joined the Party in 1937, adored quoting from his favourite French authors and had made many visits to France in the thirties, courting influential people and arranging youth congresses so successfully that he had been banned from entering France in 1939 on the grounds that he was fomenting a Fifth Column. The same civil servants at the Quai d'Orsay who had banned him then now had to court him as the most important diplomat in Paris. That his post existed at all was due to Foreign Minister Von Ribbentrop's insistence on having his own man among all the others scrabbling for power in Paris, for the role of German ambassador in a city that was not the seat of government was unclear to everyone – according to Hans Speidel, the first Wehrmacht officer to enter Paris and eventually commander of NATO Land Forces Central Europe. Initially confined to dealing with the German military command in occupied France, only later did Abetz's remit include dealing with the French themselves. Meeting Laval on 19 July, while his wife Suzanne was still busy buying curtain fabric and furnishing their apartments in the embassy, Abetz was completely taken in by the dark, dynamic Laval hammering home his personal vision of Franco-German collaboration.

The embassy staff was divided between non-Nazis like Achenbach and die-hard followers of Hitler like SS liaison officer Dr Zeitschel, of whom Achenbach said, 'Now that was someone we didn't trust.' According to Speidel, Schleier's impeccable Party credentials made him politically more powerful than Abetz. Gertsner, too, was considered by the diplomats an out-and-out Nazi, but became a mayor in Communist East Berlin after the war, like many Nazis who found no problem in changing allegiance from one totalitarian regime to another.

On 8 July Dr Carl Schaeffer was ex-officio appointed co-director of Banque de France as Director of the Bankenaufsichtsamt, overseeing *all* French banks, with powers to access and freeze any account. Resistance to what is today normal state intrusion in the banking sector vanished when twelve senior managers of Crédit Lyonnais were imprisoned for protecting clients' accounts from scrutiny.[12] Schaeffer also appointed commissioners to run the Jewish- and British-owned banks. Unlike many Occupation authorities, Schaeffer's operation was amazingly efficient, with two German officials sufficing to police 80,000 obedient bank employees. His failures included the seizure of all foreign currency in France for the Reich. The Bank of England immediately invalidated all its banknotes held abroad unless stamped by a British Consulate before a certain date, with the numbers duly noted. Schaeffer's next move was to open up the safe-deposit boxes of British citizens and confiscate the contents. French citizens needing to open their boxes could only do so in the presence of an official of the Bankenaufsichtsamt or another German officer. Family heirlooms were not taken but uncut gems and shares in foreign companies were 'taken into protective custody'.

The publisher Thomas Kernan returned to Paris in mid-July, to find *Vogue*'s offices on the Champs Elysées had been ransacked and its photographic studio and darkroom requisitioned for the production of propaganda photographs. One of the proliferating German organisations, the Propaganda Staffel, had moved into National City Bank Building at 52 Champs Elysées to control the French press, radio, cinema and theatre. Its boss, a pleasant, overweight lieutenant named Weber, who married a star dancer from the Lido nightclub, had been the pre-war Paris manager for German news agency DNB. Kernan had known him well, but when he walked along the deserted Champs Elysées to ask Weber's permission to resume publication – the US being still neutral – he was surprised to find himself interviewed by an underling whom he also knew. A former freelance Paris fashion photographer named Maier, whose work had never been good enough for *Vogue*, was now wearing SS uniform with the grand title of 'Sonderführer for illustrated magazines'.

Kernan was obliged to declare that *Vogue*'s US parent company, Condé Nast, had no Jewish capital or interests, but each time he filled in one questionnaire he was given another, with Maier inventing one set of problems because the French edition was produced and published by a French company and another because the parent company was American. Meanwhile, the marginal fashion periodical *Art et la Mode*, which had enjoyed a circulation of less than a tenth of *Vogue*'s, reappeared in a clone edition, with its editor openly telling the fashion houses that she had been given the mission of replacing *Vogue*.[13]

It was traditional in France for intellectuals, especially writers, to be politically active. Notwithstanding three wounds suffered in the First World War, author and pamphleteer Drieu La Rochelle had supported Franco during the Spanish Civil War and also attended the Nuremberg rallies alongside delegations of British fascists. He also edited *Dernières Nouvelles*, which folded for reasons unknown after a few months, leaving him free to run the well-established publishing house Nouvelle Revue Française until 1943. Collaboration came naturally to him, as it did to many younger writers such as Robert Brasillach and Lucien Rebatet, who contributed to the virulently anti-Semitic newspaper *Je Suis Partout*.

Hermann Eich, a journalist in his mid-twenties who had been on the staff of *Berliner Tageblatt*, arrived in Paris on 20 June also with the title of 'Sonderführer' to find himself working for Weber on the preparation of guidelines for the French press as to what it could, and could not, do. His *Wege der französichen Presse* was the bible, of which readings were given each week for editors. The editors never actually turned up but sent deputies, who swiftly dwindled in number, until replaced by a handful of secretaries who jotted down shorthand notes to be shared between several papers. Editors who transgressed Eich's guidelines were shut down.

With the blessing of the Propaganda Staffel, intellectual Henri Jeanson, who had been imprisoned during the *drôle de guerre* for his opposition to the war effort, took editorial control of the mass-circulation *Paris Soir*, starting with a vicious attack on Pétain and the government in Vichy. Because of a paper shortage, Jeansson was limited to a two-page format with four pages twice a week. Disdaining his tabloid public, Jeanson soon persuaded the Germans to back his upmarket daily *Aujourd'hui*, for which François Mauriac and publisher Bernard Grasset were happy to write – in Grasset's case after he had returned to Paris from the safety of the Free Zone, protesting to author Alphonse De Châteaubriand that 'however far back you go in both branches of my family, you will find neither a Jew nor a Jewess'.[14]

Too big for his borrowed boots, Jeanson refused after six weeks to put his name to an editorial committing *Aujourd'hui* to open collaboration – and found himself back in La Santé prison. His replacement, Georges Suarez, had written anti-German books before the war, but had no problem changing sides and serving German interests so well that he was among the first intellectuals tried and shot for treason after the Liberation. Released from prison, Jeanson was denounced for having written an article justifying the assassination in 1938 of a German Embassy counsellor by Hershel Grynszpan, which triggered off the violence in Germany known as Kristallnacht. Summoned to Weber's office to account for this and other anti-Hitler articles written years before, brought to the Germans' attention by his old enemies, he landed again in La Santé. Thomas Kernan commented, '[He] disappeared into the limbo reserved for renegades suspect in their own world and thus of no further use to the masters they were ready to serve.'[15]

The second Paris paper to resume publication was *Le Matin*, whose Conservative proprietor had no trouble following the shifting priorities of the Propaganda Staffel, one day attacking the Americans, the next praising President Roosevelt and constant only in its hatred of the English. Out of respect for its alliance with Moscow, the German administration authorised *L'Humanité* to reappear, but under the title *La France au Travail*, edited by De Châteaubriand, the tenor of whose editorials was saccharinely pro-German: 'It is particularly comforting in these times of misfortune to see numerous Paris workers striking up friendships with German soldiers.'[16]

As one door closes . . . Jean Luchaire, managing editor of *Le Matin*, persuaded Weber to back a new daily *Les Nouveaux Temps* – a clone of the pre-war *Le Temps*, right down to the typefaces used. Luchaire's method of doing business with ladies was on the large couch in his office. While employed as his secretary, future film star Simone Signoret spent most of her time buying flowers for German actresses entertained there and taking phone calls from Abetz's wife and Achenbach. She also 'watched a whole raft of ladies passing through the padded door [of Luchaire's office] in the winter of 1940; some because their husbands were prisoners and they wanted them back – one even returned with her husband a few weeks later to say thank you – and others because they needed a quick permit for some commercial enterprise'.[17] In November the respectable right-wing *L'Oeuvre* was taken over by Marcel Déat, a *député* who boasted that he was 'leader of the French who refused to die for Danzig'. Further right, *Le Cri du Peuple* was subsidised by Abetz to the tune of 250,000 francs a month. Its editor was ex-metalworker Jacques Doriot, the charismatic former Number 2 of the PCF, who had lectured in the USSR, backed Stalin against Trotsky and even visited China for the Party before turning his coat to lead the far-right Parti Populaire Français. Far from biting the hand that fed him, Doriot praised Laval, the New Order and collaboration with as much energy as his 45,000 followers beat up gays. Similarly, in December 1940, editor-in-chief Pierre Brisson wrote in *Le Figaro* that Pétain's priority for moral revival was 'worthy of one of the most decisive tests in our history'. He could hardly have done otherwise, since the Vichy regime was to subsidise his paper to the tune of 2,000,000 francs in 1941 alone. The most infamous Occupation rag, *Au Pilori* was anti-Semitic, anti-Masonic and hawked on the streets by malcontents who had previously sold the monarchist paper *Action Française*.[18] Its sales rose to 50,000 copies per issue by the end of 1941.

German propaganda had five main themes. It vaunted a mythical partnership between France and Germany, was generally pro-New Order and anti-English; was anti-democracy – especially American democracy – and it was of course anti-Semitic.

Weber was interested also in the quality magazines, for motives that combined profit and their usefulness as propaganda vehicles. In this shady area, the publisher of *Confidences* – a romantic confessions magazine – was invited by Sonderführer Weber to hand over 60 per cent of his shares in return for permission to publish. His refusal was followed by the appearance of a clone under the title *Votre Coeur*. Managing editor of *L'Illustration*, René Baschet, was an avid follower of Pétain and had no problem getting paper and permission to print after his second edition carried a photo-reportage of the Mers el-Kebir incident. Obliged nevertheless to accept from Weber a 'political director' who vetted every line of text and every picture, Baschet, under pressure, eventually sold out to parties unknown for much less than his magazine had been worth. The most popular woman's magazine, *Marie Claire*, had enjoyed a circulation of two million copies per issue. Its management's refusal to sell out saw another clone called *Pour Elle* on the streets within weeks.[19]

After its brief hiatus during the invasion, the French film industry was beginning a boom, with audiences avid for escapist themes. Production soon outstripped that of the Reich. Despite a decree of 9 September 1940 regulating the film business and the setting up of a state organising committee on 2 December, no fewer than 225 feature films and 400 shorts and cartoons were produced during the Occupation.[20]

Directors like Sacha Guitry, Claude Auntant-Lara, Claude Renoir, Jean Boyer, Marcel Carné and Jean Anouilh were kept busy producing the nostalgic or fantasy films that the public needed to escape reality for a couple of hours in the cinemas. But many classics were also produced during the Occupation, such as *L'Age d'Or* and *Les Enfants du Paradis*. Marcel Carné played with fire and got away unburnt with his 1942 blockbuster *Les Visiteurs du Soir*. Set in a fantasy country during the year 1485, it took the audience no time to recognise it as an allegory of occupied France, with the Devil playing the part of the Occupation forces.

Chapter 10

OF BREAD AND CIRCUSES

On 28 June 1940 De Gaulle was recognised by Churchill as head of the fledgling Free French forces. So, by 2 July, when Laval was appointed successor to Pétain, the main actors in France's tragedy were on the stage of history. Three weeks later came an unmistakable signal from Vichy. In one of the many volte-faces of postwar France, the chief prosecutor at Pétain's trial in 1945 was the first to volunteer for service on the three-man Commission for Denaturalisation, which began on 22 July to revoke French citizenship granted to foreign-born citizens. Coming out of retirement especially for this, André Mornet showed his capacity for hard work by revoking nationality from 15,154 persons, including 6,307 Jews, for whom the result was deportation and almost certain death.[1]

Many cases were brought to the notice of the police and the commission by letters of denunciation from neighbours, business competitors and the simply mad, like the woman whose New Year greetings to De Brinon concluded, 'I would beg you to excuse me from taking fizzy drinks the Jews put the powder from invisible diamonds in its unforgivable it cuts all the fibre of the intestines and the doctors say it's a natural death.'[2] Saner letters were often signed, 'A French patriot' or 'An honest Frenchwoman.'

Paris was still a ghost city of 1,800,000, instead of the normal 5,000,000. Few vehicles apart from German ones were on the streets. The café terraces were deserted. In an attempt to bring things back to normal, the Germans ordered the national railway system SNCF to run refugee specials, and were informed that the best it could manage was to transport 100,000 people per week, at which rate it would take half a year to bring everyone back. Yet by 8 August – the day on which De Gaulle was condemned to death in his absence by a court martial – 500,000 returned Parisians were queuing for the coupons necessary since 3 August for their ration of sugar, bread and pasta, and then queuing again to buy these essentials. Few of them cared that the Masonic orders had been dissolved by decree on 2 August and their assets seized by the state. Police trying to lay hands on the membership lists were for the most part frustrated to find that they had been sent out of the country well in advance.

One of the ways in which a society defines itself is by excluding alien elements: in the USSR, the bourgeoisie and foreigners; in Germany, Jews, freemasons, gypsies and 'deviants' such as homosexuals. Vichy's exclusion laws were aimed at immigrants, Communists and Jews, who were collectively blamed for the defeat. On 13 August, while Stabsmusikmeister Rupf conducted a public concert on the *parvis* in front of Notre Dame cathedral, Pétain announced in a policy speech that all secret societies were to be made illegal. So eager to please its new masters was the important Félix Potin company that it sacked a Jewish manageress after forty-two years' loyal service *before* the new legislation was enacted, from fear that 'the Germans will seize our business . . . if we keep Jews in our senior management'.[3]

Two weeks later, on 27 August, Pétain's dream of a mass return to the land was announced by posters everywhere featuring grizzled old peasants bequeathing the family plough to their sons with slogans such as 'This is a fine weapon, my son. Use it to fight the good fight.'[4] Grants were available for families choosing to return to farming. The catch was that they had to have at least one child and the expectation of more. They also had to undertake to remain farmers for at least ten years. With only 1,561 families signing up, the result was a crushing blow to Pétain's hopes.

Propaganda photographs of senior officials and politicians shaking gnarled peasant hands and presenting medals could not obscure the fact that life on the land had never been so grindingly hard for 100 years or more. Even richer farmers who possessed tractors had no fuel for them. Some were converted to run from *gazogène* generators that produced a fuel from burning charcoal. On large farms, rusted steam traction engines were hauled out of barns and fired up, but on smaller properties the farmer and his wife had to work with horses or oxen to pull the plough, the harrow and the old-fashioned reaper. Even binder twine for tying the sheaves of cut corn was nearly impossible to obtain. Grandmothers rescued their distaffs and spinning wheels from the barn and went back to spinning and weaving the wool from their flocks. Farmers overhauled oil presses that had not been used since cheap groundnut oil had begun to be imported from the colonies and once again crushed their own rape seed and poppy seed to produce cooking oil.

Two days before the end of the month an apparently innocuous organisation was set up. The Légion Française des Combatants sounded like a harmless old comrades' association; but its offspring would turn out to be far from harmless.

What was the Church doing all this time? If some individual priests were actively relieving grief and hardship, their superiors were mostly in wait-and-see mode. Gen Weygand was a devout Catholic and Pétain as a pillar of law and order appealed to the right-wing Catholic hierarchy. Cardinal Gerlier, Archbishop of France's second city – and a former pupil of Charles De Gaulle's father – declared in Lyons, 'Pétain is France and France is Pétain.' In gratitude, Vichy passed a law on 4 September repealing the anti-clerical Religious Associations Law of 1903 and returning Church properties not already sold off by the state. Bells pealed and priests were free to go about in public clad in traditional cassocks.

Earthly communications were also slowly getting easier. The major northern industrial city of Lille had suffered such damage to lines and switching centres that only twelve telephones remained connected, all in local government offices. By the end of August 640 subscribers had been reconnected. Written communication with loved ones across the Demarcation Line was permitted, but only on thirteen-line pre-printed postcards reading, 'At . . . on (date) . . . / . . . is in good health / tired / slightly, badly / ill / wounded / killed / prisoner. . . . has died / is without news of . . . The family . . . is well / needs food / money / news / baggage. . . . is back at . . . / works at . . . will return to school in . . . / has been received / to go to . . . on (date) . . . With love / kisses (signature).'[5]

More sophisticated reading material was also subject to German censorship. The first 'Otto List' of banned authors – named not after Abetz, but an eponymous Nazi professor – appeared on 27 August listing hundreds of books including translations of works by German and Austrian authors such as Thomas Mann, Lion Feuchtwanger and Sigmund Freud. Bookshop owners had to hand over every copy for destruction by French police.

Censorship of new works was less intrusive. Even before the one-sided 'Convention' of 28 September laying down the guidelines, no sane publisher wished to annoy the government or the Germans. On 8 November, his thirtieth birthday, the francophile linguist Gerhard Heller arrived in Paris to take up his posting with the Propaganda Staffel, running the Referat Schrifttum, censoring books submitted by French publishers. He was to spend the next weeks reading day and night to work his way through the backlog and issuing a *bon à tirage* authorising publication in most cases.

With Abetz's backing, Sonderführer Heller passed almost every work submitted to his office, and was proud that, despite all the other materials in short supply or unobtainable, paper was never lacking for books by approved authors. His low-profile censorship was accepted even by best-sellers like Antoine de St-Exupéry and Albert Camus – who cut a chapter on Kafka from his first popular success, *Le Mythe de Sisyphe*.

Heller recalled being sent with a colleague to the Presses Universitaires de France, to order managing director Paul Angoulvent to dump all his Jewish authors. Making the point that this was no request, the other officer took his pistol out of its holster and laid it on the desk, causing Angoulvent to go white as a sheet.[6] Heller was more subtle, as when ordering the publishing house Mercure de France to withdraw and destroy all copies of Georges Duhamel's book *Lieu d'Asile*. Off the record, he told managing director Jacques Bernard to hide some copies wrapped up and labelled 'Property of Lt Heller', so that when the time came, he could republish it without problems. Aware that the heart problems which had earned him the Paris posting would be no protection from being sent to the Russian front, Heller knew he was treading a dangerous path.

Despite the censorship, the annual output of literary, art and scientific books published between 1941 and 1944 was no less than it had been pre-1939. Included were 300 translations from German, a speciality of the Aryanised publishers Nathan and Calmann-Lévy. The figure for 1943 was the highest in the world, with the French total of 9,348 books beating US publishing's figure by more than 1,000 and UK output by 2,000. The reason? What else could one do when obliged by the curfew to stay at home night after night in that pre-television age?

The books most people were interested in were their new ration books. Curiously, the English word 'tickets' was used for the small squares that had to be cut out and collected by butcher, baker and greengrocer when selling the specified amount of food to each customer – while in Britain they were called by the French word 'coupons'.

Entitlement varied with age, sex and work. Category C covered farmhands and others doing heavy manual work, with other workers in Category T. Category A covered all other adults between 21 and 70, while those over 70 were Category V. Infants were E, but children from 3 to 21 were graded J1, J2 or J3. Babies were entitled to milk; conversely, the old received a larger bread ration. The average adult received 350 grams of bread per day, 350 grams of meat per week and a monthly allowance of 500 grams of sugar, 300 grams of coffee and 140 grams of cheese. Although rations for babies and young children were supposed to be adequate, records show that boys maturing in 1944 were seven centimetres shorter than those of 1935, while girls were eleven centimetres shorter than their older sisters. Teeth especially suffered.[7]

As in Britain during the war, the rich could still sate their hunger in restaurants. For low-income workers and the unemployed, a chain of state canteens was opened in towns, similar to the British Restaurants across the Channel. These *rescos* offering balanced three-course meals with wine for 8–16 francs were patronised by as many as 200,000 Parisians. At the other end of the market, journalist and gastronome Jean Galtier-Boissière was paying 100 francs a head to entertain his friends to oysters and beef with a good cheeseboard and wine. Alas, by 2 August 1941 he would lament in his diary having to pay 650 francs for three friends and himself to enjoy fresh sole followed by slices of mutton. He estimated that restaurant prices quadrupled in the two years from December 1940 and were ten times as high by the beginning of 1944. A contemporary joke told of a madman released after thirty years in an asylum. Appalled at the wartime menu in a restaurant, he asks for special treatment and is given lobster, mutton chops and chips, a cheeseboard and pastry to finish with. The bill comes to 1,250 francs. Aghast, he tenders in payment the only money he had on him when locked up. It is a single golden *louis d'or*. The waiter bows and returns with change of 2,000 francs.

The value of gold had increased even more than that of food, but there were some things money could not buy. When Goering dined at Maxim's, he was given a table by the orchestra, while the favourite table of the Duke of Windsor and the Aga Khan was kept vacant for their return. He enjoyed the food enough to rule that the restaurant should be closed to all except high-ranking German officers, but lost interest in the idea once Eagle Day had come and gone without the destruction of the RAF. Released from internment, one politician's British wife hired Fouquet's for her celebration banquet – after which the gentlemen repaired to the cloakroom, to toast each other in black-market whisky, while she finished her meal with a Craven A cigarette 'traded' for food by her compatriots still behind bars in the St-Denis barracks.

As time went by, prudent French gastronomes avoided La Palette in Boulevard Montparnasse, frequented by the Resistance and watched by the Gestapo. The singer Tino Rossi was among the few uncommitted patrons at the Alexis bistro near Notre-Dame-de-Lorette, where one risked finding one's table surrounded by Jacques Doriot and the top brass of the PPF. Few could do more than gaze through the windows. The *Journal Officiel* announced on 18 September a subsidy of 150 francs for seeds and tools to encourage everyone to take an allotment and grow his own food.

Just as the civilian population was thinking itself safe from the violence of war, a new enemy appeared. From bases across the Channel, RAF bombers raided ports where German invasion preparations were going on. From there, the targets spread to submarine bases, factories and airfields, many of them in or near centres of population. Between September 1940 and May 1941 the naval town of Brest suffered seventy-eight raids, causing the mayor to appeal to Pétain: 'The women and children have to take refuge at night in the caves in the cliffs around town and in a tramway tunnel.'

At the eastern end of the Channel coast in Dunkirk, where 82 per cent of houses had been destroyed in the May fighting, the first RAF raid on 28 July was followed by a massive raid on 8 August. The Occupation troops took priority in the shelters, leaving most civilians cowering in cellars beneath the ruins of their homes. Few people in Britain knew or cared that between 60,000 and 67,000 innocent French civilians were killed and around 72,000 seriously wounded[8] by bombs which bore cheeky messages scrawled in chalk like 'Here's one for Adolf'. The addressee was for the time safe; each mis-directed delivery merely adding to the misery of his French victims. After Mers el-Kebir it was yet another reason to wonder who was the real enemy, and posters all along the Channel coast asked, 'And these were your allies?'

With big business seeking new opportunities, the Occupation administration was one step ahead, requiring each section of industry and commerce in August to form a Comité d'Organisation Nationale. The initials CON were unfortunate, since *con* is both a female body part and a rude word for 'silly' – as in English. Even after it was re-abbreviated to CO, there was no doubt for whose benefit these organising committees had been set up, although they were ostensibly intended for updating business methods and re-equipping factories to prepare French firms for competition in a German-dominated United States of Europe.

A series of laws dated 18, 20 and 31 October and 9 and 16 November 1940 completely revised French corporation law. As in the European Community that Britain joined in 1973, young and ambitious businessmen snatched the opportunity to enhance their careers by working for the COs. In the absence of trade unions and parliamentary democracy, considerable power accrued to them, largely through their authority to impose sanctions on companies who failed to march in step with the New Order. The inherent problem from the start was one endemic in totalitarian economies: a proliferation of 'organising bodies' whose members had to pay the costs of a flood-tide of time-wasting paperwork. Some companies belonged to more than one CO; others had no idea to which they belonged. Many companies believed they were being discriminated against when the restricted resources were carved up. While major companies could keep abreast of all the bureaucracy, smaller ones found that they were pawns being moved now by German orders or lack of them, now by the OCPRI – the central office for distribution of industrial products. It was a dream-world, in which the Germans insisted on placing orders direct, reducing the COs' role to the compiling of statistics.

Some COs did work. Banking, then with no need of raw materials or expensive machines, was enjoying a boom in export credits to cover orders from the Reich. Henri Ardant, MD of Société Générale, considered it so vital for French banking to integrate itself into the new united Europe that he jumped at the chance to run the banking CO established on 13 June 1941. His connections with the SS hierarchy were so close that former SS-Standartenführer Helmut Knochen said at his postwar trial, 'He gave us all the information we wanted from the point of view of both banking and finance.'[9]

Money is money, whether German or French, so that remark should be taken in the context of Dr Schaeffer's memories of hospitality and warm personal relationships with the directors of most of the major banks during the time he ran the Bankenaufsichtsamt. By 15 September 1940 everyone holding a bank account had to provide proof of Aryan descent before being allowed to use it. Safe-deposit boxes of all Jews who had not returned to Paris were opened and their contents confiscated. The result was a harvest for the Reich, because in 1939 Paris had had the largest Jewish population of any city except Warsaw and New York, including 150,000–200,000 stateless refugees from Nazi Germany and Poland. That bedfellows are not always lovers is demonstrated by the management of the Banque Nationale pour le Commerce et l'Industrie being very close to Schaeffer for business reasons, yet protecting Jewish employees from the second Statut des Juifs in June 1941 by finding work for them to do at home and continuing to pay their salaries.[10]

In September the Paris Bourse reopened in Vichy, so unsuccessfully that the Germans eventually gave permission to reopen in Paris *sans* the Jewish members. On one afternoon that month, Thomas Kernan looked out of the window of his office to see gangs of what he called 'pimply youths' in the Blackshirt uniforms of the Jeune Front movement smashing the windows of Jewish-owned shops on the Champs Elysées. He watched an appalled Wehrmacht officer collar one young hooligan, but release him after being shown an SD identity card. Robert Hersant, leader of the Jeune Front, later found himself in trouble for saying, 'I don't want any Boches around me. I use the Germans, but I detest them.'[11]

On 30 September the Louvre museum reopened its doors on a collection considerably reduced by all the looting, official and unofficial. The following day, Foreign Minister Paul Baudouin noted in his diary that Pétain had been at his most intransigent in Cabinet when drafting the first Statut des Juifs, which came into effect on 3 October 1940 – from when all Jews had to register their presence at the local Hôtel de Ville. Nobel prize-winning philosopher Henri Bergson, a sick 81-year-old who had converted to Catholicism, went to register out of despair and to express solidarity with the persecuted minority among whom he had grown up.

The statute specified that no Jew was allowed to serve in the educational or judicial systems, the armed services, the civil service, press and entertainment, nor to present himself for election to public office. Jews were also forbidden to queue, without doing which they could not buy food. They had to hand in their radios and were forbidden to use telephone kiosks. The PTT was instructed to disconnect Jewish subscribers and remove their handsets.

The Director of Education for the *département* of Seine, which then included greater Paris, sent to all head teachers a circular of which this is an extract:

The Law of 3 October regarding the status of Jews stipulates as follows:
Art 1. 'Jew' in the context of this law means any person having three grandparents of the Jewish race, or two grandparents if married to a Jew.
Art 2. The following public service employment is barred to Jews:
Art 3. . . . members of the teaching profession . . .

Article 7 continued:

The Jewish state employees affected . . . will cease to exercise their functions within two months of the promulgation of this law. They will be permitted to claim their pension rights, providing they have sufficient pensionable years of service or be entitled to a proportional pension if they have served at least fifteen years. Those who fall into neither category will have their cases settled within a period to be determined by the administration.

By his circular of 21 October, the Secretary of State for Education has informed me that by 'teachers' is meant all civil servants whose professional activity brings them into regular and direct contact with pupils and whose authority affects the teaching and indirectly the pupils, viz. primary school and other teachers, heads of schools, etc.

Shortage of paper caused the circular to be issued on paper headed 'République Française' with the old revolutionary slogan 'Liberté, Egalité, Fraternité', which was hardly appropriate in the circumstances.

No less ominously, the prefects who control regional government in France were given power to intern foreign Jews. The concentration camp at Gurs, where refugees from the Spanish Civil War had been held, was among those taken over for 'foreign undesirables'.[12] Three days later, Algerian Jews were deprived of citizenship, which had been theirs by right since 1871. Towards the end of the year the Jewish-born Catholic priest Abbé Glasberg managed to get into the camp at Gurs and reported the 'inhuman conditions' to his superiors. On the instructions of Cardinal Gerlier, Monsignor Guerry went to Vichy in December to hand a protest at this unchristian treatment of the detainees to the Minister of the Interior, but got no further than the minister's *chef de cabinet*.

On 12 October Wehrmacht sappers blew up the monument in Rheims to the coloured colonial soldiers who had died for France in the First World War, exposing in the granite base a document acknowledging their important contribution to victory. In Paris, the sappers also dismantled the statue in Denys-Cochin square of General Charles Mangin, a hero of that war. The reason? When commanding his regiment of Senegalese soldiers occupying the Rhineland in 1918, Mangin had ordered mayors in his area to supply whores for military brothels and overruled their protests by saying, 'Don't worry, *meine Herren*, German women are none too good for my Senegalese soldiers.'

In September and October Laval travelled repeatedly to Paris for meetings with the Germans, which enabled his many enemies in Vichy to turn the Marshal more and more against him. On 22 October Laval met Hitler at Montoire in central France, to prepare the way for Pétain's meeting with the Führer two days later. Hitler was on his return journey from a meeting with Franco, at which his expectation that the *caudillo* would repay German help in the civil war by offering military support had foundered on the German refusal to promise in return control of French North Africa. On 25 May Laval would tell his dinner guests, 'My meeting with Hitler at Montoire was a moving surprise. Rejecting any idea of vengeance, Hitler is prepared to admit France into the [New Europe] he will create when the war is over.'

After the Hitler–Pétain meeting, photographs of the two shaking hands at Montoire made the front pages of newspapers all over the world. In a letter thanking Cardinal Baudrillart for supporting him, Pétain wrote, 'I want [the people] to trust me blindly, as three million of them did when I was their commander when they faced the enemy. Later, they will come to understand what my plan was.'[13] On 30 October Pétain broadcast an appeal for collaboration as a way of 'making the best of it'. Prophetically, he added, 'I went freely to talk to the Führer. I was subjected to no diktat or pressure. A collaboration, which I accept in principle, has been planned between our two countries. It must be sincere. This policy is mine. It is me alone that history will judge.'

If most of their elders were too numb or too self-interested to react, the youth of Paris thought it was time to protest when the German authorities ordered the Rector of Paris University to forbid any demonstration on 11 November – the anniversary of the Armistice that ended the First World War.[14] The Sorbonne had reopened in July to prevent its buildings being requisitioned. Handwritten notes were passed hand-to-hand among secondary school and university students, summoning thousands to a rally at the Tomb of the Unknown Soldier beneath the Arc de Triomphe. The demonstration was suppressed by French police and German troops, with a force that seemed excessive to at least one Wehrmacht officer. The book censor Gerhard Heller was ordered to leave his office and join troops re-establishing order. When four apprehended students were placed in his custody, he marched them inside the building at pistol-point – but then told them to make themselves scarce.

On the following day, the university was closed down. It was a black day even for the dark years, as far as education was concerned. A purge of left-wing teachers included PCF member Georges Guingouin, who refused to toe the pro-German party line and went underground, organising resistance in the Limousin area. Another independent-minded young Communist, 18-year-old student Pierre Daix from Rennes, was arrested on 26 November for his part in the Armistice Day demonstration. Emerging from prison in March 1941, Daix became a member of one of the PCF action groups after Hitler invaded the USSR in June of that year. Arrested in January 1943, he was deported to Mauthausen concentration camp, where he was lucky not to be murdered by other Communist prisoners for not blindly obeying orders from Moscow.

On a more trivial level, the law also caught up with Thomas Kernan in November 1940 – for a minor infringement of blackout regulations committed way back in June! The wheels of Justice were grinding as slowly as usual and the cataclysm of defeat did not stop him being fined. Cycling home from the tribunal in November, he counted the cars on the streets. One passed every five minutes.[15] The silence was that of the countryside, broken only by birdsong and crickets in the gardens. At night, the stars could be seen again from the centre of Paris for the first time in a century, so little illumination was emitted by the blue-painted panes of the street lamps and similarly blue-lensed cycle lamps.

Hitler's love of animals earned a respite for the French circus. Deprived of fodder for their herbivores and meat for their carnivores, the great names of French circus were hiring out docile animals to pull ploughs in anticipation of a bleak war until the Cirque d'Hiver and Cirque Medrano, made famous by Toulouse-Lautrec's paintings, and where Buster Keaton would make his comeback in 1947, were taken over by the enterprising Busch family. On 20 December the Cirque d'Hiver added 'Busch' to its name and opened with matinees and evening shows each day except Sunday, when continuous performance was the rule. Nobody seemed to notice that one of the white-face clowns had two small squares of black on his upper lip, remarkably reminiscent of the moustache of a certain Austrian ex-corporal. To compensate for the missing international acts, music-hall turns were added to the bill, with Charles Trenet and Les Petits Chanteurs de l'Opéra performing between the elephants and the lions. From there, it was a logical step to go on tour in the Reich, where the fodder rationed in France was freely available for a travelling circus.

Two weeks after the Marshal's meeting with Hitler at Montoire came proof, if proof were needed, that Hitler's handshake did not mean he was going soft on the self-confessed master-collaborator: 70,000 Lorrains who did not wish to be German were expelled from their homes and dumped by special trains in Lyons on a one-way ticket. Furious at the way Laval had made him Hitler's dupe, Pétain decided to get rid of him. On 13 December the last straw came when Baudouin hinted that the German invitation for the Marshal to attend a ceremony at Les Invalides marking the return of the ashes of Napoleon's son the Duke of Reichstadt from Vienna on 15 December was a plot between them and Laval to kidnap him.

The Marshal invented a subterfuge. Asking all the ministers at that day's Cabinet meeting to write a letter of resignation that would not be accepted, but held 'just in case', he then told Laval and one other minister that their resignations had been accepted. Laval turned white with anger. 'You are a weathercock,' he yelled, 'which turns with the wind.'

After he stormed out, slamming the door, Pétain scribbled a note that smacked of a commanding officer reprimanding a wayward subaltern: 'M. Laval will be confined to his quarters for two days.'

The Hôtel du Parc was packed with a new breed of secret police – the so-called Groupes de Protection (GP). Laval's office phones were dead. At 10.30 p.m. the American UPI correspondent appeared, somewhat roughed up by them, to inform Laval that his driver had been arrested and his car confiscated by the GP. Trying to leave the building, Laval was detained by the head of the Police Nationale and General Laure, who showed him Pétain's note, which they were treating as a warrant to place him under house arrest. Driven under escort to Châteldon, Laval found himself, his wife and daughter prisoners in their own home. Thus neither the head of state nor the head of government attended the midnight ceremony at Les Invalides, the French government being represented by Darlan and De Brinon. Hitler was furious at being spurned, but popular reaction in France to this non-event was, 'He should have sent us some of our own coal back, not just these useless ashes.'

By an oversight, Laval's radio had not been removed from the château, so that he heard the Marshal broadcast the severing of relations with him 'for reasons of internal policy'. On the Tuesday, *chef de cabinet* Du Moulin arrived at Châteldon to announce that the family was free, confessing that Laval had been the victim of a conspiracy playing upon Pétain's paranoia. In the privacy of the Pavillon Sévigné back in Vichy, the Marshal apologised, saying that he had no idea Madame Laval and her daughter had been inconvenienced. In the same breath he offered his erstwhile prisoner the Ministry of the Interior, which was turned down, followed by those of Agriculture and Industrial Production – both of which Laval also rejected, as Pétain had known he would.

In a prison cell after the Liberation, preparing the defence he was not allowed to present in court, Laval wrote of this time, 'I learned from . . . the Police Nationale, who had guarded me [at Châteldon] that on Thursday [19 November] the official guard [on my house] was to have been replaced by a unit of the GP, of which a man called Norey was instructed to shoot me on the false pretext that I was trying to escape.'[16] He was convinced that Pétain's sacking him cost months of extra captivity for hundreds of thousands of French POWs and that the Germans had been about to reduce the Occupation costs from 400,000,000 francs per day to 180,000,000 francs, had he been left in office.

Chapter 11

COURAGE OF A QUIET KIND

W hile the intellectuals talked, the politicians manoeuvred and the businessmen schemed, a number of ordinary people living less than 15 kilometres from the author's house in south-west France decided independently of each other to do what they could to keep the fluttering flame of freedom from being extinguished altogether.

Georges Chabrier returned home to St Pey de Castets after being demobilised in Pau to find that his home was 300 metres on the wrong side of the Demarcation Line. Volunteering under-age in the First World War, he was twice wounded during three years at the front. Demobilised in 1918 aged 20 and with a leg troubled for the rest of his life by pieces of German shrapnel, his respect for authority survived the hardships of the twenties and thirties. Called up again in 1940, he served with a unit of other wounded veterans in Pau until demobbed at the Armistice. Believing that the Marshal had saved his life at Verdun, Chabrier supported him as legal head of state, but nevertheless decided that his duties as a patriotic French citizen were not yet discharged, whatever the generals and politicians had decided.

Picking up the pieces of his peacetime life, he spent weekday mornings as an auxiliary postman; in the afternoons he worked as a carpenter and the local road-sweeper and school caretaker. Collecting the mail from the nearby town of Castillon, where it arrived by train, he cycled back with it to the village of Pujols, where there was a sub-post office inside the thirteenth-century castle built there on the orders of England's King John. After the incoming mail had been sorted, Chabrier set off on his bicycle again with his bag of letters in order to deliver them to the homes of the addressees.

St Pey and Castillon were in the Occupied Zone, Pujols in the Free Zone, but Chabrier farmed a piece of ground divided by the Line and had a pass from the local Kommandantur entitling him to cross it at any time between 8 a.m. and 8 p.m. The first risk he took was to carry across the line, for ex-servicemen whom he knew, letters slipped inside the wrappers of newspapers and magazines. Most covered family matters too complicated or too intimate for the official printed postcards; others were business correspondence that the writers did not want to be seen by German censors. If caught, the routine penalty for this was seven days in prison, and two weeks for a second offence but, had any of the letters contained military information, the penalty would have been a firing squad or deportation to a concentration camp.

Georges Chabrier's permission to cross the Demarcation Line.

For a man with wife and children, whom he was also putting at risk, to take this decision required a very steadfast kind of courage. Twice Chabrier was denounced: on the first occasion, the guards searching him did not think to look inside the newspaper wrappers; on the second occasion, the Germans arrived to search his carpentry workshop while he was having his hair cut by the village barber. Luckily, a neighbour secreted the post-bag, including a bundle of clandestine mail, below a deep pile of wood shavings. The Alsatian sniffer dog sneezed several times at the pungent resin in the pitch-pine shavings, but his handler did not think of digging into the pile.

'The Germans searched everywhere in the house and the barn,' Chabrier told a fellow *résistant* later. 'They took away all the letters I had written my wife while in uniform, and kept them two weeks before telling me I could have them back. By God, I was frightened that time!'

Running the village telephone kiosk and cooking lunch for sixty-three pupils in the village school, his wife looked after him and their two sons. She was soon pregnant again, but the couple had to move out of their bedroom into the spare room when two German soldiers patrolling the line were billeted on them. One of the lodgers was the driver of the Oberleutnant who had signed Chabrier's *Ausweis*. Having been a German teacher in Paris before the war, he spoke excellent French, confessing to his involuntary hosts with a conspiratorial wink that he hoped one day to join his wife and children in America. Judging that his consistent under-performance in the Wehrmacht made him a likely candidate for the eastern front after the launch of Operation Barbarossa, he drove the car into the Free Zone one day and was never heard of again.

With two less amenable Wehrmacht men sleeping in the house every night, Chabrier's next step was even more courageous. Although bona fide refugees were allowed to return home in the summer of 1940, once the controls were tightened up there were many thousands of people who wanted to cross illicitly. The risk of being caught was high and only local inhabitants knew when the mobile patrols were likely to pass a given point, so Chabrier quietly informed his ex-service friends that he was prepared to help people who needed to cross without papers.

French *gendarmes* and SS troops checked the identity of all passengers alighting at Castillon station because it was the last stop before the frontier. Line-crossers therefore left the train at the previous stop, St-Magne, leaving their bags on the train. Railway staff turned a blind eye when Chabrier's 15-year-old elder son arrived at Castillon station to load the luggage onto his father's cart pulled by a rather aged mare and brought them home, where they were hidden until nightfall. While the two Germans slept in the main bedroom, he then reharnessed the mare, and drove the luggage quietly through the curfew to a bridge over the stream that ran along the line. There, he loosed the family's ancient sheepdog to cast about sniffing for anyone nearby. Since the guards had orders to shoot to kill, it was only when the dog was satisfied there was no one around that the boy carried the bags across and hid them on the other side.

His father meanwhile rendezvoused with his friends bringing the refugees and led them across the line between patrols. They collected their luggage – sometimes far too much of it – and followed him up to Pujols on its hill, where he discreetly left them with the local café-owner before retracing the dangerous route homewards to snatch a few hours' sleep before dawn.

'You had to be careful,' Chabrier said, 'because you never knew which neighbour might send an anonymous letter to the Gestapo.'

No one kept a record of how many people father and son helped in this way. All Chabrier would say was that they included women with babies and children, escaped POWs and even an English colonel. Usually, he was warned to expect a group by the mayor of Libourne or the Procureur de la République, a sort of District Prosecutor. Having belonged to no organised group, neither they nor Chabrier received any medals or commendations after the Liberation; nor did he or his elder son ever talk about what they had done.

As to why so many people wanted to cross into the Free Zone, where they were still far from safe, a large part of the reason was simply ignorance of

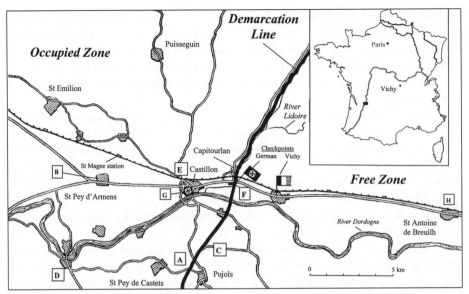

One small corner of France: the area of Castillon. **A** The place where Chabrier and his son helped refugees to cross the Line; **B** Home of Chabrier's friend Teyssier, who was tortured and killed; **C** Where Chabrier's friend Darfeuille was shot dead; **D** Home of Chabrier's cousin Sabre, killed in a death camp; **E** Home of Coupry, killed in a death camp; **F** Rambaud's farm, where Col Rémy was caught by a German guard; **G** Gestapo HQ, where Demetrio tortured his victims; **H** Rémy's rendezvous at Château la Roque with Louis de la Bardonnie.

conditions there, due to the unavailability of Vichy newspapers in the Occupied Zone and the frequent attacks on Pétain in the German-controlled press in Paris, which made life in the Free Zone seem attractive. In a sense it was preferable: Simone De Beauvoir noted on a visit to the Free Zone in 1941 the availability of foreign newspapers and American films no longer available in Paris.[1] For immigrants at risk there was also a powerful magnet at Vichy in the presence of US and other neutral diplomatic missions, from whom a visa might be forthcoming.

On one occasion an attractive and well-dressed woman in her mid-thirties with a Parisian accent arrived at Chabrier's house out of the blue carrying a small suitcase and saying that she worked in the War Ministry and needed to cross the line, but had lost her papers. With his wife still in bed after the birth of their third child, Chabrier played the part of a stupid peasant, ignoring the woman's show of distress and explaining that all she had to do was go to the German Kommandantur and ask them for a duplicate pass. His instinct was proved right a couple of weeks later when she was seen in uniform at the checkpoint in nearby Capitourlan, strip-searching women crossing the line there.

Had Chabrier needed any reminder of the penalties for the risks he ran, it came when an old service comrade named Teyssier living a few kilometres to the north of St Pey was caught, tortured and returned dead to his family. Chabrier's cousin Sabre, who was the butcher in another neighbouring village, 'died in a death camp crematorium' – as did Coupry, another friend caught in August 1944 taking people across. A fourth friend, Darfeuille, was taking some documents across when shot dead by the guards several hundred metres inside the Free Zone.

Some were just unlucky, but who betrayed the others? Chabrier said:

It wasn't just the vigilance of the guards and German customs officers . . . Other *passeurs* who worked for profit – 10 francs for a letter and as much as 10,000 francs for taking a person across – denounced those of us who did it for free. Nobody will ever know how many bodies of rich Jews who had been carrying all their wealth with them were fished out of the Lidoire (a tributary of the Dordogne, along which the line passed) after being killed by these people.[2]

At the trial of Maurice Papon in 1997 an old lady, whose parents, grandmother and younger brother were deported, recalled being entrusted to a *passeur* who raped and abused her.[3]

Another veteran of 1914–18, who had spent time in a German POW camp, Raoul Laporterie was mayor of Bascons in Les Landes, living on the Vichy side of the line, but with four clothing stores to manage on the other side, which required him to cross and recross it every day. Like Chabrier, he also began by taking a few letters across for people he knew. Because this sector of the line was near the strategic Mont-de-Marsan airfield, thousands of trees were chopped down to make it more difficult for people to slink across. Laporterie decided that the best way to get people out of the Occupied Zone was to do it openly by abusing his powers as mayor and using blank identity cards and genuine rubber stamps in his office to create new identities for them.

Since the Germans were suspicious of any obviously new cards, he had the brilliant idea of resurrecting the population of the cemetery to make new identities that would stand up to scrutiny. In one year, the population on paper of Bascons thus grew from 450 to 1,850, to the benefit of Edith Piaf's husband Jacques Pills and André Malraux' wife Clara. It was easy enough to scuff and crease the cards Laporterie made, but an apparently old card in a new wallet attracted attention, so the 'price' he demanded from each line-crosser was the old cellophane wallet in which the genuine ID card had been kept.

On 10 October 1940, Laporterie's help was sought by 'Colonel Olivier,' a Free French officer parachuted back into France the previous night on a mission to survey the airfield, from where the Luftwaffe's long-range Focke-Wulf Condors flew missions to attack British shipping and vector U-boats based in French ports onto convoys far out in the Atlantic. With the neighbouring race-track taken over to extend the runway for Condors with supplementary drop-tanks that would give them the range to bomb Canada and the USA, constant updates were required in London, the biggest scoop coming when a friend of Laporterie was handed detailed plans of the base by an anti-Nazi Austrian officer on the airfield.[4]

As the first winter of the Occupation drew nearer, country folk were better off than townspeople because their heating and cooking was mostly by wood from the forests hauled home, sawn and split by hand. Town-dwellers faced a bleak, coal-less winter; Simone De Beauvoir recounted how it was so freezing in their apartment that she went early each day to the Café Flore to grab two little marble-topped tables near the stove, on which Sartre and she worked by the light of acetylene lamps.[5]

It was for most people a sad Christmas that marked the end of the first half-year of the Occupation, summed up by a rhyme parodying a Christmas carol. No one knew where it originated and there were several versions, but it went something like this:

Christmas has been cancelled, the Virgin and Child evacuated.
St Joseph is in a concentration camp and the stable has been requisitioned.
The angels have been shot down. The Wise Men are in England.
The cow is in Berlin, the ass in Rome,
and the star has been painted blackout blue[6] by order of the Blockleiter.

Governments depend on the fact that most citizens quickly accept new rules and regulations. Already France was effectively two countries: to the west and north of the Demarcation Line the population was subjected daily to the sight of armed German soldiers and the rhythm of life was set by the Occupation authorities; in the predominantly agricultural Free Zone, most people had yet to see their first German soldier.

In Paris and other main cities on the first day of 1941 not only was the pre-war roar of traffic absent but, the French service of the BBC having asked every patriot to keep off the streets at 3 p.m., from five minutes to the hour Germans sobering up after their Sylvesternacht celebrations found themselves in a ghost city during this uncanny demonstration that actually broke no laws and therefore incurred no punishment.

A rhythm that haunts the soundtrack of every film set in wartime France was first heard two weeks later when Victor De Laveleye of the BBC Belgian service used the Morse code for letter V, which is dot-dot-dot-dash, in his programme of 14 January, asking listeners to display next day a letter V – standing for *victoire* in French and *vrijheid* meaning 'freedom' in Flemish. The same rhythm being also the opening bar of Beethoven's Fifth Symphony, the BBC adopted this, played on timpani, to begin its broadcasts to occupied Europe from 22 March onwards.

On 3 January 1941 Paris University reopened after its two-month closure. Two days later the sound of clogs on pavements rang out once again all over

France. With most leather requisitioned for boots, belts and harness for the Wehrmacht's hundreds of thousands of draught horses, shoe rationing came into force on 5 January, after which storekeepers attempted to convince customers that wooden-soled shoes and clogs were actually quite fashionable, with compressed cork a quieter alternative for those who could not stand the noise.

At the top end of the fashion market, in the haute couture salons the spring collections were sparse, each designer being limited to seventy-five patterns. Rochas' idea of a gesture of economising cloth was a daring long-sleeved dress in black taffeta with one shoulder provocatively bare. Belts were limited to a maximum width of four centimetres to save cloth. Germaine Grès' audacity in exhibiting a jersey dress using far too much material for Vichy's austerity measures cost her licence to trade – which was restored only after the personal intervention of Jean Cocteau, Sacha Guitry and a host of other luminaries.

To ease the shortages by recycling, a decree dated 23 January forbade throwing out old metal, paper, skins, rubber, feathers, bones, animal skin and leather, which all had to be put out for collection by municipal employees driving horse-drawn carts. Made from traditionally secret and presumably unrationed ingredients, perfume continued to be the luxury present always obtainable by those who had the money: Schiaparelli, Guerlain and the other great names knew a boom after the arrival of the Wehrmacht.

By January 1941 membership of the Compagnons had risen to 20,000, and this success had attracted the attention of the taxman: Dhavernas was detained in Paris for several weeks to explain to the Inspection des Finances where all the money had gone. The coming spring was to see a split in the movement, reflecting the inappropriateness for town life of a daily timetable designed for tents and campfires. The emphasis on physical work in the rural *chantiers* was replaced for the town-dwelling *compagnon* by service to his neighbours, with urban companies renamed *companies normales* – in whose curriculum physical education, amateur dramatics, choral singing and organisation of morale-raising events for the population replaced labouring in the fields and forests.

Depending on the instructors, the level of achievement could be high: the producer Michel Richard took his 'gang show' on tour with sixty-six performances in the Free Zone and also to Angers, Le Mans, Tours and Paris in the Occupied Zone. Six thousand copies of the Compagnons' songbook were sold. With vocal training taken as seriously as the other activities, the movement's most popular choral ensemble was named in September Les Compagnons de la Musique, eventually becoming world-famous after the war, when it toured the world initially under the patronage of Edith Piaf as 'Les Compagnons de la Chanson'.

January also saw the first flyers produced on a child's printing set by a group of young people who sought to rebut the political and religious differences dividing the population. For the name of their network of protest they chose the place where an unexpected victory over the Prussians had unified the French people 150 years earlier. The Valmy network's first slogan that mushroomed on walls all over the capital was 'We have one enemy: the invader'. More success went to the second, more snappy, slogan, 'Hitler's Hoover is emptying our country faster than you know'.

On 24 January Paris Prefect of Police Roger Langeron was arrested by the Germans for his uncooperative attitude and divested of his office. His two successors were to suffer the same fate, because it was virtually impossible to exercise the functions of the office without becoming either a lackey or an enemy of the SD. Yet Marcel Déat, who had been a close associate of De Gaulle in 1935–6,[7] was not alone in wanting larger doses of Hitler. On 1 February he launched the far-right Rassemblement National Populaire, accusing the Vichy government of being 'in the pay of the Judeo-Anglo-Saxon conspiracy'.

Berlin had been pressing for the reinstatement of Laval ever since Pétain engineered his resignation in December, and finally, on 9 February, forced the resignation of Pierre-Etienne Flandin, who had replaced him in the Cabinet. Refusing to reinstate Laval, Pétain chose as his new prime minister a man whose anti-British credentials were impeccable. Charged also with the portfolios of the Interior, Foreign Affairs, Information and the Navy, Admiral Darlan was in addition designated the official *dauphin* or successor to the Marshal as head of state. Travelling in appropriate style, on important visits the little admiral was preceded by a special train carrying his own chef and a band of forty musicians,[8] but his days as Vichy's Number 2 were nevertheless numbered, because Hitler wanted Laval back in power.

On the cultural scene, with Friedrich Von Schiller declared a French citizen in 1792, the end of the month saw the Schillertheater company celebrate the somewhat unequal partnership of the two countries with a production of *Kabale und Liebe* at the Comédie Française. It was scant comfort for most people when fish, chocolate, tobacco, clothing and wine were rationed the following month, and the French had to get used to eating swedes, used only as cattle-feed before the war. The novelist Colette, whose husband Maurice Goudeket[9] was Jewish, kept a low profile during the Occupation, but did go public with her recipes for salads of edible weeds, recommending rubbing swede juice on the skin to prevent wrinkles and stitching a layer of newspaper into one's winter underclothes to cope with lack of central heating. Whether working-class neighbours appreciated her advice to wear gold jewellery for additional warmth is doubtful; the luckier ones bought an over-vest of cat-skin or any other fur, and hardly needed her counsel in *Paris de ma fenêtre*: 'Go to bed. Get the meal over and done with and the household chores finished, and go to bed with a hot-water bottle for your feet.'[10]

Even smart city-dwellers took to keeping rabbits and chickens, feeding the latter on scraps and taking them for walks on a lead to scrabble for worms and snails in the parks. More exotic avian species, which needed all but unobtainable bird seed, got eaten. On 5 March 1941 all the oats in the *département* of Eure-et-Loire were requisitioned with the exception of the amount calculated to be necessary for sowing the next season's crop and an allowance of 3 kilograms per day per workhorse. Feeding oats to any other animal was an offence, the denunciation of which led to a charge of sabotage being judged by a German military court.[11]

To symbolise the unreality of attending school and taking exams seriously with soldiers patrolling the streets with loaded rifles, fashion-conscious girls and boys defied clothing restrictions to create *le style zazou*, which foreshadowed postwar youth fashion, with its overlength jackets, baggy trousers and exotic hairstyles, greased with salad cream in the absence of hair oil. The girls had padded shoulders, making them look bulkier than the boys, and both sexes carried a perpetually rolled umbrella, whatever the weather. They clustered in student bars drinking fruit juice and jiving to swing music, their only outdoor sport being the baiting of public figures such as the gay Pétainist Minister of Education, Abel Bonnard. Nicknaming him '*la Gestapette*' ('*tapette*' meaning 'gay'), they greeted him with chants of '*Gestapette, aux chiottes!*' A polite rendering would be 'Gestapo gay, off to the bogs!'

The marriage of French bureaucracy and Nazi regulations spawned a million different passes, permits and identity documents, one of the most coveted being the *Service Public* sticker that had to be displayed on the windscreens of the 7,000 private cars licensed in greater Paris. Drivers got used to being stopped for identity and permit checks and booked for traffic violations by Feldgendarmerie NCOs toting sub-machine guns; they came down especially hard on motorists using illicit petrol coupons. Insisting that French policemen on traffic duty copy exactly their less elegant but very precise hand signals, they relaxed only on Sundays, when no private French vehicles were allowed on the streets of Paris.

Accused of being part-Jewish, star entertainer Sacha Guitry protested publicly that his name was not a corruption of Gutman. Perhaps as compensation for his hurt feelings, Abetz made sure he had not only the all-important sticker for his windscreen, but also some petrol coupons from time to time and a special allocation of coal for heating – two favours that would be held against Guitry after the Liberation, when it was assumed that he had done something underhand to merit them. He was also among those privileged to receive graciously couched invitations on embassy stationery from Frau Suzanne Abetz: 'Ambassador Abetz and his wife invite you to lunch . . .' It was always luncheon, to avoid problems of getting home after dinner before the curfew. After lunch, her favourite excursion was to a fashion show, for the business of haute couture continued to function despite textile requisitioning, thanks largely to new artificial fabrics invented in Germany.

For the less well-connected, in the absence of taxis, ancient *fiacres* pulled by bony old hacks reappeared on the streets and *cyclo-taxis*, pedalled by men and women, also plied for hire on the former taxi-ranks. When it rained, the 'driver' had only a cape for protection, but the trailer compartments – some closed-in and more comfortable than a motorcycle side car – might hold as many as three adult passengers. Some people who before the Occupation would not have walked more than a few paces took a pride in ignoring these expedients and walking everywhere.

On 28 January the Gestapo claimed its first major success in France by arresting nineteen members of a network based in the Musée de l'Homme in Paris. After escaping from a POW camp linguist Boris Vildé had returned to Paris and sounded out several colleagues, including anthropologist Anatole Lewitsky and librarian Yvonne Oddon. They in turn contacted three Socialist lawyers, André Weil-Curriel, Maurice Nordmann and Albert Jubineau, with a view to setting up escape routes for people at risk for racial or political reasons to get to Britain via Spain. A contact in the US Embassy was also fed military information destined for London. The third activity of the group was duplicating digests of BBC broadcasts and foreign press reports in the endeavour to counteract the flood of German propaganda. Their sentences were to be exemplary.

Those with a nose for business sniff every wind. The shortage of conventional motor fuel impelled the Société Imbert to buy a franchise for the production of German *gazogène* generators. Mounted behind vehicles or towed on trailers, the wood-fuelled *gazogène* produced a weak combustible gas that allowed a car or truck with an adapted carburettor to travel at medium speed on the flat and pant its way up any incline. Buses and other commercial vehicles in the major cities were converted to run on town gas. As in wartime Britain, the drivers had to refill the enormous collapsible reservoirs on their roofs at specific 'gas stations'.

The business community rapidly came to terms with its new super-client. Starting in February 1941, increasing numbers of senior executives went on state-sponsored trips to glean know-how and technology from their counterparts in Germany – especially in the use of artificial substitutes for natural products in short supply – that would serve France well after the war. On 17 March the Paris Stock Exchange reopened and experienced a continuous upward trend in share prices over the next two years. Boards of management took advantage of Vichy's fixed low interest rates to refinance loans and take out new ones. To these advantages would be added the Charte du Travail on 4 October 1941 – a charter of labour that banned strikes and made free trade unions illegal.

On 18 May a new chief was elected by the leaders of the Compagnons. Guillaume de Tournemire had been the youngest cavalry officer in the army and a hero of the colonial war in the Rif Mountains of Morocco. Affirming his personal loyalty to Pétain, he made it clear to Pucheu and Darlan that the Compagnons were not a Hitler Youth clone. Formally installed as Chief Compagnon on 25 August, Tournemire afterwards undertook a tour of inspection covering 9,000 kilometres, quietly spreading the word that the Compagnons were 'a fighting force'.

Although the PCF would later claim to have been in the forefront of the anti-German struggle from the very beginning, its first tracts were spuriously backdated to 2 July 1940 and signed by the party's second-in-command Jacques Duclos in the absence of Maurice Thorez, who was safely ensconced in Moscow for the duration.[12] They were in any event simply ranting accusations of British and French politicians blamed for causing and losing 'the imperialist war', according to the Comintern line into which the Party was locked until Hitler invaded the USSR in June 1941, when Charles Tillon, who became head of the FTP, estimated at no more than fifty the number of Communists in greater Paris capable of using a weapon.

In Marseilles, Captain Henri Frenay, founder of Combat and protagonist of the Mouvement de Libération Nationale, betrayed a certain ambivalence by writing a full year after the Armistice, in May 1941:

May Marshal Pétain give us the benefit of his authority and unequalled prestige for a long time. We are totally devoted to the work of the Marshal.[13] We believe De Gaulle's movement is wrong. One defends a country better by staying in it than leaving it. Many undesirable elements are clustered around De Gaulle. In short, the MLN has no links with Gaullism and takes no orders from London.[14]

If the home-grown Resistance was slow in getting off the ground, this early in the Occupation few agents from London were active in France. Considering that accounts by agents began to appear soon after the end of hostilities in Europe, it is surprising that no two authorities agree a figure for how many were sent, how many caught or killed at the time of capture, or died under torture and in concentration and death camps afterwards. Part of the confusion is due to the reluctance of successive British governments to admit the scale of losses. Another reason why figures are hard to find is the internecine squabbling and betrayals of one service by the others. British Intelligence, Colonel Buckmaster's Section F in Special Operations Executive (SOE) and De Gaulle's Bureau Central de Renseignements et d'Action (BCRA) often defied elementary security by sharing the same RAF flights to infiltrate and exfiltrate their agents, but each organisation had its own networks and agendas.

The best guess is that around 1,600 agents were sent from London into France.[15] Of these, fifty-two were women. Despite the feeling in the intelligence community that women were liable to change allegiance for emotional reasons and were physically vulnerable when caught, Buckmaster used them particularly for the dangerous job of operating clandestine transmitters because he thought them less liable to be suspected than men when moving their bulky sets from one hideout to another. Of the seventeen women who were caught, twelve died – four of them at Natzwiller, a winter sports resort in Alsace that had been converted into a concentration camp.

Even in the *réseaux* set up by SOE and controlled by its agents who also operated the vital radio links with base and gave instruction in sabotage techniques, the couriers, informers, saboteurs and safe-house providers were mostly unvetted French men and women, with all that this implies in terms of double agents and betrayal. Many networks collapsed through their own success: the bigger they became, the greater the risk of detection or betrayal.

The chief of De Gaulle's BCRA[16] was André Dewavrin, who took the *nom de guerre* of 'Colonel Passy'[17] One of his first recruits to work in France was Gilbert Renault, a thickset, balding and very dynamic 35-year-old with a prodigious memory, who founded the Confrèrie Notre Dame network under the alias 'Colonel Rémy'.[18] Starting in autumn 1940, he regularly crossed the Demarcation Line carrying bulky envelopes of military intelligence collected by his informers in Brittany and along the Atlantic coast, and had no illusions what would happen to him if caught. Once in the Free Zone, Rémy passed the information to Louis De La Bardonnie, who lived only 12 kilometres from the Line at his family château overlooking the Dordogne Valley. With the help of a small group of personal friends, Bardonnie made sure this got to Pau, where it was handed to the guard of a train leaving for Canfranc in Spain. From there, a French customs official took it to Jacques Pigeonneau, the Vichy consul-general in Madrid, who forwarded the vital envelope to London.

While Rémy risked only his own life, Bardonnie and his friends of both sexes had families to worry about. By having a transmitter furnished by Rémy, weapons and at times up to 10,000,000 francs in secret funds on his property, which was also being used as a base by three different RF agents,[19] Bardonnie also placed at risk his wife Denyse and their nine children. One of the group was a refugee from Alsace who had lived through the German occupation of the province in 1914–18, studied in Germany and worked there for French Intelligence under cover as a journalist. Knowing the enemy that well, Paul Armbruster persuaded Bardonnie to go underground using false identities after initiating proceedings for divorce to protect Denyse and the children. He also assured the Bardonnies that their children would be left alone by the Germans because of their blue eyes and blond hair.

Two other members of Bardonnie's *réseau* were anti-Pétainist freemasons working as pilots for the port of Bordeaux, who brought the U-boats up the treacherous Gironde estuary into port at the end of each foray and took them out again. Their traffic intelligence radioed to London by Bardonnie resulted in the RAF destroying eleven subs caught at the mouth of the estuary. Their great frustration was that the immense U-boat pens being built by the Organisation Todt were never bombed during construction because, once completed in autumn 1942, they were bombproof. Grand Admiral Doenitz considered the failure to destroy the pens along the Atlantic coast while they were still vulnerable one of the greatest mistakes of the RAF bombing campaign.[20] However, Bardonnie's pilots were eventually able to claim the credit for eleven U-boats destroyed by Allied aircraft, only diverting suspicion from themselves by repeatedly telling their German masters that they must be the victims of a mole inside their own port administration!

Even for a man with Rémy's nerves of steel, each line-crossing was an adrenalin trip. One he particularly recalled later took place in the spring of 1941. To avoid identity checks at Castillon station, he had himself driven right up to the line by a doctor with a permit to travel in the frontier area. A farmer named Rambaud living just inside the Occupied Zone was to guide him from there to a neighbour living on the other side of the line. Seeing more activity than usual at the checkpoint, the doctor lost his nerve, set Rémy down on the main road and departed visibly terrified. Walking the rest of the way, Rémy had hardly sat down to an early supper with Rambaud and his elderly mother, when an armed German customs official rode up on his bicycle, his suspicions aroused by the doctor's behaviour. In basic French, he ordered Rémy to accompany him back to the post.

Rémy was using his genuine identity card, bearing his mother's address in Brittany. The card in the guard's pocket, he was then marched off to the control point in the village of Capitourlan, desperately trying to work out what to do with his bulging packet of papers. Where the path ran alongside a sheer drop of several metres into tangled brushwood, Rémy wrapped the papers in his floppy Basque beret, thinking to throw it into the bushes or even to hurl himself down the bank and attempt to escape. Before he screwed up courage to make a bolt for it, the appearance of a second armed customs guard made him realise that if he had run, he would have been gunned down like a rabbit bolting from a sheaf of corn.

At Capitourlan, he contemplated slipping the papers to a girl who smiled at him, but knew that many people trying to cross without papers had been betrayed by the villagers in return for the German reward. Waiting in the control post while the French-speaking lieutenant finished his meal, Rémy searched desperately for anywhere to secrete the papers with the two customs men keeping an eye on him. By now, he was soaked with nervous perspiration and fear was making him tremble. His wife and children were waiting for him in Ste-Foy-la-Grande, a mere 18 kilometres away in the Free Zone. Would he ever see them again?

'What were you doing in that farm by the line?' was the lieutenant's first question.

'Trying to sell Monsieur Rambaud some fire insurance.' Rémy picked up his ID card and pointed to his declared profession, *Inspecteur d'assurances*.

'*Also, Versicherung*! And what company do you work for?'

Wanting to be out of the border post as quickly as possible, Rémy blurted the name of the only German-sounding company he knew, 'Zurich Assurances.' It was the right thing to say. The bored lieutenant waxed lyrical about the beauties of Zurich for a few minutes, handed back the identity card and waved goodbye. Hardly able to control his legs and not daring to look behind him, Rémy headed back to the farm with the uncomfortable feeling that the first guard was still watching him. Only by dint of reciting prayers unused since he had left junior school did his breathing return to normal and the trembling stop. Back at the farm, he decided to borrow Rambaud's bicycle, ride into Castillon and take the bus back to Bordeaux which would at least corroborate his story of being there on business and keep Rambaud out of trouble.

Certain that Rémy would be picked up for breaking the curfew if he did that – and suspecting the guards were simply letting the dog run to see where it headed – Rambaud insisted that his dangerous guest must cross the line immediately, without waiting for darkness. Minutes later, while the old woman kept watch for anyone approaching from the road, their hot-potato guest was across the Lidoire stream – but not yet safe because anyone caught within 7 kilometres of the border was automatically handed back by the French guards on the other side. Hardly had Rémy concealed himself in the bushes than the first guard reappeared at the farm with a squad of soldiers. At the top of his voice, to make sure Rémy could hear what was going on, Rambaud cursed them for bothering him when there was still two hours to go until curfew. Roughed up by the soldiers, who took him for a drunken old peasant, he succeeded in distracting them while Rémy put more distance between himself and the Lidoire.

A few weeks later a party of Germans arrived to search the farm and outbuildings thoroughly. Nothing was found, but Rambaud was arrested on the grounds that he 'received too many visitors' and was driven away to Libourne prison, where he spent several weeks before being released for lack of evidence against him.[21]

Chapter 12

OF CULTURE AND CROPS

On 15 March 1941 the SS pulled off a political coup, fusing Deloncle's MSR with the followers of Marcel Déat in the Rassemblement National Populaire, a far-right party to which Laval gave some undercover financial support at the beginning because it made him look like a liberal alternative.[1] On 1 April, with Darlan officially installed as deputy prime minister, one of the first laws that passed across his desk undid the loophole through which Reynaud had hoped to find marital bliss with the late Comtesse de Portes. In keeping with the importance Pétain attached to the family as a social institution, and to reward the Church for its support, divorce was made more difficult once again.

There was an ominous foretaste of future violence in the report dated 9 April by the gendarmerie commandant in Blainville-sur-Orne in occupied Normandy: 'Immoral behaviour by wives of POWs is to be seen wherever [German] troops are stationed. Girls still in their teens are becoming prostitutes. This behaviour is difficult for officers to control, given the German protection certain women enjoy.'[2] Apart from promiscuity, women's motives varied. Although one of the Marshal's slogans was 'I keep promises, even those made by others,' it was now evident that his undertaking to 'bring the boys home' was empty talk and the wives and families were suffering: with a factory worker earning 1,200–1,800 francs per month, the allowance to a POW's wife with one child was a mere 630 francs; it increased to 830 francs for two children and to 1,060 for three children, but was still insufficient as inflation bit.[3] With military personnel enjoying better rations that the civilian population, hunger alone motivated some women to find a German boyfriend, even before the adult bread ration in the Occupied Zone was reduced on 14 April from 350 grams a day to 275.

Along the Channel coast, nightly bombing raids by the RAF added to the misery. Yet public opinion largely blamed the Germans for making the ports into strategic targets. Throughout the Occupied Zone, people who listened to the BBC passed on its news. A spate of V signs chalked on walls provoked frightened house-owners to hastily scrub them off. Convinced Pétainists – and the vast majority of the population still supported the Marshal – took to carrying a chalk in their pocket, ever ready to add two more strokes to a V and turn it into M, meaning *Vive le Maréchal!*

The screw of anti-Semitism in the Occupied Zone was given another turn on 26 April with the proclamation by General Otto Von Stülpnagel of the second anti-Jewish ordinance. On 9 May the first of Vichy's scapegoats for the defeat were brought to trial at Riom near Clermont-Ferrand in a courtroom packed with 300 enemies and with no chance of a fair hearing from a military tribunal headed by a judge who had been a member of Action Française. Only six witnesses appeared for the defence, including serving officers who courageously confirmed that defendant Pierre Mendès-France had been *ordered* to go to North Africa. One of the seven judges had the moral courage to dissent from the judgment that Mendès-France be stripped of his parliamentary privileges and sentenced to six years' imprisonment. A second Jewish defendant from the *Massilia*, Jean Zay, was sentenced to deportation, while of two gentile *députés* who had been serving officers when travelling with them to North Africa one was given a suspended sentence and the other acquitted.

That month, Darlan travelled to Berchtesgaden for secret talks with Ribbentrop and Hitler, seeking a reduction in the crippling Occupation costs as a quid pro quo for French help in Syria: in defiance of France's neutrality, French airfields there had been placed at the disposal of the Luftwaffe flying support missions in Iraq for the uprising led by Rashid Ali against the British occupation of his country. Darlan's second, economic, argument was that only 1,500,000 soldiers were garrisoned in France and not the 4,000,000 men originally budgeted for. Hitler's Delphic reply indicated a possible 25 per cent decrease in daily Occupation tax of 400,000,000 francs a day, which was enshrined in a protocol signed at the end of May in the Paris Embassy. It was indeed reduced to 300,000,000 francs a day, but increased to 500,000,000 francs on the German occupation of the southern zone in 1942 and to a crippling 700,000,000 francs after D-Day.

Hearing a BBC broadcast in May, during which President Roosevelt expressed disbelief 'that the French people was collaborating with its oppressor', a group of theological students at a seminary in Lyons wrote a simple statement: 'The French people does not collaborate.' Signed with their initials only, it was to be posted or handed in at the US Embassy, but became duplicated as a tract, inciting the Vichy paper *Action* to ask, 'But who is financing all this?'

On 22 May Herbert von Karajan celebrated Wagner's birthday by conducting *Tristan und Isolde* at the Palais de Chaillot. Karajan was a frequent visitor during the Occupation, as were Eugen Jochum, Wilhelm Kempff and many other conductors, along with soloists of the quality of Elizabeth Schwarzkopf and Lore Fischer. A new event was added to the cultural calendar when the Berlin Chamber Orchestra performed in the courtyard of the Palais Royal for Mozart Week, held in July. Of German conductors, only Wilhelm Furtwängler refused to come, saying that he preferred to conduct in Paris when asked by the French and not the Wehrmacht.

On 23 May, together with eight members of his network, Gaullist naval intelligence agent Count Henri Louis d'Estienne d'Orves was condemned to death by a military court. Betrayed by his radio operator shortly after returning to France from London in December, he had been arrested in Nantes on 21 January. Before his execution at Mont Valérien on 29 August, he pleaded for clemency to be shown to the Breton sailors implicated in his arrest on the grounds that they had been motivated purely by patriotism. They were all deported to Germany. His last letter to a service comrade ended with his explaining that he had to cease writing because he and the two men to be shot with him were too busy telling each other jokes. On the reverse of a photograph of his wife and five children, taken at Quimper in Brittany, he wrote: 'To my dear children I return this photo which gave me such joy in August 1941'.[4]

With the Red Army observing German preparations for Hitler's invasion of the USSR, the PCF and the parties in Holland and Belgium were brought into play by the Comintern although still officially supporting Franco-German friendship. A strike, ostensibly over wages, introduction of new technology and poor food, spread from the Belgian coal mines into France like a powder trail sparking from pit to pit in May and early June. German military governors reacted severely, deporting 224 activists and taking ninety-four hostages, of which nine were shot.[5] A pay increase of 18 francs per day was conceded before the last men eventually went back to work on 9 June.

On 2 June 1941 Pétain tightened up his first Statut des Juifs with a second statute, obliging heads of Jewish families in both zones to register with the local town hall, which records later proved invaluable to the Milice and the SS in scooping up victims. The list of professional activities barred to Jews was now so long that it effectively left them unable to earn a living. The only statutory exceptions were for those who had rendered exceptional service to the French State (an ambiguous term by then) or whose family had been in France for at least five generations and rendered exceptional service to the French state during this time. Other restrictions were reflected in letters all account holders received from their bank managers in the week of 13 June, requiring them to send an attestation of racial purity. Failure to do so for any reason resulted in seizure of the account.

The doyen of the Paris bar, Maître Pierre Masse, wrote to Pétain on learning that Jewish citizens might no longer be officers in the armed services:

I should be obliged if you would tell me how I withdraw rank from my brother, a lieutenant in 36th Infantry Regiment, killed at Douaumont in April 1916; from my son-in-law, second-lieutenant in the Dragoons, killed in Belgium in May 1940; from my nephew, J.-F. Masse, lieutenant in 23rd Colonial Regiment, killed at Rethel in May 1940. May I leave with my brother his Médaille Militaire, with which he was buried? May my son Jacques, second-lieutenant in the Chasseurs Alpins, wounded at Soupir in June 1940, keep his rank? Can I also be assured that no one will retrospectively take back the Saint Helena medal from my great-grandfather?[6]

Courage availing nothing, Masse was deported in 1941 and later died in Germany.

These and other heart-rending appeals for protection by the state they had well served were forwarded from Vichy to Pétain's avidly pro-German official delegate in Paris, Fernand De Brinon. How many letters were actually seen by the Marshal is an unresolved question. The probable answer is not very many, since Ménétrel personally sorted all mail to ensure nothing untoward arrived on his master's desk. A later letter that was acknowledged came from Victor Faynzylber, who also sent a photograph of himself wearing both the Croix de Guerre and Médaille Militaire and standing with the help of the crutches he needed since losing a leg in the 1940 defeat. With him in the picture are his two children, the 7-year-old daughter bearing her yellow star in conformity with the German ordinance. The plea was not for the veteran himself, but for the release of his wife, held at Drancy. It went unheeded, both she and later her husband being killed after deportation to Germany.[7] On 11 August 1941 a group of eighteen veterans wearing a total of seventy medals came to Vichy to request that anti-Semitic propaganda be dropped in official army publications, but no one listened. Not even when Pétain himself had signed the citation did a medal protect – as in the case of André Gerschel, dismissed as mayor of Calais.[8] Retired General Staff officer Jacques Helbronner had personally lobbied for Pétain's advancement in the First World War, but his personal appeal to the Marshal did not save him or his family, all deported and gassed at Auschwitz in 1943.

For some tastes, the anti-Semitic laws were far too lenient. Le Petit Parisien commented, 'The Jews wanted this war and have thrown the world into a hideous conflict, in the light of which crime the present measures seem benign. . . . It seems impossible that these people, running 80 per cent of the black market should spend their money so shamefully earned while the great majority of the French people have a very hard life of it at the moment.'[9] The reference to the black market was echoed in a current poster that showed two caricature Jews swapping a loaf for cash.

In Paris, Hauptsturmführer Danneker's fan mail after the second ordinance included a letter from 'The Group of Anti-Semitic Friends' asking him to do something to stop Jews riding in cyclo-taxis pedalled by Aryans, having their baggage carried by Aryan porters or their shoes shined by Aryans. The imagined risk of contamination for bootblacks was lessened each day, as more and more people were obliged to wear shoes with wooden soles and uppers of artificial textiles that needed no polishing. The annual Grenoble Fair was declared the 'first fair of the Ersatz', introducing among other delights street signs that were no longer made in enamelled metal but Bakelite, first of the plastics family.

At the beginning of June, eleven young women and nine young men from various walks of life were shipped off to Drancy for mocking the yellow star ordinance by wearing either stars marked Jew or French or similarly shaped yellow objects on their clothing. Hailed as heroes by the other detainees, they were held in the camp for three months to give them a taste of what it actually meant to *be* Jewish. On 21 June, convinced that his captors intended to kill him eventually, Pierre Mendès-France escaped from Clermont-Ferrand prison. Refusing to go with him for fear of reprisals against his family, his cell-mate Jean Zay was murdered by the Milice in June 1944.

News of the escape was overshadowed by events of greater import. On 21 June a handful of Germans in the know suggested with a wink to French friends that they should listen to the radio next day, when the hot news was the launch of Operation Barbarossa, Hitler's invasion of the USSR. On 30 June 1941 Pétain severed relations with the USSR, but most French people were far more interested in the introduction of clothes rationing the next day, which came with a national appeal for them to hand in unwanted or outgrown garments, in return for which they would be given extra clothing coupons. This fell on deaf ears, anyone with surplus clothes preferring to trade them for a few eggs or a loaf of bread.

That summer's Paris shoe fair boasted shoes made from wood, straw and synthetic leather, with fashion designers backing the skirt-culotte as the smart garment for chic Parisiennes to wear on their bicycles, with the advantage that they could bend down to pump up their tyres and cycle home without fear of an importunate breeze revealing intimate secrets to male eyes. And cycles there were, everywhere. By the end of the Occupation, 2,000,000 were registered in Greater Paris, where new ones cost the price of a car before the war.

On 13 July De Gaulle asked over the radio that every patriot should go out next day sporting the national colours of red, white and blue. In the seaside town of Arcachon Renée De Monbrison did so, her children similarly dressed. A less courageous stranger sidled up to her, whispering, '*Salut, bonne Française.*' In Paris a handful of men wearing tricolour handkerchiefs poking out of their breast pockets were arrested. While more prudent folk preferred not to show in public they were listening to the BBC, just how many did is illustrated by a current joke. 'Question: What would you say if I told you a Jew killed a German in the street at 9.30 p.m. and ate his brain? Answer: First, a German has no brain. Second, Jews don't eat pork. And third, no one's in the street at 9.30. Everyone's listening to the news on BBC.'

The Church disapproved: Cardinal Liénart of Lille said, 'Do not listen to London or [the German station in] Paris. Listen to Lyons and Toulouse [in other words, the voice of the Church hierarchy].'[10] German propaganda attempted to discredit the BBC by a poster campaign showing it as a maiden aunt, *La Tante BBC*, whose initials stood for 'Bobard-Boniment-Corporation' – the Corporation of Lies and Humbug.

On the surface, everyday life was still normal in some respects. Although Renée was technically Jewish under the German ordinances, her husband's family was an old Huguenot one. The children had been brought up as Protestants and were not legally Jewish. Thus, a pass to be had for the asking

SCHULAUSWEIS

(LAISSEZ-PASSER SCOLAIRE)

nur gültig vom 15 Juni bis 5 Oktober 1942

(valable seulement du 15 Juin ou 5 Octobre 1942)

Schüler _____ den _____
(écolier)

Schülerin ____ de MONBRISON ____ Françoise ____
(écolière)

geb am 18-6-1925 ____ in Paris (16ème Ar^t)
(né (e) le ____ à

besucht die Schule ____ LYCÉE MICHEL-MONTAIGNE
(fréquente l'établ scolaire) ANNEXE D'ARCACHON

Signature
du Chef de l'établ.

Inhaber dieses Scheines ist berechtigt, die Demarkationslinie
einmal und zurück
zu überschreiten.

(le porteur de ce laissez-passer est autorisé à franchir la ligne de démarcation
une fois aller et retour)

Bordeaux, im Juni 1942

The vital school holiday pass that enabled Françoise to cross the Line.

enabled her daughter Françoise to cross the Demarcation Line in order to attend the convention of the Protestant Scouts in Nîmes.

Strip-searched when crossing the line between Langon and La Réole, Françoise was already naked and about to take off her second sock, in which was hidden a letter she was bringing across for an old family friend, when the German policewoman told her she could keep her socks on. Had Françoise known about it, there was a wall among the vines 2 kilometres away exactly on the line with an unguarded door, through which several hundred local people had simply walked unmolested into the Free Zone.

Now that the Germans allowed only the owners of houses situated in the coastal zone to stay there, Baboushka had fled inland to the village of Sablé, still in the Occupied Zone, and was surprised how hard it was to find a hotel room. With the coast off-limits for holidays, inland hotels were full, with any empty rooms taken by German soldiers billeted on the hoteliers. The couple running Baboushka's hotel were both Pétainist and anti-Semitic, yet business was business, so they made a point of always addressing her by the non-Jewish part of her name as 'Madame Robert.'[11]

On July 11 Déat and Doriot launched La Légion des Volontaires Français contre le Bolchevisme (LVF), with Deloncle as president. Recognised by Darlan on 3 August, the movement had the support of the Institut Catholique, Monseigneur Jean Mayol de Lupé going so far as to enrol himself as chaplain-general with the SS rank of Sturmbannführer, greeting his Sunday congregation with, '*Heil Hitler! Et pieux dimanche, mes fils!*' ('Heil Hitler and a devout Sunday!') Among his spiritual sons were Abbés Verney and Lara, who volunteered as chaplains to accompany into Russia the LVF units hailed by Cardinal Baudrillart as 'the finest sons of France'. Mistrusting the idea of French soldiers in German uniform, Hitler limited LVF numbers to 15,000. He need not have worried: 173 recruiting offices were opened, but of 10,788 volunteers in the next two years only 6,429 were able to pass the medical, such was the toll of food shortages on general health.[12] Doriot departed for the eastern front, doing his political career irredeemable harm by absenting himself from France for eighteen months.

Governments of the Third Republic had been preoccupied with the declining birth-rate. Pétain's regime took this one stage further. While elevating motherhood as a career and encouraging Mother's Day by national propaganda, the old Marshal's brand of National Socialism also looked after the family unit, in which it had common cause with the Church. Three months after the Armistice, one of many magazine articles signed by him stated, 'The rights of families precede and override those of the state and individual rights. The family . . . is the essential unit of social structure.'[13]

The strong Marian cult in the Church naturally approved. Smiling priests were photographed with children reciting prayers they had written asking Jesus to protect the Marshal. The image of the Good Shepherd was applied to him, and on 24 July 1941 the Church bestowed its final blessing on Pétain and all his works in a statement read out in every church: 'We venerate the head of state and ask that all French citizens rally round him. . . . We encourage our flock to take their places at his side in the measures he has undertaken in the three domains of family, work and fatherland.'[14] No head of state could have asked for more. On 12 August Pétain denounced as an 'evil wind blowing through France' those who refused to collaborate. 'In 1917,' he said, 'I ended the mutinies. In 1940 I put an end to the rout. Today, it is from yourselves that I wish to save you.'[15]

On 13 August Communist demonstrators came to blows in Paris with French police and German Feldgendarmerie units at Porte St-Denis and Porte St-Martin. The following day, sober bespectacled Pierre Pucheu, appointed Minister of the Interior by Darlan in July, expanded the Service de Police

Anti-Communiste (SPAC) created by Daladier in 1939 by the formation of *'brigades spéciales'*. The ambiguous title concealed a nationwide machinery for arresting and trying Communists with no appeal system and only one verdict: death. Seeking to justify himself at his trial for collaboration in Algiers during 1944, Pucheu claimed that he had accepted the Interior Ministry under compulsion, and selected hostages to be shot from lists of known Communists in order to spare the lives of 'good Frenchmen'; but those who knew him at the time saw a man eaten hollow by the worm of ambition.

A legally trained observer, who arrived in Paris on the day of the demonstrations to take up his posting on the staff of Von Stülpnagel in Operationsabteilung 1A, was former law student Albrecht Krause. While convalescing after being wounded in the chest near Leningrad, he had attended the trial in Strasbourg of nineteen Alsatian and French Communist activists. After hearing Roland Freisler, president of the Nazi Volksgerichtshof, ranting and raving against the accused, allowing neither them nor their lawyers to speak, Krause left the hearings appalled and was taken to lunch by the GOC Strasbourg in a smart hotel where they saw Freisler and his cronies enjoy a three-hour feast before returning to sentence the seventeen men to death and the single female defendant to life imprisonment. On the spot, Krause decided that pursuing his law studies under such a regime was impossible.

Because the German occupants are usually cast as villains in media depictions of the Occupation, it is interesting that Krause found Otto von Stülpnagel an urbane and civilised soldier trying to fulfil an impossible task. As Militärbefehlshaber in Frankreich, he was not only the highest ranking Wehrmacht general in France, but also responsible for ensuring that the troops under his command observed the provisions of international law including the Hague Conventions, which for the most part they did, to begin with. The Waffen-SS was, of course, a parallel army, and not part of the Wehrmacht structure.

Krause found life on Von Stülpnagel's staff rather genteel, indeed old-fashioned. Although known officially as *Stabshilferinnen*, most of the secretaries came from good families and were nicknamed *Edeltippsen*, or 'noble typists'. To avoid illicit liaisons, they were strictly segregated except during working hours, had separate sleeping accommodation and their own canteen. Refusing the posting to his HQ of any officer who could not speak good French, and discouraging contact with Abetz's staff in the embassy and Oberg's SS in Avenue Lannes and Avenue Foch, Von Stülpnagel had a number of intellectuals on his staff and enjoyed discussing history or mathematics with them in his private dining room of the Hôtel Raphaël. He also encouraged junior officers to use permanently reserved boxes at the opera and the best theatres when no high-ranking visitors claimed them. On these occasions, they wore civilian clothes in order not to disturb the audience.

In his spare time, Krause used a Nansen passport to attend classes at the Sorbonne, which was forbidden for German personnel, and there continued his studies of Hebrew and Arabic, paying his teacher for one-to-one lessons with food and clothing.[16] Speaking fluent French, Krause found contacts with ordinary French people very relaxed but, in common with many other Wehrmacht officers, was wary of approaches by French collaborationists. His arrival in Paris was perfectly timed to witness the start of the PCF campaign to tie down in France tens of thousands of German personnel who could otherwise have been sent to the eastern front. On 13 August Communist activists Maurice Le Berre and Albert Manuel killed a German soldier with a chopper and a bayonet near the Porte d'Orléans. Six days later a German firing squad executed two other men arrested during a PCF demonstration – Henri Gautherot and Szmul Tyszelman, an immigrant only naturalised in 1939 and known in Party circles as 'Titi' – who were also accused of thefts of explosives.

On 21 August during the morning rush hour at the Metro station Barbès-Rochechouart a 22-year-old Communist agitator and veteran of the Spanish Civil War who styled himself 'Colonel Fabien' assassinated a Kriegsmarine lieutenant in charge of a clothing store – allegedly to avenge the death of Titi. Pierre Georges, to use Fabien's real name, may have been praised for this by fellow Communists, but throughout the Occupation until the Allied landings the population generally disapproved of acts of violence against German personnel, asking themselves what did killing one or one hundred Germans achieve, except invite reprisals?

They were right to ask. On the morning after the assassination, on every street corner Parisians perused a bilingual poster in German and French, in which Von Stülpnagel's deputy Lieutenant-General Schaumburg promulgated the Hostage Ordinance.

With minor differences between the French and German texts, it read:

On the morning of 21 August a member of the Wehrmacht was the victim of assassination in Paris. I therefore order as follows: 1. On and after 23 August any French person under arrest for whatever reason shall be considered a hostage; 2. On each future occasion a number of hostages corresponding to the gravity of the crime will be shot. Paris, 22 August 1941

Initially, forty-eight hostages were shot at Châteaubriant, Nantes and Paris. Von Stülpnagel realised the PCF campaign was concerted by Moscow to alienate the population from the occupying forces but, in the absence of convicted perpetrators of assassinations, he could not fail to take reprisals without inviting his forces to take matters into their own hands – as frequently happens in such situations. Although many innocent people were randomly executed during the next three years in reprisals for sabotage and attacks on German personnel, a large number of those shot were in fact previously arrested Communist activists. One compromise way out was to blame the Jewish community, which was fined 1,000,000 francs[17] on the logic that the PCF activists ordering and executing the outrages were mainly

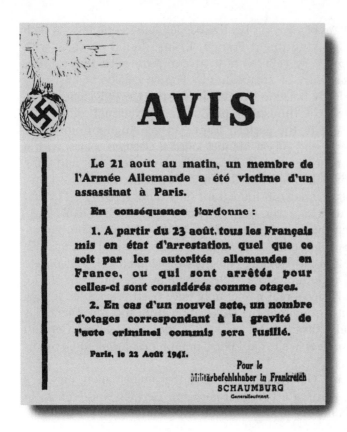

French text of the
hostage ordinance.

Jewish immigrants, like Tyszelman, and illegals, like Abraham Trzebucki, who
was arrested while collecting money for an underground organisation, rapidly
tried by one of Pucheu's new courts and guillotined on 27 August.

That was a day of bloodshed, some of it unlamented. Pierre Laval and
Marcel Déat were at the Borgnis-Desbordes barracks in Versailles reviewing
the first contingent of the LVF in their new Wehrmacht uniforms with a
distinguishing tricolour badge and 'France' on their left arms when a
21-year-old recruit in the parade pulled out his revolver and fired five shots at
them. Although neither target was badly wounded, the initial outrage at the
attack triggered a witch-hunt for the Communists responsible. In fact, recruit
Paul Colette was a far-right renegade and probably the hit-man for Déat's
rival Deloncle, the body of whose secretary was found floating in the Seine,
after she had been killed to stop her telling what she knew.[18]

When, in September, saboteurs set fire to haystacks and standing crops in
the Occupied Zone, prefects of police blamed Communist saboteurs. As a
government poster made plain, less corn meant less bread on the family table.
The mathematics were simple: since the Germans took their 20 per cent levy
of the total crop, it was the French who suffered the shortfall.

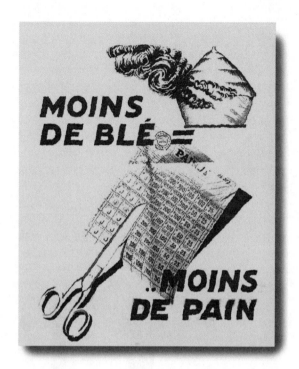

Sabotage of crops meant less bread – for the French, not the Germans.

In Moissac, Mayor Delthil had been one of the senators who voted dictatorial powers for Pétain, and the Prefect of Tarn-et-Garonne considered him to have handled his town's problems wisely. Yet old political enemies manoeuvred him out of office in January 1941 for 'creating an island of resistance against the policies of the Marshal' within the town hall.[19] The plan misfired when compromise candidate Dr Louis Moles replaced Delthil on 31 March.

Although the town council dutifully voted to change the name of 'la rue des franc-maçons' to 'la rue des Compagnons de France' nobody bothered to change the road signs. As the Prefect dryly noted, 'respect for the person of the head of state does not entail support for his policies of collaboration'.[20] More importantly, as far as local people were concerned, the potato harvest had been poor at 3 kilos per person and long queues at the butchers' shops and groceries caused grumbling. All over France posters appealed to those fed up with waiting to be served to let war-wounded men, pregnant women and mothers of small children go to the head of the queue. Hungry people who had traditionally had full stomachs might be expected to blame their leaders, yet senior Vichy official Pierre Nicolle noted on a visit to Paris how Parisians seemed to have stopped thinking for themselves altogether, being interested only in where their next meal was coming from.

Chapter 13

SAVING THE CHILDREN

In France the Scout and Guide movement was divided by religion into Protestant, Catholic and Jewish organisations, all under the Vichy-approved umbrella of Les Scouts de France. With the backing of the Jewish scouting organisation, Eclaireurs Israélites de France (EIF), an extraordinary Romanian Jewess who had come to France in 1933 to study medicine persuaded the authorities in Moissac to let her set up a reception centre for children at risk in the refugee centre at La Maison de Moissac.[1] From that humble start, Shatta Simon managed on a shoestring budget to save the lives of 865 children. One thing they all recalled in later life was her smile of welcome.

Laure Schindler-Levine, who was 13 at the time, recorded her journey from the mud and malnutrition of Gurs concentration camp, where she had lived for months as an orphan after her mother was deported to be gassed in Auschwitz and her father disappeared into the men's part of the camp. When Laure and three other released children were taken into a café by their guards on the way to the train station,

> it seemed extraordinary to us to be able to sit down at a table on real chairs and simply ask for food. We devoured the coffee and rolls, with the inevitable result that we had to run for the toilets. Then we took the train for Moissac with our chaperone. This was on 8 May 1941. We arrived [at Moissac] in the evening. Shatta gave us her wonderful smile and really became my 'living mother' at that moment. There were no embraces [because the children from the camps were verminous and probably carrying disease].
>
> Shatta called resident nurse Violette, to shave the heads of Eric and me because we were infested with lice and fleas, after which we were doused with insect powder. For a girl it was doubly humiliating. Because I had scabies too, Violette scrubbed me so hard that it hurt and then rubbed me all over with an evil-smelling sulphur ointment. From sheer exhaustion and fear and grief and pain and humiliation, I cried the whole time.[2]

With so many diseases they might have brought with them, two weeks' strict quarantine then ensued before newcomers from camps could join the other children. They emerged with memories of deprivation and horror fresh in their minds, to find themselves in a world of Scouts and Guides, where everyone used the familiar form *tu* for 'you' – even to Shatta and her husband Bouli. The food was pretty basic, with lots of beans and vegetables that would have been fed to the animals in peacetime, but it seemed to malnourished newcomers like feasting every day. As did many others, Laure saved some her rations to send to her father, now transferred to the concentration camp at Noé.

Food shortages and missing ration books made catering at La Maison de Moissac a constant headache. In addition, many children came from Orthodox families and had never eaten non-kosher food; others refused to eat it. Many could not speak French and used German or Yiddish. Some were traumatised by having to leave one or both parents behind in the camps, knowing they could be deported at any time; others had no living relatives. Many of the youngest did not know their own names. A helper trying to identify one 4-year-old asked who he was, to receive the reply, 'I'm Alex's brother.' Alex was dead, and the boy did not know his own name. The helper tried another angle: 'What did the concierge call your father?' 'She called him Monsieur,' the boy replied.

Once her hair began to grow again, Laure entered more easily into communal life with the other girls in her patrol, all detesting the obligatory daily dose of cod liver oil and adoring the family atmosphere fostered by after-dinner singsongs, the Friday night dinners and festivals. Daytime at the Maison de Moissac was as happy as Shatta could make it, while Bouli was the stern but caring housefather. After months of incarceration, newly arrived children were amazed to discover that the front doors of No. 18 and the overflow houses were never locked. They were free to come and go; but where could they go? At night, memories returned in dreams. The problems the more disturbed children presented for their adult carers surpass the imagination. The following extracts from personal files preserved after the war in the archives of the Maison de Moissac at the château de Laversine give some idea:

ROGER – Father deported in August 1942. No known relatives.

ISAAC – Very sweet and affectionate little boy. Arrived in Moissac aged 7 after being in Gurs and Rivesaltes concentration camps May 1940 – April 1942. Both parents deported in August 1942. No news since.

BELLA – Mother depressed since father and son both shot. Mother refuses to take care of her daughter. The child has several times run away.

ALFRED – Unidentified orphan sent to us by WIZO.[3] Has no idea who he is.

HANNAH – Father caught in a *rafle* in Paris 1941. Escaped from Pithiviers concentration camp, managed to cross into Free Zone and reach Moissac, where he worked as a tailor. Five months later, wife and children managed to join him here. In 1943 both parents caught in a *rafle*. Mother deported. Father escaped again and returned to Moissac, but was denounced. Escaped again, but was caught and sent to the mines. Caught by the Milice, taken to Drancy. During all this time, Hannah has been in Moissac.

LÉON – A good lad who wants to go into farming. To be sent to a rural group. Has one sister, who became insane after parents' arrests.[4]

Given the political situation, it sounds unreal today that the Moissac 'children's house,' or *colonie* as the locals called it, was run on the lines laid down in Baden-Powell's blueprint for the Scout movement, as adapted by EIF. Organised in patrols, children slept in dormitories with their patrol leaders. Each day began with fifteen minutes' gymnastics, after which all but the youngest children had to make their beds and tidy the dormitories before washing in communal washrooms. Bouli's morning room inspections were legendary: each mattress had to be turned each day. To prevent cheating, there was a mark on one side which had to be on top on even dates and underneath on uneven ones. The child who cheated, by just pulling up and smoothing the blankets, found all the bedding thrown onto the floor, and had to start all over again.

After breakfast, the day followed a strict timetable, with children of school age setting off just like any coevals for a day in the classroom. The younger ones marched along the main street in a crocodile to the junior school, holding hands and singing Hebrew songs. If they adapted easily to the French curriculum, many older ones had academic difficulties. Freddy X recalled starting school in Düsseldorf with lessons in German, before his parents fled in 1938 to Belgium. There, he attended school for two years, speaking Yiddish in the playground and Flemish in the classroom. For the next two years he had no lessons while in concentration camps. At Moissac, he began French schooling. His answer to how he and those with similar backgrounds coped was, 'We copied everything the others did or said, without understanding anything at first.'[5]

Older children who could not cope with school attended workshops where they received practical instruction, which might for the girls be making clothes for themselves and the little ones under the supervision of a professional *couturière*, while boys were taught a useful trade. Both also had lessons from French and refugee volunteer teachers. From November 1941, this is a sample of their weekday routine, which was no soft alternative to school:

6.45 – 8 a.m.	–	wake-up, toilet, breakfast
8 a.m. – 12 noon	–	workshops
12 noon – 1 p.m.	–	lunch
1 – 3 p.m.	–	siesta in summer/reading in winter
3 – 6.30 p.m.	–	physical training in the open air
7.30 – 8.30 p.m.	–	dinner
9 – 10 p.m.	–	studies or bed according to age
10 p.m.	–	lights out

After the Friday night *seder* meal, Saturday was the Sabbath:

8.30 a.m.	–	Getting up, toilet, breakfast
9.30 a.m	–	sports
1 – 3 p.m.	–	free time
3 – 6 p.m.	–	Jewish history
6.30 – 7.30 p.m.	–	Leisure activities[6]

Sundays were reserved for scouting activities, outdoors whenever the weather permitted.[7] Older boys and girls, who would have been Rover Scouts and Ranger Guides in peacetime, acted as the *routiers*, meaning literally 'rovers', travelling hundreds of kilometres by public transport, by bicycle and on foot to bring children to Moissac and take them on to safer hiding places, when these had been arranged. They also regularly visited children placed with foster parents, both for contact and to bring the vital food coupons, without which town-dwelling families' meagre rations would have been insufficient. As to where the documents came from before these extraordinary scouts and guides began manufacturing their own false papers, the answer is, from local mayors' offices and even on one occasion from the office of Prefect François Martin in the *département* capital, Montauban. After Shatta personally explained to him her desperate need for identity papers, he promised her 150 ID cards, plus the food coupons to go with them, and despatched them to Moissac by the hand of Dr Moles, so that she ran no risk of being caught with them at a checkpoint.

Until his resignation in 1943, Prefect Martin epitomised the many public servants at all levels who were paid to obey and implement the laws of Vichy, yet chose to remain in office so that they could temper some of the worst excesses. Daily, they confronted dilemmas that no servant of the English Crown or parliament has known for centuries. In some villages and country areas the local gendarmerie was more than cooperative to the rescue operation, closing its eyes to the presence of unregistered children or those whose papers were obviously false, warning of imminent searches and sometimes sheltering fugitives from Vichy justice. When caught, the penalties for those in the uniforms of law and order were even more severe than for others: during the Occupation, over 800 were deported to camps in the East; 338 were decapitated or shot by the Germans in France.

On the other side of the coin, when the new assistant commissioner in Moissac read the census list of 208 'persons known to be Jewish or reputed to be such', registered as living in the town, he sent for Madame Simon and informed her coldly that he was an anti-Semite and a personal friend of Darquier de Pellepoix, an anti-Semitic journalist whose proposals in an extremist newspaper in 1937 could have served as a draft for the first Statut des Juifs. As such, he warned her, he would carry out all the orders he was given without compunction. Yet on one occasion when two police inspectors came to arrest some of 'her' children, Shatta admitted that the children were present, but asked the officers to obey the dictates of their consciences, after which they went away empty-handed.

With the biggest heart and greatest reserves of courage in the world, money is still what fuels such an operation. Like a number of other children's homes of EIF, La Maison de Moissac was subsidised by the Jewish Consistory, Baron Robert De Rothschild and the Comité d'Aide aux Refugiés. The Joint American Distribution Committee, known as 'Le Joint', also contributed 400 francs per child per month, although after the German occupation of the southern zone in 1942 this money had to be smuggled into France from Switzerland at personal risk to those involved.[8] However, the regular funding never covered more than bare necessities, so when it came to buying books for the library, tools for the workshops or any other 'extras', Madame Simon had to beg previous benefactors to be generous again. Alternatively, there was some 'trading', as when the metal-workers earned themselves a workshop by overhauling the forge of a local blacksmith in return for its use. The output of some workshops, like the book bindery, could have been sold for much-needed cash, but the Simons wisely decided against this, not wishing to antagonise local tradesmen.

The children's house was a fragile shelter, as they were well aware. In the Free Zone, Jews did not have to wear the yellow star, but on 5 September in Paris the exhibition 'Le Juif et la France' opened at the Palais Berlitz on Boulevard des Italiens. After it closed to go on provincial tour four months later, Director of the Institute for Jewish Questions Captain Paul Sézille wrote to Vallat at the Commissariat Général des Questions Juives that paid attendances had totalled 500,000, which because of free and reduced price admissions meant a total attendance of close to one million. Abetz's figure of 250,623 visitors was closer to the truth. Sometimes propaganda achieves the reverse of what its authors hope: a 28-year-old history teacher with a Jewish husband visited the exhibition on its provincial tour in Lyons and was so horrified by all the lies that she decided to 'do something about it'. Lucie Aubrac was to distinguish herself later in the Occupation.

Most Parisians were more interested in the annual Paris Fair that opened on 6 September, with the *gazogène* stand the biggest draw for would-be motorists who had no entitlement to petrol coupons. A strange exhibition-in-reverse that ran from February to October at the Petit Palais was a German shop window exhibiting not products for sale but products the Reich sought to buy. Of 12,000 different items required by the military, tenders were received for 80 per cent; likewise 75 per cent of the civilian requirements. With 26,000 tenders received, the organisers congratulated themselves on holding out exactly the right carrot to bring into line any proud laggards in French industry. For every carrot, there is a whip – in this case the alternative to working for the Reich was to see precious machinery shipped off east of the Rhine, against which accepting German orders was the best defence.

On 16 September Wehrmacht officer Captain Scheben was shot dead on the Boulevard de Strasbourg in Paris. Reflecting the mood of the population, journalists of all shades except the Communists deplored the assassination, author Pierre Audiat commenting, 'It was by no means clear how the elimination of a German soldier who . . . was only there in obedience to military discipline might . . . influence the outcome of the war. Had some truly heroic gesture been at stake, the murderer should have fulfilled his patriotism by being right out in the open.'[9] His readers saw the curfew brought forward to 9 p.m. from 21–23 September, before which Maître Antoine Hajje, a 39-year-old Communist lawyer arrested on 25 June, was executed in reprisal by firing squad with eleven other hostages, some after interrogations and torture at 11 rue des Saussaies.

On 18 September 1941 a new law made it compulsory to harvest Spanish broom, whose fibres could be treated to replace hemp and flax, possibly even cotton and wool. Bones, too, were wanted by the state. Like Scouts in Bob-a-Job week, pairs of Compagnons knocked on doors collecting them; for one kilo of bones, they were given a bar of soap or a packet of washing powder, passed on to elderly householders who had helped them.

On the night of 2 October, while Von Stülpnagel was still debating how to handle the assassination campaign, SS-Standartenführer Helmut Knochen's SD in Paris took matters into their own hands by providing explosives and vehicles with curfew passes for a group of Deloncle's MSR toughs to blow up six Paris synagogues. A seventh, where the charge failed to explode, was blown up in broad daylight next day, allegedly for reasons of public safety. As ever, the different German intelligence organisations were spying on each other and Von Stülpnagel, briefed by the Abwehr on the truth of the operation, reprimanded Knochen, who pretended the explosions were the work of anti-Semitic civilians.

Furious, Von Stülpnagel cabled Berlin demanding the recall of Knocken, Brigadeführer Rhomos and another SD officer named Sommer. A spate of cables hissed vituperatively between the SD in Paris and Himmler and between Stülpnagel and OKW in Berlin, each side trying to outmanoeuvre the other. Confirming Knochen's independence from Wehrmacht control, his boss Reinhard Heydrich told OKW that Von Stülpnagel should mind his own business because Knochen and Rhomos were key personnel in the important campaign that would rid France of Jews. As a sop, the junior officer involved was sent home.

In October the Swiss closed their frontier, to make it more difficult for refugees to flee France. The flautist Marcel Moyse, living at his country home in Franche-Comté, had regularly travelled to teach at conservatoires in Geneva and La Chaux-de-Fonds. With this no longer possible, and since he was wary of returning to the Paris Conservatoire, where his name might be mistaken for Jewish – Moïse being the French for Moses – he earned money by travelling to Lyons and playing live concerts on the radio with his son and daughter-in-law. The nerve-racking downside of these paid engagements came at the end of the broadcasts. Well after the curfew, they had to return on foot to a friend's apartment where they were staying. Armed with appropriate passes, they took care to walk in the middle of the street so that no German patrol would shoot them as curfew-breakers. Their wisdom was proven when another musician was spotted hiding in a doorway on the way home and gunned down without even being challenged.

The nadir of Moyse's war came when he was subsequently denounced to the Gestapo as Jewish, but released after a *collabo* musician vouched for his racial purity. When Moyse asked why he had done this, the reply was simply that the *collabo* had admired his playing for twenty-five years. Armed with a Certificat de Non-Appartenance à la Race Juive, Moyse was safe for the rest of the Occupation, but stunned to discover that he had been denounced by a former student, at whose wedding he had been best man.[10]

When appointed Minister of the Interior in July, Pucheu had boasted of his intention to execute 20,000 Communists. After the assassination of a German colonel in Nantes, he personally selected ninety-eight hostages to be executed on 22 and 23 October at Châteaubriant, Nantes and Bordeaux. Roughly half were Jews taken from Drancy, enabling Pucheu to justify his action by claiming that otherwise the Germans would have shot French veterans. Among sixteen hostages shot at the firing range of Bêle, near Nantes, was one of many bemedalled heroes abandoned by the country they had served in one or both world wars.

Léon Jost, a director of the biscuit company Lu, had lost a leg in the First World War and since devoted much time to ex-servicemen's and other welfare work. Arrested on 15 January, he had been sentenced on 15 July to three years' imprisonment for helping to organise an escape line to Britain via Douarnenez. As there was a three-hour delay in taking the men to the firing range, Jost added a series of postscripts to his last letter, all neatly numbered, as in the minutes of a meeting. In the first, he apologised for his writing, having given up his spectacles and pen. In the last, he asked his wife to write for their children a memorial of his life with her. 'I was marked out by fate,' he wrote, 'but we loved each other greatly, didn't we, my darling?'[11]

Like all the other terror machinery of the Reich, the hostage executions generated their own bureaucracy. Désiré Granet, shot at Châteaubriant on 22 October, wrote just before his death to his 11-year-old son Raymond, 'I ask you to keep the promise you made me, to work hard at school and to love your mother, who has loved me and whom I love so much.' A confused and anonymous Oberleutnant (signature illegible) in the Feldkommandantur at Nantes wrote on 9 December to Granet's wife Yvonne. Addressed in error to the dead man, the letter read: 'In reply to yours of 28th inst, the Kommandantur informs you that your husband, shot as a hostage at Châteaubriant on 22 October was buried in the cemetery of Russigne [*sic*]. Your request for re-possession of his effects has meanwhile been passed to the

Prefecture. Your request to remove the body has been refused.' A form letter from the mayor of Châteaubriant advised her in scarcely warmer tones: 'It is permitted to place flowers on the graves. It is not permitted to remove the bodies, nor to place a gravestone on the grave with the deceased's name. Any pilgrimage or demonstration is forbidden.'[12]

Some of the questions one cannot help asking oneself about these executions are answered in an eyewitness report of the execution of Granet and twenty-six other men at Châteaubriant written immediately afterwards by Abbé Moyon from Béré-de-Châteaubriant:

It was a warm and sunny autumn day. Being a Wednesday, the town was bustling with the activities of the weekly market when my lunch was interrupted by Monsieur Moreau, director of the concentration camp at Choisel. Hearing that the hostages were to be shot, I agreed to go with him to be with them in their last hours. At the camp, the hostages had been placed in a special detention hut, surrounded by both German soldiers and French gendarmes when I arrived. The *sous-préfet* had already given the men the news and suggested they should immediately write last letters to their families.

I had the feeling that some of the men only truly believed they were going to die when they saw me arrive (in my soutane). I told them that I had come not only as a priest for the believers, but to give what consolation I could to them all and execute any last wishes. For forty-five minutes I listened to them talking of their families, their hopes and cares, but I was unable to answer their most urgent question: when, where and how they were to be executed.

The door of the hut, which I had closed to give us some privacy from the guards, was thrown open to admit French gendarmes with handcuffs for all the condemned men and a Wehrmacht chaplain, who told me to leave. All the other prisoners had been locked in their huts, and from every hut came the sound of men singing the '*Marseillaise*'. The handcuffed hostages were led into waiting trucks, joining in the '*Marseillaise*' and also singing the '*Internationale*'. I tried to keep up with the execution convoy in my car, but was left behind, my last contact being the sound of the condemned men singing. At the quarry chosen for the execution they were divided for execution into three groups of nine, all the men refusing to be blindfolded. The youngest, a boy of 17, fainted before the volley rang out.[13]

The abbé was careful to keep a neutral tone in his account, for this was still the honeymoon period for Pétain and the Church hierarchy, with religious schools eligible for state finance and every school once again allowed to hang a crucifix on the classroom wall, which had been forbidden for thirty-five years as part of the separation of Church and state in the Third Republic. While other demonstrations and mass meetings were forbidden, pilgrimages and other religious assemblies were tolerated. On the first anniversary of the Vichy Légion, Bishop Piguet of Clermont ordered all the church bells in the diocese to be rung – which did not save him from arrest in May 1944 on the charge of having sheltered a priest on the run from the Milice.

Shortly after the executions at Châteaubriant newspapers all over France carried an announcement headed 'Attention, all those who are eating cat-meat!' The warning boiled down to advice to cook the cats well to avoid being contaminated by microbes from rats they had eaten. In November, food shortages led to an expansion in the black market, condemned by Vichy and the Church. However, for hungry people the morality was obscure, with Bishop Dutoit of Arras declaring, 'When a producer has furnished at the legal price the quantity of foodstuffs or merchandise he is required to produce, it seems to us that it is not against the law to ask a *slightly* higher price for his surplus. But justice and charity are opposed to any increase in price that constitutes an exploitation of the need or credulity of the buyer.'[14]

If the Church was in love with the Marshal, many French intellectuals were still infatuated with Hitler's New Europe. In November, Pierre Drieu La Rochelle and Robert Brasillach, respectively contributor and editor of the newspaper *Je Suis Partout*, were living it up at a writers' congress in Germany. A more commendable motive for travelling there was that of Captain Hans Speidel – later to be NATO Supreme Commander, Land Forces Central Europe. Sent by Gen Von Stülpnagel to Hitler's HQ in East Prussia to request permission to relax the Hostage Ordinance because the scale of reprisals was playing into the Communists' hands, Speidel returned empty-handed and later commented, 'Von Stülpnagel was too correct for the Party.' For his 'correctness', the unhappy Militärbefehlshaber in Frankreich was to pay a double price, squeezed out of office the following year and later accused of war crimes, awaiting trial for which he committed suicide in February 1948.

On 16 November 1941 six Communist activists were shot in the citadel of Lille, not as hostages, but for crimes committed. Félicien Joly, found guilty of fifty sabotage missions and other anti-German activities, had been extensively tortured at Valenciennes, but was able to think clearly of his loved ones' future as it would be. To his fiancée, he wrote, 'When the rhythm of life overwhelms memories of me, embrace the future, be happy in another man's arms and do not weep for what we have done together.'[15]

On 17 November the Franco-Polish Interallié resistance network was rolled up by the SD. Among those arrested was Mathilde Carré – a petite, pretty, well-dressed, green-eyed law graduate of the Sorbonne, who began the war as a nursing aide for the French Red Cross while in the process of divorcing her reservist officer husband. Confessing in her memoirs, written during the twelve years she spent in British and French prisons during and after the war, that she had been driven by 'the animal pleasure of the body which my soul disdains',[16] she was called at her trial 'a dangerous nymphomaniac'. Her accuser in question was Polish undercover agent Roman Czerniawski, who had no complaints about the months she had spent as his mistress, working for *Interallié*. Mathilde's denial that she also slept with other comrades was countered at the trial by one witness offering to tell the court where on her body she had a beauty spot, 'except that she doesn't have one anywhere, and that is the truth'.

Mathilde was dubbed *La Chatte* (the She-Cat) by her unfortunate comrades and became known by the even more cuddly nickname *das kleine Kätzchen*, meaning 'Little Kitten', to the Abwehr officers for whom she worked after being 'turned' by an unassuming Scharführer in the Geheime Feldpolizei named Hugo Bleicher, who perfectly merited the description of a 'grey man'. Of average height and build with prematurely greying hair, he passed unnoticed when in civilian clothes, the only distinguishing feature his thick spectacles that hid the pale, unsmiling eyes in his impassive face. When, after the war, he ran a small tobacconist's shop near Lake Constance, not far from the Swiss border of the Federal Republic, no one guessed that the man behind the counter wearing a beige cardigan and peacefully smoking his pipe had put behind bars more Allied agents than any other Abwehr officer in France – and been so respected by them for his humane and intelligent methods of questioning that he was even invited to the wedding of his two most famous captives, Odette and Peter Churchill.

No stranger to imprisonment himself, Bleicher had been a POW of the British during the First World War, after which he was employed as a bank clerk and later an import–export businessman in Morocco. Speaking fluent, slightly accented French and English, he never rose beyond NCO rank, despite often being referred to as 'Colonel Henri'.

Mathilde epitomised the women so feared by British Intelligence, who would let their feelings or desires override political loyalty at the drop of a garment. After one night in a freezing cell at La Santé prison, she was installed in Bleicher's comfortable quarters, and had no qualms about opting for comfort. Asked by the judge at her trial whether she was compelled to go to bed with him that first night, she replied, 'What else could I have done?' Swiftly convinced by Bleicher that Britain's eventual defeat was a matter of time alone, she had no wish to be shot in La Santé. Asked her feelings for the men and women she had delivered to imprisonment, torture and, in thirty-five cases, death, she replied, 'There was nothing I could do about it.'[17]

One of her victims was army officer Pierre d'Harcourt. In 1942 he was living near the Porte d'Orléans. Recruited by a personal friend, he was told to hand over his information to a contact from another network who was in radio communication with London. The woman he met in a restaurant was Mathilde Carré. Unaware that he was being watched from that first rendezvous, d'Harcourt continued passing information after she handed him on to 'Felix', an Austrian who claimed to be working for the German electrical giant Siemens. Walking home from a rendezvous with this new contact, d'Harcourt was accosted by two men in black suits, one of whom

1. In 1940, General Charles De Gaulle was a lone voice crying in the wilderness. Few French people had heard of him, or heard his appeal for resistance to the German occupation launched over the BBC on 18 June 1940.

2–3. An official portrait of Marshal Philippe Pétain in typically benign pose. He was the popular and legitimate head of state, who mistrusted his devious, collaborating Prime Minister Pierre Laval, seen with him, right.

4–5. *Left and above*: One man who did hear De Gaulle's broadcast appeal for resistance in 1940 was farmer Louis De La Bardonnie. Among the first to fight the German occupation, he risked not only his life but also those of his wife Denyse and their nine children.

6–7. *Left and below*: While De La Bardonnie was on the run with false papers under various identities, including railway inspector Borin and a priest, Denyse had to file for divorce to protect herself and their children from deportation to the death camps.

8–9. *Above and left*: Louis De La Bardonnie's first cumbersome Type 3 Mk 2 transmitter was hidden at Château La Roque in a bedroom on the first floor (right-hand window). The earth wire is still there.

10–11. *Left and below*: After the Liberation De Gaulle came to thank the Bardonnie family (left, flanked by Louis and Denyse), but the only thanks Bardonnie received from Britain was a printed certificate bearing Field Marshal Montgomery's signature.

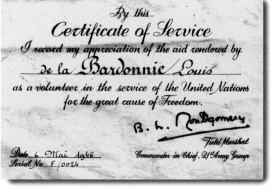

By this
Certificate of Service
I record my appreciation of the aid rendered by
de la Bardonnie Louis
as a volunteer in the service of the United Nations
for the great cause of Freedom.

B. L. Montgomery
Field Marshal
Date 6 Mai 1946   Commander-in-Chief, 21st Army Group
Serial No. F/0024

12–13. *Above, left*: Marius Bouchou's widow (front row, right) returned from Ravensbrück concentration camp broken in health and spirit, unable to smile even for the camera at the wedding of her daughter Cathérine to Robert Hestin. *Right*: Mayor's secretary Marius Bouchou (in naval reservist's uniform) provided *résistants* and refugees with false identity papers, but was betrayed by his friend Faytout after the fatal arms drop. Deported to Germany, he died of starvation and ill-treatment.

14. Ordinary people did extraordinary things. Georges Chabrier was a village postman by day. At night he risked death for himself and his son to save refugees' lives by smuggling them across the Demarcation Line into the Free Zone.

15–17. Some of the weapons that cost Marius Bouchou and his friends their lives. *Above left*: parachuted Mk 2 Stens, two Lee-Enfield .303s and a MAS 36 rifle; *top*: 9mm ammunition; *above right*: .303 ammunition and a Browning pistol hidden by one of the men who never returned to reveal their hiding place. The cache was found by accident in 1998.

18. The road to hell began at the Gestapo HQ in Castillon, where the tortures of SS Lieutenant Helmut Demetrio and his brutal subordinate drove some victims to suicide.

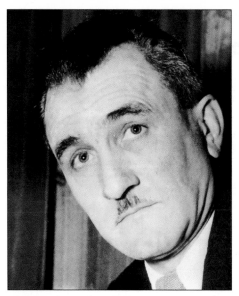

19–20. *Above left*: Collaboration took many forms. Joseph Darnand directed the murderous activities of the Milice and escaped at the Liberation with Vatican help. *Above right*: Politician Eugène Deloncle cheated his SS protectors and died a gangster's death.

21–2. *Below left*: An everyday scene all over France in 1943 when French police and German soldiers worked side by side because national police chief René Bousquet (*below right*) took his orders directly from SS General Karl Oberg (back to camera).

23. *Right*: Victor Faynsylber lost a leg fighting for France. He sent this photograph to Marshal Pétain, invoking the legal entitlement of a wounded veteran for his family to be exempted. Officialdom was deaf: with his wife and children, the one-legged ex-soldier was gassed at Auschwitz.

24. *Below*: The day of shame, 16 July 1942, when French police rounded up 12,884 people for the SS, including 4,051 children and 5,802 women, most of whom met their death at Auschwitz. Here, Jewish detainees leave Vélodrome d'Hiver for Drancy camp.

25–7. *Above, left to right*: De Gaulle's military deputy General Delestraint was shot in Dachau. His political counterpart Jean Moulin was France's youngest prefect before going underground as art dealer 'Max'.

28. *Left*: Sadist Klaus Barbie (in Feldgendarmerie uniform) caught Moulin and tortured him to death.

29–31. *Below, left to right*: Renée De Monbrison spent four anguished years keeping her children out of Barbie's clutches, while Captain Frenay and Colonel Pommiès were equipping and training a secret army for the Liberation.

32–4. *Above*: German heroes? Yes! Kriegsmarine Feldwebel Heinz Stahlschmidt proved his love for his French girlfriend by saving 3,000 lives in Bordeaux. *Right*: Less romantic, but no less heroic, was the last military governor of Paris, 49-year-old General Dietrich von Choltitz. He put his own life on the line in August 1944 by defying Hitler's orders to destroy the city, through whose traffic-free streets (*below*) goose-stepping troops and military bands had been parading daily for the previous four years.

**Place
Bouli et Shatta SIMON**

Avec l'aide de la population de Moissac et en dépit du danger,
ils ont pu sauver plusieurs centaines d'enfants juifs de la barbarie nazie.

35–7. *Above left*: In 1940 Prefect François Martin condemned the selfish attitude of the inhabitants of Moissac, 'interested only in selling their agricultural produce'. But the town council gave La Maison de Moissac (*below right*) to Shatta and Bouli Simon as a reception centre, enabling them to save several hundred children and adolescents from deportation and death, as the plaque (*above right*) witnesses. Breaking his own laws, François Martin gave the couple genuine identity cards that helped to save 150 lives.

38. *Below left*: Shatta Simon had scant time for her own son. Pregnant again and warned that she risked losing the child if she did not reduce her crippling workload, she replied, 'What does one unborn child matter, when thousands of living ones are at risk?'

39–43. Many of the children had lost all their relatives. They came from hiding or concentration camps to live as Scouts and Guides in Moissac and participate in school classes, music lessons, camp fire sing-songs, and even trade training for the older ones. *Above left*: Defying Vichy's anti-Semitic laws, France's Chief Scouts came to show solidarity with the work of La Maison de Moissac. *Above right*: Some of Shatta Simon's girls camping. *Right*: A group of Moissac EIF scouts singing. *Below left*: a young recorder class. *Below right*: Older boys learning metalwork.

44–6. *Above*: After Major Helmut Kampfe (*left*) was assassinated by *maquisards* in June 1944, his friend Major Adolf Diekmann (*centre*) unleashed his men of 3 Company SS Regiment Das Reich on the civilian population of Oradour-sur-Glane. Regimental commander Colonel Stadler (*right*) threatened a court martial, but Diekmann was killed fighting in Normandy days later.

47–8. *Below*: Time stopped on Saturday 10 June 1944 in Oradour-sur-Glane. Every building was burned to the ground leaving a scene akin to nuclear devastation. *Left*: In France's shrine to the victims of the German retreat the butcher's shop remains as a burned-out shell.

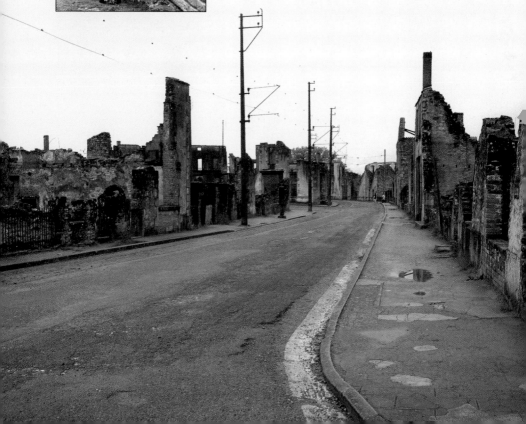

49–53. The SS herded 240 women and 205 children, including the infants' class (*above*), into the church (*top*). They panicked, choking in the smoke from asphyxiating grenades, and in their attempt to escape the SS fired on them through the windows, as bullet holes in the 1914–18 memorial plaque (*below left*) testify. The only survivor was Madame Rouffanche (*below right*), who climbed through the centre window above the altar (*above right*) and hid in bushes, severely wounded, while the killing continued. On the same day, the SS burned 197 adult males alive in barns.

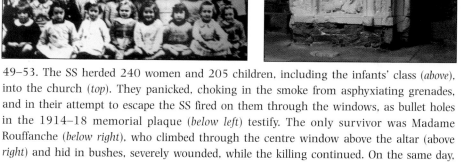

54–6. *Left and above*: The fashionable winter sports resort of Natzwiller-Struthof in Alsace was turned into a concentration camp where prisoners were worked to death in the quarry and hauling a road-roller (top) weighted down with rocks to level mountain roads.

57–8. *Below left*: Camp commandant Josef Kramer was given a Christmas bonus for watching women prisoners die in his gas chamber so that their skulls could be added to Dr Hirt's collection. Arrow indicates gas extraction chimney. No one knows how many died more slowly in medical experiments at the camp because they were designated *Nacht und Nebel*. At the Liberation 17 whole bodies and 166 quartered bodies were found in Dr Hirt's vats of preserving fluid. *Below right*: Kramer hanged countless prisoners on these gallows during the roll calls that lasted hours, summer and winter.

59–61. The Atlantic coast resort of Royan was in the German pocket of resistance interdicting Allied use of the port of Bordeaux. On 5 January 1945 the bombing mission order was to destroy the town 'occupied by German troops only'. Two waves of RAF Lancasters dropped 1,589 tonnes of high-explosive and incendiary bombs. In the attack 284 female and 158 male civilians were killed, but only 37 Germans. Royan's elegant Edwardian casino (*top*) was unrecognisable after the raid (*above right*). *Below*: The town and harbour the day after the raid.

62–3. The bombing made no difference to the outcome, except for the wounded and dead. Manned by many nationalities in German uniform, like these Sikhs who changed sides after capture in the Western Desert (*above left*), the Royan pocket of resistance held out until Berlin capitulated on 8 May 1945. The exhaustion on the face of this surrendering Wehrmacht soldier says it all (*above right*).

64–5. Most of the FFI men containing the pockets of resistance were civilians like these three *maquisards* (*above left*) with their parachuted Stens, but De Gaulle sent regular forces to take over and claim the victory, for which he decorated General De Larminat (*above right*).

thrust a pistol into his back, while the other told him in poor French that he was under arrest. Making a dash for it, d'Harcourt was shot and wounded, to find himself confronted in captivity by the very people he had thought Resistance agents, next stop Buchenwald.

Another victim of *La Chatte* was Christopher Burney, a young French-speaking English officer who arrived in France in May 1942 to contact an RF network already rolled up by Bleicher and Mathilde without London's knowledge. Living on his wits, Burney managed to evade capture for eleven weeks before being picked up in a casual check of papers. Thrown into a sparsely furnished cell in the rue des Saussaies, expecting to be summarily shot, he was instead beaten up with his hands cuffed behind him and shuttled back and forth in black vans between Fresnes prison and various interrogations.

Still miraculously alive, either because of his military rank or value as a hostage, he was eventually deported early in 1944 to Germany in the company of thirty-one male agents and four women. The women were shot in Ravensbrück and the men hanged in Buchenwald shortly before the war in Europe ended, with the exception of the few like Burney who managed to escape after nearly two years of starvation and ill treatment.

Mathilde's defence in court rested entirely on her claim that a woman did not have the same choices as a man. That her inevitable death sentence handed down by a French court in 1949 was commuted and she was released is due to the lateness of her trial. By then, everyone in France had had enough of the war. Five years later, Mathilde – now a rather dumpy little woman approaching her fortieth birthday – disappeared. Whether an old enemy had caught up with her at last, or she changed her identity so that none of them could, remains a mystery.

After the departure on 19 November 1941 from Paris Gare du Nord of the 100,000th French volunteer worker for Germany, enticed by promises of higher pay and better food, one might think Goering would be all smiles on meeting Marshal Pétain a week later at St-Florentin. Yet, blocking all the Marshal's requests, Goering shouted, 'Tell me, Marshal. Who won this war? You or us?' Visibly shaken by this gross discourtesy, Pétain replied with a quiet sarcasm that escaped Fat Hermann, 'I had not previously been quite so aware how badly we had been beaten.'

More or less at the same moment, the 1st Battalion of the LVF was taking its first four casualties under fire 60 kilometres from Moscow. Doriot, who was present, later described the fighting in a frozen birch forest: 'The thermometer showed −10 degrees in the morning, but it was down to −37 by dusk, and −41 the following day. Men don't function at those temperatures. Hands are too numb and joints all stiff. In the front line, the ground is as hard as stone and you can't dig in. Automatic weapons become unreliable.' Another LVF man described the problem of urinating at those temperatures: 'Each guy has to have a mate holding his gloves, because by the time he's finished pissing, his hands are too frozen to put them on for himself.'

On 1 December in Paris Ernst Jünger was depressed after censoring some last messages written by executed hostages. If death came to the mutilated bodies of convicted *résistants* as a mercy after long torture, many hostages selected at random were still hoping to live right up to the last moment. Shot by soldiers wearing the same uniform as Jünger, they had written to wives and sweethearts and children and parents, spelling out their small cares to avoid mentioning the main thing on their mind. One said only, 'I am leaving about 615 francs, which please give to the relief of the POWs.' A hairdresser wrote: 'Come to Vannes to collect my suitcase. Alfred must look after my bicycle because when he is old enough to work, it will belong to him. As to the clippers and scissors, do what you like with them. Be good to each other.' Another man's postscript read: 'Ask the Kommandantur to release my body so that you can bury it at home.[18] I die innocent. Remember me.'

Jacques Grinbaum, aged 21, having been selected as one of fifty-three hostages from Drancy to be shot with forty-two others at dawn on 15 December at Mont Valérien, wrote to his parents and sisters aged 12 and 14 a letter that reads like a school essay. As his last night drew on towards dawn, he added: 'It is 3.15 a.m. I am calm, very calm, waiting. . . . It is 5.40 a.m. Still holding up. I have made my confession. I love you Daddy, Mummy, Jacqueline and Yvette. Please keep my things which you can get from the Kommandantur and the Red Cross. Courage. Good luck!'[19]

That month, safe in their literary bubble, the august members of the Prix Goncourt jury deliberated as was their custom, come war or peace, after a good lunch in the Drouaut restaurant. Outside, on the streets of Paris, the pace of attacks on German servicemen and French policemen accelerated, with civilians also killed and wounded by stray bullets and grenade fragments. As the assassination campaign brought forward the shoot-on-sight curfew to 6 p.m., large bilingual posters announcing death sentences in red print with black borders were everywhere to be seen. The four weeks to Christmas included attacks on French and German police on traffic duty, grenades thrown into a Wehrmacht canteen, a bomb in a café frequented by off-duty soldiers, sentries attacked with revolver and grenade, a Wehrmacht medical officer wounded on the Boulevard Magenta, a lieutenant wounded on Boulevard Péreire, a major twice wounded in the rue de la Seine and various attacks on collaborationists. In default of the culprits, on one day alone – 15 December – ninety hostages were shot at Mont Valérien and another twenty-five in the provinces.

The last consolation for some after 7 December, when the Japanese attacked Pearl Harbor, and the US declaration of war against Nazi Germany next day, was that the course of the war in Europe was altered inexorably. Thinking ahead to when they might need them as a bargaining counter, on 12 December 200 Gestapo and 360 Feldgendarmerie arrested 743 French Jewish VIPs and scooped up another 300 from Drancy, transporting them to the German-controlled concentration camp at Compiègne.

Danneker had brought two Viennese Jews to Paris to set up a French Judenrat, or Jewish council, that would organise the elimination of French Jewry on the same pattern that was working so well in Eastern Europe. Entitled L'Union Générale des Israélites de France (UGIF), its first task was to amass a fine imposed on the whole community of 1,000,000,000 francs for the murder of German soldiers. In his note to Abetz dated 7 December, Danneker considered this entirely logical because the men had been killed by preponderantly Jewish Communists. UGIF was henceforward to re-group all the existing agencies and be the sole channel through which Jews could communicate with those who wished to destroy them. Approving Danneker's use of anti-Semitic Paris police inspectors to hunt down Jews in the capital, Pucheu now created a force specialising in this work – La Police aux Questions Juives (PQJ).

The mass of the gentile population had more immediate problems than concern with these measures. Reporting a protest demonstration at Frozes, near Grenoble, on the night of 16 December, Gendarmerie Captain Piozin reported: 'Milk supplies in the area are so irregular that the population is getting violent. Only children under six get even a part of their allocation. The demonstration was broken up by the Gendarmerie.' In Corsica, bakers were reportedly selling bread at 30 francs a kilo – way above the legal price – and peasants were routinely slaughtering undeclared pigs to sell the meat on the black market.[20]

In Moissac, Dr Moles' recipe for combating black marketeers was to set up a municipal market where vegetables had to be sold at the official prices – and a subsidised canteen where the poor and homeless could find at least one decent meal a day. In the following month he went a step further and created a municipal depot where everyone could buy milk for their children. When whole truckloads of black-market produce were occasionally stopped at routine checkpoints, the offenders were prosecuted, with prison terms likely. The grey market, however, was widely patronised by poorly paid gendarmes, who bought direct from peasant producers what they could not find in the shops, and usually turned a blind eye to others in the same situation.

One of the trades enjoying business-as-usual throughout the Occupation was ladies' hairdressing. Women careful of their appearance forewent food if necessary to have their hair done professionally. The parents of Marie-Rose Dupont[21] were church-going peasants with a small property not far from Moissac who prospered in the grey market boom. But life had been so hard for them before the war that when Marie-Rose was only 14 her mother, desperate to be rid of a mouth to feed, tried to engage her to a well-off older man. For the first time in her life, Marie-Rose refused to obey her parents. Since the alternative to marriage was to earn her own living, she started work as a hairdressing apprentice and two years later in 1936 opened her own salon in Moissac. A hasty marriage to a work-shy alcoholic husband who sold off all her possessions left her in 1939 divorced with a 12-month-old son.

After the defeat in June 1940, she was relieved to find that the regular customers still had their hair done regularly. Even refugee women seemed able to find money for this. Apart from the problem of procuring shampoos and dyes, which were in very short supply, life had never been better for Marie-Rose. The problems of being a single working parent were alleviated by her parents' help looking after her son in the daytime and she was able to spend all her Sundays with him. All the family was pro-Pétain, so when the Marshal came to Moissac and addressed a full house in the local cinema, Marie-Rose heard him repeat the phrase, '*J'ai fait à la France le don de ma personne*,' and felt like weeping. Around her, many people did shed tears. This was the Messianic side of Pétain.

Although the salon was prospering, the country was in mourning – for the defeat, for the hundreds of thousands of POWs languishing in Germany, for its own self-esteem – and public gaiety was frowned upon, especially dances. Since they could not be organised publicly, *les bals clandestins* took their place, organised by word of mouth. Friends whispered of a rendezvous in a house with a room large enough for a dozen or so couples to dance to the music of a portable wind-up gramophone and, for an hour or two, the war was forgotten in the arms of one's partner.

Marie-Rose was not just good-looking, but extremely beautiful, immaculately made-up and coiffed. As owner of her own salon, she could always swap a free permanent wave or hair-do for an article of clothing, so she was also well-dressed. But she turned down all propositions for more than just a few dances. Given the total non-availability of contraception, casual sex was out of the question and she was certain that she never again wanted to be tied to a husband. For a single mother from a peasant home, she had good reason to feel pleased with her life – and no thought of what the future might hold. Why should she, when the only interference from Vichy was the visit of a gendarme on 27 March 1942, bringing her a harmless extract from the *Journal Officiel* obliging her and all other salon proprietors to collect hair clippings for mixture with rayon fibres in a specialised factory in Calvados producing up to 40,000 pairs of slippers a month?

It was not only hairdressing that was paid in kind. Dr Paulette Gouzi recalls treating adults and children from the *colonie* and elsewhere who came to her door with bronchitis, stomach ailments, worms – but with no money. 'Many people were very poor. It was normal for us to treat them and not be paid. But a few days later they would return with some eggs perhaps, or a rabbit they had snared – or even a chicken.'

In both zones, food was replacing money in the parallel economy. The Prefect of Tarn-et-Garonne expressed concern at the growing rift between the poor town-dweller consumer and the peasant producer, who was thriving in this time of universal shortages. So much so, that on 13 July 1942 he signed a decree requiring the gendarmerie to *force* producers to take their vegetables to open markets where prices were controlled. Like most such legislation, this was more honoured in the breach than the observance. Another area of social conflict that worried him was the growing xenophobia, directed not at the Italians who had arrived at the beginning of the century, but the Spanish refugees – especially those who did not work but lived off handouts from the Mexican legation, and therefore had both the money and the time to go hunting for extra food.

Yet, in the big cities, some still ate very well. Widely criticised after the Liberation was the extravagant way top French executives wined and dined their German clients in the best restaurants when they came to France, themselves accepting reciprocal hospitality when in Germany. By the end of 1941, 7,000 companies were accepting and fulfilling German orders for both civilian and military products. It was a figure that would double before the end of the Occupation, when virtually all firms with fifty or more employees and many smaller companies were working 100 per cent for the Reich. In around fifty major companies, German commissioners were appointed, to intervene directly in management decisions.

What was the alternative? French industry was in a German vice. Since the Occupation administration controlled the allocation of raw materials, any firm that refused their orders would have been obliged to lay off its workforce. Not only did working for the occupiers mean business, German contracts also made for a truce between management and labour, since the single-union representatives could literally see on which side their bread was buttered: the Occupation authorities released extra food for factory canteens where the workers were behaving the way they wanted. A full stomach being a powerful argument, initial reluctance of management and labour to deal with the only client in the market dwindled rapidly. Commercial giants like Paribas, Rhône-Poulenc, Ugine, Crédit Lyonnais, Société Générale and many others were, according to historian Annie Lacroix-Riz, more than eager to do business with the Reich.[22]

A few refused to compromise. At the top of the scale, the enormous Michelin company had both the advantage of being based in the Free Zone and the clout to keep the invader at arm's length. When Germany offered to release supplies of artificial Buna rubber to replace unavailable supplies of natural rubber from Indo-China in return for shares in the company and taking over subsidiaries in Belgium and other Axis-occupied countries, Michelin found a thousand ways to wriggle out of such a deal because its Board foresaw the impossibility of a *final* German victory, whatever the next few years might bring. The price for such resistance was often harsh: when the President of Crédit Commercial de France refused to hand over to the Germans 440,000 shares in Galeries Lafayette formerly owned by a Jewish shareholder, he was fired.

To understand the policies of the biggest companies requires sitting for a moment in their boardrooms, where the war and the Occupation were seen as temporary complications that required only modification, and not abandonment, of long-term policies. Louis Renault, the shrewd head of the automobile empire, guessed wrongly that Germany and Britain would soon make peace to avoid weakening themselves by a prolonged conflict that would leave them both wide open to Soviet invasion or American economic domination. His decision to accept orders for vehicles from the Wehrmacht was to cost his life after the Liberation, but how could he have refused, after making trucks and tanks for the French Army and having both the skilled workforce and the necessary machinery? Getting into bed with the enemy did not always mean love, however. The Peugeot family supported Pétain for the first two years of the Occupation and accepted orders from Germany, yet refused such blandishments as extra food for its workers, because of the German propaganda that came with it.[23]

Aluminium Français advised Vichy in June 1941 that it had been approached to jointly build and operate a smelting factory out of range of RAF bombers in the Free Zone. Interestingly, in view of the early date, it argued that the new factory would have no effect on the outcome of the war because it could not be completed before the end of 1942! The board also advanced the long-term argument that failure to go along with this German initiative would result in the factory being built in another occupied country where *after the war's end* it would be operating in competition with the output of Aluminium Français.[24]

In the dye industry, the German chemical giant IG Farben pressured French competitors to form a cartel in which it would own the majority shareholding, in return for which French companies ended up collectively the fifth largest shareholder in IG Farben. In a series of tortuous boardroom manoeuvres, the French chemical group Ugine saw its market value multiplied fifteen times in two years after becoming a partner in IG Farben's pesticide manufacturing division, which produced the Zyklon B gas for the extermination camps.[25]

Chapter 14

THE WOMEN'S ORDEAL

On 13 January 1942 General Guibert of the Gendarmerie Nationale ordered all units in the Paris region to adopt 'the system of repression practised by the Paris police, to give all assistance to the police in case of terrorist attacks, and to pursue the aggressors by all means, and capture them dead or alive'.[1] Words, however, were not enough for the Germans or government in Vichy. Two months earlier, in November 1941, La Légion des Combattants had been renamed Légion des Combattants et Volontaires de la Révolution Nationale, with membership open to all, whether ex-servicemen or not. This made it effectively the only political party in the Vichy state. To create an ultra force prepared to stamp out the left-wing Resistance using its own methods of kidnapping and murder, members of the Légion were invited in January to join a new Service d'Ordre Légionnaire, vaunted as a modern order of chivalry with uniforms like those of the SS (except for the inevitable berets), torchlight oath-taking ceremonies and parades with waving banners. This forerunner of the Milice was set on course by the appointment of Joseph Darnand as its Inspector-General.

In Paris, the trial of the Musée de l'Homme network ended with ten death sentences. Léon-Maurice Nordmann, his spirit undiminished by long confinement, retorted to the judges, 'We risked death every day on this battlefield. I consider that we have been at war with you from the beginning.'[2] Symbolising the political darkness, on 18 January the power cuts in Paris were so bad that twenty-four Metro stations had to be closed, adding to the misery of food shortages and restrictions.

Two months later, after going clandestinely to London to meet De Gaulle, Christian Pineau – Socialist founder of the Libération-Nord network and publisher of the clandestine weekly *Libération* – wrote, 'I found De Gaulle's thinking entirely military. When I explained that Pétain had substantial support, and that we were also up against the Communists playing their own game, he was unmoved by the dangers we were running. For him, [it was normal for] every combatant to risk his life whether in a tank in North Africa or posting handbills on walls in France.'[3] It never occurred to De Gaulle that most Frenchmen then saw little difference between the LVF serving the Reich in German uniform and the Free French wearing British uniform with a shoulder flash reading *France*.

One of his handful of agents on the ground was Jean Moulin, who had landed by parachute on 1 or 2 January at Eygalières, in Provence. His mission was not military like Rémy's, but political. Like everything else in France, the existing Resistance organisations were, as Hitler had foreseen, divided by class, politics and religion. Moulin's mission was to unite them all under an umbrella organisation: Le Conseil National de la Résistance. An accomplished sportsman with a reputation for Socialist sympathies, Moulin was to prove the ideal man for the job, except for a fatal tendency to take unnecessary risks.

In the first days of February Jacques Doriot vaunted the prowess of the LVF on the eastern front, from which he had just returned, to a rally of PPF supporters in Paris' massive indoor cycle track, le Vélodrome d'Hiver. The PPF claimed an attendance of 50,000; a Propaganda Abteilung report said 30,000; independent estimates reckoned only 20,000 turned up, but the turn out was still impressive, and presaged well for the exhibition 'Bolshevism against Europe' that opened in Paris on 1 March.

In mid-February, Heydrich imposed SS-Brigadeführer Karl Oberg as Höherer SS- und Polizeiführer Frankreich, to oversee the work of Danneker and Knochen. A tubby little caricature of Himmler, Oberg had been responsible for police repression in Poland and now took overall responsibility for security work in France. Since he could not speak French, he used Knochen to control French officialdom.

That month the underground newspaper *Défense de la France* – which would become *France Soir* in 1944 – published an article condemning women who slept with the enemy: 'You so-called French women who give your bodies to a German will be shaved, with a notice pinned on your backs *Sold to the enemy!* So will you shameless girls who trip around with the occupiers be shaved and whipped. On all your foreheads a swastika will be branded with hot iron.'[4]

Who were these shameless women and girls? If some were amateur prostitutes, others were single mothers needing a protector, a source of money or extra food; others again were just young girls seeking some fun in the dark years when a new dress or a pair of pretty shoes was otherwise only a dream. But a good number were respectable women employed in hotels, restaurants and other places where the clientele was German. Even if they tried at first never to smile or to reply other than frigidly to questions, daily contact soon made it plain that most German soldiers had no more desire to be in Hitler's armed forces than the French had to see them in France.

Raymonde Z worked in an abbatoir near St-Malo, plucking and gutting twelve chickens an hour. It is easy to see why she fell for her elegant lover Fritz, in his dark blue Kriegsmarine uniform. After the Liberation their son Gérard grew up with all the other children at school singling him out as *le fils du Boche* and his mother abusing him daily as the incarnation of her shame. Interviewed for *L'Express* aged 55, he said bitterly, 'She should have aborted me, or given me away.'[5]

Perhaps some of the women sought to escape from the crushingly patriarchal Pétainist philosophy in which they had no political rights or representation, no influence of any kind outside the home. But many others genuinely fell in love, never thinking that there would be a price to pay for the hours or weeks or months of happiness before their lovers were posted, perhaps to die shortly afterwards on the Russian front. One such was Thérèse Y, who worked in her mother's bar at Lillebonne, halfway between Rouen and the coast. Her mother slept with Germans for cash, and turned a blind eye to what her 17-year-old daughter was up to with Josef, a music-loving pharmacist who sang operatic arias to her after the bar closed at night. To have a sexual relationship with a racially inferior French woman outside an approved brothel was an offence under military law, so her dream ended when she told him she was pregnant.

After he stopped seeing her, she found a job as waitress in a requisitioned château where, among the men she served at table was her ex-lover, pretending not to know her. His regiment posted elsewhere, Josef vanished, only to reappear in Lillebonne three days after the lonely birth, apparently full of remorse. After briefly holding in his arms the daughter who had been christened Marie-José after him, he vanished forever, leaving a baby girl who grew up wondering, 'When will Daddy come back for me?' Unlike many of France's war babies, Marie-José was told the truth by her mother when young, but it was not until 2002 that they travelled together to the WASt – the Wehrmacht Archives Service – and there, among 18,000,000 files they found that of Josef, who died unmarried in 1984.[6]

On 19 February at Riom the Supreme Court began hearings of 'those responsible for the defeat of 1940'. Thus, only 35 kilometres from all the foreign correspondents in Vichy, Edouard Daladier stood in the dock beside Léon Blum and Gen Maurice Gamelin, indicted for military incompetence. It was a costly error on Pétain's part. An adroit parliamentarian, Blum defended himself partly with counter-accusations that the Marshal shared responsibility for French unpreparedness, having been Minister for War in 1934. This received widespread circulation abroad and clandestinely in France.

On 23 February the long wait of Boris Vildé and the six other men of the Musée de l'Homme network ended in a volley at Mont Valérien, the three women condemned with them being deported to the camps. In his last letter to his wife, Vildé hoped that no one would hate the Germans for his death. 'Forgive me for deceiving you,' he continued, 'when we shared that last kiss. I knew the execution was for today. Try to smile when you receive this letter, as I am smiling while I write it. I just looked in the mirror and found my face quite normal. A little quatrain runs through my head: As ever, impassive / and brave pointlessly / I'll have twelve German rifles / pointing at me.'[7] It was typical of a linguist like Vildé to make a final pun: the French word *impassible* means both 'impassive' and 'not punishable'. He ended, 'Keep my engagement ring [CENSORED]. It is a beautiful thing to die healthy and lucid, in possession of all my spiritual faculties – so much better than falling at random on a battlefield or dying slowly, eaten away by illness.'[8]

On 24 February diplomat Ernst Achenbach was despatched by Abetz to Vichy with the message that Admiral Darlan *must* be replaced by Laval, now recovered from the assassination attempt. His unbeatable trump was the bluff that refusal to reinstate Laval would result in Hitler appointing Reinhard Heydrich as Gauleiter for France.

At La Maison de Moissac, Laure Schindler was too excited to sleep when at last given permission to visit her father in the camp at Noé. On the appointed day she was up and dressed hours before her chaperone was ready to leave. Called into Shatta's office at the last moment, Laure wept to hear that there was a serious epidemic at Noé, as a result of which the camp was temporarily closed to visitors. There was no epidemic – or at least, nothing worse than usual. It was Shatta's way of breaking gradually to Laure the news that a parcel of food scraps she had sent her father had been returned marked 'Addressee deceased'.[9]

On 2 March Shatta and the children welcomed Chief Scout General Lafont, who came with the head of the Protestant Scout movement on an official visit to show solidarity. They pronounced themselves impressed with the work being done and the educational activities. After lunch and singing of Hebrew and French songs including '*La Marseillaise*', the afternoon was marred by a visitor who had come looking for trouble. Lawyer Guy Botreau-Bonneterre found in the Lion patrol's dormitory a portrait of Pétain apparently being threatened by exercise clubs arranged on both sides of it. He reported the childish prank as an act of treason to the Prefect in Montauban, who was obliged to appoint a Special Branch commissioner to conduct an enquiry, which found 'no evidence of dissidence'.

Fortunately the spiritual head of Shatta Simon's little community was the philosopher Edmond Fleg, who placed a great emphasis on the importance of manual labour for character building. For twelve months his 'rural group' of adolescents had been reclaiming a 58-hectare estate near the town that had been uncultivated for years. Epitomising the ideal of the Marshal's unsuccessful back-to-the-land programme, the project earned the Maison de Moissac Brownie points with the authorities.

Just over a month later Gen Lafont was obliged to inform the heads of the various scouting organisations in France that EIF had ceased by law to exist. Mastering the double-talk necessary in the Vichy state, he continued, 'There will be no further mention of EIF on future publications of the movement. EIF will not participate in our events unless they are specifically invited by the authorities. [However] internal relationships within the movement will continue to be governed by the spirit of scouting fraternity.'[10]

Obliged to dismiss Otto Von Stülpnagel for his vacillation over the execution of hostages, Keitel at OKW replaced him in March by Karl Heinrich Von Stülpnagel, a cousin of Otto working with the Armistice Commission in

Wiesbaden. With the similarity of name, the French civil population hardly noticed the handover.

In March a bevy of the most popular male and female French film stars travelled by train to show solidarity in Germany. They had return tickets; not so the 1,112 deportees who followed them on 27 March, when a column of gaunt and famished prisoners was herded from the concentration camp at Drancy in the Paris suburbs to Le Bourget railway station, where they were loaded in freight trucks at a siding called '*le quai aux moutons*' because it was normally used for sheep being transported to the slaughterhouse. Among the crowd of local residents watching them shuffle past were wives who had travelled out from Paris to say goodbye after hearing on the prisoners' grapevine that their menfolk were about to be deported. Although no Germans were present – the camp was under the aegis of the Paris Préfecture de Police – the gendarmerie guards would only allow them to wave farewell from a distance. Half of the deportees had French nationality, giving the lie to Vichy's pretence that sacrificing foreign Jews was saving French lives. As the Wehrmacht refused to supply guards for the train, the gendarmes were replaced at the last moment by sixty Feldgendarmerie men, commanded by a triumphant Theodor Danneker, who stayed on board for the three-day trip to Auschwitz before returning to France to continue his mission. Only twenty-two of the unwilling passengers on that train came back.

This was the first of eighty-five transports from the Paris area, involving 75,721 prisoners of whom less than 3,000 survived the camps. In the process, 69,619 Jewish homes, of which 38,000 were in Paris, were emptied of all personal belongings, theoretically sent east for Germans setting up home in the occupied territories. In practice, much disappeared into neighbours' possession or was filched on the way. Many richer Jews had taken the precaution of moving to the Italian-occupied pockets in south-eastern France because Mussolini refused to have anything to do with the Final Solution. The *département* of Alpes Maritimes had 12,217 Jews registered in the 1942 census, causing anti-Semites to jibe that Cannes should be spelled Kahn, a French variant of Cohen. However, when the mayor of the town sounded out opinion among his councillors over action to be taken, the influential hotel-owners and shopkeepers protested that the refugees were their best customers for years.

For the few German civilians in France, life was far more relaxed and pleasant than at home. Thanks to the influence of an uncle who was a Luftwaffe general, but whose advice to become a *Blitzmädchen* she had refused, on 1 April 21-year-old Ursula Rüdt von Collenberg took up a civilian post with the German Archive Commission. She was stunned to find American and English books and neutral newspapers on sale in Paris. Another pleasure was to find silk and other fabrics for sale – at a price – and a White Russian émigrée dressmaker to extend her wardrobe way beyond what she could have afforded in Germany.

Ursula's job was to extract from files in the Quai d'Orsay dating back to the time of Cardinal Richelieu any documents useful for propaganda, for example clashes with Britain in nineteenth-century colonial Africa. Von Ribbentrop's Foreign Office had requisitioned the Hotel d'Orsay, where she lived in style with a suite all to herself. An ample breakfast and dinner were eaten there, but an equally plentiful lunch was eaten at the embassy in the rue de Lille. Most of her colleagues were anti-Nazi but patriotic, genteel to the last man and girl; when a photocopyist looted some gold-tooled leather wall-hangings from the Quai d'Orsay, she was immediately dismissed. With her well-connected German friends in Paris, Ursula visited the opera, theatres and art exhibitions. Using public transport, she explored the north of France as a tourist, finding no hostility anywhere, and continued enjoying life in France until October 1943.

It's not just the English who keep a stiff upper lip. When nearly 200 people were killed by an RAF raid on Longchamps racecourse on 4 April, the PA commentator signed off with thanks to the organisers for a good day's racing 'despite a slight contretemps at the start of today's card'.[11] The previous day the RAF had targeted the Renault factory at Boulogne-Billancourt, where production of vehicles for the Wehrmacht was temporarily reduced by 40 per cent at a cost of 367 civilians killed and 361 badly injured.

On 16 April Paris high-school pupils from the Lycée Buffon defied the prohibition on demonstrations to protest against the arrest two weeks previously of Raymond Burgard, a teacher at the school and founder of the Valmy network. The teenage protest march was brutally broken up by the police with many arrests. Five of the youths would be shot at Mont Valérien on 8 February 1943, their sacrifice being pointless: Burgard was deported and eventually beheaded in Cologne on 15 June 1944.

Furious that the trial of Blum and the others at Riom had provided a public platform on which the policy of collaboration could be attacked, Hitler ordered Abetz to have the trial called off. It was suspended on 14 April, but that was not the end of the affair. Whether or not Hitler blamed Darlan for organising the trial, Abetz used that excuse to finally manoeuvre the admiral out of office as head of government, although he remained the Marshal's *dauphin* when Laval was reinstalled as head of the government on 18 April.

The author George Orwell broadcast over the BBC that day:

Laval is a French millionaire who has been known for many years to be a direct agent of the Nazi government. Since the Armistice he has worked for what is called 'collaboration' between France and Germany, meaning that France should . . . take part in the war against Russia. There is a very great danger that at some critical moment Laval may succeed in throwing the French fleet into battle against the British Navy, which is already struggling against the combined navies of three nations.[12]

This was pure propaganda. As Laval told his judges after the Liberation, he had zero authority over Darlan's navy at any time. A letter he wrote on 22 April to US ambassador in Vichy, Admiral William Leahy, explained his increasingly pro-German policies as opposition to the UK–USSR alliance: 'In the event of a victory over Germany by Soviet Russia and England, Bolshevism in Europe would inevitably follow. I believe . . . that a German victory is preferable to a British and Soviet victory.'[13]

However, his draft text of a broadcast implying that the Germans would win the war caused Pétain to snort derisively, 'You are not a soldier, Mr Laval. So how can you know? You may say that you *hope* for a German victory. That is all.'

Laval not only said that on air, he also ordered the COs to direct companies to send teams of workmen under their own foremen to Germany, where they would acquire new skills and knowledge. This was another of his attempts to get back the POWs on a one-for-one basis, news having reached him that French and Belgian POWs who refused to work, had been caught escaping or were suspected of planning escapes, were transferred to a complex of camps around Rawa-Ruska on the Polish/Ukrainian border, where conditions were so appalling that men died like flies from malnutrition and overwork in the quarries, being buried in mass graves with hundreds of thousands of Soviet POWs. Approximately 25,000 western European POWs were eventually killed off in this way. Laval's initiative flopped when an approach by the CO of the leather-processing industry was turned down by the Wehrmacht, in whose camps the POWs were detained.

A few POWs were still managing to make a home run. On 17 April General Henri Giraud escaped from the castle of Königstein near Dresden – a sort of Colditz for French officers – after thirteen months' captivity. With his photograph in every Gestapo and SD office, he reported, 'The Alsatians were ready not only to give a prisoner money, but to risk their lives for him. Without knowing a single person there or being helped by any organisation, I passed right through Alsace without problem.'[14] The province having been declared German by force, helping escapers was high treason, punishable only by death, as Lucienne Welschinger and four accomplices found on 29 January 1943 at the High Court in Strasbourg. Their *réseau* mainly of women had helped several hundred escaped POWs through Alsace and Lorraine on their way home. The execution of the women did not discourage Father Mansuy, a veteran who had lost an eye and an arm in the First World War. In August 1940 he had delivered a sermon on the text of the Good Samaritan to a congregation of restive POWs, ending with, 'If you ever need a Good Samaritan, here is my address.' When he was arrested after sheltering 2,500 escapees, the Gestapo said finding him had been easy because his address was in every camp.

Reporting for duty in Vichy, Giraud was received by Pétain on 28 April 1942 and on 2 May accompanied Darlan and Laval to meet Abetz at

Moulins. High on his success in getting Laval back into power, Abetz sought to grease the wheels of collaboration by suggesting Giraud join the French delegation in Berlin, but the general refused, stipulating that he would return to Germany after 400,000 married POWs were released to rejoin their wives and families.

One of Laval's first appointments made the young and brilliant Prefect of the Marne *département* Secretary-General of the Police Nationale. René Bousquet had been decorated with the Légion d'honneur at the age of 21 for saving lives during severe floods, and had also won a Croix de Guerre during the Battle of France in 1940. He left the Marne with a reputation of being anti-Masonic and anti-Communist, but with no taint of anti-Semitism. Indeed, he claimed later to have organised food parcels for the detainees in the German concentration camp at Compiègne.

Himmler's deputy, Reinhardt Heydrich, visited Paris not to see the sights but to impose a tighter collaboration with the French police and gendarmerie, demanding that they all be placed under Oberg's orders – for which a precedent existed in Belgium. He also introduced to France the Teutonic concept of *Sippenhaft*, or kin-punishment, under which the members of a terrorist's family would be punished for his acts.

Under this ordinance, all male parents, grandparents and children of 18 upwards of arrested 'terrorists' were to be shot, and all adult female parents, grandparents and children condemned to forced labour, with children under 18 being sent to an approved school. At a conference in the Ritz Hotel with Heydrich and Oberg, Bousquet agreed to speed up the arrest and deportation of Jews. On 5 May journalist Louis Darquier de Pellepoix replaced Vallat as head of the Commissariat Général aux Questions Juives (CGQJ). Darquier's wife was British, and he had only added the aristocratic 'de Pellepoix' to his name for reasons of vanity. Despite an excellent service record, in 1939 he had been given a three-month sentence for inciting racial hatred. He was the ideal man for the job, Vallat having been judged too squeamish.

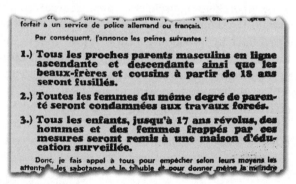

Heydrich's brutal recipe for stamping out the Resistance: male relatives to be shot, female ones sent to forced labour, children to be sent to special punishment schools.

Cardinal Baudrillart having departed this life, on 26 May 1942 the diplomat and author Paul Claudel addressed to Cardinal Gerlier a letter:

Your Eminence,

I have read with great interest the account of the splendid official and religious funeral ceremonies for His Eminence Cardinal Baudrillart. A wreath offered by the Occupation authorities was apparently to be seen on the coffin. Such homage was clearly the due of so fervent a collaborator.

On the same day I heard the report of the execution of twenty-seven hostages in Nantes. Having been loaded onto trucks by collaborators, these Frenchmen started to sing 'La Marseillaise'. From the other side of the barbed wire, their comrades joined in. They were shot in groups of nine in a sandy hollow. Gaston Mouquet, a youth of seventeen, fainted but was shot anyway.

When the cardinal reaches the other side, the twenty-seven dead hostages at the head of an army that grows daily larger, will slope arms and act as his guard of honour. For Baudrillart, the French Church could not find too much incense. For those sacrificed Frenchmen, there was not a prayer, nor a single gesture of charity or indignation.[15]

From 29 May 1942 Jews in the Occupied Zone aged six and over were obliged to wear, firmly stitched onto the left breast of their outer clothing, a yellow star the size of a man's hand that had to be purchased with their precious clothing coupons: three stars cost one ticket. *Dérogations* or certificates permitting holders not to wear a star were hard to come by from the CGQJ, even by bribery or personal connections. When leaving her country home, the wife of Fernand De Brinon was careful to carry everywhere with her a pass bearing the magic formula: 'The Commandant of the SIPO and the SD . . . hereby certifies that Madame De Brinon, née Jeanne-Louise Franck, born on 23 April 1896, is excused from . . . wearing the Jewish star, until final clarification of her origins.'[16]

She was in rather limited company. Pétain personally intervened on behalf of three friends; eight fixers working for the German procurement offices were exempted; the Gestapo and anti-Jewish police gave out thirteen other certificates to people working for them. Strangely, Jews with British or neutral nationality were not required to wear stars. The rich and famous could ask a friend like Sacha Guitry for help and he would call on Abetz or some other high functionary to help in this way, among others, Colette's husband, Clémenceau's son Michel and the wife of General Alphonse Juin, the Commander-in-Chief of French forces in North Africa. Cafés, restaurants, cinemas and museums were out of bounds to them in case they contaminated subsequent gentile visitors – as were telephone kiosks and lifts. The same 'logic' confined these people to the last carriage of Metro trains.

In the south-west, the yellow star ordinance was followed by the appointment on 5 June of Maurice Papon, an ambitious graduate of the high-powered Ecole de Sciences Politiques, to the post of Secretary-General in the Préfecture at Bordeaux, where he would sign deportation orders for 1,690 adults and children, many of them French citizens. Although her children were not technically Jewish under the German ordinance, Renée De Monbrison wanted them safe from the likes of Papon, who now had thousands of Jews behind wire in twenty concentration camps all over France.

To lessen the anguish of families divided by the Demarcation Line, the government had arranged with the German authorities for schools in the Occupied Zone to issue travel permits for children to visit relatives in the Free Zone during the long summer holidays. Renée obtained *laisser-passer* for hers to go to their great-uncle's château of St-Roch, near Moissac, where their demobilised father Hubert was based, when not living a clandestine life as 'Monsieur Casaubon', collecting military information about the German dispositions in the Bordeaux-Irun area for onward transmission to London.

Unable to accompany them, Renée swallowed her anxiety and said goodbye to 14-year-old Françoise, 11-year-old Christian, 7-year-old Manon and 6-year-old Jean, knowing that they would never return to the Occupied Zone. Living alone in the villa at Le Pyla, she had to wear a yellow star each time she ventured outside. With that and '*JUIVE*' stamped in red letters on her identity card, no Germans offered her a seat on a bus; now she was obliged to give her seat up to them. More importantly, there was no way she could cross the Line legally to be with the children.

There was another relative for whom Renée felt responsible. The identity papers of her aged Aunt Loulou Warshavski would shortly be a one-way ticket to the gas chambers. A few weeks after the children's departure, she therefore took the old lady 'on holiday' to Hagetmau, a village lost in the largest forest in Europe, La Forêt des Landes. Arriving there with one small suitcase each, they went to the house of a *passeur* who worked for money. A local child was bribed with sweets to hold the old lady's hand as though taking a walk with her grandma. The child paid off with more sweets at the end of the village street, they continued in pouring rain towards the Line, the aunt under her umbrella with the *passeur* carrying her suitcase and Renée with a young officer on leave, who had volunteered to walk with her arm in arm as though lovers out for a stroll, despite a torrential downpour which they hoped would keep curious people indoors.

The noise of a motorbike rapidly approaching from behind caused them a bad moment, but the Wehrmacht despatch rider did not stop, perhaps because of the rain. On paper, it was as easy as that, but one can imagine the heart-stopping anguish as the motorcyclist approached or the sound of a voice or barking of some farm dog seemed to presage a patrol of armed men and dogs.

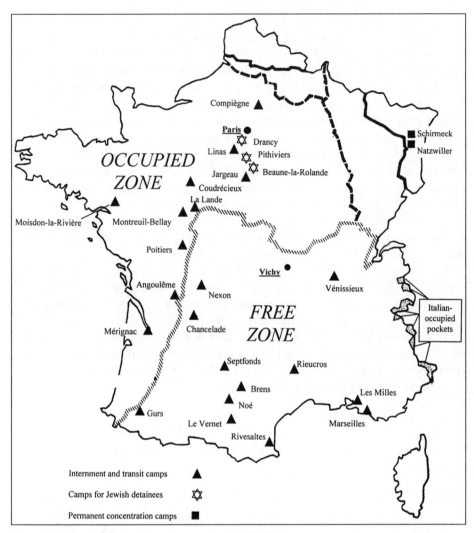

Concentration and deportation camps, August 1942.

Once across the Line, Renée and her aunt were welcomed into a farmhouse belonging to friends of the *passeur*, but knew they were not safe until 7 kilometres inside the Free Zone. Next day, after a long bus journey to Pau, Renée tried to persuade a Protestant priest who was a friend of her husband to find room for Aunt Louise, but his house and outbuildings were already overflowing with Jewish refugees and the best he could offer was to lay another mattress on the floor of the dining room if Renée could find nowhere else for her aunt.

Françoise and Manon were now at boarding-school in Pau, making poor progress due to worrying about their mother, but at least they were safe there. After a brief visit, she set off to see her sons at Chambon-sur-Lignon in the Auvergne. Accessible only by a single road and a railway winding its way through difficult mountain country, the village was fiercely Protestant. Like Roger Delthil in Moissac, its mayor Charles Guillon had asked all inhabitants in 1938 to open their hearts and homes to refugees from the Spanish Civil War and those fleeing Nazi repression. Thirteen pastors in the parishes of this upland area – of which the tall blond André Trocmé, Edouard Theis and Noël Poivre were the most active – organised shelter for 5,000 refugee children and adults, almost every house and farm opening its doors to them. Each month, several trains brought groups of children with false papers identifying them as city kids from poor families having a well-merited holiday in the country. Whenever the gendarmerie was to pay a visit, Trocmé received a warning, giving time for children living in the village to be sent to outlying farms. Renée's sons were staying in the home of Monsieur Eyraud, who was – as she later found out – head of the Resistance in the area.

In the Dordogne, the Bardonnie family was under surveillance day and night. The German search of the house was by an SS unit stationed just across the line in Castillon. Denyse was absent at a clandestine meeting with her husband, so it was 14-year-old Guy who 'welcomed' the visitors armed with machine-pistols. Sixty years later, he still remembers the rush of terror on being roughly lined up against a wall at gunpoint with his younger brothers and sisters, desperately hoping that 'Uncle' Armbruster's faith in their blond hair and blue eyes would be justified – as it was that time.

Chapter 15

'WE HAVE LEARNED OF THE SCENES OF HORROR . . .'

With Hitler's Minister for Armaments, Albert Speer, complaining that the manpower shortage in the Reich was critical as losses on the eastern front sucked almost every fit German male into uniform, on 21 March 1942 Fritz Sauckel was empowered to drain the occupied territories of workers. Later hanged at Nuremberg for the brutality of his slave labour programme, he was an insignificant man who had grown a Hitler moustache to give him what passed for an air of authority. Meeting Laval on 16 June, he demanded 2,060,000 workers from France in addition to the 1,600,000 POWs used as cheap labour in Germany.

A week later Laval announced that he had finally done a deal: in return for every *three* volunteer workers heading east, one POW would be released to return home. Called *La Relève*, or 'the relief shift', the scheme was a failure, enabling him later to claim that it was because of him that only 341,500 actually left, earning the release of 110,000 POWs, including 10,000 disabled. Sauckel's hunger was unsated, and he forced Vichy to introduce conscription for labour service in the Reich – Le Service du Travail Obligatoire (STO).

On 2 July Bousquet got the impression at a meeting with Oberg and senior SS aides that no one liked being pushed around by Adolf Eichmann, who was growing impatient at the slow progress of the Final Solution in France. Minutes of the meeting taken by Oberg's interpreter, SS-Major Herbert Hagen, record Bousquet's point that Pétain disliked using French police for arrests in the Free Zone, while not protesting about the arrests per se. On 6 July Danneker cabled Berlin the news that Laval would allow children in the Free Zone to be deported with their families, and had said that the fate of Jews in the Occupied Zone and other 'enemies of the regime' was of no interest to him at all.[1] By saying this, he gave the green light for the most monstrous single outrage of the Occupation, of which details were thrashed out in meetings on 8 and 10 July between the Gestapo and French police led by Bousquet's deputy for the Occupied Zone, Jean Leguay.

On a lighter note, Ernst Jünger noted in his diary how the feet of the nude dancers at the Tabarin were rubbed raw by the wooden-soled shoes they had to wear in daytime. After a copious dinner at the famous La Tour d'Argent, he also reflected that the simple fact of eating well in a luxury restaurant conferred an immense feeling of power when one knew that most people on the street outside were hungry, day after day. For Jean Cocteau's friends at Louis Vaudable's establishment in the rue Royale, a good dinner always ended with 'jam'. The opium so designated arrived by a route protected by Danneker, who found its distribution useful for blackmail.[2] For most people in the looking-glass world of Vichy, the rule was definitely 'jam tomorrow and jam yesterday, but never jam today'. Shortages and rationing were hurting so much that on 14 July housewives in Marseilles followed their Parisian sisters who had protested on 31 May against all the problems of trying to feed a family. They chose the wrong place to demonstrate; from inside the PPF headquarters hard-liners opened fire, killing two women.

In Paris, Simone De Beauvoir's intellectual Jewish friends ignored the prohibition on entering public buildings and still spent hours debating in the Café Flore. Nor did they bother to wear the star in Montparnasse or St-Germain des Prés.[3] Those in less privileged *quartiers* were hearing rumours of a pending massive round-up. On 15 July the Paris public transport service was ordered by the police to reserve hundreds of buses for special duties next day. With UGIF officials having been ordered to stockpile blankets and what provisions they could get their hands on, roughly printed tracts in Yiddish and French were passing hand to hand hours before the first knock on a door, which gave time for one hundred of the victims targeted by Bousquet and Leguay to commit suicide. More would have done so, or tried to escape, except for the belief that the Germans would only take men for labour in the east. This time, whole families were to be arrested.

Official records say less than 5,000 Paris police were involved; eyewitnesses put the number twice as high. As Prime Minister Lionel Jospin admitted on the fifty-fifth anniversary of the most infamous *rafle*, no German personnel were directly involved in the arrests.[4] Jean Leguay was later reinstated in the Corps of Prefects after denying any personal involvement or participation by police or gendarmerie, yet all arrests were carried out by his officers, paired with colleagues they did not know, and therefore could not trust. Typically, the knock on the door came at dawn, when two police officers arrived at the apartment of Madame Rajsfus – her former neighbour, *agent* Marcel Mulot, and a plain-clothes inspector. They told her to pack and come along. More loquacious arresting officers told victims that they were being sent to work camps in German-occupied Poland. That afternoon, held with 100 other people in a nearby garage for several hours awaiting transport to the cycling stadium Vélodrome d'Hiver – the largest covered space in Paris – the Rajsfus children were told by their mother to slip out and go home. There, 14-year-old Maurice and his sister found the concierge already looting the apartment[5] and the evening papers devoting as much space to the *rafle* as to the gala opening of the cabaret *Le Florence*.

Their mother and thousands of other men, women, children and infants were eventually bussed in full view of passers-by to the stadium, which swiftly became a scene from hell as adults and children clamoured for news, for the sight of a friendly face, for a lost parent or child, for a piece of bread or a drink of clean water. The few toilets were swiftly blocked and too soiled for use. Only two doctors were allowed into the stadium to treat the sick and those driven insane. The first of eleven suicides was a woman who threw herself from the upper stands onto the concrete below and twenty-four other deaths during the eight days before everyone was shipped out included two women who died in childbirth.

A handful of those rounded up were rescued by the very men ordered to arrest them. In Soissons, north of Paris, Monsieur and Madame Glas were warned in advance about the *rafle* by *agent* Charles Letoffe, who sheltered them in his home between 18 and 26 July. Louis Petitjean was an inspector in the Paris branch of Renseignements Généraux, the equivalent of Special Branch. Ordered to report for duty at 4 a.m. that day, he was given the name and address of a woman to arrest. Petitjean and his watchdog duly arrested a Madame Fuhrmann and her 7-year-old son in their apartment at 6 a.m. The boy clung to his mother, screaming, 'They're going to deport us!' While the other officer was conscientiously checking that gas and electricity were turned off, Petitjean whispered to the woman to trust him and he would save her.

With mother and child left at the local assembly point to await transport to the stadium, Petitjean went home and returned that afternoon, using his RG card to convince a sergeant-major in the elite Garde Républicaine, in charge of the PA at the stadium, that Madame Fuhrmann and her son were required in connection with an ongoing criminal investigation. After several announcements almost inaudible in the general chaos, they eventually appeared. So physically difficult was it to clear a passage through the press of desperate people, climbing over benches and the sick lying on the ground, that Petitjean told her to leave behind her suitcase, but she refused, because it held all her remaining possessions. Once outside, he led his two charges to the Bastille Metro station, bought them tickets and said goodbye, discovering many years later that they had survived the war and emigrated to Israel.

Gitla Szapiro was 10 years old when arrested with her parents despite the fact that she and her younger sister had French nationality. In the stadium, she noticed some Red Cross helpers trying to alleviate suffering. Transported to Pithiviers concentration camp between Paris and Orleans, she watched her father and brother having their heads shaved. The father's beard was also shaved off before the two males, an older sister and the children's mother vanished for ever. Taken to Drancy, Gitla was left to look after her 5-year-old sister, both of them constantly ill from the atrocious food and sleeping on soiled, lice-infested mattresses. Hearing their names called for deportation, they were terrified, with the younger girl crying that they were going to be shot. On an impulse, Gitla took her hand and got off the bus to walk back into the camp. Miraculously, no one called them back and thanks to the intervention of an uncle, who had managed to obtain an *Ausweis* stating that he was a *wirtschaftswertvoller Jude* or economically valuable Jew, they were released into the care of an organisation for Jewish orphans. The uncle had been trying to get all the family released, but was too late to save the older children and parents.

Those left behind in Drancy were accommodated in unfinished and unfurnished council flats. Children were lodged in vast 'dormitories' with no toilets on the same floor, but buckets for their use at night. The food was mainly cabbage soup, tolerable for an adult stomach, but not for children. The smaller ones with diarrhoea had either to wait in agony until an older child or adult came to help them, or foul themselves. What clothes could be washed could not be dried, so they had to stay naked or put them on still wet. Approximately 5,500 children passed through this nightmare between 21 July and 9 September, one in five needing medical treatment.

On 28 July Charles Wajsfelner wrote from the camp to his family's former neighbour, Madame Salvage, the local baker, asking her to take care of his little brother Maurice, his message showing that he at least had no idea what lay ahead. 'Thank you very much for what you gave us the day we had to leave. . . . Tomorrow morning Daddy, Mummy and I leave for an unknown destination. I shall write you our news as soon as I can. I ask you a favour – to help my aunt, her daughter and Maurice. We shall pay you back one day. Please say hello for us to all the people in our street.'

On 18 July SS-Oberstürmführer Heinz Röthke proudly informed Berlin that 12,884 people, including 4,051 children and 5,802 women, had been taken either to Drancy or other camps. The irony of *la rafle du Vel d'Hiv* is that France was the first European country to treat Jews as full citizens: after the Revolution, the atheist Maximilien Robespierre supported Henri Grégoire, a Catholic priest whose parish lay in eastern France where many Jews lived in poverty, in claiming before the National Assembly equal rights for Jews in accordance with the Declaration of the Rights of Man.[6]

It is sometimes alleged in defence of those who participated in the round-ups that nobody knew the truth about the deportations, and that they all

Charles Wajsfelner's last postcard from Drancy transit camp. He had no idea what lay ahead in Auschwitz.

believed the victims were being sent to work camps in the east. The lie to this
is given by a letter from Bouli Simon to the other leaders of the EIF written
shortly after Vichy had agreed to hand over to the Germans 10,000 foreign
Jews living in the Free Zone:

'The official version is that they are supposedly being sent to construct a
"Jewish state" in central Europe. . . . Yet you know that recently in Minsk
35,000 Jews were machine-gunned to death and during the German
occupation of Poland 700,000 Jews have been killed – men and women, the
old and the young – whether in massacres or the gas chambers.'[7]

Certainly Shatta was under no illusions when she ran all over Moissac to
track down some Rovers included on the arrest lists. Mika X crossed the
Napoleon Bridge and 'hid in the broken country on the other side of the river
for three days with two or three other lads. Then we were taken to a campsite
15 kilometres from Moissac, where some Protestant Scouts looked after us.'[8]

Despite the brotherly solidarity of other Scouts, Mika's troubles were far
from over. On 15 September he was led across the Swiss frontier just after the
federal government had passed a law requiring the repatriation of all refugees
over 15. Aged 20, Mika was arrested by the Swiss police, dumped back on the
border, re-arrested and taken by train in handcuffs to Rivesaltes concentration
camp, where he refused to work. On 8 November – the day the Allies landed
in North Africa – Mika was summoned to the camp commandant's office,
handed a train ticket and shown a four-word telegram purporting to come
direct from the office of Interior Minister Pucheu: 'Liberate immediately
Itzhak Michalowicz'. The telegram, Mika learned long afterwards, was a fake
sent by an optician in Metz with the complicity of the prefect of police. At the
time, all he could think of was to get as far away from Rivesaltes as possible.

Hesitating whether to head back to Moissac in case he was the bait in some
Kafkaesque trap, he was walking round the streets of Toulouse, hungry,
inadequately dressed and very cold, but with no money to buy food or a room
in a hotel, when a stranger tapped him on the back and thrust 400 francs
into his hands before vanishing among passers-by. In one of life's
coincidences, thirty years later Mika was Israeli Ambassador in an African
country and received an invitation from his French opposite number to come
and meet an inspecting officer from the Quai d'Orsay who had just arrived.
The inspector turned out to be the man who had given him the money, that
dark night in Toulouse.

But back in 1942 the hunt was well and truly on. The Rovers and Rangers
now had both to save themselves and help to get all the children of an age to
be arrested into safer homes. They called this le planquing, or 'stashing'. Alone
or in small groups, they travelled the country, knocking on doors of priests,
ministers and others who might be able to help. From sometimes unexpected
quarters, help did come in the nick of time. Hearing that some Jewish
children without papers were camping in the commune of Monboucher near
Limoges, the mayor's secretary left her office with all the official stamps

and blank identity cards on her desk long enough for them all to have new papers.

In Moissac on the fateful morning of 26 August, Shatta had been forewarned to expect the knock on the door that came at 8 a.m. She opened it to find herself facing the chief of police from neighbouring Castelsarrassin with a list of the 'illegal' children to be arrested. Behind him was a row of dark vehicles in which they were to be taken away.

'I'm afraid they've all gone,' Shatta said.

A search revealed the house to be empty, which led to the question, 'Where's their travel permit?'

Shatta apologised for having mislaid the paper on which should have been noted their present whereabouts. Her excuse was accepted and the *agents* departed empty-handed. Not so lucky were four adult refugees picked up by the police elsewhere in Moissac, none of whom returned from deportation. One search team was stopped by a cyclist who remarked, 'Feeling proud of yourselves today, are you?' A father of nine children, his sarcasm earned him a summons to the sub-Prefecture in Montauban, where he diplomatically apologised for his spontaneous outburst and was allowed to go.

No sooner had the police from Castelsarrassin departed from the Maison de Moissac, than Shatta headed for the local police and gendarmerie HQs, to be reassured in both places that there was no more danger for the moment. Some of the children returned to the house by the bridge, to be reclaimed by their parents in the Occupied Zone on the strength of a clever disinformation rumour to the effect that families with children were not, after all, going to be deported. Bouli and Shatta did not believe a word of it and ignored more than eighty desperate telegrams from parents. Instead, they summoned enough Rovers and Rangers to accompany an emergency convoy of forty children across 500 kilometres of 'enemy territory' to the Swiss border and across it.

When 15-year-old Kurt Niedermaier was ordered to present himself at the concentration camp of Septfonds, less than 50 kilometres distant, she hurried on her bicycle from Moissac to Castelsarrassin and confronted Lieutenant Tanvier in the gendarmerie there with the news that his son's closest school-chum was to be deported. Tanvier quietly 'lost' the boy's paperwork and Kurt was safe for the time being. When it came to saving lives, Shatta had no scruples, using bribery and threats of what would happen 'after the end of the war' – a prospect that seemed infinitely remote in 1942. She even managed to 'corrupt' the anti-Semitic assistant police commissioner into so compromising himself that after the Liberation he came to her for an attestation that he had done his bit for the Resistance.

In Chambon-sur-Lignon, pastors Theis and Trocmé did everything possible to prevent an official visit on 10 August of Minister for Youth Lamirand. Considering it inevitable, Unionist Chief Scout Jean Beigbeider tried to smooth things over. The scant official meal over, the cortège drove through the village with no people in the streets and no flags waving or hanging on the houses.

At the football ground, the prefect frigidly quoted Romans 13, verses 1–7, on the respect due to those in authority. After a religious service, all the pupils read an open letter from Trocmé that was on every noticeboard:

Monsieur le Ministre,
We have learned of the scenes of horror three weeks ago in Paris when the French police obeyed the occupying power and arrested in their homes all the Jewish families in Paris to dump them in the Vel d'Hiv. Fathers were torn from their families and deported to Germany and children torn from their mothers, who suffered the same fate. Since we know that the decrees of the occupier will soon be applied to the Free Zone, where they are presented as the spontaneous decisions of the Head of the French State, we fear that deportations of Jews will soon be occurring in the Free Zone.
    We hereby inform you that a number of Jews live among us. We do not differentiate between Jews and non-Jews for that would be contrary to our evangelical teaching. If our comrades, whose sole fault is to have been born in another religion, are ordered to be deported or even registered, they will disobey and we shall hide them as best we can.

Hearing the text read out aloud, Lamirand blenched and replied, 'This has nothing to do with me. Take it up with Monsieur le Préfet.' The following exchange then took place in public:

Prefect: 'Monsieur Trocmé, you are sowing dissension on what should be a day of national harmony.'
Trocmé: 'There can be no national harmony while our brothers are threatened with deportation.'
Prefect: 'In a few days, my staff will come to Chambon to register all the Jews.'
Trocmé: 'We do not know who is a Jew. We only know people.'

When the police arrived two weeks later, the head teacher refused to supply a list of Jewish children. Asked how many there were, he replied, 'None.' Trocmé was summoned to the town hall, where he told the police, 'If I had a list of these people, I should refuse to hand it over to you. They have come in search of aid and protection from the Protestants here, whose pastor I am. A pastor is a shepherd and it is not the job of the shepherd to denounce the lambs entrusted to him.'

Chapter 16

THE PROTESTS GATHER STRENGTH

O n 11 August 1942 Laval agreed to furnish 150,000 workers for STO. The Germans would eventually bring their requirement for French workers to the astonishing figure of 1,575,000 plus the POWs out of a total population of around 40,000,000. However, it is estimated that only 785,000 men and women actually left France under the scheme, half of them deserting on their first home leave.[1] Even before bombs started falling regularly on industrial targets all over the Reich, it was impossible to keep secret that the conditions of work in Germany were far from those promised. The *requis* lived in poorly heated dormitories often adjacent to the target factories; they worked alongside prisoners and forced labourers from a score of conquered territories with no common language; few German women would have anything to do with foreign men; there was little wine and meals were *Eintopf* – a single dish instead of the traditional five-course French lunch and dinner.

The summons from the STO arrived couched in elegant officialese: 'I have the honour to inform you that the joint Franco-German Commission . . . has selected you for work with the Todt Organisation / to work in Germany. I invite you to present yourself at the German Labour Office on . . . to learn the date and time of your departure.' The sting was in the tail: 'Failure to comply with this posting is punishable under the provisions of the law.'

The Todt Organisation was the biggest enterprise in Europe, employing 2,000,000 workers at its peak. If working for it in France was the better of two undesirable alternatives – and a worker could earn in any factory working for the Germans twice the normal rate elsewhere – one German spokesman for the organisation announced in Moissac that, whereas so far Germany had limited itself to taking only half of French production, it would in future take all. So, if one wanted to eat well, the best plan was to work in, or for, Germany. The STO caused severe rifts between the business community and Vichy because the only factories that could keep their labour force intact were those fulfilling German orders and their subcontractors. With no political intent, thousands of young men went underground on receiving their STO call-up. Some lived rough in the forests, and would become the core of the Maquis. Others had it easier. Some neighbours of the author set out for the STO train in a *gazogène* car that conveniently 'broke down' in front of the village gendarme, who obligingly issued a *procès verbal* confirming the breakdown. They continued their journey to the railway station, arriving after the departure of their train. The *procès verbal* stamped a second time, they returned home and were not called again.

The police, gendarmerie, fire services, railways and Civil Defence all offered shelter from the STO, and knew a rush of volunteers. In Moissac, Louis Fourcassié signed up with Le Service de Surveillance des Voies. The wages were low but compensated by extra ration cards. Wearing a blue-and-white armband, equipped with a torch and whistle and a bilingual *Ausweis*, he and a friend patrolled the rail-tracks at night, ostensibly to prevent sabotage. In the event, the guards told *résistants* they encountered to hit them a few times and tie them up, as their alibi for doing nothing.[2]

At Vichy on 4 August an official delegate of the American YMCA protested about the *rafles* and deportations. A few days later Pétain received Donald Lowry, head of the coordinating committee for many charities. The Quakers, refusing to let a sword sleep in their hands, also protested. Slowly and quietly, Catholics and Protestants all over France began deliberately to impede the deportations by hiding Jews – especially children. Many Jews suspected their motives, but very few children followed the adolescent protected by priests at his high school in Orleans who converted and became Cardinal Aron Lustiger, senior churchman of France. The success of this low-key but widespread movement is that a quarter of a million Jews survived the war in France despite the collaboration of police and gendarmerie.

On 12 August 1942 Vichy newspapers made much of the first convoy of prisoners released under La Relève de-training at Compiègne the previous day, but made no mention of the deportation of stateless Jews and other immigrants from the Free Zone At Noé, Rabbi René Kapel's belief that they were going to labour camps took a hard knock when the old and the sick who could not walk were carried in freezing rain more than a mile to the train station. Local residents were so horrified at the emaciated appearance of the prisoners that future departures were arranged at night. A Catholic social worker who witnessed the scene went to Archbishop Jules-Gérard Saliège in Toulouse to ask for his intervention. Saliège, a partially paralysed 72-year-old who had supported the cause of the Spanish refugees, showed more courage than his pope by issuing a pastoral letter condemning Vichy's treatment of its Jews. The letter was read out on 23 August in most parishes of the Haute-Garonne *département*, in which Noé lay. A week later, Cardinal Pierre-Marie Théas, archbishop of Bousquet's home town of Montauban, issued a second pastoral letter protesting against the violations of human dignity. It was read out in every church and would also have been read out at a Mass for the SOL in front of the war memorial in the town but for the diplomatic intervention of Prefect François Martin. He reported all this to Vichy, noting that the population had overwhelmingly approved of the contents of the cardinal's letter.

In the third week of August 1942, 5,000 more Jews were arrested in the Free Zone, police in Nice and Monaco rounding up 548 adults and twelve children, who were sent across France to Drancy en route to Auschwitz. That there were not more children was due largely to the Marcel network founded with the help of Bishop Rémond of Nice by Syrian-born Moussa Abbadi and the woman who would become his wife, Odette Rodenstock.

When shown in Lyons, the Paris winter collections, featuring wasp waists, fitted busts and exaggerated sleeves in artificial fabrics, attracted foreign buyers for the first time during the Occupation, causing the fashion editor of *L'Illustration* to gush that the ingenuity of making little go far was 'the crowning glory of our race'. Whether or not Lyons' Cardinal Archbishop Gerlier read the fashion pages is unknown, but he had often been quoted in the press for hailing Pétain's regime as the New Jerusalem after the corruption of the Third Republic. His realisation that under Vichy's racist legislation Jews were being deported not to labour camps but killing factories in occupied Poland and elsewhere came after 'the Night of Vénissieux'.

Eight kilometres from the centre of Lyons, Vénissieux was the site of an internment camp in some respects worse than Drancy. On one night alone, twenty-six detainees committed suicide. The complex of factory buildings surrounded by five-metre walls was guarded by Vietnamese troops under French officers. Inside the walls, conditions were so appalling that the officials departed, leaving to the volunteer workers of the ecumenical charity Amitié Chrétienne the job of drawing up lists for deportation. They had to deal with 1,300 cases – soul-destroying work, compounded by their commitment to find foster homes for children whose parents had been, or were going to be, deported and killed. In the absence of 'proper authorities', they ignored Bousquet's orders to ship all the detainees to Drancy for onward routing to Auschwitz, and managed to save some 500 adults and 100 children by forging identity papers, altering them to show false ages, arranging escapes and sending 140 people to hospital with faked medical certificates. Many of the children were smuggled out of the camp hidden in the beaten-up old Citroën car belonging to the Jesuit Abbé Alexandre Glasberg. An unlikely-looking hero, with his short, stout build and thick-lensed spectacles, Glasberg was himself a converted Ukrainian Jew, who understood anti-Semitism all too well. Working with him in the camp was the Jesuit Father Pierre Chaillet, from whom Archbishop Gerlier of Lyons learned all the gruesome details.

They could do nothing to save the rump of 545 people who were transported to Drancy, but on the night of 29 August, they packed the camp bus with children and managed to get 108 of them to the Lyons headquarters of EIF. There, twenty or so were kitted out as Scouts and Guides to be sent on a camping trip in the remote countryside, the others being hidden in private homes, for the most part Catholic. Prefect Alexandre Angeli of Lyons furiously demanded that the eighty-four children be handed over. As the patron of Amitié Chrétienne, Cardinal Gerlier backed up Chaillet's refusal to divulge names, after first making a statement that he was still a loyal citizen. Father Chaillet was confined in a psychiatric clinic for three months, in conditions that were no better than they had been in the camp – Vichy had an appalling record for neglect and maltreatment of the mentally handicapped.

At Montauban Prefect François Martin felt and acted very differently from his counterpart in Lyons. Receiving orders to arrest 1,700 Jews shown on the census list, he and his staff did everything possible to ensure that the people affected were warned. This was not simple, for one careless word could reveal him as the source of the warning. So many children were being moved long distances that Shatta had to attend a planning meeting with other organisers in the Hôtel des Alpes near the main station in Grenoble. In the middle of the meeting, two policemen knocked on the door and quickly detected the false ID papers, for which the penalty was torture to uncover the source. Shatta kept her nerve and told them, 'Yes, they are false papers. But we are meeting here to try and save the lives of 200 Jewish children under threat of deportation. You must do what your conscience bids you.' After delivering a warning not to stay so close to the station again, the officers left; their intended victims breathed normally again and took the advice to heart.[3]

Reading an article about police and gendarmerie collaboration in *L'Express* of 6 October 2005, Lucien Janvoie wrote that many gendarmes, such as his own father, made a practice of warning those they were to arrest and turned a deaf ear to denunciations of refugees in hiding once they had realised the fate of those rounded up. In at least one case, at Gap in Provence, an entire company of gendarmes enlisted together in the Maquis and worked against the authorities.[4] Others were engaged on more mundane tasks. The hunt for metal was one: by September 1942 cities had long since lost their bronze statues, but the copper shortage led to a bizarre campaign advertising a reward of a litre of wine for every 200 grams handed in. The logic was that without copper sulphate solution to kill mildew on vines, there would be no grapes next year.

On 2 September Cardinal Gerlier issued a proclamation to read in all the churches of his diocese. It was carefully worded to avoid construction as an attack on Pétain, but the message was clear. Through ecumenical links, Pastor Marc Boegner, as Chairman of the Protestant Federation, wrote to Pétain using the Marshal's own language to equate the inhumane treatment of the Jews with 'moral defeat' and 'an attack on the honour of France'.

The action of the Catholic leaders was doubly courageous in that they were dependent on funds from Vichy for many purposes, including religious schooling. One Catholic historian, Renée Bederrida, reckons that of the eighty or so bishops and archbishops only five or six made public protests after the Vénissieux scandal.[5] Indeed, Cardinal Suhard of Paris, who had married Pétain in a proxy ceremony, and continued to collaborate, was shunned by De Gaulle after the Liberation when eight bishops were obliged to resign.

Lower down the ladder, people from all walks of life played their parts, not always with the total cooperation of their charges, some of whom refused to eat non-kosher food or cut their side-locks, which were an immediate give-away in the street and constituted a terrible risk for their protectors. Those prepared to integrate were found work on remote farms as labourers or au pairs. Sometimes groups were sent to Annemasse on the Swiss border, only 4 kilometres from Geneva, where professional *passeurs* took them across for 300 francs a head. When the professionals judged it was too dangerous, Georges Loinger, a sports *moniteur* working for Les Compagnons de France, devised an unusual way of getting more of these children to safety in Switzerland by refereeing a football match near the border and slipping the children across, one by one, during the game. The actor Marcel Marceau developed a mime routine that would delight the world after the war as his cover for escorting 'theatre groups' of children eastwards. Others were escorted across by Jewish Scouts and Guides.

Pro-Vichy prefects all over the Free Zone attacked this humanitarian initiative, claiming that it had no popular support because most of the population blamed the Jews for the black market, but the Prefect of Montpellier warned that public opinion had been disturbed by the pitiless nature of the persecution. Not all senior public servants were acquiescent rubber stamps: 200 prefects were among the several thousand civil servants dismissed as unreliable. Even the RG reported widespread disapproval of the government's handover of residents in the Free Zone.

Wary of the powder keg that was Lyons – the PCF was particularly active in France's second city – Laval put a brake on the deportations, informing Oberg on 2 September that the Church's attitude meant a slowing-down of the Final Solution in France, but not its abandonment. Oberg seems to have taken this in good part, knowing that Laval had other troubles. On 4 November the multi-venue annual congress of Doriot's PPF brought to Paris 7,198 delegates from eighty-eight collaborationist organisations. Their in-fighting on hold for the moment, Eugène Deloncle shared the platform at the Vel d'Hiv with Doriot and Déat, whose Hitler moustache made him look more like the Führer than ever when his lank hair fell forward over his temple as he thumped the rostrum to hammer home his points.

So many PPF members were marching through the streets in their SS-type uniforms that Laval feared a coup was brewing and Abwehr officer Oskar Reile was paying 160,000 francs a month to a mole inside PPF headquarters to let him see files on Doriot's ever-closer ties with the SS and SD.[6] To keep the balance of power, Abetz now backed Laval in forbidding Doriot to make the closing address of the congress in the Vel d'Hiv, stirring 20,000 supporters to gather near PPF HQ in rue des Pyramides. Those within earshot heard Doriot say that Pétain should ask Germany to defend French interests in North Africa. Was he prescient, or was there a security leak? This was four days before the Allied landings in Morocco.

The PPF's enemy at home was an easier target: transports totalling 10,522 prisoners had transited from the Free Zone by 15 September, the shortfall being made up by greater police activity in the Occupied Zone and a bending of the rules so that previously exempt categories could be arrested. A total of 2,000 Greek and Romanian Jews were arrested in Paris and *rafles* carried out in twenty provincial cities of the Occupied Zone to fill the cattle-trucks of the forty-second and forty-third transports, which dragged their cargoes of misery eastwards on 9 and 11 November 1942 after an article on 8 November in *Au Pilori* by political editor Maurice De Séré stating that 'the Jewish question must be resolved immediately by the arrest and deportation of *all* Jews without exception'.[7]

That month Jan Karski arrived clandestinely from Warsaw with eyewitness reports on the Polish ghettos and Belzec extermination camp. During two weeks spent in Paris, what shocked him most was the apathy of the French population to the Occupation – a fact commented on by Abetz and others, and which was largely a result of people's preoccupation with getting the next meal, or extra clothing coupons, or grey-market food at the weekends. The diary of a Parisian housewife for October 1942 goes some way to explaining this.

7.30	At the baker's. Got bread. Rusks later.
9.00	Butcher says only meat on Saturday.
9.30	Cheese shop. Says he will have some cheese at 5 p.m.
10.00	Tripe shop. My ticket No. 32 will come up at 4 p.m.
10.30	Grocer's. Vegetables only at 5 p.m.
11.00	Return to baker. Rusks, but no bread.[8]

At 4 p.m. she had to be back at the tripe shop. At 5 p.m. came the dilemma: cheese or vegetables? And so it went on, day after day. In addition, there were effectively three price levels:

	legal price	grey market	black market
1 kg butter	42 F	69 F	107 F
12 eggs	20 F	35 F	53 F
1 kg chicken meat	24 F	38 F	48 F

On some items the mark-up was grotesque: farmers sold potatoes for 3 francs per kg; in Paris they cost five times as much. With average wages frozen at 1,500 francs per month for men and 1,300 francs for women, shopping around was time-consuming and exhausting.[9]

In September it became known that the appalling overcrowding, lack of sanitation and medicine and inadequate rations at Rivesaltes camp had claimed the lives of 60 of the 140 infants in the camp during the preceding two and a half months.[10]

Among the children released as a gesture to improve conditions, fifteen were sent to a Catholic orphanage near Montpellier, to put some fat on their emaciated bodies before travelling two weeks later by train to Moissac. In the camps, the inadequate rations were often seized by the guards and sold to detainees with money. Prisoners without money or food parcels from outside were close to starvation. A letter from Röthke to RHSA Ref IV B4 dated 6 November 1942 annouced the departure from the station of Le Bourget of convoy 901/36 to Auschwitz under the command of Feldwebel Ullmeier. According to the last sentence, it included '1,000 Jews with rations for fourteen days.'[11] Since the deportees were given no food for the journey, this poses the question, was everyone on the take, even up to Röthke's level?

In the early hours of 2 October the flash of a torch from a field near Vendôme, midway between Orleans and Le Mans, was spotted by the pilot of an RAF Hudson whose passenger waiting to drop was one of the tragic players in what Kipling romantically labelled 'the Great Game'. Colonel Buckmaster of SOE's F Section was sending in an agent to build the largest network of the Resistance, for which Francis Anthony Suttill, a 33-year-old lawyer qualified in both Britain and France, had chosen the name of a fifth-century theologian, Prosper of Aquitaine. With no idea that his Prosper network was to be a cynical deception plan costing the lives of several hundred French patriots, he immediately set about recruiting agents throughout northern France with very poor security until several *thousand* people were involved. At the same time, another far too large network known as Scientist was growing in the south-west.

At Norfolk House in St James's Square in London was the office of Chief of Staff to the (future) Supreme Allied Commander. COSSAC was also the umbrella beneath which several shadowy sub-organisations lurked – in particular, the London Controlling Section. The ambiguous title cloaked a deception factory run by Colonel John Bevan, among whose creative brains was Wing Commander Dennis Wheatley, later to be a world-famous author. The first Controlling Officer, Colonel Oliver Stanley, had resigned rather than deliberately misinform Resistance agents regarding the Dieppe raid with a view to letting them be caught and reveal, under torture, their false information in order to convince Hitler that the raid was a prelude to a full-scale invasion.

A stockbroker in civilian life, Bevan was made of sterner stuff. Like De Gaulle, he considered that in total war civilian lives could be spent with no more compunction than a general feels when sending his men to certain death in a militarily justifiable operation. It was already known in London that an invasion of the Continent could not be made before the spring of 1944, but Bevan's plan was to use SOE's Section F to pass to its agents in France 'confidential' information about an invasion in the spring of 1943 – as Churchill had promised Stalin. Some would be caught and divulge this information, causing Hitler to keep in France more forces than necessary, and thus weaken his eastern front. The name of the game was Operation Cockade.[12]

On 8 November 1942 the Allied landings in North Africa caused Pétain to require the departure of Ambassador Leahy, who handed the embassy building over to chargé d'affaires Somerville P. Tuck. Tuck had been lobbying the Marshal to let 5,000 children at risk emigrate on State Department visas, but the initiative came to nothing.[13] At the time of the landings, Gen De la Porte du Theil was making a tour of inspection of the Chantiers *groupement* in Algeria commanded by regional commissioner Van Hecke, an ex-Foreign Legion officer. Shortly before leaving France, the general had been informed that Van Hecke had had 'compromising' contacts with US Consul Robert Murphy in Algiers but, true to his policy of leaving subordinates the maximum freedom of action, he did not broach the subject during the visit.

Van Hecke was in fact one of the 'group of five' officers conspiring with Murphy to smooth the path of the invading Allies. De La Porte du Theil decided to fly back from Constantine to France the very next day but, before leaving, delegated full powers to Van Hecke and ordered him to disregard any orders he might be obliged to send after his return to France. In Vichy, De La Porte du Theil reported to Pétain and Gen Weygand, who was arrested the following day by the Germans and deported as a hostage. At that moment, the creator of the Chantiers had no reason to think that he would one day follow in Weygand's footsteps.

PART THREE

1944 – THE BEGINNING OF THE END

Chapter 17

SOAP AND SABOTAGE

The last pretence of Vichy's autonomy disappeared on 11 November 1942. Not even Laval could hope for a favourable outcome of an eventual peace conference after Hitler tore up the Armistice agreement and his forces drove across the Demarcation Line to occupy the whole of France, save only the Italian pockets in the south-east and Corsica, also occupied by Italy. Support for Pétain dwindled overnight to a diehard 30 per cent, most of his supporters only continuing to believe in him *because there was no one else.*

On 12 November the tired old man in the pin-striped suit told Guillaume De Tournemire, 'I've decided that my duty is to stay here. I'm aware that I have lost my prestige, but by doing this I shall protect France from some of the misfortunes she would suffer without me.' De Tournemire protested his personal loyalty while adding that it would not stop him working against the occupiers. Pétain replied, 'Do all you can, but be prudent for the sake of your young members. I shall do what I can to help. Good luck!' Three days later, Pétain received his former *chef de cabinet* Roger De Saivre, who told the Marshal that he intended making for North Africa to get back into the fight. Pétain embraced him, saying, 'If I were your age, I'd do the same. But, as it is, my place is here. Good luck, my son.'

With the Allied invasion of North Africa, OKW had no choice but to secure the southern coast of France from the Spanish border to Italy. The next step, on 17 November, was Operation Lilac: the disarmament of Vichy's puny army, one unforeseen consequence of which was that many officers and men decided to act according to their own consciences, forming the disciplined Armée Secrète, separate from the political factions of the Resistance. Based in Pau, Captain André Pommiès had created a network of arms dumps throughout the south-west. Yet, within a week of the invasion, many dumps had been betrayed by local informers. So the strategy of Armée Secrète was simple: the Germans could only police directly one-quarter of French territory, leaving the remaining three-quarters to a network of informers, *miliciens* and pro-Vichy functionaries. If the underground army terrorised these *collabos* into changing sides, the Germans could control only where they had a physical presence.

In demobilising the 2nd Dragoons at Auch, Lt Col Schlesser told each man to keep in touch with comrades and hold himself ready for the call. Some demobilised men slipped away from their homes in darkness; others made

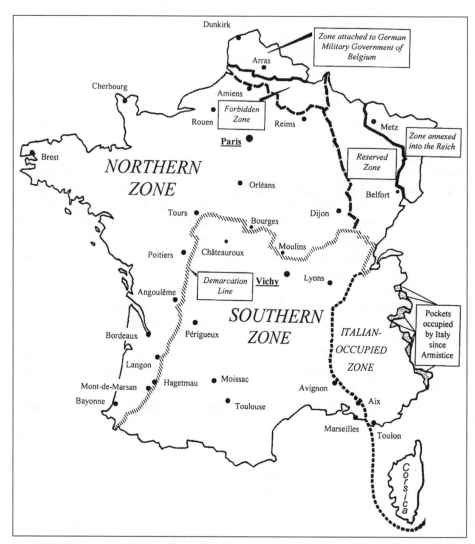

Occupied France after 11 November 1942.

gestures of defiance, like Lieutenant Narcisse Geyer who rode out of 2nd Cuirassiers barracks in Lyons on horseback in full uniform and kept riding until contacting a Maquis unit in the bleak limestone uplands of the Vercors. In Algeria, Van Hecke posted the 40,000 young men serving in the Chantiers to the army, where they began weapons training immediately, later fighting the Afrika Korps in Tunisia alongside Allied forces and participating in the invasion of Italy in 1943 and France in 1944.

De Saivre was travelling in company with Prince Napoleon and his personal secretary. Officially exiled from France as pretender to the throne, the prince had volunteered for the Foreign Legion in March 1940, only to have the recruiting sergeant reject his Swiss nationality and accuse him of being a French deserter! The three had met up while unsuccessfully trying to find a flight from Geneva to London and were planning to cross the Pyrenees and make their way to Britain. During their journey south from Toulouse in the rear of a butcher's van, they were nearly caught by a German patrol. Once in the mountains, slowed down by De Saivre suffering agony from his new boots, they were tracked down, arrested and driven to the town of Foix, where the Prefect sneered, 'So you're Prince Napoleon? Where's Joan of Arc? And you're De Saivre, the Marshal's *chef de cabinet*? Take them away!' Their next four months were spent in a succession of German prisons.[1]

By now it was nearly impossible to find a Breton fishing boat on which to sail away to England one moonless night. Although an estimated 30,000 people escaped over the Pyrenees during the Occupation, half of them in 1943,[2] they risked among other things betrayal by their guides. On 24 November five men from Paris paid to be taken over the mountains without being caught by the Austrian ski and dog patrols. First stop was Henriette Courdil's hotel at Ussat-les-Bains, where she emptied two dozen books from the suitcase of newspaper editor Jacques Grumbach and told him to carry only essentials in his backpack, which was also full of books. At the last moment an English driver from the Paris branch of Rolls-Royce joined them, as they left the hotel with Spanish guides Lazare Cabrero and Valeriano Trallero.

Grumbach was soon exhausted by the weight of his pack. At 1 a.m., in a mountain refuge with a temperature of −10 degrees Centigrade, Cabrero forced him to dump more books. At dawn, Grumbach fell for the hundredth time and broke an ankle. With the others resting higher up, Cabrero returned to Grumbach, shot him with his revolver and took his watch and wallet after hiding the body behind some rocks. Pretending he had not been able to find the laggard, he announced on rejoining the group that they owed him 25,000 francs each, if they wanted to be taken the rest of the way. They argued that they had already paid 35,000 francs each. 'Not to me,' retorted Cabrero. 'I don't get any of that. So make your minds up.' By scraping together all the money they had with them, the five men raised 40,000 francs, which Cabrero accepted with the addition of a promissory note for 100,000 francs signed by Pierre Dreyfus-Schmidt, the *député* for Belfort. Grumbach's body was not found for eight years, although Cabrero meantime confessed to Madame Courdil that he had 'done in the guy with glasses, who could not keep up'.

The Marshal's confusion after the German takeover is illustrated by his broadcast to the nation a week after giving De Tournemire his blessing and only four days after sending De Saivre and the prince on their way. 'I have decided to increase the powers of Mr Laval,' he announced ingenuously. 'But I remain your guide. You have only one duty: to obey.' On 13 December, Laval was kidding no one when he declared, 'A German victory will save our civilisation from falling into Communism. An American victory would be a triumph for the Jews and Communists.'

The biggest prize the Germans coveted in invading the southern zone was the French Mediterranean Fleet in Toulon harbour, getting their hands on which might have changed the course of the war. At 4.40 a.m. on 27 November the first German troops attacked the naval base. At 5.25 a.m. the doors of the arsenal were blown in by German shells. Immediately signals were sent by radio and semaphore to scuttle the fleet and crews abandoned ship with the exception of sabotage teams. The town was rocked by explosions sending 235,000 tonnes of prime seagoing force to the bottom of the harbour. Some of the cruisers continued to burn for several days. One small surface vessel braved the German minefields to make for the high sea with five submarines. Despite the atrocity of Mers el-Kebir, Admiral Darlan had kept his word to Winston Churchill.

With the Wehrmacht came the German security services. Establishing himself in the luxurious Hôtel Terminus adjacent to Lyons' main railway station, SS-Obersturmführer Klaus Barbie was a psychopath who enjoyed whipping prisoners, pulling out finger and toe nails, pistol-whipping faces and burning his naked victim's sensitive body parts with heated pokers. When bored, he interrupted interrogations at which he had been fondling his French mistress and played the piano for her pleasure. This was the man who was recognised by a personal citation from Himmler on 18 September 1943 and the award of the Iron Cross first class with oak leaves and swords on 9 November 1943.[3]

Forty years later, *résistant* Jean Gay trembled when recalling how he was trussed to a pole unable to move for two consecutive days, suffering severe cramps while repeatedly nearly drowned in alternately scalding and near-freezing water. To add mental agony, Barbie informed him that his two sons had been arrested and were being tortured in cellars below the hotel. Prisoners in the vermin-ridden, unventilated cells of Lyons' Montluc prison regularly saw their predecessors at Barbie's interrogations return bleeding, unconscious, with broken limbs and eyes literally gouged out. To demonstrate his contempt for the *Untermenschen* he was terrorising, Barbie strolled without a bodyguard after interrogations to dine in Lyons' famous gourmet restaurants.

With one extraordinary exception, there were only two ways out of his private hell: summoned 'without baggage', a prisoner knew he was to be shot; summoned 'with baggage', he was en route to a concentration or death camp. Just before Barbie left Lyons, 100 corpses were found floating in the rivers Rhône and Saône, some shot, others beaten to death. It is necessary to recount these obscenities in order to comprehend why many captives confessed before torture even started.

To detect Jews with false papers, the Gestapo paid Ukrainian and White Russian anti-Semites to spot victims in the street and at railway stations – one of whom was Simone Veil, who survived deportation to become first president of the European parliament. A handful of brave young men calling themselves L'Armée Juive were so successful in assassinating these human sniffer-dogs that the supply of volunteers dried up completely.

Much has rightly been made of the heroism of people who helped downed Allied aircrew. Around the end of November 1942 – the dates are difficult to establish, since all those involved paid with their lives – a politically uncommitted truck driver named Gaston Brogniard picked up a Canadian airman, whose aircraft had been shot down near Le Touquet. Concealing him in the rear of the truck, he took him home, despite knowing the penalties, and asked his friend André Baleuw to procure a false identity card. For greater safety, the unidentified Canadian was then transferred first to the house of a friend, Madame Duquesnoy, and then to another friend, surnamed Illidge, who was the wife of a British POW in a camp near Breslau. Another friend called Roger Snoek made contact with an escape network based in Paris. The dates become clearer after Brogniard and his little group of friends were betrayed and arrested by the Gestapo on 27 December. Interned at Le Touquet's Hôtel Westminster and in Boulogne prison, they were condemned to death at Loos-lès-Lille on 18 February 1943. Brogniard, Baleuw and Snoek were shot on 20 July 1943. André Lagache and Madame Illidge were deported to Germany on 9 August 1943.[4]

In Paris, the rich were getting richer and the poor hungrier. On 11 December the sale of the Viau collection at the Hôtel Drouot realised a record total of 47,000,000 francs, including 5,000,000 francs paid by a German purchaser for Cézanne's *Montagne Sainte-Geneviève*. Among celebrities handing out food to the needy in the street outside was Maurice Chevalier, but Sacha Guitry was too busy: having block-booked the restaurant Carrère in rue Pierre-Charron for his private New Year party, he wittily listed the menu as 'Maybe fish, Perhaps roast beef, Probably poultry, Sort-of vegetables, Possibly salad, Theoretically dessert. Wines: red, white and blue.'

In the last six months of 1942, the seven gendarmes stationed in the village of Collonges in the Rhone-Alpes, 4 kilometres from the Swiss frontier, arrested more than fifty people walking along the N206 road or across country and charged them with violating their 'assignation to a forced residence'. One of their victims, Szandla G, confessed that she had paid 38,000 francs to a guide to take her and her two daughters safely across. 'I had the impression,' she told the arresting officers sadly, 'that our money interested him more than getting us across the border.' A week later she and one daughter started the long journey to Auschwitz.[5]

When the same gendarmes interrogated the proprietor of a local workmen's restaurant, he admitted taking 5,000 francs or more from each refugee he put in touch with a *passeur*, who had to be paid separately. At the end of August, two families hiding above a watch-repair shop were introduced to a young man of 23, who offered to take them across the border. A price was agreed and paid, but he betrayed them at the frontier wire –

according to the gendarmerie report 'because my oath to the SOL made it my duty'.[6]

Immediately after the occupation of the southern zone, few Germans were seen in Moissac. Seeing men in field-grey walking with Frenchwomen in Montauban and Toulouse, Marie-Rose Dupont was disgusted because her father had brought her up to think of *les Boches* as the enemy, having himself been a POW in Germany in 1914–18. In the northern zone, it was a far more common sight. By mid-1943 80,000 French women had claimed child benefit from the German authorities and asked that their offspring be given German nationality because fathered by a German soldier.[7]

One busy morning a civilian entered Marie-Rose's salon, flashed a Gestapo ID card and asked to step into the apartment behind the salon, to talk in private. She explained that it was let, without saying that her tenants were a Jewish refugee couple recommended by Shatta Simon. The *gestapiste* refused to talk in the street, because it was 'too public', and said he would return when she closed at noon. She could not imagine what he wanted, unless it was in connection with the grey marketing essential for running the salon. When he returned at 12.15 p.m. there was still one elderly lady under the dryer. 'Get rid of her,' he ordered. 'I can't,' Marie-Rose explained. 'Her hair's still wet, but she can't hear anything with the blower on. What can I do for you?'

He showed her a list with four names on it. The woman under the dryer pushed the hood back and shouted at the top of her powerful peasant voice, 'Why are you bothering my daughter? Go away and leave her alone!' To Marie-Rose's amazement, the *gestapiste* blushed and fled in confusion, leaving the list on the cash-desk. 'That's the way to treat those swine,' observed her client, calmly pulling the dryer back over her head.

One of the names on the list was of a man working opposite the salon, so Marie-Rose hurried across to warn him. He disappeared that afternoon, and presumably so did the other three, but she never knew what that was all about.

Arriving in Marseilles by the same train as Oberg on 22 January, Bousquet personally supervised the cordoning off of the whole city, with 12,000 police assembled for a thirty-six-hour *rafle* that filtered 40,000 people through ID checks. The police having passed warnings, only thirty known criminals and Resistance workers were interned in a special camp near Fréjus. To turn failure to triumph, 2,200 immigrants were arrested, including numerous Czechs and Poles who had fought in the Foreign Legion during the Battle of France. Many were Jewish, and it was no coincidence that the Final Solution's transport expert Adolf Eichmann was on the spot to organise their transfer to Drancy. The Old Port of Marseilles, a maze of narrow streets and alleyways following medieval street patterns, which both Vichy police and the Germans considered a haven for criminals and *résistants*, was demolished by German sappers on 24 January.

On 30 January Darnand's SOL became the Milice, backed by the Catholic credentials of Philippe Henriot, who proclaimed that recruitment was open to physically suitable men 'of good will who wish to serve their country'. In a broadcast on 30 March over Vichy radio, he announced that the Milice was to be 'an order of knighthood [implementing] the Marshal's national revolution to give France back her soul'. Defying the open disapproval of Cardinals Gerlier and Suhard, the *abbé* Bouillon appointed himself its national chaplain. Honoured with the rank of SS-Obersturmführer, Darnand now had his own army equipped by the Germans and trained alongside men of the LVF. By the end of the year, it numbered 10,000 men and women with their own training school and newspaper called *Combats*.

On 11 February, 210 young Alsatians of both sexes gathered by the calvary outside the village of Riespach. Twenty-three lost their nerve and returned home but the others, armed with two hunting rifles and two revolvers, made it safely through 15 kilometres of broken country to safety in Switzerland. The following night another group from Ballersdorf – 12 kilometres further from the frontier – was not so lucky. Surrounded by German troops, the eighteen boys returned fire with four rifles. One only escaped to Switzerland; the others were shot in the sand-pit above the entrance of the nearby concentration camp of Natzwiller and incinerated there.[8] On 13 February two police officers arrived in Chambon to arrest pastors Trocmé and Theis, escorting them to the concentration camp at St-Paul-d'Eyjeaux near Limoges. After five weeks' confinement, they were released a few days before all the other prisoners were deported. It is thought that none returned.

On 15 February men coming of age in 1940, 1941 and 1942 were called up for STO. In the southern zone, one-third of them were serving in the Chantiers de Jeunesse, where De La Porte du Theil issued them with fifteen-day leave passes and a written instruction to report for STO at the end of their leave. Roughly half of them interpreted this as tacit permission to desert. Resistance tracts proclaimed that going to work in Germany meant living under Allied bombs and that leaving France was treachery. For once the Communists and the Church were on the same side. On 21 March Cardinal Liénart announced in Lyons that turning up for the STO was not a duty of conscience, while in the street posters of the Feldkommandantur threatened 'pitiless sanctions' for those who did not present themselves at the recruitment centres and railway stations to catch their trains. One alternative was to find a job with a German agency in France, so 2,000 joined the Kriegsmarine as fitters and guards and 1,982 donned German uniform as drivers in NSKK Motorgruppe, freeing Germans for more military tasks. The Organisation Todt employed 3,000 more in uniform as armed guards for construction sites, where the labour was a mixture of local *requis*, who were paid a reasonable wage, and slave labourers from the East. On 7 October that year, Laval did another deal with Speer, under which 10,000 factories were designated 'S' and their workers exempted from the STO.

At Vesoul in Franche-Comté only three of 400 STO conscripts reported for duty; in the Jura twenty-five out of 850; in Seine-et-Loire only thirty-one from 3,700.[9] The attitude of many police officers towards arresting defaulters was summed up by Lieutenant Theret, head of the detachment at Paris' Gare d'Orsay. He warned his men on 9 March 1943 that he 'would not find a single STO dodger and counted on them to do likewise as good Frenchmen'.[10]

The word *maquis* meant simply 'scrubland'; STO runaways were said to *prendre le maquis* as in the report by Gendarmerie *chef d'escadron* Calvayrac in Haute-Savoie dated 22 March 1943: 'No-shows for STO are so numerous that only fifty of 340 reported in. Many men have abandoned their homes, their work and their family *to take to the maquis* instead.'[11] From there, *maquis* came to mean collectively 'those hiding in rough country' and *maquisard* was coined to mean 'a man hiding in remote country'.

Another expression achieving legitimacy in the Petit Larousse dictionary was 'black market', defined for the first time after the law of 15 March 1943 detailed severe penalties for illicit trafficking. As an example of inflation, an egg cost 1.75 francs in 1941; now it cost in Paris as much as 11 francs – more than a skilled worker earned in an hour. When the two neologisms collided, the result was bloodshed. PCF member Georges Guingouin now effectively governed a remote area of the Limousin, where his printed communiqués, signed in his own name as 'Prefect of the Maquis', fixed agricultural prices and banned black marketeering. The penalty for transgression was not a fine, but a bullet. He also used traditional trade unionist methods to slow down industrial and agricultural production in the area, rather than open sabotage, which invited reprisals.[12]

On 20 March Italian Inspector-General for Racial Policy, Guido Lospinoso, arrived in Nice, backed up by the debonair Under-Secretary of State for Foreign Affairs, former ambassador to the Court of St James, Giuseppe Bastianini. The latter had arranged the escape of 17,000 Jews from Dalmatia when he was Governor-General of the occupied province. Lospinoso and Bastianini informed the Germans in Nice that Italy was going to take responsibility for the Jewish question in the south-east because the French were dragging their feet. The truth was quite different: on 21 March the Italian army of occupation received the following instruction: 'The Number One priority is to save Jews living in French territory occupied by our troops, whether they be Italians, French or foreigners.'

A first convoy of 2,500 Jewish refugees was bussed from the coast to Megève, St-Gervais and other Alpine resorts, where the Italian authorities accommodated them and provided new identity cards. Italian–German relations deteriorated after Lospinoso ignored several protests from Knochen in Paris, and SS officer Heinz Röthke planned to kidnap banker Angelo Donati, a central figure in the Italian rescue operation. André Chaigneau, the newly appointed prefect in Nice, declared his willingness to work with the Italians, but not the Germans or his own master, Bousquet.

On 5 April Vichy handed Daladier, Blum, Reynaud, Mandel and Gamelin over to the Germans as VIP hostages. On 11 April the Vel d'Hiv was packed with thousands of uniformed PPF members reaffirming their loyalty to the Party with Hitler salutes in protest at Allied bombing raids. On 15 April, to combat the rise in prices of goods wanted by the German purchasing agencies, all German offices closed at midday, cancelling all pending deals. Although that day was a Thursday, to get around a ban imposed by the Feldkommandantur of Dunkirk, a memorial Mass was celebrated there for René Bonpain, who had been the parish priest in the suburb of Rosendaël. An enormous crowd of believers and unbelievers stood in and outside the church of St-Martin in silent tribute. Bonpain had been condemned for his intelligence-gathering activities. After prolonged torture by the Gestapo in neighbouring Malo-les-Bains, he had been shot with three other members of the Alliance network the previous month.[13]

In Paris on 16 April 1943 a second agreement was signed between Bousquet and Oberg, with Article 5 stipulating that the Feldgendarmerie would henceforward deal only with discipline and protection of German personnel, while the French police services would take over repression in both zones. While the agreement was being signed, at 4.08 p.m. British bombs rained down again on Nantes. Whatever had been the theoretical target, 600 civilians were sufficiently injured to be taken to the main hospital where thirty-six doctors and nurses lay dead in the ruins. The total of deaths rose to 1,150, plus injured who had lost limbs, eyesight or otherwise had their lives blighted.

Also in April the daily ration of bread was reduced to 120 grams per adult and the quality can be judged by the requirement that bakers produce 134kg of bread from 100kg of flour, additives including sawdust. By early summer 1943 green vegetables were rationed, meat was unobtainable except on the black market and 1kg of butter cost 350 francs, as against 250 in May 1942. With salaries frozen at the 1940 level, 71 per cent of Parisians' income was devoted to food, if one can believe the statistics produced at the time. The Institut Dourdin published its survey of incomes on 5 July: of 2,600 sample households totalling 6,729 people, 83 per cent had more than one wage-earner and more than 30 per cent had supplementary pensions or allowances. The most telling statistic was the average monthly income per person: at 876 francs, it was approximately the black market price for two kilos of butter! Deaths from malnutrition, hypothermia and lack of medicine pushed civil mortalities to 169 per cent of pre-war levels, which so alarmed the Propaganda Staffel that it recommended a forced exodus to remove 1,000,000 'useless mouths' from the capital.[14] Aperitifs, tobacco, bed linen, shoes, torch batteries and shaving cream had become unobtainable in shops. The money economy was failing; barter became the rule, with people rhyming, 'The cobbler's got some ribbon, the hairdresser's got cheese. Everybody's got to swap in times like these.'

On alcohol-banned days, known as les jours sans, or 'days without', regular patrons at a café or restaurant in Paris ordered 'my usual coffee' with a wink to the waiter and found in the cup a black-market digestif or apéritif.

Cartoonist Aldebert drew a smirking waiter whispering in a client's ear, 'In the soup, Monsieur, you'll find a whole chicken stuffed with two mutton chops.' People joked, 'Save paper! Don't throw away your used Metro ticket, but use it to wrap your weekly meat ration after sealing the perforations, so the meat doesn't fall through.'[15] Behind the jokes was a national propaganda campaign against the black market.

Nobody lucky enough to have cigarettes threw away the dog-ends, which were kept to re-roll for another smoke. Extraordinary ersatz tobacco mixtures were sold, the most bizarre being 'Belgian tobacco', a concoction of gossamer spider silk said to resemble 'the pubic hair of Venetian blondes'![16] Real soap had disappeared, and the substitute blocks disintegrated on contact with water to a gritty paste. Workers in dirty jobs had the right to extra 'soap', but the repeated queuing to collect it took up a working day, which they could ill afford. No wonder that in July 1943 Captain Flouquet of the Lyons gendarmerie reported that 'the mood of the population is very negative. People criticise every initiative of the government and listen favourably to English radio. They consider the Germans to be the main enemy.'[17]

An instant hit on the BBC French Service was *The Partisans' Song*, which everyone thought had been written by a few *maquisards* around a hidden campfire, the chords being plucked out on a guitar. The truth is more prosaic. The BBC wanted a pompous signature tune for the programme *Honneur et Patrie*, but Emmanuel Astier de la Vigerie and a group of other Free French in London disagreed. On 30 May, between midday and 4 p.m. somewhere in the London suburbs, *The Partisans' Song* was written by Maurice Druon and his uncle Joseph Kessel, who had escaped together from France at Christmas 1942, with music by singer-songwriter Anna Marly. It was a call to arms: 'Come up from the mines, comrades. Come down from the hills . . .' There was no ambiguity about its message: 'We break the bars of our brothers' prisons . . . If you fall, a friend will take your place.'

In May, there were 1,284 Allied air raids against 793 different towns, with Cambrai bombed eleven times and Douai nine times. In June, 2,307 raids hit 1,572 targets. By the end of August an estimated half a million high-explosive and 35,317 incendiary bombs had dropped on French towns. In Le Havre all the water mains had burst, leaving the fire service to lay hoses from canals and the sea, until they finally ran out of diesel fuel for the pump engines and had to beg some from passing Germans. Equipment was so worn out now that units borrowed car batteries from garage-owners to feed emergency lighting. Civil Defence trucks toured the devastated areas with food, drinking water, clothing and fuel for heating and cooking. The Red Cross and the Refugee Service also did what they could. Central government could do little except despatch special crisis trains to the worst-hit areas, each with its own operating theatre, a thirty-bed emergency ward, a midwifery section, a kitchen able to provide 14,000 meals and supplies of clothing and bedding for the homeless.

Chapter 18

CASUALTIES IN THE GREAT GAME

In the northern zone very little stockpiling of arms had been possible. There was a desperate need for weapons, explosives and ammunition, which the RAF was ordered to deliver. Weighing 2.5 tonnes, a typical consignment included six Brens, twenty-seven Stens, thirty-six .303 rifles, five automatic pistols, 18,000 rounds of ammunition, Mills grenades and 8kg of plastic explosive with detonators, plus medical kits. Sometimes chocolate, money and cigarettes were stuffed into empty spaces.

Each mission required a reception party on the ground willing to hide the matériel. In May 1943 Rodolphe Faytout, a farmer in Pujols-sur-Dordogne persuaded Pierre Mignon and a dozen other friends that 'it was time to do something'.[1] None of them knew how he communicated with London, but all were exhilarated by the first drop. Transported in Faytout's small van, the consignment was dispersed on several different properties. For each subsequent operation, a different small field was chosen in this area of woodland and mixed farming, always distant from the towns where the Germans were based. The group undertook no military action, but as the months went by, the hidden stocks mounted steadily, distribution helped by the relaxation of travel restrictions across the Demarcation Line after 2 March 1943.

The BBC coded personal messages confirming each 'shipment' were listened for by 17-year-old Cathérine Bouchou in the hamlet of St-Antoine-de-Queyret.[2] Since her father was the mayor's part-time secretary, she helped him make false papers with genuine ID cards and the Mairie's rubber stamps. Cathérine's mother and younger sister knew nothing of this and, like many people unwilling to get personally involved, Mayor Chanut simply turned a blind eye.

On 21 August after the news from London, Cathérine heard, *'Jacqueline a une robe rouge. Je répète. Jacqueline a une robe rouge.'* Jacqueline's red dress was to be 'Annette', a radio operator arriving to replace an arrested predecessor working for SOE officer George Starr, code-name 'Hilaire', who was staying in the Bouchou house. 'Annette' was Yvonne Cormeau, widow of a Belgian RAF officer killed during the London blitz when a bomb destroyed their house while he was home on leave. Mother of two young children, she joined the WAAF and volunteered to work for Maurice Buckmaster's F Section as a way of avenging her husband.

The drop was to take place in the meadow behind the Bouchou home at 1 a.m. on 22 August. Cathérine recalls a full moon that night, and the aircraft flying in so low on its first pass that Faytout's little group thought it was going to hit her house. Anxious not to drop 'Annette' in the surrounding woods, the RAF pilot over-corrected, landing her in the Bouchous' vineyard, where she lost a shoe and tore her skirt on the stakes before recovering the transmitter and a suitcase of money dropped with her. Beneath each of nine other parachutes blossoming in the moonlight swung a man-size container. With their contents hidden in the Bouchous' barn, Faytout's group split up and returned home. The original intention to disperse the weapons next day was prevented by an ancient Heinkel HE 46 biplane used as a spotter plane flying low-and-slow over the area.

Determining the position of a transmitter requires only two direction-finding vans: spaced apart, their bearings intersect at the source of the transmissions. In an alarming lapse of security, 'Hilaire' kept 'Annette' transmitting his backlog of messages from Cathérine's bedroom for five days. Her SOE set was so large and cumbersome that on one occasion when stopped at a German checkpoint, 'Annette' convinced the bored soldiers that it was X-ray equipment, in keeping with her current cover identity as a district nurse. With a combination of nerve and luck, she went on to make a record 400 transmissions over thirteen months without being caught, not seeing Cathérine again until they met during a *This is Your Life* programme devoted to Yvonne Cormeau's life on 8 November 1989.

Faytout's group received several other drops, unaware that SS Officer Helmut Demetrio, based in the former savings bank adjacent to the Hôtel des Voyageurs in Castillon, had them in his sights. His slender build, spectacles and habitual slight smile did nothing to soften Demetrio's face, marred by duelling-type scars on upper lip and chin. With his interpreter Heinrich – called 'Cosh' because of the way he punctuated questions – Demetrio had already tortured many suspects and line-crossers who fell into his hands.

The fatal drop took place on 20 October at the farm of Lucienne Beaupertuis and her husband near Pujols, after which the ammunition and weapons were hidden in a woodshed for dispersal when fog grounded the spotter plane. The arrest next day of Faytout, followed by that of Pierre Mignon and several others, made it plain that Faytout had talked. As to how much he had given away, the answer came swiftly. Lucienne's husband was arrested while she was out shopping. At his trial post-Liberation, Heinrich the Cosh said proudly, 'That one I played with, like a cat plays with a mouse.' Four days after his arrest, a black Citroën drove up to Lucienne's farm. Faytout got out and indicated the shed where the arms had first been hidden. French-speaking SS men jumped down from the truck behind the Citroën and started hunting for them, but they had already been buried elsewhere, despite the spotter plane. When Demetrio and Cosh came into the farm kitchen, the latter's first words to Lucienne were, 'Your husband has spilled the beans. He said you would tell us where the arms now are.'

She knew that was a lie, because if he had cracked they would already know. Seated on the kitchen table with a loaded pistol pointed at her, she was roughed-up and questioned for four or five hours. Knowing that one of her arrested friends had been found hanged in his cell with an eye torn out of its socket after interrogation by these two men, she became so traumatised that her throat dried up completely and she could neither speak, nor move hand or foot. Faytout was called in to break the deadlock, but could only stare at the floor in silence until told to 'piss off back to the car' by Heinrich the Cosh.

With a mine-detector from Castillon the arms were soon found, Lucienne trusting her husband not to have involved her, even under torture. At dusk, everything was loaded onto the truck. Some time after the Germans' departure, Lucienne's paralysis wore off and her voice returned. Realising that she had forgotten all about her daughter, who should have been home from school long since, she ran to a neighbours' house, hoping she was there. Without opening the door, they warned her to keep away, in case she was being watched, so she spent the night anguished for her husband and child, only learning next morning that other neighbours had heard about the raid on the farm and taken her daughter home with them.

One by one all the others were picked up, including Cathérine's father, Marius Bouchou. There were not many cars on the road in that rural area, so she clearly remembers the black Gestapo Citroën taking him away. A few days later, her mother heard the distinctive *gazogène* engine returning and told her two daughters to run across the field behind the house and hide in the woods. Concealed there, they saw her taken away too, leaving the old grandmother alone in the house. That day marked the end of family life: Marius had been working hard to buy the rented house, but with both parents gone and no income, the sisters and their grandmother had to spend all their savings on rent. The families of the arrested men, who included Mayor Chanut, received no news of them as they were designated NN – *Nacht und Nebel* prisoners existing only as numbers, their identity and whereabouts unknown outside the camps' administration. What follows is taken from Pierre Mignon's notes, written as a record for his children and grandchildren.[3]

On arrival at Fort du Hâ prison in Bordeaux, all were facially unrecognisable after the beatings of Cosh, which turned out to be an apprenticeship for the constant, senseless violence of *kapos* and guards and the degradation of slowly starving in the filth of the death camps at Neue Brem, Buchenwald, Neuengamme, Mauthausen and finally Dora. During one transfer in cattle trucks, Marius Bouchou died in Mignon's arms, worn out with beatings, overwork and starvation.

At Camp Dora, Mignon toiled with Lucienne's husband for months in underground factories building V-weapons, allowed out into daylight only to witness the hanging of fellow prisoners. On the death march westwards as the Red Army approached, 2,400 prisoners were locked inside a barn in a half-track park that was heavily bombed by Allied aircraft. Mignon and

ARTICLE 1er – Sont nommés dans l'Ordre National de la Légion d'honneur :

AU GRADE DE CHEVALIER

DEPORTES-RESISTANTS

Armée de Terre

LOBRE   (Marie-Jeanne) Veuve Bouchou – Sous-Lieutenant des Forces Françaises Combattantes.

"A été déportée en Allemagne pour son action dans la résistance contre l'ennemi au cours de la période d'occupation.

"En est revenue grand invalide à la suite des privations et "sévices subis.

After surviving deportation, broken in health and spirit, Cathérine Bouchou's mother Marie-Jeanne was awarded the Légion d'honneur.

Beaupertuis were among 337 survivors next morning. Back in France, Lucienne could not recognise her husband in the hospital: the powerful peasant farmer who had weighed 102kg when arrested was reduced to a skeletal 43kg. Cathérine Bouchou's mother also returned from the camps prematurely aged and with broken health, unable even to smile for the ritual photograph at her daughter's wedding.

None of the survivors spoke of their experiences, even to each other. There are many stories like that of Faytout's group, on which the author stumbled when a cache of arms was found in 1998 beneath a concrete wine-press near his home in Gironde, where it had been hidden by one of the men who never came back. It comprised an assortment of Mark 2 Sten guns, Browning pistols, Lee-Enfield and French MAS 36 rifles with a large quantity of .303 ammunition, plus 9mm rounds for the Stens and Brownings. Most of the weapons were no longer in working order, because of rust, but the ammunition was mint-condition in waxed cardboard boxes marked 'Winchester Repeating Arms Co, New Haven, Connecticut.'

On the other side of France, Klaus Barbie was targeting bigger game than Faytout's little group. In November 1942 Jean Moulin had drawn the three main movements of the southern zone – Combat, Libération-Sud and FTP – into a loose federation titled 'Les Mouvements Unis de la Résistance' (MUR). As the plurality of the title indicates, command was divided, with Frenay refusing to subordinate his Combat organisation to the FTP and both FTP and Libération claiming he was a militaristic dictator. The differences between the various leaders were complicated by the infiltration into the other movements of undercover Communists nicknamed 'submarines'.

Since none of the leaders agreed to work with the others, Moulin harnessed them loosely to his troika by doling out subsidies from funds parachuted with arms drops – and then withdrawing support when someone became difficult. In the first five months of 1943 his subsidies totalled 71,000,000 francs.[4] As

ARTICLE Ier — sont nommés dans l'Ordre National de la Légion
d'Honneur : A TITRE POSTHUME

AU GRADE DE CHEVALIER

. . . .

BOUCHOU Marius - Sous-Lieutenant.

"Résistant aux sentiments patriotiques les plus purs. A trans-
"porté et camouflé des armes chez lui, ainsi que des postes émetteurs
"A hebergé des radios, le chef du réseau Hilaire et des réfractaires
"S.T.O.
"Comme chef de secteur, mettait au point l'organisation d'une
"compagnie de combat lorsqu'il a été arrêté le 23 octobre 1943 à
"ST ANTOINE DE QUEYRET.
"Déporté à NEUENGAMME où il est décédé le 10 janvier 1945.

Cathérine Bouchou's father Marius never returned from the death camps. He was awarded the Légion d'honneur posthumously.

to what was done with this money, researchers run into blank walls, since most Resistance operations at this point cost no more than a few bullets.

Doriot declared in August 1944 that 600 of his men had been 'treacherously gunned down by terrorists'. The first to die was Paul De Gassoski, killed by the Resistance on 24 April 1943. In his memoirs, Abetz stated that the first three-quarters of 1943 saw 281 Germans, 79 French police or gendarmes and 174 *collabos* assassinated. Whatever the actual figures, the real price was paid by the hostages executed in reprisal: historian Robert Aron quoted the tally of the German chaplain at Fresnes prison: 1,500–1,700 men and women shot in Paris prisons alone during the Occupation.

A neutral picture of Milice activities at the time comes from a report of 11 May 1943 by Prefect François Martin, writing from Montauban to Laval about an incident when *miliciens* stopped people in the street at gunpoint and demanded their papers. Martin had the courage to state categorically that, had he been present at the time, he would have ordered the arrest of individuals arrogating to themselves police functions in this way.[5]

Although Moulin's brief from London ran only in the southern zone, like many other agents in the field, he also made unauthorised contacts – for example, with the PCF hard core in Paris, working directly for Moscow. Suspecting as much, Colonel Passy defied all the canons of Intelligence work by parachuting into France at the end of February 1943. Instead of working with him, Moulin chose the moment to return to London and did not go back to France until 21 March.

On 7 June in Paris the Gestapo arrested Moulin's military counterpart, General Charles Delestraint, code-name Vidal, who understood German and was fully aware of his position. There could be no question of denying his mission or identity, since he had on him when arrested identity papers in his true name. Detained with him was *résistant* René Hardy, who was liberated a few days later with no marks of ill-treatment, but did not tell his comrades what had happened. On 27 May Moulin committed the worst mistake possible for a clandestine agent, who already knew he was being hunted all over France, by calling a meeting in Caluire, a suburb of Lyons, of *all* the Resistance bosses, any one of whom was likely to be under surveillance. It is hard to find a sane reason for such a major error.

The venue, in the house of a dental surgeon, was chosen because it was thought they could enter and leave unnoticed among his patients. Frenay, in London for a briefing, was represented by his Number 2, Henri Aubry, who brought along René Hardy, who was most likely to have told Klaus Barbie the time and place, as well as the fact that Moulin would be present. The house was already staked out before they arrived and the meeting had just begun when Barbie's men burst in and handcuffed everyone, including genuine patients awaiting treatment. As they were being herded into closed vans, Hardy made a run for it. Despite several Gestapo men turning automatic weapons in his direction, he escaped with only a slight leg wound – a remarkable achievement with one's wrists cuffed behind the back. Despite two postwar trials, his exact role in the betrayal was never resolved.

In the torture chambers Barbie now used in the Ecole de Santé Militaire, Moulin claimed he was Jacques Martel, an art dealer from Nice. To prove it, he gave the address of his genuine art gallery there. Barbie replied by calling him by his Resistance code-name, Max. What happened in the following thirty hours is best left to the imagination. The local French police reported the arrest routinely, between reports of ID cards stolen from a *mairie* and an increase in thefts of vegetables from gardens. On the evening of 23 June in Montluc prison the 'trusty' prison barber was called to shave an unconscious man, who had obviously been tortured nearly to death, and whose flesh was cold to his touch. Moulin mumbled something in English and then asked for water. The guard rinsed out a shaving mug and the barber held it to Moulin's mouth, but he could only swallow a few drops before losing consciousness again.

Driven to Paris, he was briefly lodged in a cell at 40 Boulevard Victor Hugo, a suburban villa in Neuilly used by Boemelburg's men as an interrogation centre. Prisoners André Lassagne and Delestraint were brought there from Fresnes prison to be shown Moulin lying on a stretcher. Noting that his skin had turned yellow and his respiration was hardly noticeable, Lassagne denied knowing him. The dignified Delestraint replied to the guards' question with, 'How do you expect me to identify a man in that condition?' Officially, Jean Moulin died in a train taking him to Germany on 8 July 1943, aged 44. Gen Delestraint was transferred to the concentration camp at Natzwiller and from there in September to Dachau, where he was shot and cremated on the morning of 19 April 1945, aged 64. In one successful operation the SD had neutralised both the military and the political leaders of the Gaullist Resistance.

On 10 June 1943 SS-Hauptsturmführer Aloïs Brünner, fresh from annihilating the 35,000-strong Sephardi Jewish community in Salonika, arrived in Paris. Three weeks later, he replaced the corrupt and brutal gendarmes guarding Drancy by Feldgendarmerie soldiers, whose 21-year-old commander SS-Sturmführer Ernst Heinrichsohn had the body and grace of a ballet dancer. He took pleasure in attending the selections for deportation slapping a riding crop against his boots. When short of victims for his next transport, Heinrichsohn drove to the Rothschild Hospital and had thirty-five patients aged between 70 and 90 dragged out of bed to make up the number. Of 536 adults and sixty-three children in that transport, only two survived to return to France.

Brünner also set up thirteen interrogation sub-stations in Paris manned by members of the *carlingue* who had no qualms about torturing suspects. The most infamous was at 93 rue Lauriston, run by a violent gangster named Henri Lafont and renegade police inspector Pierre Bonny, a 'real family man' who never spoke at home about the work at which he spent long hours each day.[6] So useful was Lafont that he was given both German citizenship and SS officer rank.

With intensive ID checks at all main stations it had become so dangerous for the Moissac Rovers to travel far that the task of visiting children in foster homes fell more and more on the Rangers – who yet found time for love. In July 1943 a 22-year-old helper code-named Sultane married Pierre Kanthine, a teacher working with the *colonie*. It was a brief marriage: on a clandestine trip to Rouffignac in the Dordogne shortly afterwards, the bridegroom was denounced by the mayor and taken hostage. In reprisal for a Maquis attack in March 1944 he was shot on the last day of the month.

Seen from London, these tragedies were unimportant to the course of the war. Colonel Bevan's Operation Cockade still aimed to keep the Germans believing an invasion imminent, so corroboratory arms drops to the Resistance built up during 1943 on a scale that could not fail to alert the Abwehr and SD. Drops of high explosive totalled 88 tons in January alone and rose to a peak of 10,252 tons in June, when 10,790 pistols, 2,353 Stens and 5,537 grenades were dropped, among other matériel.[7] In western France during April/May Suttill's Prosper network received 1,006 Stens, 1,877 incendiary devices and 4,489 grenades; in June it took delivery of another 190 man-sized containers of matériel on thirty-three landing grounds spread over twelve *départements*. The south-western Scientist network received 121 consignments of arms between May and August. During August the BBC twice broadcast coded messages alerting agents in Prosper and Scientist to an invasion scheduled for September, failing only to send the confirmation messages on the night before the spoof operation.[8]

Bilingual, having grown up in England and France with an English father and French mother, Francis Suttill may have been a good lawyer, but lacked the paranoia vital for undercover work. He remained unaware that virtually all his movements were watched by the Germans thanks to a triple agent. Flyer and con-man Henri Déricourt, listed in the SD archives as agent BOE/48, afterwards summed up Suttill as more suited to be an officer in a gung-ho cavalry regiment than for clandestine warfare. It was Déricourt who coordinated the scores of drops to Prosper, feeding times and places, and arrival and departure of agents, to SS-Sturmbannführer Boemelburg in

Paris.[9] What Boemelburg did not know was that his double agent was in fact a triple agent acting under instructions from Col Bevan that overrode his duties for Section F. This was the real dirt of Operation Cockade.

By the second week of July both Suttill and his Number 2, Gilbert Norman, were in Gestapo cells divulging the false invasion plans. Several hundred other Prosper agents were also arrested, tortured, deported or shot straight away. It seems likely that the rolling-up of Suttill's network was due to appalling security, rather than planned by Col Bevan, who intended Cockade to run right up to the real D-Day. Bevan's own security was so tight that Buckmaster was prepared to put in writing as late as December 1945 that Déricourt was innocent of any collaboration with the Germans, and 'had the finest record of operations completed of any member of SOE'.[10] The cost in suffering among the thousands of French men and women ensnared in these machinations can never be calculated.

On 5 June 1943 Laval announced the departure of another 220,000 young men including agricultural labourers to Germany, resulting in widespread comments that the Germans were going to bleed France white by taking all its young men. Yet even this did not pacify Fritz Sauckel, who reported to Hitler on 9 August, 'I have completely lost belief in the honest goodwill of French Prime Minister Laval. His refusal . . . to execute a further programme for recruiting 500,000 French workers to go to Germany before the end of 1943 . . . amounts to downright sabotage of the German struggle for life against Bolshevism.'[11]

Although exempt from the STO because employed as a Paris fireman, Raymond Bredèche decided to go absent without leave while he still had the chance, despite this making him technically a deserter from the armed forces. With a compass and rucksack filled with warm clothing and food, he took a train to Grenoble and simply walked into the countryside until challenged by a sentinel at the approach to a Maquis camp. For him, it was as simple as that. Whatever his dreams of glory, the reality was hard. The group had no weapons until an Italian unit withdrawing over the Col de Muzelle in September dumped three crates of ammunition, handkerchiefs, socks and two rifles. Only then could the band of young men pretend that they were fighters.[12] Their diet was mainly potatoes bought from local peasants, who would have preferred to sell their surplus to the black market at higher prices. It was a feast when Bredèche killed a one-metre-long *couleuvre* snake and roasted it over a fire. Maquis 'wages' did not run to restaurant meals: camp leaders received 20 francs a day; 'NCOs' had from 9 to 15 francs; the other men got 5 francs! Even this money had to be stolen from railway stations, post offices or houses of suspected collaborators or black marketeers. As late as five months before D-Day, one Maquis unit in Dordogne had a total of three Sten guns with ninety-two rounds of ammunition, seven revolvers and twenty-three rifles. Another group further north had three Sten guns, six grenades, thirty-five revolvers and thirteen rifles between them.

In most Maquis units, Reveille was at 6.30, followed by toilet and breakfast. The salute to the flag, if observed, was accompanied rarely by a bugle call, more often by accordion or mouth-organ. Cleaning camp and other chores occupied the rest of the morning; obtaining food, much of the afternoon. Often, foraging turned to robbery. The Chantiers and Compagnons camps were targets of choice to get winter clothing, boots and other supplies. One unit in the Ardennes hijacked mail bags containing several villages' food tickets and then went on to steal 150 kilos of government tobacco the next day.

On 25 July Mussolini was overthrown after the Allied invasion of Sicily. During the resulting confusion, General Lospinoso managed to acquire illicitly the Gestapo's list of Jews registered in Italian-occupied territory and hastened back to Italy, to organise a gigantic rescue operation – as Bastianini had done in Dalmatia. With the SS hard on his heels, he set up a complicated operation to ship all the refugees at risk to North Africa with American help. Arrangements were made to move a total of 30,000 men, women and children.[13] On 8 September the scheme's banker, Angelo Donati, was finalising the details in Rome when Eisenhower's HQ prematurely released the news of the Italian surrender. With the Germans immediately occupying Nice, it seemed that the rescue plan had failed.

Particularly at risk were up to 527 children hidden for short or long periods in convents and elsewhere by Odette Rodenstock and Moussa Abbadi. To keep in touch with them and bring letters from parents, Odette travelled day after day on *gazogène*-powered buses to visit foster-parents – all too often finding them at the end of their tether, not just because they were risking their lives but because the small child they had welcomed into their home would say nothing to them but, 'I want my Mummy. I want my Mummy.' Older children caused different problems. Unable to resist divulging a secret, a boy might tell a classmate, 'My name isn't really Rocher. It's Reichmann, but you mustn't tell anyone.'[14]

In August 1943, while the famous Parisian boys' choir Les Petits Chanteurs à la Croix de Bois were singing in Berlin, the insanity of the Final Solution saw eighty-seven detainees transported *westwards* from Auschwitz through Poland and Germany to Alsace. Dr Josef Hirt, director of the Institute of Racial Anthropology at Strasbourg University, wanted freshly killed Jewish bodies undamaged by bullet wounds or ill-treatment for his experiments. These unfortunates were thus to be gassed in a specially adapted gas chamber at Natzwiller. Although not a death camp designed for mass slaughter, Natzwiller and its twin camp in neighbouring Schirmeck cost the lives of many thousand prisoners by slave labour in a quarry of pink granite used for Nazi monuments. They died from overwork, ill-treatment, malnutrition, exposure in the −30°C winter weather, random killings and 'medical experiments' including deliberate burning with mustard gas and injection with lethal diseases.

Among the prisoners were Norwegian Resistance workers, German criminals, Communists, French *résistants* – and homosexuals, among them

18-year-old Pierre Seel, who had unwisely reported being robbed of his watch during a nocturnal adventure in a Mulhouse park in 1939. The imprudence was to cost him dearly: his name was on a file inherited by the Gestapo after the German invasion. Arrested, tortured and sent to Natzwiller in 1940, where he was mistreated by other prisoners and guards alike, he survived and was eventually released because his uniform was distinguished by a blue bar signifying 'Catholic' rather than the pink triangle of the homosexual prisoners. In his book,[15] he reports the death of his lover Jo-Jo, literally savaged to death after several Alsatian dogs were set on him for fun by the guards. A metal pail had been tied on his head to amplify his screams so that all the assembled prisoners would hear.[16]

Natzwiller had witnessed one of the most daring escapes of the war on 4 August 1942 when Czech Major Josef Mautner and four equally desperate detainees including a French Air Force officer and a Polish ex-Foreign Legion volunteer decided to escape before they were starved or beaten to death. Dressing in stolen SS uniforms and driving a car with SS plates 'liberated' from the camp garage by a prisoner working there as a mechanic, they succeeded by sheer nerve. Luck ran out for *kapo* Alfons Christmann when he was caught near the Swiss border one month later. Brought back to Natzwiller, he was tortured in the *Appelplatz* before the assembled prisoners – and hanged on the gallows after the trap twice failed to open. Of the others, Mautner and an Austrian Communist named Haas reached Britain via Spain and Portugal; Josef Cichosz survived to join the Free Polish Army; and Alsatian former air force officer Winterberger joined the Free French forces in Tunisia.

The prisoners from Auschwitz arriving in August 1943 found the camp commanded by Josef Kramer, subsequently promoted to run Bergen-Belsen. Hanged by the British after writing a no-punches-pulled record of his work in the Allgemeine-SS, he recorded in it testing Zyklon-B gas on the first batch from Auschwitz, to ensure the building was airtight. He ordered fifteen female prisoners to undress and go into the chamber. Force was needed to close the door on the screaming women, who had realised this was not a disinfectant facility as they had been told, one naked woman fighting back so desperately that she was shot outside. The doors closed, Kramer inserted the precise dose of crystals given to him by Dr Hirt into a special chute and activated them by pouring in water. He switched on the light inside to watch the women die through an armoured glass window, noting that they lost control of their bowels and fell to the floor after ceasing breathing in roughly thirty seconds. For this devotion to duty, he received a Christmas bonus.

By then the other prisoners from Auschwitz had all been killed in small groups, with Kramer sending the bodies to Professor Hirt for autopsy, after which the skulls were preserved in Hirt's 'racial anatomy' collection.[17] A number of such spurious anthropological institutions in France were subsidised by German money.

An
ϟ-Hauptsturmführer Josef Kramer
Lagerkommandant des K.L. Natzweiler

N a t z w e i l e r / Elsaß

Betrifft: Weihnachtszuwendung 1943

Für treue Mitarbeit hat der Hauptamtschef, ϟ-Obergruppenführer
und General der Waffen-ϟ P o h l , anläßlich des Julfestes
1943 die Auszahlung einer Zuwendung an Sie verfügt.

Beigeschlossen wird Ihnen ein Verrechnungsscheck über
RM. 500.--
übersandt.

Kramer's reward for gassing the prisoners at Natzwiller. Translation of letter to him from RHSA headed 'Re Christmas bonus 1943' and dated 8 December 1943: 'Head Office Chief SS-Obergruppenführer and Waffen-SS General Pohl has authorised the payment of a Christmas bonus to you. Please find enclosed a cheque for 500 Reichsmarks.' A receipt for the money was requested.

In Bastia prison on the island of Corsica schoolteacher Jean Nicoli spent the night of 29–30 August writing letters in his cell. Betrayed by a rival Resistance group, he had been sentenced to death by an Italian military court for running a PCF cell stockpiling arms dropped by Allied aircraft from bases in Algeria. To protect the members of the cell not arrested, he and the other prisoners pretended they had been working for money: a figure of 1,640,000 francs was mentioned during the trial and reported in the press. Told that he was to be shot at 4 a.m., Nicoli's only concern was to set the record straight after his death, so that his Party comrades would know he had taken no money for himself. He was actually not shot but decapitated instead at the Carré des Fusillés of Bastia, four days short of his forty-fifth birthday.[18] Four days after it, the Corsican Resistance rose against the Axis occupation and freed itself with the help of Gaullist forces from North Africa.

On 8 September 1943 the Germans occupied the Italian zone. Two days later Hauptsturmführer Brünner arrived in Nice with a staff of fourteen, to find the Italians completing paperwork necessary to transfer hundreds of Jews by truck across the frontier to safety. The Italian Consulate in the Hotel Continental was raided by SS troops under his command, just after all its files had been removed to Rome. All Brünner could do was arrest the consul and staff, and forcibly deport them. Unaware that thousands of refugees were being spirited across the frontier by French and Italian volunteers, he installed himself in the Hôtel Excelsior by the main railway terminal, anticipating a cull of 2,000 people a day to despatch to Drancy for transport to Auschwitz.

With the Wehrmacht refusing to help, Brünner at first showed more subtlety than in Salonika by publicising forged proof that the deported Sephardim were happily working in Poland and cynically exchanging French currency of arrested Jews for *zlotys* which they 'could spend on arrival in the East'. However, even the offer of 10,000 francs head-money to informants saw him by mid-month unable to assemble more than 2,000 victims in all, proving that without the active participation of the French police, the SS and Gestapo unaided would never have amassed so many victims. Finally, Brünner used torture to force the first refugees caught to reveal the whereabouts of their relatives and friends.

In September, too, Laval informed General De La Porte du Theil that the poor response to the STO now required him to make up the deficit by handing over all young men in the Chantiers. Refusing to accept this order, the general avoided immediate arrest by stating that he had left instructions for all conscripts to be released, should he fail to return from his visit to Vichy. Shortly afterwards, De Tournemire was forced to go underground to avoid arrest by the Germans, leaving his deputy to find subsidies to keep the movement going. Fobbed off by a succession of top civil servants, he was eventually granted a handout by Laval in the hope that he could thus gain control of the Compagnons. Refusing to resign, De Tournemire joined the Alliance network of Marie-Madeleine Fourcade, and activated an undercover spin-off of the Compagnons called Druids, whose members protected STO runaways by finding false papers for them and helped downed Allied airmen escape France. Its biggest coup was described by Professor R.V. Jones, scientific adviser to SIS, as 'the most important single piece of Intelligence in the war' after Druids member Jannie Rousseau sent to London detailed information about the V-weapon launch ramps in the Pas de Calais.

With society crumbling, parents still had problems with their children. At the end of the summer term, Renée De Monbrison had been asked to remove her daughters from the Collège Cévenole at Chambon. Having not surprisingly failed their exams because unable to concentrate on lessons, they had fallen foul of the authoritarian headmistress, who made no allowances for the exceptional times. Pastor Trocmé's daughter was a school-chum of Françoise, but he could not change the woman's mind, nor could the popular English teacher Miss Williamson. So Rénée brought the girls back with her to St-Roch and put Françoise' name down for the *collège* in Moissac, where she immediately made friends with Andrée Giraud, whose family offered her a bedroom. In Chambord, 16-year-old Françoise had been considered a child, but Shatta Simon needed every pair of hands and recruited her to guide refugee children from the train station to La Maison de Moissac, cautioning them not to speak loudly in their give-away accents in front of strangers. Twice she was stopped when carrying in her school satchel official stamps of bombed towns and places in North Africa – useful for forging ID cards as they could not be checked. Afterwards, she despised herself for flirting with the German soldiers to distract their attention.[19]

By chance on a bus, Renée discovered herself sitting next to the man who had brought back from Montauban the 150 blank ID cards. Shatta Simon's brother, Dr Djigo Hirsch, had been an eminent Parisian radiologist until debarred from practising medicine. With the help of mayors and local gendarmes, he and his wife had managed to find homes for eighty boys and girls aged 18 to 20, mostly with false papers. Once in the country, where the local gendarmes gave warning of any search and there was time to hide in the woods, many had no need of identity papers, providing they kept out of sight of strangers. However, all of them needed regular deliveries of ration cards. To help him out, Renée took the risk of persuading her uncle's estate steward to employ three of the older boys on the estate – with no idea that she was placing them in grave danger.

On the morning of 18 October Djigo and his wife were arrested in the village of St-Michel near Auvillar. Their small son was safely in Moissac when the Germans arrived, but Madame Hirsch, who had few illusions of their eventual fate, took advantage of the diversion caused by Djigo running away and being seriously shot in the arm to thrust her baby into the arms of a neighbour's daughter, so that the infant should not be taken away with them. Also rounded up were a girl with false papers living in their house and Djigo's assistant.

Hurrying down to the village with Françoise, Renée arrived in time to watch from a distance as Djigo was thrown into a truck, bleeding heavily from his wound and with face unrecognisable from blows of rifle buts. Seeing the house full of Germans in uniform and plain clothes making a thorough search that lasted until 5 p.m., they ran back to Château St-Roch and telephoned Shatta in Moissac to sound the alarm. She immediately called EIF's founder Robert Gamzon with the message, 'Djigo is very ill. He has been taken by ambulance to hospital in Toulouse.' In the simple code they used because the Milice monitored phone calls, *ill* meant 'arrested' and *ambulance* meant 'taken away.' *Hospital* meant 'by the Germans'; had it been by French police, she would have said *clinic*.[20]

Gamzon cycled to Moissac, arriving at dusk. Nothing could be done to help those arrested, but he and Shatta agreed that the urgent priority was to check whether the Germans had found Djigo's filing system. If so, the eighty children were as good as dead, for it contained their true names and whereabouts, together with their ration cards. Gamzon set off on his second long bicycle ride of the day with a helper named Roger, who told him, once they were on the road to St-Michel, that he had not wanted to alarm Shatta further by telling her about Djigo's wound. His other, more vital, piece of information was that neighbours had heard Djigo mutter, 'Tidy the *cagibi*', as he was hauled bleeding onto the truck. It had to be a clue. *Cagibi* could mean a box-room, or storage place. But where? Surely not in his house, since the Germans had spent eight hours searching it.

At St-Michel the mayor was terrified that Djigo would betray him under torture, and refused to let them break the seals the Germans had placed on the Hirsch home after threatening to shoot the neighbour entrusted with the key if there was any sign of entry when they returned. The only good omen was that none of the children accommodated nearby had so far been picked up. After dusk, Gamzon pretended to set off back to Moissac, but rendezvoused with Roger and two other boys outside Djigo's house by imitating owl calls to identify each other. Breaking in without leaving any sign was not easy. Once inside, careful to show no lights and make no noise, they found clothes and food for the eighty children thrown all over the floor; with the contents of every drawer emptied on top. After two hours of fruitless searching, one of the boys lifted a heavy old door in the attic and found the box of files where Djigo had hidden it on hearing the Germans arrive. Back to Moissac through the curfew Gamzon and Robert cycled, to give Shatta the news that the children were safe – for the moment.

On 21 October Klaus Barbie was cheated of several victims. Arrested with Jean Moulin was Raymond Aubrac, whose wife Lucie had been so angered by the anti-Semitic exhibition in Lyons. With extraordinary courage and initiative, she devised a plan to rescue her husband, based on a huge gamble: that his false identity as 'Claude Ermulin' had not been broken under torture.

Two days after the arrests, a smartly dressed young woman calling herself Ghislaine De Barbantine asked to see Barbie at the Ecole de Santé. He was smartly dressed, she afterwards recalled, in a light summer suit and pink shirt, and had a woman with him, as usual. Lucie's first attempt to see her husband failed, but she returned on 21 October and succeeded in meeting Barbie again by dint of bribes to French staff working for the Gestapo. When he asked what she wanted, Lucie cried hysterically that she was ashamed to be carrying a child by 'Ermulin' and wanted to tell him what she thought of him. As she had astutely deduced, the idea of a wronged woman tongue-lashing a detainee so appealed to Barbie's perverted sense of humour that he sent for prisoner 'Ermulin'. Apparently unaffected by his pitiful state after four months in Montluc Prison, Lucie raved at him that whatever was happening served him right as far as she was concerned, but she needed a name for her child and expected him to do the 'decent thing'.

'Ermulin' was hardly in a condition to marry anyone. The whole point of the dangerous pantomime was to have him brought to the medical school for the confrontation. As the closed van was returning him and Barbie's victims of the day to Montluc prison after interrogation, two carloads of *résistants* closed in; automatic fire from silenced weapons killed the men in the driver's cab and mowed down the guards who jumped out, save one who escaped.

By risking her own life, Lucie Aubrac had saved that of her husband. [21]

Chapter 19

HAPPY NEW YEAR!

Foreseeing the likelihood of a permanent German presence in Moissac, Shatta and Bouli decided in October 1943 to spirit away more than 180 children living in the *colonie* and find them safer homes under false names. Brothers and sister were forbidden to tell each other their new identities, so that one could not be forced to betray the other. Where possible, initials were kept the same, to account for tags sewn into favourite clothing. Some were sent hundreds of kilometres as 'child refugees from the bombing of northern towns and cities' with staff at their new schools sometimes brought into the secret and sometimes not.

At a convent school in Beaumont-de-Lomagne, between Montauban and Toulouse, 12-year-old Suzette, whose name was now Marie-Suzanne Floret, found it hard not to giggle when seated at the same lunch table as her older brother Daniel, now called Denis Forestier. Yet despite the company of three other girls from Moissac, the strain of her double life was such that she fell ill and had to be smuggled into Moissac hospital, where Dr Moles cared for her. Terrified of giving herself away, Suzette stayed mute throughout her stay. In addition to delivering fictitious sickness certificates to young men who would otherwise have been liable for STO, Dr Moles also used his travel *Ausweis* and permit to buy petrol to transport wounded *résistants* in his little car.

More resilient children met up with their new identities pretending they had never met before, and then 'made friends'. But life was never easy for 11-year-old Edith L and five other girls boarding at the *collège* or middle school of Ste-Foy-la-Grande on the banks of the Dordogne. At weekends the local children went home and gorged on whatever food was available, but the Moissac girls stayed in the school *pensionnat*, scavenging dustbins for rotten vegetables they ate out of sight in the toilets. Headmistress Madame Pécastaing had begged the mayor throughout the previous winter for kindling to light the classroom stoves and a new flagpole to replace one broken in a storm, 'so that each Monday the children can sing "*La Marseillaise*" beside it, not "*Maréchal, nous voilà!*". The school's bicycle had been stolen when the premises were occupied by the French Army in June 1940. Since suppliers could no longer deliver food and other necessaries, she had been borrowing the cleaning lady's bike to do the school shopping, but this was no longer serviceable. Since her licence to use a *gazogène* car had been withdrawn, 'Please Mr Mayor . . .'[1]

Such was life for most French people by this stage. It is all the more incredible that all the documents for each new identity were forged in time at Moissac, using official stamps, ID cards and ration tickets provided by the mayor's secretary. As the last batch of children being taken to their new homes was driven across the Pont Napoléon in the all-purpose van of the Maison de Moissac, it passed the first incoming German vehicles. For their HQ the Germans commandeered premises in the rue du Pont, only 200 metres from La Maison de Moissac. When part of the middle school was also requisitioned, Andrée Giraud and four boys aged 15 tore out some of the electrical fittings in a spontaneous act of sabotage that had the headmaster terrified it would land him before a firing squad.

A colleague of his in nearby Castelsarrassin, Adrien Favre, watched another troop of Waffen-SS arrive and clamber down from their transport. When the inevitable knock came on the door, he was informed by an SS sergeant in broken French that anyone with a spare room had to accommodate two or more soldiers. The sergeant insisted on inspecting the small school house, in which there was a spare room, but Favre protested he used it for giving private lessons after school.

'You are a teacher?' queried the sergeant.

'I'm the schoolmaster.'

Demonstrating unexpected Teutonic respect for learning, the sergeant clicked his heels and apologised for bothering the Herr Professor. No question of soldiers being billeted on him. Absolutely not.

Expecting trouble between the local Maquis and the Germans, the Castelsarrassin police were relieved that the civilian population instead withdrew into their shells, paying little attention except when armed soldiers confiscated their radios and bicycles, lacking any transport of their own after the Normandy landings. Adrien Favre was about to hand over his dilapidated bike, vital for weekend forays into the country to buy food, when the same respectful sergeant yelled at his men not to bother the Herr Professor, but to leave his bicycle alone. Favre was so embarrassed that he immediately hid his cycle and did not use it for months, in case his neighbours thought that he had done the Germans some favour.[2]

Armistice Day on 11 November sparked off widespread demonstrations. At Oyonnax in Rhone-Alpes, white-gloved Maquis forces paraded a flag-bearing honour guard, 'liberating' the town for twenty-four hours. On the war memorial, they placed a wreath in the form of the Cross of Lorraine bearing the legend, 'From the Conquerors of Tomorrow to those of 14–18'. In Grenoble, 100 kilometres to the south, German troops arrested hundreds of demonstrators, deporting 450. After MUR *résistants* blew up a German arms dump, hostages were executed in retaliation. A Polish Wehrmacht deserter named Kospiski led a Maquis attack on the Bonne barracks, killing fifty Germans and destroying tons of munitions. An FTP action group placed land-mines on the windowsills of De Brinon's home, causing substantial damage. On 23 November the Resistance claimed twenty-five *miliciens* dead and twenty-seven wounded in a pitched battle, while 30,000 fascists attended the December rally in the Vel d'Hiv to hear Déat, Darnand and Henriot speak under the slogan 'Europe United against Bolshevism'. With the arming of the Milice, France was sliding into civil war.

To punish Pétain, on 13 November the Germans banned him from making further broadcasts. Listeners' reaction to Laval becoming Vichy spokesman can be gauged from the numerous Gendarmarie reports that the population detested Laval's government and regarded it as kept in power solely by the German occupation.[3] The shift in public opinion brought a resurgence of hope among those with least expectation of survival. Prisoners in Drancy dug a 40-metre tunnel from the basement of one of the apartment blocks. Betrayed when it was within three metres of freedom, the fourteen would-be escapers and sixty-five of the 'trusty' prisoners were deported on 20 November. Nineteen of them succeeded in hacking their way through the wooden floor of their cattle-truck en route and escaping. Among many Germans disturbed by SS treatment of prisoners, a German woman working for a welfare organisation in a Paris railway station asked the American-born wife of Ernst Achenbach whether, as an embassy wife, she could do something to stop the harrowing scenes when mothers were forcibly separated from their children.[4]

On 16 December, among her other problems, Renée De Monbrison had to find yet another home for Baboushka, with south-west France being too dangerous, thanks to the activities of Papon. In desperation, she contacted the midwife who had delivered her four children, now living in Villiers-Adam north of Paris, to see whether she would accept the old lady as a paying guest. 'Madame Robert' had become Baboushka's official name now, thanks to a false identity card, and it was as such that she travelled north to Villiers-Adam. To her new neighbours' questions, she avoided an outright lie by replying that she was the widow of an employee in the Renault car factory, justifying this to herself by the fact that her husband had been a director on the board of Renault!

A few months later her new hideaway became a hive of military activity. A good night's sleep had become impossible because of RAF bomber fleets passing overhead at night in the pre-invasion strategic bombing campaign. Among their targets was the V-weapons factory near Arras, after which the war caught up with 'Madame Robert' when German engineers and French labourers were billeted in neighbouring houses while converting caves near Villiers-Adam into underground assembly plants for the rockets.

An unsung financial coup of the Resistance was the brainchild of Pierre Mendès-France. After escaping from prison in Clermont-Ferrand, he had made his way to London and served briefly in the RAF before being interviewed by De Gaulle. Appreciating the intelligence of this would-be recruit, who at 18 had been the youngest practising lawyer in the Third

Republic, De Gaulle made him 'Finance Minister' of the French government-in-exile, and had his confidence rewarded by a simple but brilliant idea from the new minister. An appeal was launched for contributions *inside* occupied France and the money poured in, especially from *collabos* seeking a receipt as an insurance policy against the now inevitable Allied victory.[5] As Mendès-France foresaw, repayment was not an issue, with the value of the franc dropping by more than 50 per cent between 1940 and the Liberation.

By late 1943 Louis De La Bardonnie's clandestine activities in both zones disguised as a railway inspector and under other aliases were attracting increasing attention. On one mission in the guise of a priest, he used a Minox miniature camera supplied from London to take 1,250 photographs of documents and scenes in the port of Cherbourg. Happily for him, the many divisions of German counter-intelligence competed more often than they cooperated. His Gestapo Paris file AT/87.878/FR 1943/44 recorded him as an exceptionally dangerous agent, to be eliminated at all costs – if possible, to be taken alive, with 1,000,000 francs reward for his arrest or betrayal.[6]

At 11 p.m. on 20 November Château La Roque was surrounded by 110 SS troops with a monocled Gestapo officer from Castillon and a *milicien* to act as interpreter. After a hail of blows on the closed shutters, 15-year-old Guy – the oldest son – re-tuned the two radios to French stations and called out to ask who was there. Opening a shutter, he had a Schmeisser machine-pistol jammed into his belly, as did his older sister. For three hours the house was searched from cellar to attics, the noise being such as to wake all except the two youngest children. The governess and nanny were also woken up and questioned at gunpoint.

When the Germans left three hours later empty-handed, the night's work was not over for Guy. The *milicien* having prised out of the local postman an address to which mail was being forwarded, he had to walk several kilometres in the dark to find a telephone before dawn that might not be tapped and pass a message to his parents in Charente telling them to leave their hideout immediately. Armbruster rightly predicted that there was no immediate danger because a joint Gestapo/SS operation on that scale would result in a report to Paris before any action was taken. It was, however, officers of the Abwehr from Bergerac who arrived at the château in January, three weeks after Denyse had given birth again. All except the youngest children had been told to pour abuse on their absent father as an unprincipled swine who had abandoned them, when asked about him at school. Shown the spurious divorce papers by Denyse, the Abwehr men politely demanded who was the father of her baby, obliging her to pretend she had a lover. Once again, Armbruster's advice and their Nordic looks protected Denyse and the children.

Most French people were unaware that on 29 December 1943 the southern zone resistance organisations united, on paper at least, with the northern ones as the Mouvement de Libération Nationale (MLN). At this point, total strength in the southern zone was 30,000 and in the northern zone 15,000 – still an infinitesimally small percentage of the population. What's in a name? On 1 February 1944 all the movements were finally amalgamated on paper as Les Forces Françaises de l'Intérieur, or Home Forces, yet the old rivalries simmered beneath the surface. It was considered fair game by FTP to hijack an arms drop intended for Combat or Secret Army – and vice versa. Worse, on occasions, one faction would 'forget' to warn another of a Milice ambush or the approach of a German column.

For young *maquisards* living in woodsmen's huts and charcoal burners' shelters deep in the forests, life that winter was hard. Harder still the life in upland units, where the guide was an eight-page booklet full of counsel such as: 'Experience in 1914–18 shows that men are not cold in a dug-out shelter occupied by a dozen or so comrades.' Some advice was straight out of Baden-Powell's *Scouting for Boys*: cooks should use only dry wood on their fires, to reduce tell-tale smoke on a still day against a blue sky; with German spotter planes regularly over-flying areas where 'terrorist bands' were known to be, converging tracks in the snow were to be avoided, and so on. Since losses were inevitable, to keep them to a minimum each unit was to number not more than fifteen men, who must always camp where they could see without being seen. The moment a man deserted or there was any other reason to feel insecure, the group was to move within the hour.

The indiscipline and sometimes criminal activities of Maquis groups resulted in a circular dated 20 January 1944 warning, 'No raids should take place without prior approval of the *département* organisation. It is not our job to punish the black marketers. We are not vigilantes. That will be the job of purge committees after the Liberation.' Ground rules were to steal ration tickets each month from only one village; tobacco was to be paid for and not smoked locally but sent to a central point for general distribution; teams sent on raids should behave correctly towards the population[7] – which implies that things sometimes happened otherwise. In one four-week period an FTP unit in central France executed one of its own men, killed a German prisoner and nineteen alleged *collabos* or *miliciens*, as well as carrying out independently six sabotage operations inviting reprisals on local inhabitants.[8] A number of Maquis chiefs were simply local warlords, like self-styled 'Captain' Le Coz in Valençay, an illiterate veteran of the Bataillons d'Afrique punishment corps with thirty-six previous convictions who used his Maquis standing to assassinate nineteen innocent people.

The New Year saw pressure from Berlin bringing pro-German broadcaster Philippe Henriot and Milice boss Joseph Darnand into the ghost of Pétain's Cabinet at its meeting on 1 January. Darnand, with the title Secretary-General for Maintenance of Order, had recently taken the oath to Hitler as a Waffen-SS Obersturmführer, and was thus that least trustworthy creature, a member of one government who had sworn allegiance to the head of another state. Having, like Darquier, been sacked because the Germans judged him 'too liberal', Bousquet was forcibly removed to Germany – luckily for him in the long run, for this enabled the architect of the greatest *rafle* of all to clear his name after the war. As a last desperate gesture, Pétain tried to halt Laval's complete takeover of power by calling a National Assembly to restore some kind of parliamentary government. When prevented by German pressure from exercising this presidential prerogative, he refused to perform any further functions as head of state.

By now the government of France was a rubber stamp for German use. Among the casualties was Gen De La Porte du Theil, arrested by the Germans on 28 December 1943 and deported to Austria, where he would remain hostage until liberated by troops of the French 1st Army on 5 May 1945. His Vichy-appointed replacement could make little headway against the concerted obstruction of the officers and NCOs of the Chantiers. Those who did not resign stayed at their posts in the same spirit with which the general had returned from Algeria in 1942 – to protect the conscripts in their care, whose rate of desertion to the Maquis rose steadily, with some *groupes* deserting en masse with their instructors.[9]

On 4 January 1944, Darnand's men knocked on the door of the humble home in Soissons of Pauline Gochperg. She was the aunt of Charles Wajsfelner, who had written from Drancy to the local baker asking her to look after his younger brother Maurice, living with Pauline and her two children. Now, the men at the door informed her that her 8-year-old son Albert and 3-year-old daughter Nelly were being arrested for deportation, as their father had been. So also was 10-year-old nephew Maurice. Although not herself Jewish, Pauline chose to go with the children. What mother could not? On arrival at Drancy, she was relieved of her precious savings, recorded in *Carnet de Fouille No 63* as amounting to 330 francs. The last evidence of her life is on the list of *Abtransporte 67* that left Drancy on 3 February. There she is, carefully listed with her children: '*389 GOCHPERG, Albert - 390 GOCHPERG Nelly - 391 GOCHPERG, Pauline.*' Several pages later we find '*1117 WAJSFELNER, Maurice*'. On 6 February, the doors of the cattle trucks were opened in the siding at Auschwitz and they were gassed shortly afterwards with 982 others from Drancy.

Gen Oberg took advantage of Darnand's expanded powers to 'request' the deployment of the Milice in the former Occupied Zone, to economise on German manpower. Delighted to agree, Darnand arranged for a council of war each Thursday in Oberg's offices, at which Jean Leguay and his other representatives in the capital took their orders directly from the SS general. In both zones the excesses of the Milice grew wilder after Darnand's elevation to Cabinet rank cloaked them in a pretension of legality. On 10 January a group of *miliciens* under Joseph Lécussan abducted from his home in Lyons at gunpoint the 84-year-old former president of the League for the Rights of Man. Victor Basch and his 79-year-old wife Ilona were driven around and humiliated until Lécussan grew tired of the sport and killed them, dumping their bodies to be found by passers-by. A chronic alcoholic, Lécussan was a tall, heavily built ex-naval officer whose hair-trigger temper matched his red hair. Rarely sober, he had indulged his hatred of Jews and Communists while Director of Jewish Questions in Toulouse by a brutality that killed at least one detainee and by extortion of funds from many others. After joining the Milice in 1943, this record was enough to see him swiftly appointed its regional head in Lyons and graduate from murder to massacre after the Normandy landings.[10]

With Laval's acquiescence, Darnand removed any remaining protection for French citizens and unleashed a spate of arrests of Jews and other 'enemies of the regime', to judge which courts martial were established all over France on 20 January. One of these dangerous people was now seven months pregnant with her third child, the other two being looked after with all the other infants of the Moissac *colonie*. Warned that she risked losing the child in her womb if she did not cut down on her heavy work-schedule, Shatta Simon told her doctor, 'What does one unborn child matter, against the lives of so many living ones?'

One of the 'living ones' was Suzanne Naudet, who was hiding in her aunt's house in a remote part of Lozère. After her younger sister was arrested by gendarmes in the village on 15 January, a friendly dairyman drove Suzanne and her aunt to the one-man gendarmerie post of neighbouring Malzieu. Instead of locking them up, Gendarme Marcellin Cazals turned his single cell into their nightly refuge and found sewing work to occupy them during the day, for which he became one of eight gendarmes recognised as 'Just among the Nations' in the Holocaust archives of Yad Vashem.

Further south, in the Lot-et-Garonne village of Montpezat, Laure Schindler was now in hiding in a house without running water or electricity; among the daily chores she shared was the carrying of water from the communal well. Her foster-parents Hélène and André Gribenski were cultured people who taught in the small private school that Laure attended with her friends Sarah and Ruth from Moissac, whose false papers named them Simone and Régine. Only with them could she relax and literally 'be herself'.

She wrote of this time:

In the evenings André read us poetry by the light of candles or an oil lamp and Hélène played the piano to professional level (returning after the war to Strasbourg Conservatoire, where she was a professor). But I resisted all their approaches with frigid politeness and they respected my need to keep my barriers intact – until the day when I came home from school to hear Hélène playing a Schubert sonata. The piano had been played nearly every day during the three months I had spent in Montpezat, but I had blocked it out of my consciousness because it reminded me too much of my home in Germany and the grand piano in our nice middle-class sitting-room, on which I had endured the hated weekly piano lessons.

For whatever reason, on this day I came home and did not go into my bedroom, but sat down near the piano. Hélène noticed me come in, but continued to play. It was not very long since I had learned that my father had died and, as I listened, it was as though Hélène and Schubert between them were attacking the wall I had built around myself with blow after blow of a huge axe, until I was weeping – not the tears of a frightened child, but of a girl on the threshold of womanhood mourning all the grief in the world.

Hélène stopped playing to embrace me, but did not try to halt the sobs that wracked my still thin body. After a while, she said, 'Let it out, girl. Cry all you want. We were beginning to despair of you and wonder whether there was anybody left there behind all your polite silences.' Then she resumed playing the sonata and I realised that if you build a wall to protect yourself from pain, there is also a wall between you and love, so that you too are dead.[11]

On the same day Eugène Deloncle got his comeuppance on returning from Spain where he had been seeking a bolt-hole for the time when his life would be forfeit in France – and possibly depositing in a safe place some of the funds received during his years of right-wing militancy from Eugène Shueller, president of the Oréal perfume empire. Arrested by the SD, who suspected him of having contacted Gaullist or Allied agents in Spain, Deloncle was interrogated and released so that a *carlingue* gang working for the SD could eliminate him with plausible denial for all his followers of the MSR. Their modus operandi was simply to break down the door of his Paris apartment and shoot Deloncle and his son dead in the guise of a gangland settlement of accounts.

On 21 January the *Journal Officiel* published a decree disbanding the Compagnons de France, which came as no surprise to the leadership after *miliciens* had occupied their HQ at the château of Crépieux-la-Pape near Lyons, as well as some regional centres. That evening a message from Guillaume De Tournemire was read out in every Compagnon camp:

The government has decreed the dissolution of our movement, but . . . the struggle of the Compagnons will continue. Continue your service to your commune, your trade and your families. The day will come when the call of the Compagnons rings out again in our country. Then, the flag that I lowered to half-mast on 26 July 1942 will be raised again to the mast-head. I am counting on all of you. Have courage! Work hard for France!

He ended with the rallying cry, '*A moi, compagnons!*'

That month in Paris electricity was cut off for the night at 10.30 p.m. For cooking, gas of indifferent quality was available only at meal times. People hesitated to take a train because rolling stock was a target of opportunity for patrolling RAF Mosquitoes. One woman arrived in Paris exhausted after spending her whole journey standing on the running board of her coach, so that she could jump off and seek shelter quickly in the event of an air raid.

On 17 February twenty-two members of a PCF action group were executed by firing squad at the Parisian fortress of Mont Valérien after allegedly being betrayed by an attractive red-haired Jewess called Lucienne Goldfarb. Recruited into the Communist Youth aged 18, Lucienne turned informer after losing her parents in *la rafle du Vel d'Hiv*. Whether or not she was working for Darnand on the Manouchian operation or for some PCF faction that wanted the independent Armenian activist out of the way, is unknown. What is certain is that she was luckier than fellow-conspirator Joseph Davidowicz, who was slowly strangled to death by Party comrades whose friends had been betrayed. The crime for which Manouchian's group was shot was the assassination on 28 September 1943 of SS-Standartenführer Julius Ritter, Sauckel's deputy for the STO in France, and they were tracked down not by the Gestapo, but by the Renseignements Généraux, who arrested Manouchian at a meeting on 16 November 1943 with his FTP boss Joseph Epstein.

Seeing everywhere in Paris the black-and-red posters announcing the death sentences, Simone De Beauvoir wrote, 'I looked for a long time (at the young faces on the poster) under the arches of the Metro, thinking with sadness that they would soon be forgotten.'[12] Headed 'Liberation? Are these liberators or an army of criminals?'[13] the posters made much of the fact that Manouchian and his immigrant comrades boasted hardly a single French surname between them. The twenty-third member of the group, Olga Bancic, was beheaded in Stuttgart prison on 10 May 1944.

From his cell a few hours before being led out to execution, Manouchian wrote to his wife,

We are going to be shot at 3 p.m. I don't really believe it, but I know I shall never see you again. I should so like to have had a child by you, as you always wanted. So please get married after the war without any guilt and have a child in my memory. My last wish is that you marry someone who can make you happy. I have no hatred for the German people or anyone else – except for whoever betrayed us and those who sold us. Everyone will have his due reward or punishment.[14]

Marcel Rayman, who died with Manouchian and for the same crime, wrote to his son, 'Be happy and make Mummy happy as I should have wanted to do, had I lived.'[15]

German posters had long since attracted adolescent graffiti, despite the risks. For example, *BOLCHEVISME* was altered to *BOCHE*, so that *SI TU VEUX QUE LA FRANCE VIVE, TU COMBATTRAS LE BOLCHEVISME* was changed from 'If you want France to live, you will fight Bolshevism,' to 'If you want France to live, you will fight the Germans'. The previous year a group of pupil-teachers at the Le Braz lycée in St-Brieuc had encouraged some pupils to tear down German posters, paint V-signs and distribute Resistance literature. After a German soldier was killed in the course of one of these teenage pranks, twenty of the pupils and pupil-teachers were arrested and interrogated by the Gestapo. Some were released, others deported, but the unlucky three lost their lives at Mont Valérien, being shot six minutes before Manouchian and his comrades.[16]

Tortured at several interrogations before his condemnation on 20 January for 'intelligence with the enemy', Maurice Pomponeau was executed on 21 February at the Montluc prison in Lyons for the unusual crime of encouraging desertion by offering false papers, civilian clothes and shelter to *malgré-nous* servicemen from Alsace and Lorraine. By profession an accounts officer in the French Air Force, his last letter to his family was a list of his insurance policies and included the advice that his salary should continue to be paid 'until the end of the war, I think'.[17]

Violent death was not reserved for captured *résistants*. In the late evening of 3 March 1944, RAF bombs aimed at the Renault factory in Boulogne-Billancourt killed 500 civilians living in this densely populated area and injured three times as many. The following day an impromptu cenotaph was erected in the Place de la Concorde, past which a queue estimated at 300,000-strong slowly filed. Another huge demonstration took place at the enormous mass grave into which the hundreds of simple coffins were tightly packed, side by side.

Murder also throve. On 11 March Paris firemen were called by neighbours to a chimney fire at the unoccupied apartment of Dr Marcel Petiot in the very respectable rue Lesueur near the Arc de Triomphe. After breaking in, they recognised the smell of burning flesh and found in the stove the remains of human bodies. After police telephoned Petiot at his surgery near the Opéra, he arrived on a bicycle, claiming to be 'a brother of the occupier' and that he was in the Resistance. The bodies, he said, were of executed traitors. Pretending there were secret files in the apartment, he told the police it was vital the whole affair be hushed up.[18] Only in occupied Paris could anyone telling such a story be allowed to leave after promising to return – and then disappear!

A further step in the moral decline of France's government came on 16 March, when fascist theoretician Marcel Déat joined the Cabinet. After five weeks of stubborn resistance, the Marshal had given in to German pressure, ceded all executive power to Laval and been obliged to accept Hitler's spy Cecil von Renthe-Fink into his immediate entourage. The Hero of Verdun was effectively under house arrest by this time, going outside only for exercise in his garden, accompanied by Ménétrel.

By the end of the month, according to a cable from Abetz to Ribbentrop, the Paris police alone had carried out 4,745 arrests, many for sabotage in factories working for the Germans. This compared with approximately 40,000 French citizens arrested all over France in the whole of the previous year. Of the 670,000 workers drafted to work in the Reich, only 400,000 now remained there, the missing quarter of a million having failed to return from home leave. Those enlisted in recognised Maquis units numbered at most 40,000,[19] so where were the others?

Some lived at home with false papers, operating in informal groups, distributing tracts or collecting intelligence to be passed on to London; others again lived rough in remote areas, but did not put their lives at risk because they had no weapons anyway. In Pellegrue, a small village in Gironde, Robert Hestin spent four months hiding in his bedroom after deserting from the STO, fearful that neighbours would denounce him if he went outdoors. Eventually unable to stand the inaction and because his political views were that way, he joined a Communist Maquis unit passing through the area and travelled with them as far as la Souterraine, north of Limoges. There, he fell out with the self-appointed officers, who tried to win him over with a soft job as their mess servant in a requisitioned château. After giving them a lecture on the inequity of PCF members enjoying the services of a cook, pastrycook and baker in the château while their men slept in barns and lived on soup, Hestin walked out in disgust and continued walking the 200 kilometres home.[20]

Decapitating the many-headed Maquis was impossible because there was no command structure. The Germans and Milice dealt with each band piecemeal, usually by infiltrating informers, so each new recruit had to be carefully vetted. When a Belgian walked into a camp near Thônes in Rhône-Alpes full of plausible details of his family being massacred by the SS, a search of his belongings revealed a hidden SS identity card. Since the Belgian would not talk, there was no alternative but to kill him. All *maquisards* had *noms de guerre*, to protect their families if caught. The one called Blanc-Blanc was elected to do the deed because he had already 'killed his first German' as the saying went. He picked up the group's single Sten gun and begged the victim to pardon him. They embraced, after which Blanc-Blanc could not press the trigger. Everyone looked embarrassed until the Belgian said, 'You can't expect me to give you the balls to do it, so please get a move on.' The leader took the Sten from Blanc-Blanc and fired a single shot at close range, his hands shaking so much that the Belgian was only wounded in the shoulder. Staunching the blood with his handkerchief, he begged them to send it back to his mother unwashed. The next bullet pierced his heart.[21]

With Maquis sabotage and armed attacks growing daily more numerous in the area, the Moissac gendarmes began fortifying their HQ. They also alerted the Maquis to German ambushes, but by no means all the civilian population supported the sabotage, as when the Toulouse–Bordeaux line was blown up in the early hours of 20 March, angering many Moissagais who could have been killed taking produce to market in Bordeaux on the 5 a.m. red-eye special.

Chapter 20

DANCING IN THE DARK

Two days later, with Hubert De Monbrison *en mission* she knew not where, and her daughters Françoise and Manon staying safely with the Giraud family in Moissac, Renée went to visit her aunt Loulou, staying at a small hotel in La Roque-Gageac, a picturesque village on the banks of the Dordogne. It was an inspired choice of date, for at 6.30 the following morning a party of Germans blew in the kitchen door of Château St-Roch, hoping to find Hubert there.

Renée's two sons looked out of their bedroom window to see another soldier prone beside a machine gun under the great cedar tree in the garden with a server kneeling beside him to feed the belt of ammunition, ready to shoot down anyone fleeing the house. Booted feet ran up the grand stone staircase. Two soldiers burst into the boys' bedroom, hauling them bodily down to the main hall decorated with the armour, swords and halberds of their father's Huguenot ancestors. There, they were lined up at gunpoint in their pyjamas with the valet, Pierre, his wife and frightened children, and a recently arrived refugee boy of 17, whom the boys pretended was a visiting cousin. Young Jean De Monbrison urgently needed to empty his bladder after the night's sleep. Christian warned him that he would be shot for trying to escape if he so much as moved, but when the attention of the Germans relaxed, 10-year-old Jean slipped into a toilet. He was hauled out before he had finished and booted back into line with the others while the building was searched.

The ancient uncle, whose senility prevented his understanding the danger in which he stood, appeared and told them blithely, 'These gentlemen have invited me to go and take breakfast with them in Toulouse.' After his valet had made the Germans understand that his master was no longer able to look after himself, the officer commanding laughingly arrested him also, so he could continue his customary duties inside the St-Michel prison in Toulouse!

The soldiers now conducted a more thorough search for Hubert, using 15-year-old Christian as a human shield. The nightmare probably lasted no more than twenty minutes, but seemed an eternity to the boy. As they shoved him ahead of them through each doorway, he was more frightened that his father might have returned in the night without waking them than of the loaded rifles prodding his back. Released to rejoin his younger brother, he saw the nephew of the estate steward who had betrayed them all being taken away by the Germans, together with the Spanish workers and the youths with false papers for whom Renée had found jobs on the estate.

After the departure of the Germans, accompanied by the usual threats to return, the only people left in the main house were the two brothers, the false cousin and a hysterical Jewish girl from Alsace. Working in the kitchen when the Germans arrived, she had the presence of mind to make coffee for the officers. Thanking her politely, they had taken no more notice of her, but her nerve cracked when she understood them discussing in German whether to shoot one of the brothers and leave his dead body on the steps of the château as bait to bring his father back in the hope of saving his other son. The terrified girl hid in the garden while the three youths ran upstairs to grab sunglasses, old hats and coats as disguise for themselves and her before jogging for 14 kilometres through the woods and fields to reach Françoise in Moissac.

She was in her bedroom doing some maths homework that had to be handed in the next day when called downstairs by Madame Giraud after her brothers and the two other terrified young people arrived, exhausted and covered in mud. Since there was no way of contacting their father, Françoise decided to set out with Christian by train to Sarlat, the nearest railway station to La Roque-Gageac, and warn their mother not to return. They arrived at Sarlat five minutes before curfew. Warned to stay in the station until dawn or risk being shot on sight by a German patrol, they slipped out and walked 12 kilometres through totally unknown country in pitch darkness, hiding in ditches each time they met a German patrol. Luckily none had dogs. Well after 1 a.m., they arrived exhausted at the hotel, to wake their mother with the news of what had happened that morning. After tears from Renée, relieved that Hubert had not been captured or killed, Christian fell asleep, leaving his mother and sister to worry about what to do next.[1]

Taking refuge in the house of an old friend of Hubert, Renée and her children were awoken early one morning by the noise of doors being broken down. Opening the bedroom shutters to escape through the garden, they found their way blocked by a civilian in black leather coat, who pointed a revolver at them and shouted, 'Police spéciale allemande!' Lined up awaiting interrogation, Renée briefed her children in whispers about her current false identity, while fully expecting to be taken away in handcuffs or even shot on the spot. However, the Geheime Feldpolizei men showed no interest in her or the children, having come for the daughter-in-law of the owner of the house, whose letters in a personal code to her husband serving in the French Army in Algieria had been intercepted by the censors. Assuming her a spy, they ignored pleas from her father-in-law to take him instead because she had two little children to look after, and hustled the terrified woman off to the Fort Montluc in Lyons, leaving her 7-month-old baby and 2-year-old son to be looked after by Renée and her daughters.

After Françoise had returned to Moissac, her younger sister Manon volunteered to accompany her back to the château without the steward seeing them, to recover some of Renée's jewellery, to be sold for food. They found the hiding place easily and thrust the jewels into the saddle-bag of one bicycle, heading for Moissac with a borrowed poodle sitting in the basket on the handlebars of the other bike. At two checkpoints on the road, they stopped and chatted to the German soldiers, letting them fondle the poodle, before riding off high on adrenalin at the risk they had taken and holding their breath for a shouted '*Halt!*' and the click of a rifle bolt behind them.

Shortly afterwards, Françoise was woken up one morning by the sound of a *gazogène* truck pulling up outside yet another temporary home. Fearing the worst, she was delighted to see her father climb down from the cab – until she heard that he was on his way to give himself up in Toulouse so that his uncle could be released. Realising that he would be shot or deported, Françoise tried to dissuade him and was left in tears as he drove off, her anguish turning to joy when he returned after a woman recognised him at Valence station waiting for the Toulouse train and whispered the news that the ancient uncle had been released that morning.[2]

In March, the critic and poet Max Jacob died in Drancy of sickness and ill-treatment after several great names on the French cultural scene had done their best to have him released. With it getting both more difficult and dangerous to plead for exemptions, among those who refused to lend their signatures to a petition was Pablo Picasso, who lived and painted undisturbed throughout the Occupation. As though excusing himself for abandoning his friend of nearly half a century, Picasso said, 'Max was always an angel. Now he will be one.'

Old and young were grist alike to Hitler's mill. Barbie chalked up another great victory on 6 April by a raid on La Maison des Roches at Izieu, isolated in the Rhône-Alpes, although only 20 kilometres from Chambéry as the crow flies. Since May 1943 French Red Cross worker Sabina Zlatin and her husband Miron had sheltered a community of 100-plus Jewish children in the neighbourhood with the cooperation of local residents. Forty-five children were having lessons in the house from five adult helpers on that sunny morning while she was out seeking more hideouts, unaware that a denunciation had brought Barbie's convoy of cars and soft-top trucks to Izieu.

With boots and rifle butts, the children were hustled onto the trucks. Toddlers unable to clamber aboard were thrown bodily in and the tailboards slammed shut. One adult survived the war; two adolescents and Miron Zlatin were transported 3,000 kilometres by train and shot at Tallinn in Estonia; the children were gassed naked at Auschwitz on 15 April. One of the women sorting clothing outside the gas chamber was Fortunée Benguigui, who had kept herself alive in the camp hoping that her children were safe in France. That morning, she recognised on a pile of clothing outside the gas chamber a pullover belonging to her son Jacques.

Life goes on. That was also the day an unknown young singer named Charles Aznavour got the break he had been waiting for at the Casino-Montparnasse in Paris, while at the ABC the Compagnons de la Chanson were singing the repertoire for which they would be famous worldwide thirty years later. Another unknown called Yves Montand came to Paris that spring to seek his fortune despite being on the run from his STO obligations and suspected of being technically Jewish. On the night after his first engagement, he was only saved from arrest by the proprietor of his hotel distracting a German military police NCO from checking his guest's obviously false ID. His first pay-checks lost at the poker tables, Montand had a second stroke of luck when Edith Piaf fell out with her current male singer. Montand detested Piaf as heartily as she sneered at what she called his 'poor singing', but when she insisted that he dress like her on stage – all in black – he decided to make this his trademark style for the rest of his career.

With 2,000 Waffen-SS troops straight from the Russian front posted to the Moissac area to regroup and refit, Madame Delmas, owner of a smart hotel and restaurant in the centre of town, with a husband who was a POW in Germany, organised *dîners dansants* for the SS officers on a Friday evening. Food and alcohol could always be found on the black market; her problem was finding attractive girls to amuse them. Each Friday afternoon she came to have her hair done in Marie-Rose's salon, so as to look her best that evening. Several times she invited her beautiful hairdresser to join the fun, promising that the food was excellent and the officers very correct: 'You'll have a good time. Nobody's going to make you do anything you don't want to, so where's the harm?' Often in the salon, Marie-Rose had heard women discussing girls who went with Germans; it was hinted darkly that they would 'have to pay for it' after the Liberation. It wasn't that which held her back: she just did not want to get involved with this very manipulative client. One Friday evening in April 1944, Madame Delmas telephoned just before closing time to say that she had been unable to get away that afternoon for her hair appointment. The plea ended, 'Couldn't you, just this once, come to the hotel and comb my hair out? I'd be so grateful.'[3]

Reluctantly, Marie-Rose agreed to help a regular customer in a fix and packed a few essentials in a bag. After arriving at the hotel, she was kept waiting by Madame Delmas until it was almost time for the guests to arrive. To escape after doing her hair, Marie-Rose used the excuse of having to look after her son, but Madame Delmas said, 'Let your parents take care of him. Stay just for a while and enjoy a good dinner. You deserve it.'

The food was ample and well cooked, the atmosphere very relaxed, with all the officers in their immaculate SS uniforms being very correct and attentive to the ladies. Several times Marie-Rose danced with a blond, blue-eyed Austrian officer. An engineer in civilian life, he told her his name was Willi. She was 23 years old, he three years older. One of the other girls present, interpreting for the officers who could not speak French, was a vivacious multilingual Jewish refugee called Masha from Latvia, whose 'racial impurity' bothered none of the SS men.

Good food, a glass or two of wine, the elegant atmosphere and the polite manners of the men chatting up the girls with champagne glasses in their hands in the moonlit garden behind the hotel, all put Marie-Rose off her guard. All she knew of Willi was that he was unmarried and came from Vienna. Yet when he asked whether they could meet again the following Friday, she blushed to hear herself say that she would like that.

It seemed a very long week. Two weeks after their second meeting they became lovers. Sometimes they met, not entirely by chance, on the street by the salon or on the beach where local families and the German soldiers went to swim in the River Tarn with an unmarked demarcation line separating the two groups of swimmers. Then they could only share a few glances, for romantic attachments were forbidden to an SS officer, even had Marie-Rose been prepared to 'come out' and let the neighbours know. Only in Madame Delmas' hotel could she and Willi openly be together.

On 20 April Pétain paid his first visit to Paris since the defeat on the occasion of a Requiem Mass in memory of the thousands of victims of the Allied bombing campaign. Received inside Notre Dame cathedral by Cardinal Suhard and senior German officers, he emerged to the acclaim of an enthusiastic crowd estimated at 1,000,000 people. Commentator Jean Galtier-Boissière reckoned that immediately after the Armistice 95 per cent of French people were for Pétain; 50 per cent remained so until the occupation of the southern zone; and 30 per cent remained loyal right up to the Normandy landings.

One reason came the following day, when the RAF raided the suburb of St Denis and the important freight-handling yards of the Gare de la Chapelle, destroying 304 buildings, damaging Le Sacré Coeur cathedral and leaving another 635 dead.[4] On 28 April Pétain was allowed to broadcast an appeal for calm and respect for German personnel, his essential impotence being evident on a visit to the Château de Voisins, south-west of Paris, when twelve of the nineteen cars in his cortège were full of German security men.[5] Nevertheless, even on D-Day+1 at St-Etienne, his rapturous reception by the crowds was both a tribute to him as a man and a gesture of appreciation for the persistence with which he had tried to find a spoon long enough to sup with Hitler. Having no intention of allowing him to be kidnapped by *résistants* after his return to Vichy, as had happened to Mussolini the previous summer, his German captors obliged the Marshal to spend each night in the Château de Lonzat, surrounded by German troops, with an inner cordon of his personal bodyguard and the château itself patrolled by French police.

On 2 May Brünner despatched to Drancy a victim more precious than he realised. Odette Rodenstock had been betrayed and arrested at her apartment by three *miliciens*. Interrogated under torture, she pretended to have lied to get her cover job as a social worker employed by the diocese – this to protect Major Rémond. Realising their mistake, the Gestapo in Nice cabled Drancy to 'continue her interrogations'. Abbadi took a train to Paris, hoping to rescue her somehow, but had to content himself with sending a food parcel. Rescue being out of the question, she was deported in Convoy 74 on 20 May to Auschwitz-Birkenau, later to survive long starvation in Bergen-Belsen.

With all the burden of looking after 527 hidden children now falling on his shoulders, Abbadi returned to Nice, to find that it was too risky to stay in his hotel room after dawn – the time when Odette had been arrested – but also too dangerous to walk the empty streets before the bars were open. He returned to the diocesan offices to ask for a list of churches with early Mass, and recalled later, with a humour that conceals the horror of his situation at the time, 'Every morning at 6.30 a.m. I was in some church or chapel. No devout Catholic ever went more regularly to Mass.'[6]

On the night of 21 May the RAF bombed Orleans, killing 150 civilians. In the absence of any organised rescue services, it was the survivors who had to clear away the ruins in a town without water or gas. British planes returned on 8 June to destroy the Vierzon rail bridge and the two main road bridges were wired for demolition by the Germans. As the real D-Day approached, the pace of RAF arms drops to the Resistance accelerated, until the Maquis in south Dordogne boasted 2,800 Sten guns, 450 military rifles, 500 revolvers, eight anti-tank grenade launchers, 100 automatic rifles and several tonnes of plastic explosives. With all this weaponry, some of it in the hands of civilians with a grudge to settle, it is not surprising that from D-Day to the end of July there were an estimated 6,000 murders in France. In some cases, whole families were wiped out for reasons that had nothing to do with the war.

After the last 3,500 STO conscripts left in July, bringing the total of French workers inside the labour-starved Reich to some 200,000 – of whom 10 per cent were female volunteers – the Germans ordered a census of unmarried women who could be conscripted. The archbishop of Toulouse spoke up, his family-centred Catholic morality outraged at the idea of single women being removed from the safety of their communities and sent to a foreign land. In occupied Moissac, the only 'incident' was on 3 June when a German soldier attempted to rape a local woman. The task of the town council had become almost impossible, torn as they were between the flow of laws and instructions from Vichy and the impositions of the Germans, but when Dr Moles tendered his resignation as mayor, he was ordered to withdraw it, so he went to a colleague and had himself given 'sick leave'.

As part of the deception campaign to convince the Germans that the invasion was going to take place in the Pas de Calais, 8,000 tonnes of bombs were dropped on 4 June in what was only a diversionary raid on Boulogne, increasing the misery of the survivors in the town. By then, even the cloud-cuckoo world of Parisian haute couture was aware that the situation was too serious for frivolity: for once no autumn collections were shown. Material for clothes had in any case become nearly unobtainable, with the latest regulations for footwear restricting the permissible materials to wood, raffia – and rattan.[7]

The story of the Normandy landings on 6 June is too well known to need commentary here. With a news blackout on French radio, many people heard of the invasion in a roundabout way. At the beginning of June, Willi had been due for fifteen days' leave and tried to persuade Marie-Rose to travel to Vienna in order to meet his parents who, he was sure, would raise no objections to their marriage after the war. Whether it would actually have been possible for her to go there, Marie-Rose never found out because she told Willi that she could not leave her son. He therefore took his leave in Moissac, meeting her discreetly in sports shirt and shorts after the salon closed in the balmy early summer evenings.

Masha earned her living by giving German lessons in Montauban and Toulouse. It had been a boom market, with Berlitz language schools' students rising from a pre-war 939 adults to 7,920 in 1941.[8] On 6 June she and Marie-Rose were driven by an Italian SS auxiliary to Montauban, where Masha was to give some lessons and Marie-Rose had to buy supplies for the salon. They arrived there before midday, took an early lunch in the Sans Souci restaurant and then split up, having agreed to rendezvous there at 4 p.m. Returning to the restaurant, Marie-Rose found Masha agog with bush-telegraph reports of the landings in Normandy. The Italian driver was nowhere to be found and all the German troops in Montauban were hastily departing, so the two women took a train back to Moissac. The streets of the town were deserted, except for the last SS men loading equipment onto trucks to head north. Willi was gone. Marie-Rose had no idea where until receiving a letter from him explaining that he had been wounded fighting with his unit on the Normandy front and invalided back to the Reich. Thus began a correspondence that lasted two years.

Maquis and Resistance groups all over France had received coded orders in the BBC personal messages on the night of 5 June to blow up rail tracks, telephone lines and bridges. For obvious reasons, let alone the restoration of national prestige, one would think that Free French troops played an important role in the first landings. On the contrary, Gaullist presence on the beaches on 6 June was limited to less than 200 French liaison officers sent in with the early waves, 180 French commandos who went ashore with the British at Ouistreham and a small paratroop detachment dropped in Brittany.[9]

De Gaulle was understandably angry at not being informed of the invasion date until hours beforehand, ostensibly because the Allied command mistrusted Free French security, but also because President Roosevelt lacked any concept of the civil unrest that might be triggered by treating all the factions in the Resistance as equal allies, once ashore. He had all along preferred to deal with Pétain or Darlan or General Giraud in preference to De Gaulle, who patently would not become a passive puppet after the war. Winston Churchill was obliged to follow suit, since it was an American ball the game was being played with. Anglo-American interest in France at that point in the war was to make it the most advantageous battlefield over which to fight Germany into unconditional surrender. For De Gaulle, the liberation of his country was the first priority.

PART FOUR

THE PRICE OF LIBERATION

Chapter 21

ATROCITIES ON BOTH SIDES

Broadcast on 6 June from London were pre-recorded messages from Churchill and Eisenhower, also printed as leaflets dropped on populated areas. Both leaders exhorted the French people to do everything possible to assist the invasion. Furious at the way he had been sidelined throughout the planning, De Gaulle at first refused to record a message because their speeches failed to acknowledge him as leader of Free France. Unwilling to fragment the Resistance by naming and condemning the factions with their own agendas, he agreed at the last moment to broadcast an injunction for the population to obey only the orders from Gaullist officers.

What the Anglo-Saxons failed to appreciate and what he foresaw all too clearly, was the hideous game about to be played in the plumb centre of France. The town of St-Amand-Montrond lay some 300 kilometres from the landing beaches, but less than 40 kilometres from the major city of Bourges, where there were important Wehrmacht, Gestapo, Milice and Vichy military units. Four local Maquis leaders met at dawn on 6 June in the house of René Van Gaver, while the alarm was still being sounded on the Atlantic Wall at the first sight of the enormous invasion armada off-shore.

With Van Gaver were Daniel Blanchard of Combat and Hubert Lalonnier of the FTP. As far as armed intervention was concerned, all four men were supposed to take their orders from COMAC, the Comité d'Action Militaire of the united Resistance movements. COMAC was controlled by PCF members Pierre Vrillon and Maurice Kriegel-Valrimont with fellow-Communist Alfred Malleret-Joinville. The confusion of titles, initials and code-names was deliberate, to obscure the long arm of the Comintern, which preferred the PCF at this stage to set the stage for its role after the Liberation through apparently popular-front organisations. If their actions succeeded, the Party could emerge and claim the credit; failure could be blamed on the other partners in the umbrella organisations.

COMAC had called upon all units not only to implement several agreed plans – Plan Green was the sabotage of railways, Plan Slowcoach the blockage of roads, and so on – but also to 'show a spirit of sacrifice' in exceeding instructions and taking local initiatives. It was that spirit of sacrifice that was to cause all the misery in peaceful St-Amand. On Sunday 4 June at a village fête in nearby Châteaumeillant Blanchard and his fellow-*résistant* and brother-in-law André Sagnelonge got stinking drunk. When

Blanchard's wife told the men to stop drinking, he told her to get lost because 'It's the last piss-up we're ever going to have.'[1]

The senior military mind in the Resistance in the Cher *département* was Colonel Bertrand, a career soldier who had been underground with the Armée Secrète since April 1943. Why had he not been invited to the early-morning meeting on 6 June, or to a preparatory meeting held on 29 May? The answer lay with the fourth man at the meeting in Van Gaver's house. A militant PCF member posing as the neutral regional organiser of the multi-party Front National, Fernand Sochet had deliberately cut Bertrand out of the line of command to prevent the colonel's professional appreciation of the situation dampening the ardour of the local young men frustrated by four years of Occupation. In the words of one Communist *résistant* involved, 'We were driving a Citroën *traction avant*, while [Bertrand] was riding a bicycle.'[2] At that moment, they should all have been on bicycles and keeping well off the main roads.

However, between the two meetings in St-Amand, Van Gaver and Blanchard did contact Col Bertrand and tell him of the planned local uprising. Bertrand was horrified: a single glance at the map was enough to show that overt military action had no hope of success, and would certainly incite German and Vichy reprisals long before any Allied troops could get there from Normandy. Moreover, he had received De Gaulle's order dated 16 May that when the invasion took place no confrontation was to be sought in the early stages because 'a general unplanned uprising [then] by the diverse factions of the FFI is likely to break the impetus of French Resistance and cause considerable harm to the general population, without any compensating gain'.[3]

Given the fragmented control of the FFI, Bertrand did not have authority to stop the local commanders from going ahead, but reluctantly agreed to request the CO of the locally based Vichy 1RF regiment that his troops not intervene, whatever happened in St-Amand. The stage was set for tragedy, and the unwitting heroine was Simone Bout de l'An, whose husband Francis was outright boss of the Milice since Darnand had been promoted to Minister of the Interior. Ironically, her husband had chosen St-Amand as a safe place to leave her and their two children because it was the sort of town where 'nothing ever happened'.

At 5.30 p.m. on 6 June De Gaulle's hastily written speech was broadcast from London, containing the ambiguous phrase that 'the duty of the sons of France . . . is to fight with all the means at their disposal'.[4] To Blanchard and Sagnelonge, pumping adrenalin after four humiliating years, he seemed to be blessing their local initiative. Thirty minutes later, some seventy men with an assortment of arms gathered at a lock gate on the canal outside town. Subsequent Communist commentators seeking to justify the label 'popular uprising' multiplied the initial numbers threefold. The Renseignements Généraux, in an attempt to justify the lack of action by local forces of law and order, multiplied them tenfold, but men involved that day are definite: a maximum of seventy.

Many of them were strangers to each other and introductions were made at the same time as weapons parachuted to a Combat group were handed out to men who had never handled anything more lethal than a shotgun. Fortunately only one *résistant* was killed before they learned how easy it was to loose a burst accidentally from the Stens. Most of them were aged between 20 and 25, on the run from the STO and looking for a way of proving their courage and manhood. The PCF members among them had been instructed that day to 'exterminate all the German garrisons and . . . kill without mercy all the murderous rabble of the Milice'.[5]

Feeling trigger-happy with weapons in their hands, but no training to use them, they surrounded the Milice headquarters and opened fire. An impressive hail of bullets struck the building, but hit no one inside. Nor did the return fire and hand grenades of the *miliciens* score a hit until a stray shot killed an innocent passer-by. The attackers having no unified command, each man kept in touch only with the others he knew, allowing one *milicien* to escape on a motorcycle and give the alarm by telephone, stirring waves in Bourges and Vichy with his vivid account of Allied parachutists dropping on St-Amand, invented to justify his running away.

Inside the building, Simone's small son was sick and needed hospital treatment. Furious at the incompetence of the men supposedly protecting her, Simone gave them all a good tongue-lashing, on the lines of 'Call yourselves men?' She then ordered the senior *milicien* to inform the FFI by telephone that they were prepared to surrender for the sake of the women and children, provided they were guaranteed their lives. Lalonnier agreed to this, without any intention of keeping his word to men who had arrested and beaten up his friends. After Simone thrust a white sheet out of a window at about 11 p.m. the *miliciens* walked out, hands above their heads, followed by the women and children. Lalonnier wanted to kill the men there and then in compliance with the FTP directive, but gave way to Blanchard and Van Gaver, who insisted they be treated as POWs and locked up in the sub-prefecture.

Because the *miliciens* had not bothered to destroy their files of informers and sympathisers, these were now used to launch a manhunt, with so many people dragged out of their houses at gunpoint that Mayor René Sadrin turned the town hall into a prison because the sub-prefecture cells were not big enough. The only Germans in the town – three civilians from the STO – were also locked up there, but not maltreated. The general euphoria was somewhat dampened when the flood of volunteers eager to join the FFI was issued only three bullets per man and a hunting gun from the store of those confiscated after the defeat, but slowly the numbers mounted until they approached 200 maximum.

Francis Bout de l'An was awoken in his Paris hotel next morning with the news that his wife and children were hostages of the FFI. Darnand, also in

Paris, told him to use all necessary German and French forces to re-take the town and liberate his family. At the same time, Van Gaver received from a patrol of 1RF outside town the disquieting news that the Allies were still bottled up in a few square miles of Normandy beachhead and neither Bourges nor any other city in France had 'liberated itself', so that the FFI in St-Amand were on their own. This was not quite true – in Guéret there was fighting between local FFI and Milice/German forces, but no help was to be expected from that quarter.

Telephoning the sub-prefecture in St-Amand in the hope of getting an update from a Vichy official, Bout de l'An found himself talking to Van Gaver, sitting in the sub-prefect's chair. The conversation rapidly degenerated into an exchange of insults that became threats. At more or less the same time, when the Allied forces were clinging desperately to the first few miles of beachhead, a 35-year-old Communist teacher known as 'Col Kléber' Chapou ordered his private army of 400 FTP and other *maquisards* to occupy the city of Tulle in central France, 160 kilometres south of St-Amand. With the nearest Allied troops fighting for their lives over 400 kilometres distant, it was glaringly obvious that the town could not be held and that killing the forty or so German soldiers in the town was an invitation for reprisal massacres. However, a mood of euphoria at being 'liberated' by their own compatriots had some of the population dancing in the streets by nightfall. Their joy was to be short-lived.

Travelling via Vichy, where he collected thirty *miliciens*, Bout de l'An headed towards St-Amand, stopping 60 kilometres short at Moulins, where the Wehrmacht commander promised to attack St-Amand in force the following morning, meantime gathering intelligence on enemy strength by over-flying a light observation aircraft, whose pilot reported that the town was in a holiday mood, with only a few barricades here and there. The FFI, having neither camouflaged their transport, nor parked it under cover, panicked at the sight of the small aircraft with Maltese cross markings and left after posting warning notices that the thirty-six *miliciens* and the women they were taking with them would be shot in the event of reprisals on the townsfolk. They were signed 'The Committee of the Resistance'. In fact, only seven women and eighteen of the male prisoners were loaded aboard the departing trucks. Simone's children had been taken to the hospital, despite her protests at being separated from them. Although her captors knew exactly who she was, and rightly considered her more valuable than all the other prisoners, she alone among the hostages showed no sign of fear, openly despising the girlfriends of the *miliciens* – or 'little sluts' as she called them.

When the inevitable German attack came in, apart from the pilot of the spotter plane hitting a tree-top and crashing in flames, all the casualties were among the population. Nineteen civilians were killed, six homes burned to the ground and 200 hostages locked up in the 1RF barracks. As one local summed up bitterly, 'On 7 June the Maquis ordered drinks all round, leaving us to pay for the drinks next day.'

Finding their three compatriots unharmed, the Germans withdrew in good order, handing the town over to the Milice, who plundered and burned the homes of the departed FFI men. And there the sorry episode would have ended, but for the hostages. Bout de l'An could hardly ignore such a challenge, although some observers considered him more interested in reasserting his authority than in reclaiming his wife for emotional reasons. Staying at a safe distance even after the shooting was over, he showed no concern for the *milicien* hostages, declaring that they should have died fighting. But the fact that his wife was still a hostage sent him into a rage in which he ordered all the 200-odd prisoners to be executed if his wife were not liberated within forty-eight hours. To save these lives, Mayor Sadrin of St-Amand and a friend volunteered to try to deliver this ultimatum, but the Maquis column had split up to be less conspicuous from the air and vanished into the countryside.

In Tulle, by 6 a.m. on 9 June tanks of the SS armoured division Das Reich were patrolling all the main streets. SS men forced entry into the houses and dragged out any men found inside, arresting also any male on the streets. André Gamblin, a 22-year-old accountant, was shopping for milk for his baby daughter when they picked him up. *Gazogène* engineer Raymond Lesouëf was having breakfast with his wife and two children when he was led away. In all, more than 3,000 men were herded inside the walls of the MAT armament factory on Place Souilhac while the SS went around the town collecting ladders and rope. They were in no hurry because this was routine work for them. Their commander, Major Kowatsch, admitted as much to Prefect Trouillé: 'We hanged more than 100,000 at Kiev and Kharkov. What we are doing here is nothing for us.'[6]

A slim, blond Belgian-born Feldgendarmerie officer, Lieutenant Walter Schmald had been in Tulle for five months and narrowly escaped assassination by the *maquisards*. It was he who conducted a triage, releasing doctors, postal clerks and others essential for running the town, and returning towards midday to divide the remaining men into two groups: those to be hanged and those to witness the hangings. After the Germans had eaten lunch, leaving their hungry victims standing in the sun, at 1.30 p.m. a loudspeaker truck toured the town, announcing that life should go back to normal. To keep the victims calm, they were assured there would be no killing of hostages, just an identity check.

Locked up in the Kommandantur, Adjutant-Chef Conchonnet and three gendarmes were released at 4.30 p.m., in time to hear a loudspeaker announcement that hostages were to be hanged and their bodies thrown into the river. The SS were in holiday mood, they noted, smoking and laughing. Seeing corpses dangling everywhere, the gendarmes were then escorted to the railway station, where twenty-one colleagues from the Lot *département*, brought along as hostages by the SS, had already taken off their ties, to speed up their own deaths. Thanks to the mayor's intervention, the gendarmes were not hanged.[7]

From behind curtains and over garden walls the women of Tulle watched one of their sex chatting freely with the SS men killing their husbands, brothers, fathers and sons. Tall, blonde Paulette Geissler was well known as the horse-riding, chain-smoking German secretary of the manager of the armament factory. From that day, the women of Tulle call her *la chienne* – the bitch – and allege that she laughed at the men being hanged and blew cigarette smoke into their faces. Father Jean Espinasse, who was with the men as they were hanged, said only that Geissler was chain-smoking as usual while she chatted with the SS, who were joking with each other to accordion music and popular songs played over loudspeakers.

A competent amateur sketch of the scene may have been done by an SS officer. Opinions differ, but the sketch shows the houses with soldiers casually walking along the pavement, silhouetted corpses hanging from each lamppost. In the centre, a busy group reminiscent of a Renaissance Crucifixion: an officer watches with hands on hips, a soldier on a ladder against a lamppost is reaching down to help a hostage awkwardly climbing a second ladder towards the noose above his head with his hands tied behind his back, another soldier steadies the victim's ladder, ready to pull it away. Three or four other victims under guard watch what is going to happen to them.[8]

The priest also described how the SS divided the condemned men into groups of ten, with their hands tied behind their backs, and how the SS man at the top of the ladder put the noose around the victim's neck when he was high enough and then ordered the second ladder pulled away. And so it went on, life after life, until every balcony, telegraph pole and lamppost along the main street had a body hanging from it, the last ones still convulsively twitching.[9]

The following day units of the same SS division immortalised its name at a large village which has become France's national shrine to the victims of the German retreat. Less than 20 kilometres north-west of Limoges, Oradour-sur-Glane is frozen in time. The roofless homes and shops, barns and workshops could be the result of an earthquake or area bombing for, as the roofs collapsed, they brought the walls down with them in many cases. Yet all this ruination was accomplished by fire and a few bullets.

At 2 p.m. on the balmy summer afternoon of Saturday 10 June, 120 men of 3rd Company of 2 SS Regiment Der Führer belonging to SS Division Das Reich cordoned off the village. Major Adolf Diekmann ordered the mayor to assemble the villagers by beating the traditional drum. One 8-year-old boy in a small school for refugee children from Lorraine hid in a garden either because he recognised the SS uniforms or because he understood what the men were saying in German: Roger Godfrin was to be the sole child alive by the end of the afternoon. The other 247 pupils in the refugee school and the main school obediently lined up with their teachers for what they were told was an identity check.

A party of cyclists – five young men and a girl seeking refreshments – were allowed through the cordon to share the fate of the villagers, as were a number of mothers living in outlying hamlets who came looking for sons and daughters after the time they should have returned home. The women and children were first herded into the church, after which the males were locked into several barns. That sounds an orderly procedure, yet evidence at the postwar trial was that groups of men, women and children were shot in the streets, some left wounded and finished off later. Several bodies were stuffed down a well only sixty centimetres in diameter.

The five male adult survivors testified that the SS shot at the mass of bodies jammed into their barn, aiming low to hit the legs and throwing straw and other combustible material on top of the bodies, many still living, before setting fire to everything with phosphorus grenades. While 197 of their male friends and relatives died of wounds or were burned alive, the five survived by throwing themselves flat when the first shots were fired and hiding in a corner of the barn that the flames did not reach, subsequently escaping into the countryside.

The SS next turned their attention to the church. The one woman to survive testified that at about 5 p.m. two soldiers carried in a large box with fuses coming from it, which they lit and retired. Inside were what were described at the trial as asphyxiating grenades that filled the church with choking smoke, panicking the press of 240 desperate women and 205 children into breaking down the door into the sacristy. There, the SS were waiting at the windows, like farmers waiting for rabbits to break from the last stand of corn to be harvested. Bullet holes in the masonry show how they shot at the trapped women and children.

In desperation, 47-year-old Marguerite Rouffanche used the stepladder for lighting the altar candles to climb up to a stained-glass window behind the altar, through which she fell to the ground outside. Another woman climbed up and threw her baby to Madame Rouffanche. It fell to the ground, both mother and child being immediately killed. Madame Rouffanche, although hit by several bullets, managed to hide behind a stone wall in the presbytery garden, where she was found by civilians the following morning.

At 7 p.m. the evening commuter tram from Limoges was halted at the SS cordon. Passengers whose papers showed a domicile other than in Oradour had come to buy black-market food. They were ordered back on board, to return to Limoges. The twenty-two inhabitants of Oradour were lined up against a wall with a machine gun pointing at them. One can imagine their feelings as they were kept there, with the smoke from every building in the burning town darkening the evening sky for miles around and their nostrils filled with the stink of burning flesh. Many of the SS were drunk on looted wine and spirits, but after three hours the hostages were simply told to go away. Entrance into the village being forbidden, they sought refuge on nearby farms or hid in the woods till dawn.

By the end of the day, out of all the 700 people who had woken up that morning in Oradour only the boy from Lorraine, one woman and five men were alive. Of the 642 people killed only fifty-two corpses were definitely identified; the others were carbonised, many not even recognisable as human. Some time after dawn, the last SS departed and the handful of surviving inhabitants of Oradour walked into the stinking, smouldering ruins that had been their homes. Every house was gutted. Six decades later, rusting motor vehicles and children's prams and bicycles have almost completely disintegrated. The melted bronze bell still lies on the church floor for tourists to photograph.

As to the reasons why it all happened, on the French side it is claimed that there was no Resistance activity in Oradour-sur-Glane and that the SS misread their maps, when they should have been at nearby Oradour-sur-Vayres, where the Maquis had been active. The German version does not differ greatly as far as the massacre of the men is concerned, but claims that the village was the right one, to be destroyed in reprisal for three local Resistance operations, in which two German officers had been kidnapped by the Maquis and an ambulance convoy ambushed. Stripped to his underclothes, Lieutenant Gerlach managed to escape after capture while his driver was being machine-gunned in some woodland. He found his way back to his unit by following a railway line, and indicated that his kidnapping had occurred near Oradour-sur-Glane. After his traumatic experience, and since he had fallen into the hands of the Maquis after misreading his map and getting lost, he may well have confused one village called Oradour with the other. Two unidentified *miliciens* also directed the SS to Oradour-sur-Glane on the morning of 10 June.

In the second incident, a German ambulance unit was attacked by *maquisards*, with the medical personnel and wounded men they were transporting burned alive in the vehicles. In the third, while prospecting ahead of his unit Major Helmut Kämpfe, a personal friend of Diekmann, was taken prisoner by a band of FTP *maquisards* led by Jean Canou. The major's personal papers were found by a despatch rider in a street in Tulle next day, where he had presumably thrown them to leave a clue while being transferred from one vehicle to another. An offer to return him unharmed against the release of *maquisard* prisoners was agreed to, but the Maquis killed him anyway. His remains were found by German war graves investigators after the war, with 10 June 1944 given as the date of death. It was afterwards claimed by the Maquis that he was killed in retaliation for what happened at Oradour.

With the *maquisards* neither wearing uniform nor carrying their arms openly – and thus not protected by military law – *Ordnung Sperrle*, the Standing Orders for dealing with Resistance attacks on German troops required the area of an attack to be routinely cordoned off, and houses from which shots had been fired to be burned, with three hostages shot for every soldier wounded and ten hanged for each dead German. Major Diekmann, commanding the troops at Oradour, claimed to have found bodies of murdered Germans on arrival there, as well as caches of weapons and ammunition. According to his account, there was no intention of killing the women and children and the men were to be taken hostage, but when the houses were set on fire, the flames spread to the roof of the church, where the Maquis had a store of explosives, which blew up and brought the flaming roof down onto the victims below, producing heat sufficient to melt the bronze bell.

Diekmann's superior, Colonel Sylvester Stadler, was sufficiently disturbed by the number of civilians killed to refer the matter to divisional commander General Heinz Lammerding, who on 5 June had issued divisional orders to arrest 5,000 hostages as 'punishment for attacks on German personnel by mobile bands of terrorists'.[10] Lammerding ordered an investigation as soon as the situation permitted. Given the urgency of getting his tanks and men to the Normandy front as swiftly as possible with insufficient wheeled transporters and a lack of many spare parts for the tanks,[11] no priority was given to this. Whatever his intention, when on 29 June Diekmann was killed in action together with many of his men who had taken part in the 'operation' at Oradour the enquiry was abandoned.

That awful Saturday when a town was destroyed, 150 kilometres to the north-east the two mediators from St-Amand were stacking up the miles hunting for the FFI, with the deadline already extended several times. On one occasion they missed a rendezvous by less than a kilometre. Meanwhile, Bout de l'An decided the local Milice were too 'soft' to carry out the reprisals he had in mind and sent for Joseph Lécussan, the man who had killed Victor Basch and his wife in January.

Drinking heavily from the moment he took command, Lécussan ordered houses blown up and embarked sixty-five hostages in motor-coaches on 11 June, destination Vichy. Inhabitants of St-Amand who had listened to the BBC against a background of the *miliciens'* explosions the previous day, caught a message from General Koenig, Commander-in-Chief of the FFI: 'Since it is impossible for us to supply you with food, arms and ammunition, I repeat that all guerrilla activity should be kept to a minimum. Stay in small groups.'[12] If only, they must have thought.

The efforts of the mediators finally bearing fruit despite the FFI calling them Milice stooges and Lécussan letting them know he considered them closet *résistants*, to be liquidated after they had served their purpose, a letter from Simone to her husband arrived in St-Amand, reading:

My dear Francis,
I am in the hands of the liberation army. I am being well treated.
Spare the hostages to avoid the worst happening. I put my trust in
God. I am worried about the children. Give them a hug for me.
Kisses, Simone

Although the term 'liberation army' implied that part of the message had been dictated, the letter proved that she was still alive, which was enough to keep the reprisals on hold. The urgent concern of Mayor Sadrin was now to arrange the exchange in a climate of extreme mutual mistrust. Finally, the FFI gave up their female hostages, but not the *miliciens*. In return, Bout de l'An kept his word to return his hostages to St-Amand, after being urged to do so by Simone, who had not been physically ill-treated. They arrived back home on 25 June, and there the sad affair should have ended with the release of the *milicien* prisoners.

But they were still prisoner on 20 July, when their captors were on the run from a massive anti-Maquis operation directed by General Von Jesser, under orders to engage and destroy all Maquis units in central France. Twice they managed to break through the cordon of German and Ukrainian troops hunting them, but never to distance themselves from their pursuers. The largest group of thirty-five men still had with them the thirteen prisoners. Because of the risk that one would escape and give them away, the group's 28-year-old temporary commander Georges Chaillaud decided to kill the prisoners. Not all his men agreed because, during the six weeks they had all been on the run, old friendships had reblossomed among men who had gone to school and played football together, even courted the same girls. Chance alone had led one to the Maquis and another to the Milice. Chaillaud actually owed his life to *milicien* Louis Bastide, who had knowingly allowed him to get rid of compromising papers some months before by flushing them down a toilet before an interrogation.

As Chaillaud admitted later,

There was no question of shooting the prisoners because the Germans would have heard the shots. So we hanged them. We made running knots with parachute cord attached to high branches. We didn't have a step-ladder or a chair, so we put the cord around their necks, lifted them as high as we could – and let them fall. When I told their boss they were going to be killed, he said simply, 'You chose England and we chose Germany. You've won and we've lost.' The *miliciens* died bravely.

Other accounts differ, some implying that Bastide begged the man whose life he had saved to let him live in return.[13]

The same parachute cords could have been used to tie up and gag the *miliciens*, leaving them to be found by the Germans, instead of thirteen strangulated corpses hanging from the trees. But then, they would have given away their captors' names, so perhaps it was fear of reprisals that caused the gruesome hangings. Some of Chaillaud's men were so nauseated that they threw away their weapons and walked home. Within hours, Lécussan received a phone call from one of them identified only as 'the Traitor', saying that eight *miliciens* had been hanged. Had this informant been present only for the first executions, before leaving in disgust? At any rate, the number is not important. Lécussan's rage would have been directed at his favourite target anyway.

There had been few Jews in St-Amand before the war brought a number of refugees to the area. Lécussan had already rounded up a number in retaliation for the murder of Philippe Henriot. Some had been tortured and killed, with their bodies left floating in the river. Determined to make St-Amand *judenrein* after the latest outrage, Lécussan organised a total round-up for the following day and summoned to his aid forty-five German soldiers and a motley band of Milice and other hangers-on, who arrived in cars and coaches, the men being catered for in the local cinema, the bosses repairing to a hotel for a large meal with plenty of drink.

That night, doors were smashed in by rifle butts and the victims dragged out in night attire or underclothes, some elderly ones not even allowed to collect their false teeth. French citizenship was ignored. There was no longer a pretence of deportation to a labour camp. One bewildered grandmother, arrested with her 3-year-old grandson, asked permission to bring her sewing things, only to be told, 'You won't need them. You're going to paradise.' Already dressed and ready for the *miliciens*, 76-year-old veteran Colonel Fernand Bernheim told them, 'You must have sunk really low to come and arrest me.'[14]

By the evening of 22 July, the prisoners were all locked in overcrowded, stifling cells in the Bordiot prison at Bourges, where eighteen people had to share one toilet bucket, emptied every twenty-four hours. The only food was dry beans twice a day. Any valuables had been stolen. In the afternoon of 24 July Lécussan arrived to oversee what he considered proper revenge for the killing of the *milicien* hostages. The full details are too obscene to recount, but in short the male prisoners were transported in a closed van to a deserted farm in a military training ground known as Guerry. In groups of six they were made to carry solidified sacks of cement and heavy rocks to a deep well, where *miliciens* waited with pistols and sub-machine guns.

Instead of shooting the prisoners so that the bodies fell into the wells, their killers made them kneel by the parapets and pushed them over alive, with the rocks and sacks of cement thrown in afterwards. The lucky ones died from a crushed skull or broken neck, others by asphyxiation as more bodies and rocks crashed down on them in a tangle of bodies that took local firemen days to extricate. Once the prisoners waiting their turn realised what was happening, they were frozen in terror with the exception of one man who preferred to die attempting to escape rather than walk like a beast to the slaughter. Charles Krameisen dodged the bullets, running barefoot through the scrub, tearing clothes and flesh on brambles and thorns. That night, he emerged from hiding shocked and dishevelled, to knock on the door of a peasant bringing up his eight children with his wife in a farm near the execution site, by whom he was taken in and given food and clothes.

It would be nice to end the story on this note of courage and humanity, but the women and children were still locked up in Bourges prison. With *miliciens* and Gestapo now mostly preoccupied by saving their skins before the Allies arrived, they might have all survived until liberation had not the local head of the Milice been assassinated on 7 August. With no chance of catching the assassin, the other *miliciens* decided to execute hostages. Since all the men from St-Amand were dead, it was the turn of the women.

For 'humanitarian' reasons, those with children were exempted, but two women who had claimed to be childless, so that their children would not be rounded up, were included in the ten told they were 'to be deported'. In the prison courtyard, as they were getting into the Milice van, a German officer saw one of them weeping. Luckily able to speak German, she explained that she was not Jewish, and was returned to the cells with another woman. The other eight and a Jewish *résistant* who had been in prison for two months were then driven off to Guerry.

Bloodstains and bullet scuffs on the parapet of the well used this time bore witness to the fact that the man and five of the women were first shot before being dumped in the well. The body of the youngest, aged 18, was naked and mutilated. She had probably been raped. The last woman to be pushed in before rocks were dumped on the bodies was the wife of Charles Krameisen. Between 9 and 11 August the Gestapo fled from Bourges. On 17 August the prison gates opened to release the twenty-five women and nine children who survived the tragedy of St-Amand, the town where 'nothing ever happened'.

Chapter 22

MURDEROUS MIDSUMMER

Laval was a lawyer to the end: his official line on the Normandy landings was that they were not French business because France was legally neutral in the war between the Allies and Germany. So whether he did ask Abetz on 14 June to expedite the return of the LVF and the Charlemagne Division to stiffen the German resistance is a moot point. The date may be a coincidence, but it was then that De Gaulle first returned to France, landing at Courseulles in General Montgomery's British sector of operations after crossing the Channel aboard the French destroyer *Combattante*. With Monty too busy to pay much attention to his visitor, after a brief motor tour to Isigny and Grandcamp in the American sector, De Gaulle re-embarked and returned to Britain, first jamming his foot in the political door by appointing his former *chef de cabinet*, Francis Coulet, Commissioner for Normandy and disproving American rumours that his presence on French soil would trigger a civil war. The Gaullist officials were rapidly accepted by the population, while the Vichy functionaries they replaced were only too happy to disappear quietly.[1]

In usually tranquil Ste-Foy-la-Grande on the south bank of the Dordogne river, the bridges vital for German troop movements had been blown up by the Maquis on 8 June after 'the fourth republic' had been proclaimed by a self-appointed 'representative of Gen De Gaulle'. By 13 June conscription had begun, the mayor being ordered to supply seventy-two able-bodied men aged 18–55 to serve 'under military discipline'. The consequences were inevitable: by dawn on 18 June the town was under fire from an armoured column on the opposite bank and *résistants* taken alive were made to dig their own graves before being shot. Jean-Adolphe Blondel, mayor of the nearby village St-André-et-Appelles, begged a passing Wehrmacht major to intervene when SS troops threatened to set fire to his village after finding wounded *résistants* being treated in the mairie. The best compromise the major could achieve was for Blondel to be shot 'as an example' and the village left unburned.

On 22 June the strategic oil reserves of the Wehrmacht at St-Ouen and St-Denis were bombed and huge clouds of black smoke darkened the Paris sky as they had four years earlier. On 28 June, after his son left to rejoin his NSKK transport unit, Philippe Henriot and his wife visited a cinema on the Champs Elysées before returning to their apartment in the Ministry of the Interior. Alarmed by threatening calls on their direct line, Madame Henriot begged her husband to request a Milice bodyguard, but he was sure they were safe inside the Ministry. According to the subsequent police report, 'At 5.30 a.m. six or seven black Citroën *traction avant* cars pulled up, disgorging thirty or so men in Milice uniforms, armed with automatic weapons.' The uniforms tricked the concierge into letting the *résistants* into the building where they killed Henriot in front of his wife.

The death of a high government official whose anti-Semitic radio tirades continued long after it was known that the euphemism *deportation* meant death presented the Church with a problem that split its ranks. At Henriot's memorial service in Paris, Cardinal Suhard agreed to officiate and pronounce the absolution but not to read a eulogy. In Lyons cathedral Cardinal Gerlier officiated at the memorial service, but also refused to read a eulogy and left before the absolution. In Limoges Monsignor Rastouil went a step further by refusing to conduct a memorial service, for which Darnand had him arrested. Confronted with the warrant, the monsignor exclaimed, 'Am I the first bishop to be arrested by Frenchmen? Is this an honour?' He was released after three days, following protests from the papal nuncio. However, in Bordeaux on 5 July Monsignor Feltin condemned the assassination by saying, 'No one has the right to impose justice without approval of the legal authorities. . . . He who claims to serve his country otherwise is guilty of murder.' And, at the far-Right end of the politico-religious spectrum, Father Tabaillé of Vienne included in his eulogy the statement that Henriot had 'fallen as a hero and a martyr'.[2]

By the end of the Liberation, the Resistance claimed 3,136 sabotage operations, with 834 derailments putting out of action 1,855 locomotives and 5,833 wagons, plus 972 other 'operations'. One of these happened on 9 June when a section of Corps Franc Pommiès blew up the rail tracks just outside Moissac and followed up by attacking a troop train guarded by military police in the station. Lieutentant-Colonel Pommiès' private army had an extraordinary record in the twenty months of its undercover war: 102 ambushes and 265 other operations, during which 4,529 Germans were taken prisoner or killed. The cost was high: 387 deaths, 1,200 wounded and 156 taken prisoner and deported, few of whom survived. After the FFI blew up a 150,000-volt high-tension pylon at Castelsarrassin on 30 June, gendarmerie reports judged the mood of the population to be 'calm' compared to people over much of France,[3] although 'the sight of girls and young women flirting with the Germans in the town will lead to reprisals by the population on these women after the Liberation which can not be far off'.[4]

Not all the clandestine weapons were fired at Germans. One 30-year-old Moissac man was arrested for robbing a farmer of food at gunpoint, but most Moissagais were more concerned with the fine weather that promised a good harvest of fruits and vegetables, although the *viticulteurs* worried about hail storms bruising the dessert grapes on the vine and making them unsellable. Grain reserves were sufficient to last until the harvest, but farmers were threatened by the Maquis with arson of their fields and homes if they handed over more than the minimum to the Germans. Bread and fats were becoming scarce and meat was distributed – theoretically – only twice a month.

Françoise Armagnac was 26 years old on Tuesday 4 July 1944 – the day she was to marry 36-year-old fellow-agronomist Georges Pénicaut at the church of St Peter in Chabanais, halfway between Limoges and Angoulême. She was a guileless, outspoken and carelessly dressed young woman, whom not even her friends could call pretty with her poor eyesight compensated by unattractive wartime spectacles, but that day she had taken care with her appearance, and was wearing a white silk dress with a diadem of pink roses in her hair.

The couple and friends set out after the ceremony to walk from the church to the house where the wedding breakfast was to be held. Nearly there, they were surrounded by a troop of FTP *maquisards*, who locked the couple and the bride's mother with the priest in one room and the photographer in another. At gunpoint all the other guests were interrogated and made to prove their identity before being released. Interrogation of bride, groom and priest lasted for the rest of the day. Towards dusk, with the photographer and the bride's mother, they were driven in a van 30 kilometres to the group's temporary HQ in the Château de Pressac. There, violence towards the prisoners was so excessive that their leader 'Colonel' Bernard threatened to shoot dead the next man who touched them.

Despite this, a mock trial was held, the evidence against Françoise boiling down to a Milice badge found in her bedroom and a diary, in which she had recorded joining the Milice on 3 May 1943. She pleaded that she had only attended a few meetings and left the organisation three months later. The page for 7 August, on which the resignation was clearly noted, was torn out of the diary by her accusers, saying that they decided what proof to take in evidence and what to disregard. The following day Françoise was constantly insulted by her captors and made to scrub floors in her soiled wedding dress. Growing tired of this around 9 p.m., they shot her, still in her wedding dress.

It was true that she had briefly belonged to the Milice – for social reasons, in the same way that she had also founded a troop of Girl Guides. According to local *résistants*, the real reason the FTP men killed her was that, as a grand-niece of a president of the Republic, her death had more impact on local people than that of lower-class Pétainists.[5]

It was a summer of atrocities on both sides, some famous, others now forgotten. At St-Genis-Laval, just outside Lyons, German troops revenged themselves on the local population by executing 110 prisoner-hostages including a boy of 18 and a young girl, all taken from Montluc prison. In groups of six, hands tied behind their backs, they were hustled into a room and machine-gunned. Petrol was poured over the bodies and phosphorus grenades lobbed on top. The wounded who managed to crawl out with flesh and clothing burning were machine-gunned in the doorway.

The dilemma of the French forces of law and order was summed up by a gendarmerie captain in Haute-Savoie: 'The present situation confronts (my men) with a delicate moral choice. They can blindly obey orders and expose themselves and their families to certain reprisals from the Maquis, or adopt a passive attitude. As most of them do not have the strength of character to adopt the first option, I believe that . . . the second is the only one acceptable.'[6] Relative inactivity was not enough for the population; 30 per cent of his men had to be transferred elsewhere after the Liberation to avoid revenge by relatives of men they had arrested. Another report of the same period criticises a gendarme who 'betrayed his uniform by consorting with a person of previously good reputation, but who was discovered . . . to be a dangerous terrorist, in the share-out of an illegally slaughtered animal to get food for his family'.[7]

In the north and west of France, innocent civilians far from the fighting in Normandy continued to be killed by British and American bombs. At St-Nazaire on the Atlantic coast, which had 45,000 inhabitants at the start of the war, 85 per cent of homes and all public buildings had been destroyed. There was no water, electricity or gas and many streets were impassable even on foot. In the Channel port of Le Havre, where sirens sounded 1,060 times between the beginning of the war and D-Day, the Parks and Gardens service recovered 3,000 corpses from the rubble. All had to be identified, transported and buried – often with no time for coffins or prayers at the graveside. When the survivors went to church on Sunday, they found their priest sleeping beneath the altar and eating at a street kitchen after the destruction of the presbytery. Instead of a sermon, he announced from the pulpit the timing of gas and electricity cuts and made appeals for information about the missing.

On 2 July 500 political prisoners in the French wing of Toulouse prison were handed over to German personnel and locked into freight wagons in the main station with planks nailed over every opening – for which SNCF added a supplementary charge to the customary invoice for providing locomotives and cattle trucks of deportation trains. In the midsummer heat, with the guards allowing them no food or water, prisoners began to die. Braving the guards, some Quakers managed to push through the small gaps between the planks one loaf and a can of sardines to share between two men. On the evening of 3 July, the train started a nightmare journey for the men locked in their stinking prisons. With the Toulouse–Brive line cut by sabotage, the train headed for Bordeaux and then back towards Toulouse, turning back again to Bordeaux after being strafed by RAF Mosquitoes. On 5 and 6 July, the guards opened the doors for fifteen minutes to allow men to relieve themselves on the line and bury the dead.

At Angoulême, the Red Cross managed to distribute fruit, bread and water. With the lines impassable northwards, it was back to Bordeaux, where they waited three days, fed by the Red Cross on a cup of noodle soup and some bread. On 12 July, they were herded through the empty streets at 2 a.m. and locked into the looted, vandalised synagogue – for three entire weeks. The Red Cross brought soup each day, except on Sunday when the Germans forbade it, but allowed the prisoners sugar, butter and biscuits instead.

On 10 August they were marched back to the station and locked inside freight wagons coupled to a long train, direction Nîmes. During the single fifteen-minute halt that day, they relieved their bowels and bladders by the tracks within sight of two wagon-loads of flea-ridden, equally filthy women prisoners doing the same. On 15 August in Provence they were again the target for Allied fighters. With the train stopped, the guards could take cover beside the track, but the prisoners could only huddle together in the wagons, each hoping that someone else's body would stop the bullets. In one raid, three died and sixteen were wounded.

Where the line had been cut by sabotage, they were forced to march along the permanent way. On 19 August – the day that St Michel prison was liberated by the Toulouse FFI and the remaining *résistants* there released – they were mobile again, but with neither food nor water. By way of Montélimar and Valence they headed up the Rhône Valley. On 21 August in Chalon-sur-Saône one bucket of water and two and a half kilos of bread had to suffice per seventy men. At 10 p.m. on 24 August with the train making 20kph, eleven desperate prisoners hacked through the floor of their wagon and dropped through onto the tracks, two of them suffering legs amputated by the wheels. The train continued without them – no one knew where to.[8]

On 6 July four captured women SOE agents called Andrée Borrel, Sonja Olschanezky, Vera Leigh and Diana Rowden were transferred from Karlsruhe prison to Natzwiller. As *Nacht und Nebel* prisoners, they were to be killed without trace. That evening the four women were individually taken to the sick bay, told to undress and, on the pretence that it was an inoculation for typhus, given a supposedly lethal injection of phenol by SS Untersturmführer Dr Werner Röhde or his assistant. Their bodies were immediately thrown into the four-body camp crematorium by Hauptscharführer Peter Schraub. At least one of the women recovered consciousness sufficiently to scar Schraub's face with her fingernails before being forced in alive and the door slammed after her.[9]

Georges Mandel served as *député* in the National Assembly from 1919 to 1924 and 1928 to 1940, holding posts in four successive governments between 1934 and 1936 and as Minister of Colonies from April 1938 to May 1940. Equally opposed to policies of the Left and the pro-German far Right between the wars, he was also briefly Interior Minister in Reynaud's short-lived Cabinet. Refusing to accept the Armistice, he sailed from Bordeaux aboard the *Massilia* to continue the fight from North Africa. Arrested by Vichy officials on disembarking in Morocco and returned to France, he was handed over to the Germans in November 1942. After a stay at the concentration camps of Oranienburg and Buchenwald, he was returned to Paris on 4 July 1944, to be kept as a hostage in the Santé prison. While being 'transferred to another place of detention' on the night of 7/8 July, in a joint operation of the SD and Darnand's Milice, Mandel was gunned down in the forest of Fontainebleau by alleged *résistants* in a deliberately orchestrated mirror-image of Henriot's killing.

On 9 July 12th SS Panzer Division was driven out of Caen by Canadian 3rd Division pushing in from the west and British 1st Division from the north. What remained of the ancient capital of Normandy was a bombed and shelled wasteland but 200 kilometres to the east in peaceful Villers-Adam Madame Robert's landlady was selling off the surplus fruit and vegetables from her garden to hungry and thirsty German soldiers passing through eastbound, who grew fewer in number until the only ones left were technicians dismantling the underground V1 factory.[10]

In Paris, police recorded between 28 July and 2 August finding nine bodies shot and left in the streets bearing a card stating, 'This man shot a German soldier. For this, he has himself been shot.' Many others had been removed and buried before the police got there.[11] Streets near major German installations were covered by a blizzard of ashes as every paper that could not be removed was incinerated. In working-class districts schoolboys and students were hacking down the lime trees that lined the boulevards and using pickaxes to prise up the cobblestones, piling them into makeshift barricades, ineffectual against tanks.

Anxious to move the twenty children she had hidden in a technical school in Toulouse, Shatta Simon asked 20-year-old Henri Milstein to organise a summer camp for these and other children in remote countryside on the Black Mountain, where the Foreign Legion now does its training. His campers eventually numbered 200 children with false papers, and tragedy gave them a near miss when a Maquis unit ambushed a German patrol nearby, killing four soldiers but allowing one to get away and lead the revenge squad back. Henri was returning from buying vegetables on a bicycle towing a small trailer, when he ran into one of the roadblocks. His identity card had been borrowed from an old classmate in Moissac, so the photograph did not resemble him. Even worse, he was using a pre-war military map to find his way around the countryside. For four hours he meditated over his likely fate until a French-speaking officer arrived to interrogate him.

The first question, 'Why all this food in your trailer?' was reasonable enough. It could have been destined for the Maquis group who had killed the soldiers.

The second was, 'Why do you have a military map in your pocket?'

Luckily for Milstein, it seems the officer had been a Scout himself before the movement was banned in Germany after 1933. Initially sceptical of a Scout camp in the middle of a manhunt, he eventually accepted Milstein's word that he had 200 hungry young mouths awaiting dinner, and waved him on his way without even querying the ID card. Not long after the narrow escape on the Black Mountain, Milstein was stopped at a Milice ID check in Toulouse railway station. With no chance of playing the Scout card there, he recalled that the tailor in Moissac whom his sister had married had a client who was a police commissioner in Toulouse. Blurting out that he was visiting the client to take measurements for a new suit, his mind went blank when asked for the commissioner's name, which he had only heard by chance. In the nick of time, it came to him, and the papers were thrust back with the ultimate benediction: 'You can go.'

It was for most French people another grim 14 July. Women queuing for bread in Paris whispered about the criminal-law prisoners in the Santé prison who had mutinied, setting fire to their cell blocks in the night, because they were at risk of being shot as hostages. At dawn, *miliciens* from Lycée Louis-le-Grand had crushed the mutiny by summarily shooting twenty-eight prisoners against the prison wall. In Nîmes, gendarmes refused to form a firing squad to execute *résistants* arrested by the Milice. Themselves placed under arrest and imprisoned in Marseilles, they were set free a few days before the town was liberated.

After Hitler was nearly killed on 22 July by the bomb planted in his map briefing room at Rastenburg, anti-Nazi Wehrmacht officers in Paris locked up in Fresnes prison all their SS, SD and Gestapo colleagues, including Generals Oberg and Knochen. When news came through that the Führer was only slightly wounded, Abetz tried to smooth things out by ostentatiously pouring champagne for all in the Hôtel Continental on rue Castiglione and pretended for public consumption that the entire event had been some kind of military exercise.[12] Although the French press carried news of the attempt on Hitler's life next morning, there was no coverage of the arrests in Paris, nor of Karl-Heinrich von Stülpnagel being ordered to return to Berlin, charged with high treason. On the battlefield of Verdun, he ordered his driver to stop the car and tried to blow out his brains with his service pistol. Managing only to blind himself, he was taken to hospital to recover and stand trial, the suicide attempt being covered in *Pariser Zeitung* by a fictitious report that he had been attacked by Maquis 'terrorists'. Von Stülpnagel was among the conspirators who died slowly on 30 August, strangled to death in Berlin-Plötzensee.

With the war now unwinnable by Germany, the strategically useless Luftwaffe was ordered to bomb villages in the sparsely populated Vercors area of eastern France, destroying several of them in reprisal for Maquis activity. Approximately 30,000 ground troops then cordoned off the area where 3,500 *maquisards* found themselves in the ultimate nightmare of a pitched battle against vastly superior numbers of trained and regular forces with air superiority. After the landing of 200 glider-borne paras in the heartland of the Maquis, men who had thought the Allies would reach them within days now realised that their only safety lay in flight by night to avoid the daylight strafing. By 23 July the Maquis of Vercors was a spent shadow.

In the defeat of 1940 the French Army had abandoned casualties to be cared for by the Wehrmacht, but that recourse was now impossible in conditions where they would be shot as terrorists. Gradually compressed into a smaller and smaller area, surgeon-captains Ferrier and Ganimède had forty volunteer stretcher-bearers carry the worst cases over difficult terrain into a cave whose entrance was hidden in scrub. After days of hiding, it was decided to attempt a break-out for the walking wounded with a small escort of medical attendants. More days of waiting followed for those left behind, with the noises of battle coming from all directions as their comrades were hunted down. Medical supplies were few; food was running out; the only liquid was moisture seeping through the roof of the cave.

In the afternoon of 27 July bullets sprayed the Red Cross flag at the entrance. Three German prisoners released as spokesmen explained that they had been correctly treated during their captivity and that there were women and wounded in the cave. It was a waste of breath. Eighteen wounded were immediately shot lying on their stretchers, and twelve more killed the next day. Ferrier and a civilian doctor were taken to Grenoble and shot with the chaplain Yves Moreau. Six female nurses were deported. Only Ganimède managed to escape after being interrogated by the Gestapo.[13]

In Paris, Edith Piaf was now earning for one appearance 20,000 francs – a white collar worker's annual salary – of which little remained at the end of each week. The little woman in a black dress who had begun by singing to theatre queues and the patrons of terrace cafés, turning tricks on occasion, spent her earnings like water on husbands, lovers, fellow artists, song-writers and a host of hangers-on. On 22 July she was due to sing at the prestige classical music venue La Salle Pleyel, but got stage-fright when shown the concert platform, large enough for a full symphony orchestra. Conquering her nerves, she went on to give the performance of her life.

For the mass of Parisians, life was somewhat more gloomy. Between 27 July and 30 August, such was the disruption in the arrival of food supplies that butter was rationed at 80 grams per person and milk tankers coming into the capital had LAIT painted on the roofs in the hope that they would not be attacked by Allied aircraft. The press hinted that women and children should leave before things got worse, but, as in 1940, there could be no mass exodus because few people had private transport and the only trains were controlled by the Germans.[14] On 28 July Laval scurried to Abetz insisting that Je Suis Partout be banned after the critic Alain Laubreaux wrote, 'Napoleon said of Talleyrand, his foreign secretary, that he was shit in a silk stocking. Now we have only the silk stocking.'

On 31 July, Aloïs Brünner's last mass deportation from Drancy included over 300 children arrested in orphanages run by UGIF and 115 wives of French POWs held in Germany, most of whom survived incarceration at Bergen-Belsen. On 1 August what remained of the artworks in the Jeu de Paume were packed in 148 cases, loaded into five freight wagons, whose numbers were noted by the indefatigable Rose Valland and passed to SNCF résistants. They, in turn, made sure the wagons were shunted hither and thither in the Paris suburbs until overtaken by Leclerc's advance units. With no further justification for staying in Paris, the art looters were scrabbling for priority jobs back home, to avoid being given forty-eight hours' notice to report on the Russian front.[15]

Ordered to leave Vichy and take refuge east of the Rhine, Pétain refused. On 6 August he wrote to Laval:

> On separate occasions I have discussed with you [reports of the Milice's actions] in the hope that improvement would result. . . . I must stress the deplorable effect on the population, which might understand arrests carried out by the Germans themselves but can never condone the fact of Frenchmen delivering their own compatriots to the Gestapo and working in collaboration with them.

When shown the letter, Darnand – to whom the Marshal should have addressed it – replied to Pétain: 'In the course of these four years, I have received compliments and congratulations from you. You encouraged me. And today, because the Americans stand at the gates of Paris, you start to tell me that I shall be a blot on the history of France? It is something that might have been thought of earlier.'[16]

On 9 August, with British and Canadian forces launching a new offensive south of Caen, Laval reached Paris in the evening. At his trial, he protested three priorities on that day: ensuring the capital's food supply in his capacity as one of the mayors of Greater Paris; persuading the Germans to neither defend nor destroy the city; and the restoration of parliamentary democracy by calling a National Assembly. Edouard Herriot, the 72-year-old former president of the Chamber of Deputies, was confined as a hostage in a nursing home, because of poor health. Laval negotiated his release on 12 August, hoping that he would head a new government, but Herriot asserted that, under the Third Republic Constitution only Jules Jeanneney, former President of the Senate, could call a National Assembly. Jeanneney, however, was in Grenoble. Herriot's subsequent re-arrest by the Gestapo infuriated Abetz and Laval, who tried to persuade Herriot to flee with him to Switzerland, receiving the reply, 'Switzerland is too expensive, and I have no money!' Had it not been tragic, it would have been comic. Herriot understated the situation by calling it 'infinitely confused' as he was driven away by the Gestapo to a secure sanatorium near Potsdam.[17]

From this moment, there was no doubt about the eventual fate of the self-made millionaire-politician from Auvergne; but Laval went down fighting. He summoned the eighty other mayors of Greater Paris and persuaded them all to sign a pledge of support for him as president of their collective and as head of the government.[18] Also in Paris was Darlan's deputy Admiral Auphan, entrusted by Pétain with one of the most useless pieces of paper ever signed by a head of state: his authority to invest his executive powers in 'a college of notables', should he be unable to exercise them. Finding such a group at this time being impossible, Auphan handed it after the Liberation to De Gaulle, who regarded it as null and void.

On 11 August 1944, in what should have been the ultimate act of insanity, Klaus Barbie packed 650 prisoners into his last deportation train to leave Lyons' Gare Perrache. With the disruption of the rail network by strategic bombing and Resistance sabotage, the nightmare was to last even longer than for previous shipments. The filthy cattle-trucks became stinking ovens in the summer heat, and the train was repeatedly re-routed and shunted into sidings while priority traffic was allowed to pass. The journey was made even longer by a diversion to off-load the *résistants* at Natzwiller camp, the Jewish prisoners being bound for a destination further east. On 10 August all the Communist-organised railway workers had been called out on strike. Two days later, all civilian rail communications between Paris and the outside world were cut, with the unions demanding a pay increase, better food distribution and the release of their comrades arrested by the Milice. Despite a feeble bleat about their 'selfish attitude' from Vichy, the strike was maintained.[19]

On 13 August, with Allied armoured spearheads only hours away from Drancy, Aloïs Brünner assembled his last victims for deportation. At this stage in the retreat, collective insanity is the only reason that can be advanced for his being allocated a locomotive and forty-eight freight wagons from a railway system in severe crisis, where priority should have gone to evacuating the wounded and moving vital military resources. Unimpressed by Brünner's SS uniform or his mania for killing Jews at such a time, a sane Wehrmacht colonel requisitioned the train at gunpoint for his men and equipment, leaving Brünner stranded – an action that saved 1,416 of the 1,467 prisoners.

In Paris that day the Resistance learned that the Germans had commenced disarming French police in St-Denis, St-Ouen and Asnières. 'Colonel' Rol, the PCF Resistance boss and De Gaulle's Paris representative Alexandre Parodi jointly instructed senior police officers to bring their men out on strike, to cease maintaining order for the enemy, and to stop arresting *résistants*. On no account were they to allow themselves to be disarmed. Police who did not obey the instruction were to be considered 'traitors and collaborators'.[20]

Chapter 23

'HELL IS THE OTHERS'

O n the night of 14 August 1944 a fleet of 396 C-47s took off from Italian airfields to drop 5,000 US paratroops on southern France. In the second stage of Operation Anvil, after a violent naval and air bombardment of the German defences, 25,000 French, French colonial and US soldiers landed between Toulon and Cannes after dawn from an invasion fleet of 2,000 transports and landing craft escorted by some 300 warships. On the same day, the Police Nationale went on strike to ingratiate itself with the increasingly active FFI. In Toulon and Fréjus gendarmes were told to go home and stay there until the fighting was over; in Hyères most of their colleagues lay low on their own initiative until the conflict had passed through. In many places FFI fighters occupied police and gendarmerie stations *manu militari*, refusing to hand them back.[1]

The confidence engendered by news of the landings in the south sometimes went too far. Six young *maquisards* in the little Girondine village of Landerrouat attached a French flag to a car and drove through the village in triumph – to be greeted by German machine-gun fire. Rapidly hitting reverse gear, the driver headed out of the village. Two of his passengers jumped out and legged it across the fields. Their four comrades, with the Germans from Landerrouat in close pursuit, drove slap into another column of Germans coming towards them, and ended what was to have been the morning of triumph left dead on the road for their relatives to find.

SS officer Alexander De Kreuz was placed in command of a squad sent to the Paris station at Pantin, to remove from a deportation train five men, including De Gaulle's former military representative in Paris, Colonel André Rondenay. The SS drove their victims outside Paris to Domont and shot them, ordering Feldgendarmerie soldiers to bury the bodies while they returned heroically to the base in rue des Saussaies to drink champagne, as was the custom after SS executions. For most Parisians, even drinking water was in short supply. The Metro no longer worked at all and electricity and gas supplies were totally unpredictable. Like the Milice gathered in Vichy's spa buildings with their families and an assortment of livestock they intended taking with them on their flight to the east, the capital's Doriotists huddled in the PPF HQ on rue des Pyramides with their families, waiting for Wehrmacht transport to rescue them while some party comrades in Gironde rounded up all the Jewish refugees they could find on 5 August by lying in wait outside the free restaurant of Ste-Foy-la-Grande at lunchtime. After driving them across the last remaining bridge over the Dordogne in brilliant sunshine, they gunned them down in a vineyard overlooking the town and returned, singing marching songs from the First World War – 'Auprès de ma blonde' and 'En passant par la Lorraine'.

In the Paris Embassy, Abetz was obligingly issuing travel documents to anyone who wanted to head for Germany before the Allies arrived. He also took the time to send a telegram to Ribbentrop protesting that Kommandant von Gross Paris General Von Choltitz was acting with disgraceful brutality – this to deter Berlin from replacing him with a hard-line Nazi, who would implement Hitler's mad plan to detonate explosives placed on the bridges, in Notre Dame and other churches, in the Senate, at Les Invalides and the Opera.[2] Thanks to Von Choltitz's genius for procrastination, they were never blown.

Following news that the Americans and French under Gen De Lattre de Tassigny were moving out from the Operation Anvil bridgehead, Déat, De Brinon, Darnand and Doriot joined the lemming-rush to the east. In Lyons, Klaus Barbie lined up sixteen Jews in front of a firing squad at the Fort Montluc in an another act of senseless murder. At Drancy, Aloïs Brünner had to content himself with one cattle truck for fifty-one VIP prisoners and a couple of passenger coaches for himself and his staff, attached to a train reserved for an anti-aircraft battery. Transport 79 – the final instalment of Drancy prisoners for the gas chambers – was Auschwitz-bound at last when the train pulled out of Bobigny station at 5.30 p.m. and slowly progressed eastwards along the Seine.

Among Brünner's prisoners was aircraft constructor Marcel Bloch, arrested under his cover name Dassault.[3] Also in the wagon was a 12-year-old boy and Henri Pohoryles, who had left the colonie in Moissac to join the Armée Juive commando who had assassinated the Ukrainian Gestapo aides. Shrewd enough to note that there were in Paris a month after D-Day at most 300 Resistance members with arms and the training to use them, he had nevertheless been tricked into bringing the Armée Juive leaders to a false-flag meeting in Paris, where the man he thought a British agent revealed himself as German Intelligence officer Karl Rehbein and clapped them all under arrest. Surviving to found the Dassault Aviation company, Bloch later recalled his fellow passengers divided in adversity on the journey, with the Communists huddling at one end of their uncomfortable moving prison to leave a gap between themselves and the VIP 'rich Jews', neither group speaking to the other.

On the night of 16 August, curious curfew-breakers noticed a small convoy of trucks heading out of Paris westwards. They were no last-minute reinforcements for the front, but an execution squad that cut down thirty-five young Frenchmen with machine-pistols in the Bois de Boulogne and left the bodies for passers-by to find under the trees.

Impatient with the stop-go progress on the severely disrupted railway network, Brünner commandeered a car and continued his personal funk-flight by road, leaving Milice and SS guards in charge of his prisoners. Security relaxed with his departure, after which prisoners were allowed to find drinking and washing water at stops. Twenty-seven of the fifty-one escaped at about 1 a.m. on 21 August; of the twenty-four others, the obviously Orthodox were gassed on arrival at Auschwitz, with the 12-year-old boy taken to Neuengamme concentration camp near Hamburg as one of a battery of children used for medical experiments. Dr Kurt Heissmeyer injected them regularly with tuberculosis bacilli 'in the interests of science'. Fifteen days before Germany surrendered he gave them all their final injection. Had it been simply to stop them accusing him in an Allied war crimes court, he could have used something more immediately lethal than tuberculosis. However, when British troops liberated Neuengamme, they found the twenty children hanged – a slow death when the weight of a child's body has been reduced by malnutrition.

With the police on strike, German loudspeaker vans patrolled the streets of Paris warning that disorder would be dealt with by force. Few civilians ventured onto the streets as the exodus of Germans choked the main thoroughfares with overloaded ambulances, staff cars, trucks and vehicles of all descriptions. Warned by Abetz to leave for Germany voluntarily if he did not want to be taken there under arrest, Laval called a last ghost of a Cabinet meeting before spending his final night in the Hôtel Matignon. On the morning of 18 August Abetz formally closed the embassy and promised the concierge he would soon be back, before leaving with an escort of SS officers to pick up Laval and his wife. Also in the cortège was Abetz' mistress and a certain amount of loot the ambassador had managed to accumulate for his personal use. Laval takes up the story:

'About ten o'clock the German Ambassador appeared at the Hôtel Matignon, together with the chief of the German Police. The cars of the Gestapo were lined up before the door. A notice of the order of arrest was served on me. Such were the conditions in which I was forced to leave Paris.'[4]

Were they? Or was he stealing Pétain's alibi? Informed by Renthe-Fink at 10 p.m. that he would be taken to Germany by force if he did not consent to leave immediately, the Marshal played for time. The departure was delayed until 5.30 a.m., then 6.00 and 7.00. Meanwhile, Ménétrel tried to persuade his master to slink out of a service entrance of the Hôtel du Parc disguised as a workman, but Pétain retorted, 'Such an escapade is fit neither for my age nor the dignity of my position.'

He spent his last night in Vichy dictating a political testament and a final *Paroles aux Français* before going to bed. At 7 a.m. the papal nuncio and Swiss Minister Stücki arrived as requested to witness before history that he was leaving under compulsion. Stücki played the main part, ensuring that the 'violence' should be sufficient to show that Pétain had not gone of his own free will and yet provoke no shooting by the Marshal's bodyguard. The farce was played out when Gestapo officer Detering arrived with 200 SD, who surrounded the hotel and forced open the revolving door, jammed with a couple of chairs. The security gate on the stairs was also forced in front of the guards, who took no action.

Outside the door of the Marshal's suite, Detering knocked politely, but two inner doors had to be forced before he came upon the head of state in shirt and trousers, doing up his shoelaces. Ignoring the intrusion, the Marshal finished dressing, took his breakfast and was escorted out of the building at 8.15, the small crowd of onlookers piping up an unhappy '*Marseillaise*' in his honour. His destination and Laval's was the Hohenzollern fortress town of Sigmaringen between Stuttgart and the Swiss border where, in the ruins of the Reich, some authorities put as high as 30,000 the number of big and small fry from Vichy who had held out until the final collapse.

The regime that had started as comic opera ended as a real-life première of Sartre's stage play *Closed Circuit*[5] – a metaphor for hell, in which the waiter in a windowless but comfortably furnished hotel room explains to four mystified characters, '*L'enfer, c'est les autres!*': hell is the others, with whom they are locked up for eternity.

Back in the capital Pétain and Laval would see again only as the setting for their trials ending with death sentences, the Hôtel Majestic was deserted. In the Hôtel Meurice on rue de Rivoli Gen Von Choltitz sat calmly chatting to his staff. Having decided not to comply with Hitler's order to destroy the city, he would, as Helmut Rademacher observed, have been condemned to death on return to Germany and had nowhere else to go.

On the façade of the nearby Hôtel de Ville the tricolour flag flew again for the first time in fifty months, the FFI having occupied it after killing the drivers of two broken-down Wehrmacht trucks at Levallois in the north-west of the capital and thus acquiring four machine guns, twelve sub-machine guns, 250 pistols and ammunition. The Paris police fortified the Préfecture opposite Notre Dame cathedral, but all the months of planning for this moment between the various factions of the Resistance in the capital were now revealed as empty talk. When the Communists declared a 'general insurrection' against the remaining Germans in the city, the Gaullists asked sarcastically what weapons they intended to use.

The entire stockpile amounted to only 600 small arms, until weapons could be taken from German prisoners and casualties. In one early attack a truckload of German grenades was 'liberated'. When the nervous drivers of two fleeing German trucks collided near Place Clichy, the loot included nine machine guns, fifteen sub-machine guns and eight Mauser pistols. The Hotchkiss arms factory yielded twenty sub-machine guns. During the next six days a force of about 3,000 men and women – it was afterwards claimed to have been 7,000 or even 20,000 – was armed piecemeal in this way, to man the barricades of furniture, sandbags, paving stones and trees, where they captured a few unlucky Germans who had lost their way.

At 7 o'clock on 19 August 2,000 Paris policemen in civilian clothes assembled on the *parvis* between Notre Dame cathedral and the Préfecture. Accustomed to receiving orders, they milled around aimlessly with no one in charge. A truck arrived, from which a few automatic weapons and rifles were distributed. A sentry opened the main door of the Préfecture. They poured inside to sing the '*Marseillaise*' as a tricolour flag was hoisted on a flagpole. The PCF's would-be commander of Paris, 'Colonel' Rol, arrived on his bicycle with his home-made uniform in a brown paper parcel, furious that the police had not waited for him. Hastily changing clothes in an office, he emerged with the intention of taking command, but they had other ideas.

In distant Auch, Renée De Monbrison and her children were staying in yet another borrowed home. For days, they had been watching open trucks heading north carrying German wounded. On 19 August the German garrison drove out of the town with orders to regroup further north. One imagines the civilians at moments like this huddled in cellars, awaiting the ceasefire. Reality is so often different. Renée had packed the children off that day to the local swimming pool with a picnic. She heard them come running back to the house yelling, 'Auch is liberated!' Her 18-year-old daughter, Françoise, who spoke perfect English, jumped into the first Allied jeep to enter the town and kissed a wounded British liaison officer sitting in the rear seat, Captain T.A. Mellows. Colonel Hilaire of the Armée Secrète and an American officer also got a kiss, as did the Polish driver, before Françoise was told to get down and behave herself because they were there to kill Germans, not to be kissed by pretty girls.

Throughout her wanderings, Renée had kept intact her last packet of tea in the assumption that her liberators would be English and in need of a good cuppa. When she now proudly presented them with her precious gift, the result was laughter all round: tea was one thing they had aplenty. Despite the public relief in Auch that the enemy had gone, Mellows warned the family that they were not far away, having been halted at a barricade on the bridge at Isle-Jourdain manned by local Maquis units. Dusk came with a stalemate, the Germans unable to cross and the Maquis unable to prevail. After dark, the FFI 'Armagnac battalion' arrived and completely surrounded the German positions. At dawn, sporadic firing intensified until the arrival of the Corps Franc Pommiès. Now outnumbered, the scattered groups of Germans surrendered, one by one.

Since that left no armed enemy forces in the *département* of Gers, everyone congratulated themselves on having liberated their part of France without Allied intervention. Groups of musicians were playing in the streets of Auch, with people of all ages dancing from sheer joy. For the De Monbrison family, the joy was tinged with sadness at the news that Capt Mellows had been killed in a skirmish only a few kilometres away.

Elation after years of fear combined with a sleepless night to trigger one of those shameful scenes of the Liberation where young women with shaven heads were driven through the streets with babies in their arms by jeering neighbours, most of whom had never lifted a hand in anger for the past four years. The worst excesses of stripping girls naked and painting swastikas in tar on their breasts were avoided in Auch that morning when *miliciens* and other male *collabos* were rounded up and forced to parade around the town with some forty women accused of various crimes.

Most of the women were shorn, the majority because they had gone with German soldiers. While this was regarded as permissible business activity for prostitutes, those girls and women guilty of falling in love with a German were universally punished, while wives of POWs absent in Germany who had had a German boyfriend risked prosecution as well. In the crowd screaming at and spitting on its victims, 18-year-old Madeleine Martin was so carried away by the general excitement that when a neighbour accused a women of having denounced her husband, who had been deported to Germany, Madeleine took the scissors from her and continued hacking off her victim's hair until she was completely bald. Now Madeleine says, 'What a terrible thing it was to do! But at the time, I just wanted to hurt someone to make up for all the fear and unhappiness.'[6]

A former Abwehr major extrapolated from his own experience to estimate at 30,000,000 the number of anonymous denunciations made during the Occupation.[7] Most of the letters were never opened because there would not have been time. Judging by the handwriting and spelling of those that were, the majority had been written by the poor and underprivileged to get even with those above them in society or enjoying some advantage they lacked. Specific motives varied from the desire to be rid of an inconvenient wife, a violent husband or a business competitor to family feuds and the hostility of the steward at Château St-Roch towards Renée and her family, whose arrival threatened to expose his illicit selling of estate produce on the black market. Many of those betrayed in turn delivered others to the Gestapo to save their own skins. A high proportion of the anonymous letters came from women seizing the power of life and death over spouses and neighbours. When those denounced were male, one might argue that in a country which denied women the vote or any other participation on public affairs, the writers were collectively teaching a lesson to the men who had voted for the men who had voted for Pétain in the casino at Vichy.

What is strange is not that the *collabos* should have been summarily punished at the Liberation, but that the violence usually died down after the crowd had had its understandable moment of triumph. A few men were lynched, many beaten up, others later put on trial, but after the humiliation of the women in Auch there was no escalation of violence, although the new police commissioner in Moissac noted the possibility of a later 'personal settling of accounts by those to whom the official punishment did not seem severe enough'.[8] With much weaponry and explosives hidden away after the cessation of hostilities, it was inevitable that a number of *collabos* saw their shops or houses dynamited. In the worst reported incident, 'ten masked persons went to the home in Moissac of two women recently released from imprisonment (for collaboration), shaved their heads and attempted to rape the younger one'.[9]

The liberation of Moissac took place on the day after Auch. When an FTP Maquis formation joined up with the Corps Franc Pommiès to infiltrate into the town and clear it of Germans, heavy machine-gun and mortar fire greeted them from the Carmelite monastery on a hill dominating the town. Three civilians who strayed into the streets were accidentally killed and two others shot by a German firing squad. That night the Germans were trigger-happy, understandably seeing 'terrorists' everywhere, but before daybreak the sound of firing died away as the enemy withdrew, dumping in the canal large quantities of arms and ammunition and leaving all their personal baggage behind to be looted by the locals.

The FFI ordered the gendarmes to stop the looting and tried to keep some control over the jubilant population because there were still many German troops in the area. Proving the point, that afternoon they took prisoner 150 bewildered young non-German conscripts left behind without orders or transport. Church bells were ringing far and near and the spirit of revenge was unleashed. Eighty-three alleged *collabos* were arrested and despatched to the concentration camp at Septfonds, now used to intern those who had sent others there during the dark years. At 1 per cent of the population, this was about the national average – and interestingly mirrored the proportion that had been in the Resistance for any length of time.

Being a Sunday, Marie-Rose Dupont was with her son at home when a black Citroën with four men carrying rifles and wearing FFI armbands stopped outside and she was ordered to get into the back of the car. Neither then nor at any time later was she accused of anything, nor did anyone mention Willi. One of the men in the car was Albert Dumas, whose family were clients of the salon; the others she knew by sight. They drove her to the *collège*, now vacated by the Germans, which the FFI had made their temporary headquarters, and locked her up in a classroom with twenty or thirty other men and women. Unable to look at the others, she huddled in a corner with eyes closed, praying to the Virgin Mary to let her be released so she could return to her son. Two days later all the detainees were driven by the FFI to the gendarmerie in Lauzerte, 22 kilometres to the north. Since there were far too many prisoners for the cells to hold, they were locked in an office where they had to sleep on the floor, suffering frequent verbal abuse from anyone who felt like dropping in, but not otherwise maltreated.

In Paris, although German forces returned fire in self-defence, Von Choltitz refused to order reprisals against the FFI. Swedish consul-general in Paris since 1905, Raoul Nordling had heard that in the retreat from Caen 200 prisoners had been shot because there was no transport to evacuate them, and was concerned for the fate of the 4,213 prisoners held by the Germans in

Paris prisons. He arranged a bizarre deal with Von Choltitz, by which all the prisoners were to be released in return for the release of five Germans per head. Von Choltitz knew perfectly well that the FFI had nothing like this many prisoners, but wanted the agreement to look good in Berlin.

A piece of paper was one thing, but Nordling was a man of action, who hurried to Fresnes, Cherche-Midi and Drancy to oversee the release of prisoners there. He arrived at Romainville in the nick of time, for the Russian SS guards were drunk and already planning a massacre before leaving. At Compiègne, he just missed a train of prisoners pulling out eastbound, but was able to have it stopped before the German border. Returning to Von Choltitz on Sunday 20 August after a thunderstorm so violent that many Parisians thought the city was being shelled or bombed, Nordling negotiated a general truce, during which the last Stabshelferinnen 'grey mice' were evacuated after selling their bicycles and stores of tinned food in a buyers' market.

Despite the attempts of Alexandre Parodi to prevent an uprising that would invite wholesale reprisals, the truce, announced by loudspeaker from joint patrols of German soldiers and FFI fighters, was continually broken between 22 and 24 August by Communist factions under Rol's provocative slogan '*A chacun son Boche!*' ('Let everyone kill his Kraut!')

The resultant deaths on both sides were militarily purposeless, the Protestant bodies being laid in state at the Oratory and the Catholic ones at Notre Dame des Victoires. At one point during the truce, Parodi and two other Resistance heads were taken prisoner and conducted to the Hôtel Meurice, where Von Choltitz ordered their release and offered to shake hands as between officers and gentlemen. They refused the courtesy.

Until 23 August Eisenhower planned to outflank the Germans in Paris without entering the inner city, because he did not want to be burdened with having to feed the population. It was planned for General Omar Bradley to take the city 'sometime in September'. Credit for changing this plan and advancing the date to prevent the FFI-Wehrmacht conflict escalating dangerously goes largely to Consul-General Nordling, who persuaded Von Choltitz to allow him to take a motley delegation including an otherwise unidentified Monsieur Armoux, said to be 'head of British Intelligence in Paris', through the lines. By sheer force of personality, Nordling managed to get his team to General Patton, who flew them to Bradley, who personally cleared an earlier liberation of the capital with Eisenhower. Nordling now sought De Gaulle's approval, which was not forthcoming: he disliked being confronted with a fait accompli but for political reasons it was decided to let General Jacques Philippe Leclerc's 2nd Armoured Division be the first Allied troops seen in Paris.

While most PCF members obeyed Party instructions during the Liberation, the renegade Georges Guingouin was one of only twelve later honoured with the title Compagnon de la Libération for disobeying PCF orders to attack the city of Limoges in July because he judged it pointless to 'liberate' the city for a few hours and retreat, calling down reprisals on the population. When his forces, totalling about 20,000 men on Mount Gargan, found themselves in a pitched battle with Von Jesser's motorised columns, he managed to extricate them from certain annihilation, suffering ninety-two casualties to the enemy's 340. His caution was vindicated when, instead of the massacres caused by the PCF in Tulle, St-Amand and Oradour, the German commander in Limoges surrendered the garrison bloodlessly to him on 21 August.

Proving that disobeying orders was not a French prerogative, a Kriegsmarine chief petty officer from Dortmund single-handedly saved the major port-city of Bordeaux from widespread destruction and many deaths. With the Allies driving east from Normandy and northwards up the Rhône valley from Provence, there was a danger they would join and cut off the retreat of German forces in the west of the country. Lieutenant-General Nake of 159th Division had orders to demolish the port of Bordeaux and sink every ship there before withdrawing, and to blow every bridge over the Garonne, Dordogne and Isle rivers behind his last troops.

Feldwebel Heinz Stahlschmidt, who was in charge of the demolition stores, takes the story from there:

> I asked a French docker to put me in contact with the Resistance, and met these guys. They knew who I was and offered me 100,000 francs to destroy the demolition fuses stored in a secure magazine. Without the fuses, the charges were useless. I didn't want the money. I wanted them to promise me a new identity, so that I could go underground and stay in Bordeaux with my girlfriend when the Wehrmacht and Kriegsmarine pulled out. On the night of 22 August I set a charge that blew the magazine sky-high. After that, there was no going back. I didn't return to Germany until twenty-seven years later, to explain my actions to the family. People thought I was a traitor, you see.[10]

However, the charges were still in place, so on 23 August in a typically Bordelais business deal wine exporter Louis Eschenauer, who had sold wine worth 10,000,000 francs to the Germans during the Occupation,[11] agreed to talk to the German harbour-master who, in civilian life, was a Berlin wine importer with whom Eschenauer had done business for years, and with whom he lunched each week. His friend Commander Kühnemann agreed that the planned destruction of the port was pointless since Allied use of the Gironde estuary was interdicted by the Royan pocket of resistance. He revealed the contact to his superior, Lt Gen Nake, who shared this opinion, but was himself ordered to carry out the destruction with what fuses remained. He then received an offer of a deal from the FFI through Prefect Sabatier and the mayor of Bordeaux: the Resistance agreed not to harass the German withdrawal if the Wehrmacht and Kriegsmarine refrained from *any* demolition. Nake himself dictated and had printed the following announcement:

Notice to the population

As supreme commander of German forces in the Bordeaux region, I declare that no destruction will take place in greater Bordeaux, and that the harbour and bridges which are mined will not be destroyed, if the population refrains from all acts of sabotage in greater Bordeaux until the withdrawal from Bordeaux of all German forces.

(signed: Nake, Lt Gen)

On Saturday 26 August the notices were displayed throughout the city. It was on the reverse of one of them that the second stage of the deal was written by hand after being agreed between Kühnemann and Major Rougès, local commander of FFI:

It is agreed as follows:

All the German Occupation forces must have left the city of Bordeaux by 2400 hrs on Sunday 27 August. The city, the port, port installations and bridges must remain intact. American and Allied troops and the Maquis may only occupy the city from 0001 hrs on 28 August 1944.

(signed) Commandant Rougès / Hafenkommandant Kühnemann

There was little more to it than that, apart from a few uneasy moments on both sides. On 28 August Bordeaux was liberated bloodlessly only a few hours after the departure of Nake's last troops. With habitual modesty, all Stahlschmidt said after emerging from hiding to marry his French girlfriend was, 'It was the best thing I ever did.'[12]

Estimates based on the liberation of Marseilles and Grenoble on 23 August are that he saved the lives of 3,000 people, German and French. In the evening of the following day, after Patton's tankers had pulled off the roads to allow three columns of Leclerc's 2nd Armoured Division to be first into Paris, the lead tanks drove into the suburbs, accepting the surrender of German strong points, more often delayed by the delirious welcome of civilians than by enemy action.

Vichy, however, was not liberated until 26 August. Six days after Pétain's forced departure, Xavier Vallat was the last Cabinet minister left in the Hôtel du Parc, deserted apart from him and a small detachment of guards on the ground floor. Limping next door to the Majestic for lunch, Vallat saw French flags being hastily removed from the façade – a measure of prudence sparked by rumours that a German column was heading that way. About 4 p.m., standing on the balcony of his office, Vallat watched demonstrators in the street chanting '*Vive De Gaulle!*' while a sad little cluster of Pétain's faithful quietly intoned the anthem '*Maréchal, nous voilà!*'[13]

Chapter 24

A CARPET OF WOMEN'S HAIR

With Wehrmacht communications non-existent on the evening of 24 August, fortunately French long-distance lines were still working in Paris, enabling Von Choltitz to take a call from the local Luftwaffe commander, who had been ordered to bomb the capital.

'By daylight, I presume?' Von Choltitz queried.

'That's too dangerous. It'll be by night.'

'In that case, you'll miss the targets.' Von Choltitz knew the lines were monitored by the Gestapo. 'I'm not going to have my soldiers killed by German bombs, so I'll have to withdraw them. Will you accept responsibility for that?'

The answer was a categorical *'Nein, Herr General!'*

On such a slender thread hung many lives on the final night of the German occupation of Paris. Next morning a Free French Army lieutenant entered Von Choltitz's room and asked if he would order the ceasefire. Relieved that his lonely mutiny was over, the last military governor of Paris replied without quibbling over their difference in rank, 'Since you are already in my bedroom, it's a bit late for that.'

Escorted outside, the small party of German officers suffered catcalls from civilians in rue de Rivoli before being ushered into a Red Cross van and driven to the Préfecture de Police. Expecting to be shot, Rademacher was surprised to find his captors polite and correct. In return, he agreed to accompany a Free French officer in uniform to a number of strong points where elderly reservists were still holding out, since there was no other way to cease their resistance.

There were actually two surrender protocols signed in Leclerc's temporary HQ, a draughty little office at the Gare Montparnasse. On the first, he insisted that, as senior officer present, his signature covered all French forces. With an eye to history, Rol and Kriegel-Valrimont argued that Rol was commander of all FFI units in Greater Paris and not Leclerc's subordinate. To avoid the danger of their men refusing to cease fire, Leclerc signed a second copy of the document below Rol's signature.

Predictably, there were some incidents when unarmed Germans were attacked and killed after surrendering. In the worst, a grenade was thrown into a column of prisoners near the Place de l'Etoile, after which a lone machine gun mowed down several survivors. At 4 p.m. De Gaulle was driven into Paris in an open-topped car and spent the night in the War Ministry, where the office out of which he had walked as under-secretary for war in May 1940 was as he had left it, right down to the names on his internal phone buttons.

His walkabout next day down the Champs Elysées defied sniper fire from rooftops. The official line was that this was the work of German stay-behinds. In fact, some *miliciens* reckoned they had nothing to lose by a 'heroic last stand', and on 29 August nine of them were lined up and shot without trial in Paris' Roman amphitheatre by the Hôtel Lutetia, but since the main bursts of firing on the day of the walkabout were co-ordinated at 5 p.m. on the Place de l'Etoile, the Hôtel de Ville and Place de la Concorde,[1] it was widely accepted that the snipers were PCF hardliners deterring the population from going into the streets to manifest support for De Gaulle as enthusiastically as they had cheered Pétain sixteen weeks earlier. The ploy succeeded.

At Troyes prison in central France, detainees tapped out on the heating pipes 'American tanks are in Paris!' But the SS guards continued like automata calling out the names of men to fill their last remaining truck, driven to the peaceful fields of Creney just outside town, where they were machine-gunned before their killers returned for another insane 'selection'. Hostage Roger Bruge bade farewell to the men in his cell one by one as they were taken away, leaving him alone. When the footsteps returned and his cell door was thrown open, he braced himself. But this was no guard. In the corridor stood a volunteer fireman and a blonde girl, who hurried him away. In the confusion of people running along the corridors, a distraught man caught up with them and asked for news of his brother.

'Taken away an hour ago,' Bruge replied.

'Hurry,' said the blonde girl. 'They may come back.'

The SS returned just after the last prisoner had fled, but forty-nine still warm bodies lay in the fields at Creney.[2]

On August 30 'Madame Robert' saw the first US troops arrive in Villiers-Adam. Disappointed that they were not English or French, she hurried to greet them, but the sole fell off one of her worn-out shoes. Hobbling back into the house, she re-emerged to embrace an American officer, who was relieved to find someone who could speak English and through her told the villagers to take down home-made Allied flags hung at their windows, in case a German unit chanced through, with the front still very fluid. Sweets for the children and cigarettes for the adults from the soldiers were reciprocated with fruit from the villagers and drinks of well-water. There had been no piped water for days, nor electricity, so this was the first 'Madame Robert' heard about the liberation of Paris on 25 August. The last candles having been used up long since, people went to bed at nightfall as usual.

Life for 'Madame Robert' changed, as did her identity, when a British officer walked up the garden path and introduced himself as Victor Rothschild, whom she had known as a child. Freshly arrived as British Ambassador in

Paris, Duff Cooper had asked him to 'drop in' and tell her it was safe to return to the capital. After travelling back in her old clothes and shoes on a train crowded with refugees, life resumed pretty much where it had left off in June 1940 the moment she walked into the Rothschild mansion on Avenue Marigny. At that moment, she became the elegant Madame Cahen d'Anvers again, although even those lucky enough to be invited into a Rothschild residence had to wait until Saturday for a bath, because there was no hot water for anyone on other days. Her greatest joy was the reunion with her daughter Renée and granddaughter Françoise. After a journey of thirty-six hours from Montauban, which included crossing the river at Tours on a temporary footbridge because both road and rail bridges over the Loire had been destroyed, they brought the news that no one in the immediate family had been killed or deported during the Occupation, although many other relatives were dead.[3]

Back in Moissac after nearly two weeks' confinement in Lauzerte, Marie-Rose Dupont was interrogated by FFI men hunting a *collabo* who had gone to ground. Unable to tell them anything, she emerged with cuts and severe bruising on her legs from blows with the butts of their rifles. On the Sunday – exactly two weeks after the liberation of the town – she and three other female detainees were taken out of the *collège* and led through the streets to the square in front of St Catherine's Church, where a wooden dais had been erected. Praying that none of her family was there, Marie-Rose stared straight ahead as she was led through the large crowd waiting to see the fun.

A colleague of hers who ran a barbershop in the town was supposed to shave the women's heads, but could not bring himself to do this to Marie-Rose, with whom he had been at school. Unable to look her in the face, he handed the clippers to one of the FFI men, who did not know how to handle them. Her public humiliation was thus clumsy and painful as she tried to block out the ugly noise of the crowd's insults by praying to the Virgin. By keeping her eyes raised to the sky, she avoided looking at the people below, but recalls that one of the girls on the dais was an 18-year-old prostitute from a local *maison close*. Since in general whores were not troubled, presumably this girl's crime was to have fallen in love with a German client. It is interesting that well-connected Madame Delmas, at whose *diners dansants* Marie-Rose had met Willi, was denounced neither then nor later.[4]

Armed FFI men roughly bundled their victims off the platform and onto the back of a flatbed truck. With two armed guards, their shame was then paraded around Moissac for two hours, the klaxon blaring to attract maximal attention. For the same reason, the driver made a long halt outside the hairdressing salon, where a number of Marie-Rose's clients were watching. None of them showed what they were thinking, but the mild-mannered little music teacher who had taught her in the *collège* came up to the truck and took both her hands in his. Ignoring the FFI men and the crowd staring at them, he said, '*Courage! Ça va bientôt se terminer.*' ('Bear up, it'll soon be over.')

It was his sympathy that broke the dam of her self-control. Tears streaming down her face, Marie-Rose was driven away with the other shorn women and again locked up in the *collège*. A guard whom she knew told them their ordeal was over and they would soon be released. Neither of her parents came to visit Marie-Rose, but her brother brought food several times during the next four days' confinement. At 6 a.m. one morning, the women were released, the time being chosen because few people would be in the streets. Setting out to walk the few miles back to her parents' home, Marie-Rose was given a lift by a Spanish refugee who had lived in Moissac since the civil war. On the way, he tried to comfort her with the reflection that most people soon forget everything, both the good and the bad.

For a week she dared not set foot outside, but then courageously decided that the first step in restarting her life was to make herself a wig and get back to work. As she says, 'I was lucky. At least I knew how to do that for myself.' Reopening the salon, she found that far from losing customers, all the regulars came back as though nothing had happened and a whole crop of new customers booked appointments as a tacit gesture of sympathy from the women of the town.[5]

Other women's lives were irrevocably shattered in a few minutes by the scissors or clippers wielded by their tormentors. The Liberation lasted eleven months, from 6 June 1944 to the signature of the unconditional surrender by General Alfred Jodl on 7 May 1945 in Rheims, when the last pockets of resistance in France gave in. Throughout this time, over 20,000 women were humiliated as Marie-Rose had been, reaching a peak in August and September 1944.[6] If the majority were aged between 17 and 34, cases were recorded as young as 15 and as old as 68.[7]

Mademoiselle Z was also sentenced by a purge court to ten years of 'national indignity' for 'passing intelligence to the enemy'. Today, her daughter Line speaks out at the monstrosity of the sentence: 'She was 17 years old! What political motive could she have had? She was condemned for bearing a German's child. After five years in Troyes prison and at the camp of Jargeau where they put all the undeclared prostitutes, when she came out, she was completely unstable. Her life was ruined.'[8]

As another of the 'children of national shame' said, 'If it had been a one-night stand, there was always the traditional way out of the problem: single mothers left the baby on the doorstep of an orphanage, a convent or the local presbytery. But our mothers chose to keep us, so there must have been love.'[9]

Certainly Anne S showed devotion for Günther, her German MP lover. Throughout the four years of their relationship, as a daughter of a railway worker, she repeatedly travelled free by train to wherever he was posted. During the Liberation he was taken prisoner and imprisoned near Lyons. To help the father of her child, she persuaded her brother-in-law, who had made false ID papers for *résistants*, to make a set for Günther, but he broke a leg while escaping, which led to Anne being sentenced to six months in prison, during which time her only joy was to see through the bars of her cell once a week her small son being carried in his grandmother's arms along the street outside the prison. Anne's mother paid the owner of the local paper not to report the affair and shame the family, but he printed it all the same.

Anita A brought up her German lover's child in an abusive household. Married to an alcoholic ex-*résistant* who exploited her shame by repeated beatings and other humiliations, she accepted the abuse as atonement and spent hours alone in her room praying for forgiveness. Only after the husband committed suicide in 1999 did her daughter find on going through family papers that her birth certificate bore the stigmatic 'Father unknown'. Among her mother's papers were dozens of exercise books filled with the repeated phrase 'I must atone, I must atone . . .'[10]

The humiliation of women continued throughout the Liberation, which did not end until the last pockets of resistance on the Atlantic coast capitulated in May 1945. Even later, some women who had been *requises* working in Germany had their heads shorn on return to their home towns.

After the capitulation of the La Rochelle pocket, on 7 May 1945 the little seaside resort of Fouras on the Atlantic coast saw thirty or so local women dragged by neighbours to the picturesque Victorian bandstand where concerts had been given for summer visitors before the war. Renée X was cleaning the tables in her aunt's neighbourhood restaurant that had been requisitioned by the Germans as a mess when four male neighbours ordered her to come with them. Forced up the steps to the bandstand, she and the other women were kept standing there, in her words 'like sows in a market pen'; except that sows do not get spat on or have fists shaken in their faces.

With clippers and scissors, the self-appointed justiciars started cutting hair – blonde hair, dark hair, red hair, she remembers – until the women were standing on a carpet of their own hair, symbolising the femininity they were accused of soiling.

'Afterwards,' recalled Renée, 'I walked back to the hotel. It was not far, but it seemed a long way. My little daughter Mylène was there with my parents. There was no need for her to see that.' Renée had been 16 when she fell in love with Mylène's father. Posted elsewhere, he left his signet ring as a token and departed unaware that she was pregnant. His daughter, now a middle-aged woman herself, wonders whether 'people will ever understand that not all Germans were swine who raped women, and that not all French women who slept with them were sluts? My mother has felt guilty all her life.'[11]

The standard punishment for sleeping with the enemy in twentieth-century Europe seems to have begun in Belgium after the German withdrawal of 1918, and was widely used during the occupation of the Rhineland after the First World War, when German women suffered the same fate for relationships with French soldiers. It also occurred during the Spanish and Greek civil wars.[12] The victims were being humiliated for having enjoyed preferential treatment in terms of food, clothes, make-up, but there is more to it than that. Young girls naturally fall in love with young men, especially those in uniform, which is seen to endow them with all the masculine virtues. If many thousands of French girls flirted with, or had affairs with, German soldiers while most boys of their own age were away in POW camps, with the Maquis or in Germany with the STO, was that treason? Estimates are that between 49 and 57 per cent of the women punished were accused of no other crime,[13] so for what exactly were they being punished?

The only theory that makes any sense of the shearing of women's hair in liberated Denmark, Belgium, Holland, the Channel Islands, Italy, France and elsewhere is that the child-bearing potential of women's bodies is regarded as common property, so that the woman who uses hers against the common will must be shown the error of her ways – as continues to happen in peacetime to girls of strict religious or racial communities wishing to 'marry out'. Perhaps also, the collective need to punish *anybody* vulnerable seized upon the women during the Liberation as victims because the act of shearing is a physical and psychological violence with a strong element of fetishistic pleasure that can easily be sanctioned because it seems less permanent than retributive violence directed against guilty men, who have to be beaten, injured or killed. The catharsis felt by the crowd after women had been shorn seems to indicate that all these explanations are partially true.

Since the act of punishment was always sanctioned, and usually executed, by men – although with women approvingly present, some with small children in their arms – it can be seen as their way of reclaiming the masculinity lost in military defeat by disciplining the guilty women, as though subjugating the vulnerable 'guilty females' of the herd demonstrates that the males are no longer themselves subjugated to a more potent enemy.[14] That the act of shearing was inflicted for many other offences on women,[15] but very rarely on men, is taken to mean that shearing was a sexual punishment for a crime, rather than a punishment for a necessarily sexual crime; one victim at the Liberation was the singer Vera Valmont, whose only known 'crime' was accepting engagements on Radio Paris.[16]

Illicit affairs with German personnel during the Occupation resulted in 30,000 declared births. To this figure must be added all the children who, on paper, were 'fathered' by an unwitting or consenting French partner of the mother. Conservative estimates put the total above 70,000, which compares with 5,500 known births to German fathers in Denmark with a population one tenth the size of France's,[17] but it may well be higher: the Propaganda Abteilung reported to Oberg on 14 September 1942 that some 3,000 children had *already* been fathered by German personnel in Normandy alone.[18] Whichever figure one takes, if pregnancy resulted in only 5 per cent of cases, there must have been several hundred thousand emotional liaisons with 'the occupier'. Viewed by the French as the ultimate national shame, this is only now being discussed and written about openly, two generations later.

What strikes one on looking at photographs of the shorn women, whether clothed or naked, swastika-branded or with a 'confession' pinned to their blouses, is the range of facial expression. Old and young, pretty and ugly, some show lip-biting anguish; others, submission or bewilderment; a few glare angrily at the camera or defiantly brush the hair clippings off their shoulders; very few weep; and some, like Marie-Rose, have eyes downcast as if praying for the nightmare to end, unthinking that their hour of shame was frozen for ever by an unforgiving camera lens. Photographs of the women shorn in Bergerac were even printed as a souvenir set of postcards on public sale.[19]

Chapter 25

DEATH OF A TOWN

The liberation of the Atlantic coast pockets had scant priority with an Allied command intent on driving into the heartland of the Reich as rapidly as possible without incurring an unacceptable level of casualties. This implied by-passing strongly held areas not impeding the advance and the pockets of resistance around ports of lesser importance in the race to Berlin. Thus, the main thrust evolved by the beginning of September 1944 into the shape of a fist with the accusing index finger pointing at the vital industrial complex of the Ruhr valley.

Leclerc's Free French forces being under Allied command, the liberation of the rest of France was not a tidal wave of freedom washing rapidly across the map, for there was no way that the unassisted FFI could tackle the heavily fortified pockets of resistance around the Atlantic ports. Thus, when French troops entered Strasbourg on 23 November – the German border had been briefly crossed by US forces early in September – there were many hundreds of thousands of French civilians still living under German occupation in conditions worse than ever as rations were reduced, German paranoia understandably rose and RAF and US air forces diverted resources to 'keeping the enemy's heads down' and reducing morale to the point where surrender became acceptable to the pocket commanders ordered by Hitler to hold out to the last man and bullet.

Le Havre was not liberated until 12 September, Boulogne on 22 September and Calais on the last day of that month, with their civilian populations suffering great privation during this time. At Le Havre, where Allied bombing continued until the day of liberation, each evening after a day's work in appalling conditions even those few civilians whose homes were still habitable took a bus or train to spend the night in nearby villages less likely to be bombed. Each night 2,000 people pushed their remaining belongings on wheelbarrows into an unfinished road tunnel, where they cooked supper over hollowed-out swedes filled with sump oil by the light of carbide lamps and slept on their mattresses laid on the damp floor.

On 5 September 1944 the tonnage of high-explosive and incendiaries dropped on the town was such that a fire-storm engulfed half the built-up area, melting and igniting road surfaces to produce a column of superheated gases that blew human remains and other large and small debris as far as 30 kilometres away. Even those taking refuge in the deep tunnel were not safe, an uncounted number having broken through the safety barriers into an unfinished section to find room to lie down for the night. Engulfed by a subterranean river of earth liquefied by the explosions, rigor mortis turned them into a mass of mud and flesh that had to be cut apart by volunteer firemen, after their officers had refused to order anyone to do it. Survivors were trapped for forty-eight hours without food or water. In the Atlantic port of Brest the entire Sadi-Carnot shelter literally blew up on 9 September, when an unknown projectile hit a German arms dump in one section of the shelter, killing 350 French civilians in less than a second.

Keenly aware that more of France had been liberated by men in US, Canadian and British uniforms than by Gen Leclerc, De Gaulle wanted to see the strategically unimportant south-west of France liberated by men in French uniform. The three pockets around La Rochelle, Royan and Pointe de Grave totalled 710 concrete blockhouses surrounded by extensive minefields and barbed-wire entanglements, defended by 30,000 men in German uniform including anti-British Sikhs from the Indian Liberation Army. On 18 September 1944 at Saintes, De Gaulle congratulated Colonel Adeline, provisional commander of FFI forces in the south-west, on the way his men had been containing the Germans in the pockets. 'However,' he continued, 'I want no local armistice of any kind. The German pockets must, and will, be reduced by force of arms.' The armistices referred to were exchanges of wounded on the front line under flags of truce, for the skirmishes along the coast produced casualties in this forgotten war – forgotten outside France even while it was being fought, the world's media being focused on the Allied drive into Germany.

'A French armoured division will be sent here,' De Gaulle promised. 'When I cannot say, but in the near future.'[1]

He could not say when armoured reinforcements might arrive because that required Eisenhower's consent. After notifying Supreme Allied HQ on 21 September of his intention to liberate the two pockets blocking the port of Bordeaux, De Gaulle ordered Gen De Lattre De Tassigny on 7 October to relinquish two divisions for this campaign, but Eisenhower made clear who was in charge by not agreeing until the end of November to let them go, effective 25 December – perhaps as an ironic Xmas present.

By then De Gaulle had given General Edgard De Larminat command of the Forces Françaises de l'Ouest (FFO), as from 14 October 1944[2] tasked with the liquidation of the pockets as a matter of national honour. Significantly, De Gaulle baptised the operation 'Independence'. There was more to this than personal arrogance, for once the US military presence was installed in France, it was to take him twenty-two years to eject his transatlantic allies.

Not until 23 October 1944 did the White House and Downing Street recognise De Gaulle's government 'subject to the military requirements of the Supreme Commander'.[3] Three days later he decreed that all FFI units not incorporated in the uniformed services or under military command must hand

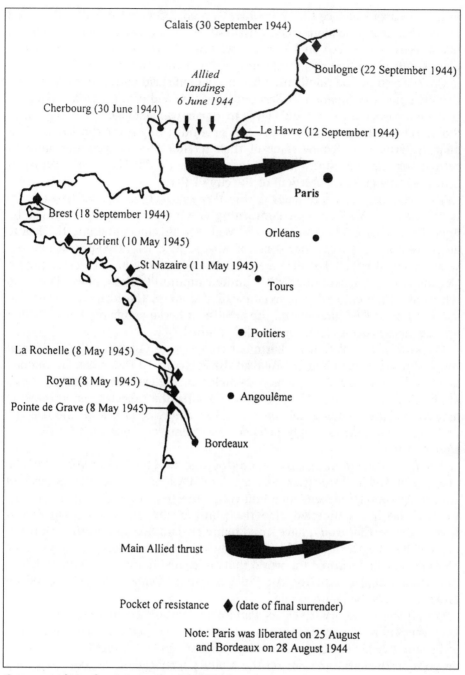

German pockets of resistance after June 1944.

in their weapons or face the consequences – an order that was directly aimed at the Communist factions. Since, as head of the provisional government he had already announced on 15 September that 'Vichy war criminals' would be placed on trial, all that remained was to define who was a criminal.

On 7 November De Gaulle used his newly confirmed authority to demand a French zone of occupation in Germany after the end of hostilities, explaining that he also needed a million POWs to repair war damage in France. Since Stalin refused to give up any of 'his' ground, this meant the UK and US allowing France to occupy some of their territory in occupied Germany. In return for his sometimes wavering support, on 12 November Winston Churchill was given the freedom of the city of Paris.

To invest the landward sides of the three pockets in the south-west, De Larminat had 10,700 men containing the 16,000-man garrison at La Rochelle. Another 5,000 were on the Médoc peninsula containing the Pointe de Grave pocket. The major pocket of Royan, with its 5,000-plus defenders, was contained by 10,040 FFO men. Their few artillery pieces were captured German or Italian cannon, with limited ammunition supplies. The only advantage they enjoyed was freedom of the air in the form of occasional support from Allied aircraft and the *promise* of aerial bombardment to 'soften up' the pockets before an eventual all-out attack.

It was to plan this that De Larminat conferred at Cognac with US General Ralph Royce commanding 1st Tactical Air Force on 10 December. He claimed afterwards they discussed intensive bombing of the exclusively military zones of the Royan and Pointe de Grave pockets after the expected reinforcements arrived. Yet the bombing mission was misleadingly described on the teletype as 'To destroy town strongly defended by enemy and occupied by German troops only.'[4]

The first of the promised armoured troops arrived on 12 December, but the opening of Hitler's Ardennes offensive four days later caused Eisenhower to cancel Operation Independence and recall the troops already in the south-west. If he had cancelled also the planned air support for Operation Independence, that would have saved many civilian lives but, in the confusion caused by the German offensive, coming only a couple of days after Montgomery had assured the world that Hitler had no reserves with which to undertake a major initiative, Air Chief Marshal 'Bomber' Harris received no order to cancel the planned raid.

On Friday 5 January 1945 six Pathfinder Mosquitoes and 217 fully laden Lancasters plus a Lancaster crew as master bomber took off from aerodromes in Britain, headed for Royan. Between 0350 hrs and 0400 hrs the first bombs dropped *on the town*, and not on the military fortifications outside. A second wave of Lancasters appeared at 0530 hrs and dropped their cargoes onto the flaming debris below, causing high casualties among civilians who had emerged from shelters to rescue the first victims. A total of 1,576 tonnes of high explosive and thirteen tons of incendiaries destroyed the town centre.

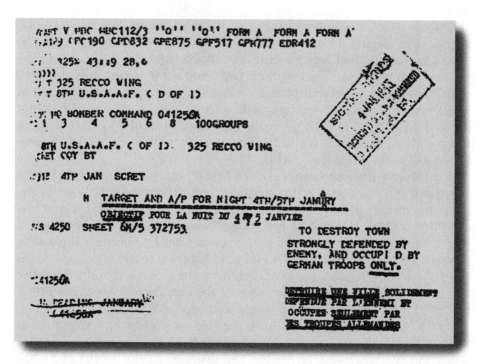

The fatal teletype that killed the people of Royan.

Trapped in the burning debris were bodies of 284 female and 158 male civilians – and thirty-seven German bodies.[5] The exact number of French civilian wounded was never agreed. The declared number of dead was also modified as body-parts were recovered during reconstruction up to five years later. The cost of all this destruction with hardly any damage to the 249 blockhouses in the Royan pocket was seven aircraft shot down by German flak crews.

Allied embarrassment resulted in alibis ranging from poor visibility over the target confusing the marker aircraft to an accusation that the French casualties must have been *collabos* and deserved what they got. As to the first alibi, the town was clearly visible by the bomb-aimers during the raid, due to the marker flares and parachute flares. Even more embarrassingly, the navigator's maps found in shot-down Lancasters had aiming points exclusively in the town area,[6] as indicated by the mission teletype. As to the second, many people remaining in Royan at this late date – after hundreds of civilians had been allowed to leave, to reduce the numbers the Germans had to feed – were refugees living there under false identities or with no papers at all, and of whom there were no records. It was little consolation that anyone could now obtain papers claiming to have been born in Royan, since all the *état civil* registers had been destroyed in the raid.

Historian Peter Krause avers that Gen Royce's adjutant in Vittel asked De Larminat in Cognac to give the go-ahead the previous evening, after the 'target for tonight' had been decided once meteorological conditions over the Continent were known. The telephone line being out of action, the adjutant's signal was encoded and sent by radio, being received at De Larminat's HQ at 1950 hrs on 4 January. Because staff were at dinner, the signal was not decoded until 0040 hrs. There was a further delay until 0530 hrs when it was translated and finally handed to De Larminat at 0800 hrs, by which time Royan was a smoking pile of rubble.

Apart from a truce between 9 and 18 January, during which the Red Cross supervised the evacuation of the wounded and all remaining civilians in the town, the tragedy did nothing to stop the fighting on the ground. The status of FFI men taken prisoner, at first judged terrorists under the Armistice of June 1940 by their captors, was only resolved after De Larminat threatened to shoot ten German prisoners for every FFI fighter executed after capture. At first the Germans refused, but then agreed, on the grounds that the Armistice had been vitiated by their own invasion of the Free Zone in November 1942, that all FFO forces taken prisoner would be treated as POWs.[7]

On 14 April 1945 – the day after the raid on Dresden – a second huge bomber fleet took off from UK bases: 1,200 B-17 Flying Fortresses headed down the Atlantic coast of France and dropped 7,000 tonnes of bombs generously distributed throughout the Royan pocket. De Larminat's men cowering in their shelters on the landward side of the minefields reckoned there were more 'Amis' above the pocket than Germans in it. This was followed up twenty-four hours later by a final US raid, in which three-quarters of a million litres of napalm were dropped in the first use of this new weapon on French soil. Photographs taken afterwards of the town centre of Royan, which had rivalled Biarritz for elegance before the war, resembled those of Ground Zero at Hiroshima – an unbroken wasteland where only a few twisted metal girders poked above the ruins to show where major buildings had stood.

It is hard to arrive at total casualty figures for the Royan pocket, but in the assault on the Pointe de Grave pocket across the mouth of the Gironde between 14 and 20 April French losses were approximately 400 dead and 1,000 wounded, with 600 dead, eighty missing and 3,230 taken prisoner on the German side. All this was to restore national pride, because the German capitulation was signed just over two weeks later.

Chapter 26

AFTER THE WAR WAS OVER ...

All over France, after the violence of the Purge, it was left to the authorities to prosecute where appropriate those who had betrayed and collaborated. For the most part, those who had been enemies during the dark years became neighbours again and did business with each other, not mentioning the past. Having had more than enough of fear and death, even those who had suffered and lost their nearest and dearest decided to live and let live, if only because spoiling today because of yesterday risks ruining tomorrow. But the main actors in this history could not so easily live down their past.

Otto Abetz was sentenced by a French court to twenty years' imprisonment in 1949, but was released in 1954. He died in a car accident in May 1958.

Ernst Achenbach successfully practised law in Germany after the war. Retained by IG Farben and claiming amnesty for alleged war criminals, he would have probably represented his country at the European Commission but for evidence of his wartime activities assembled by German lawyer Beata Klarsfeld.

Klaus Barbie was employed postwar by US Intelligence and allowed to escape to Bolivia under the name of Klaus Altmann. In 1971 a Munich court ruled it impossible to prove he knew what happened to his deported victims. After an attempt to kidnap him failed, persistent campaigning by the Klarsfelds resulted in his extradition to France in 1983 on trial for crimes against humanity. During the 1987 trial Barbie showed no emotion, even when confronted with witnesses he had sadistically tortured over long periods, and whose relatives he had killed to make them talk. Condemned in July 1987 to life imprisonment, he died of cancer on 25 September 1991.

Paul Baudouin left politics in 1941 to work for La Banque d'Indochine. Condemned in March 1945 to five years' hard labour for his role in the Armistice, he was released in January 1948 to return to his banking activities.

Karl Boemelburg left France with Pétain in 1945 and disappeared completely.

Pierre Bonny's bolt-hole was betrayed by his rival Joseph Joanovici; he was condemned and shot at Montrouge on 27 December 1944.

René Bousquet was tried in 1949. Scores of high functionaries and dignitaries including bishops and archbishops testified to his pre-war civic record and his non-collaborationist attitude during the Occupation. Even the president of the Jewish community of Châlons, who had spent the war in Switzerland, said he had 'heard nothing against' Bousquet, while admitting that all the Jews left in Châlons had been deported, with only one survivor. Acquitted, with his Légion d'honneur returned to him, Bousquet throve as adviser and later secretary-general of the Banque d'Indochine, also serving as director of UTA airline and standing unsuccessfully as an anti-Gaullist candidate for the Marne *département*.

In 1977 the French lawyer Serge Klarsfeld published documents proving Bousquet's active participation in the genocide of French and foreign Jews. Accused of crimes against humanity, 84-year-old Bousquet was assassinated by a mentally unstable writer on 8 June 1993 just before the scheduled start of the trial. Whether coincidence or conspiracy is unproven, but the death did prevent a trial in which he might have said embarrassing things.

Francis Bout de l'An was never prosecuted, and died of natural causes at his home in Italy in 1977.

Aloïs Brünner was rescued by the Vatican ratline and given asylum in Damascus, protected by Syrian security services until 'outed' by the Klarsfelds in 1982. French demands for his extradition in 1989 were refused, but Brünner was condemned in his absence to life imprisonment for crimes against humanity on 2 March 2001.

Lazare Cabrero was charged with murdering Grumbach with intent to rob. His defence was corroborated by Madame Courdil saying that a French colonel, conveniently deceased, ordered the *passeurs* to kill refugees who could not keep up, in case they were found by the patrols and forced to divulge details of the escape network. On 29 May 1953 Cabrero was acquitted.[1]

Collaborators executed without trial during *L'Epuration* – the purge after the Liberation – were conservatively numbered at 105,000 between the Liberation of Paris and February 1945 by Adrien Tixier, a postwar Minister of Justice.[2] Some 300,000 other persons were accused of various crimes, of which 124,613 received prison sentences and 6,763 were sentenced to death by military tribunals and approximately the same number were condemned in civil courts; 767 were executed. Fifty thousand others were stripped of civic rights, but most of the tens of thousands of civil servants dismissed or suspended for collaboration were eventually reinstated and recovered pension rights.

Theo Danneker hanged himself in prison in 1945.

Joseph Darnand enlisted the rump of the Milice at Sigmaringen in the SS Division 'Charlemagne', escaped to Italy with help of priests, but was extradited and shot on 10 October 1945.

Louis Darquier de Pellepoix lived undisturbed in Spain despite a death sentence imposed by a French court in his absence. He disclaimed all responsibility for the *rafle du Vel d'Hiv* by accusing Bousquet of having made all the arrangements, yet famously announced during an interview by

L'Express in 1978 that 'at Auschwitz, only fleas were gassed'. He died on 29 August 1980.

Marcel Déat escaped from Sigmaringen into Italy with his wife, helped by priests. After awaiting his turn on the Vatican ratline to South America for two years in Genoa, he moved to Turin in 1947 and died there on 5 January 1955.

Fernand De Brinon claimed he had acted to prevent a repeat of the slaughter he had witnessed on battlefields between 1914 and 1918. At Sigmaringen, Darnand, Déat and Luchaire wanted to go down fighting with the SS Charlemagne Division, but De Brinon fled. Learning of Pétain's trial while staying at Innsbruck, he decided to return to France, saying, 'They will shoot me, but at least I should like the chance to explain myself.'[3] Arrested in Bavaria, he was condemned and shot on 15 April 1947.

Alphonse De Châteaubriant left Sigmaringen for Austria in 1945 and lived there under the alias of Dr Alfred Wolf. Condemned to death in his absence on 25 October 1945, he died of natural causes in a Tyrolean monastery in 1951.

Roger Delthil was first reinstated as mayor of Moissac and a senator after the Liberation, but in the in-fighting between the parties post-Liberation was then divested of his public functions a second time for being one of the senators who voted full powers to Marshal Pétain at the casino in Vichy.

Jacques Doriot died when his car was strafed by Allied aircraft in Germany on 22 February 1945.

Pierre Drieu La Rochelle went into hiding at the Liberation and committed suicide in Paris on 15 March 1945.

The Drancy guards got off lightly. Ten were accused, two disappearing while on bail before trial, together with their commanding officer. Despite harrowing evidence of maltreatment of old and sick detainees, five gendarmes who had stolen prisoners' meagre rations, maltreated the sick, run the black market and escorted deportations, were reintegrated into the force; two men awarded two years' imprisonment were released after one year.

Marie-Rose Dupont waited for twelve months after the shame of being exhibited to the crowd in Moissac, until her hair was fully regrown. She was still corresponding with Willi, but never mentioned her public humiliation to him. Leaving Moissac, she found work in a hairdressing salon at Nice. When a male colleague fell in love with her, she told him about Willi and accepted his decision to tear up all her letters and photographs, saying, 'We'll pull the curtain on the past. It's all over and done with.'

After setting up home in Moissac, she to reopen her salon and he as travelling rep for a hair products company, it seemed that everyone had forgotten the shearing – until the day she came into the salon and found her 8-year-old son sitting in one of the chairs with a pair of clippers in his hand, totally bald. Of her humiliation in September 1944, she never spoke again until interviewed by the author in January 2006.

Rodolphe Faytout was sentenced to hard labour for life, but pardoned by President Coty and released in the fifties. Forbidden to return to his home in Gironde, he nevertheless did so and kept a low profile for the rest of his natural life, treated with disdain but never attacked by his surviving victims or the relatives of those whose deaths he had caused.

Lucienne Goldfarb was rewarded for her role as police informer by protection that continued after the Liberation during the years when she ran a highly lucrative brothel known as 10-bis on rue Débarcadère in the Paris 17th *arrondissement* – during which time her professional name was Katia la Rouquine or Red-haired Katie. She sprang to fame again at the age of 74 – half a century after the deaths of Manouchian and his twenty-one comrades, when in November 1997 her friend Christine Deviers-Joncourt, ex-mistress of Foreign Minister Roland Dumas, gave her 1,000,000 francs 'to look after my mother and children' because Deviers-Joncourt expected to be sent to prison for her part in the petroleum bribes scandal that caused Dumas' fall from power.

Georges Guingouin was elected mayor of Limoges by its grateful population in 1945, the PCF leadership having done everything possible to undermine his election campaign. Labelled a Titoist deviant, he was expelled from the Party in 1952 and thus deprived of its political protection. In the aftermath of the 1953 amnesty for collaboration crimes, many counter-accusations were levelled at former *résistants*. Guingouin was among those arrested for alleged assassination of collaborators during the Liberation. He survived a murder attempt in prison before being released in June 1954. Not until 1998 did PCF leader Robert Hué publicly apologise for the harassment of this renegade Communist. Asked for his reaction, Guingouin replied, 'I've reached the age of serenity. It's a problem for the Party and no longer concerns me.'[4]

Dr Josef Hirt, the collector of Jewish skulls from the Natzwiller gas chamber, is thought to have committed suicide in the Black Forest on 2 June 1945.

Helmut Knochen was sentenced to death by a British court in Germany during June 1946 for a massacre of Allied aircrew. Extradited to France, he received a second death sentence, also commuted to life imprisonment. After serving seventeen years, he was released in 1962, returned to work as an insurance agent in Offenbach, married a second time and retired in Baden-Baden to die there on 4 April 2003.

Joseph Kramer was condemned and hanged by a British court at Hassel on 13 December 1945.

Inspector Henri Lafont was, like Bonny, betrayed by Joanovici and shot at Montrouge on 27 December 1944.

Gen Heinz Lammerding was never brought to trial, despite abandoning an alias to live as a civil engineer under his true name in Düsseldorf. He died on 13 January 1971 at Bad Tölz, Bavaria.

Pierre Laval cabled the Spanish government on 17 April 1945: 'It is neither the statesman nor the friend who is asking your help, but simply the man. I ask you in my own name as well as in that of my wife and my faithful friend

Maurice Gabolde, for permission to enter Spain and await better days. Today it is a tired and worn-out old man who is writing to you, and in memory of our long friendship, I thank you in advance.'[5] Returning from Spain to give evidence at Pétain's trial, he was tried by a court that refused to hear his defence and shot in Fresnes prison on 15 October 1945.

Jean Leguay, the key planner of the *rafle* of July 1942, pursued a successful postwar career with the perfumery company Nina Ricci in the US and later in France. He was never prosecuted before his retirement in 1975, but subsequently became the first *collabo* to be indicted for crimes against humanity, dying on 3 July 1989 before being brought to trial.

Jean Mayol de Lupé, the ageing chaplain of the LVF, was arrested by the Americans in March 1945 and condemned by a French court on 14 May 1947 to fifteen years' imprisonment and confiscation of his property. Released in May 1951, he retired to Lupé and died there in June 1956.

Bernard Ménétrel, Pétain's doctor, was imprisoned in Fresnes on his return to France in May 1945, but released for health reasons in 1946 and died accidentally the following year.

Karl Oberg was condemned to death in Germany, but returned to France for a second trial with Knochen in October 1954. His death sentence in 1954 was commuted to twenty years' imprisonment. In 1965, he was granted a presidential pardon and returned to Germany, where he died the same year.

François Papon throve in civil service until 1981, when evidence linked him with Jewish deportations. Accused in January 1983, he displayed scant respect for the court or his judges and exploited his poor health to delay hearings. Sentenced to ten years in prison for his role in sending 1,560 Jews of all ages to their deaths, he was released after three years thanks to a specially introduced law of March 2002 permitting liberation of prisoners whose health was endangered by incarceration. Of nearly thirty prisoners over 80 years of age in French prisons, Papon was the second to be released. On 25 July 2002, the European Court of Human Rights declared his trial to be 'inequitable'.

Philippe Pétain returned voluntarily to France in April 1945, by then partially incontinent and not truly lucid. He was sentenced to death on 15 August for high treason and aiding the enemy, but De Gaulle commuted the sentence to life imprisonment. Transferred to a military prison on the island of Yeu, Pétain survived to die aged 95 in 1951.

Dr Marcel Petiot was identified and arrested at a Paris Metro station on 31 October 1944. To the examining magistrate, he defended himself vigorously as head of fictitious Resistance network 'Fly-Tox,' but no *résistant* had ever heard of him. A story of having provided false medical certificates for STO evaders likewise rang false when he could not name a single man helped in this way.

The mystery of the burning bodies in the rue Lesueur was unravelled when it was discovered that Petiot had been arrested on 23 May and spent the eight missing months in Fresnes prison for allegedly helping people escape from France

– which posed the question why he had not come forward at the Liberation to claim his reward as a patriot. Petiot's military discharge papers of 1918 recorded signs of mental disturbance, which had not prevented him from qualifying as a doctor. So popular was his first practice at Villeneuve-sur-Yonne in Burgundy that he was elected mayor in 1927 – until dismissed for petty theft and shoplifting, with a suspicion of drug trafficking as well. After that, he fled to the anonymity of Paris, opening the consulting room near the Opéra in 1933.

Police investigations connected numerous missing persons with Petiot. When more than forty suitcases filled with men's and women's clothing were found at the home of a friend of his, the truth came out. Telling Jews threatened with deportation to come to the apartment in rue Lesueur with only their most precious possessions, he gave them a lethal injection under the pretence that it was a sedative – and banked the proceeds. Charged initially with twenty-seven murders, of which he admitted nineteen, he eventually confessed to having killed sixty-three people in this way, and was found guilty on 132 of 135 indictments. Sentenced to death, he called across the courtroom to his wife, 'Avenge me!'

Petiot was guillotined on 25 May 1946.[6]

Louis Petitjean was arrested in February 1944 for helping refugees and escaping Allied aircrew and other Resistance activities. He was unable to obtain his release until May 1945, even though the superior officer who had him arrested was himself sentenced to twenty years' hard labour after the Liberation. Reinstated in the RG, Petitjean lost fifteen months' seniority and pension rights for the time spent in jail.[7]

The Police-Gestapo cooperation, according to an interview Knochen gave to *Historia* magazine in 1972, was crucial after the Wehrmacht's refusal to round up Jews because the task would otherwise have been impossible. Around 30,000 police worked directly for the German security organisations: in Marseilles, 1,000 French supported a German staff of fifty; in St-Etienne there were 344 French for only ten Germans.

Pierre Pucheu was displaced by the return to power of Laval in April 1942 and slipped through Spain to North Africa, hoping to change sides. Arrested in Casablanca on 11 August 1943, he was condemned to death by a military court and shot near Algiers on 20 March 1944.

Louis Renault surrendered himself in ill-health to a judge on 23 September 1944 and was jailed at Fresnes. Beaten up during the night of 4 October by left-wing activists, he died in hospital on 24 October 1944 from head injuries. In 1945 De Gaulle nationalised the Renault company. Not until 1967 were the family shareholders compensated. In contrast, the company Sainrapt et Brice was permitted to keep as legitimate earnings profits of 360,000,000 francs from construction contracts for the Wehrmacht.[8]

Heinz Röthke, who had declared that even a baby born in Drancy must be gassed in Auschwitz because it was a 'future terrorist', died peacefully in 1968 in Wolfsburg, where he had a legal practice.

SS Division Das Reich: Of the hangings in Tulle, in which they participated, SS officer Wulf and Sgt Hoff had 'no recollection' at their trial in July 1951. Sentenced to ten years and life respectively, they were freed the following year. Lt Schmald, who had made the selection of those to hang, was shot by the Maquis in August 1944, muttering, '*Ich hatte Befehl*' ('I was ordered to do it').[9]

The killers of Oradour were tried – some of them – by the Haut Tribunal Permanent des Forces Armées sitting in Bordeaux from 13 January to 12 March 1953. Strangely, Gen Lammerding was not extradited to give evidence, although known to be practising as a civil engineer in the British Zone of Germany. Forty-three members of 3rd Company were condemned to death *in absentia*, most of them having been killed during the subsequent fighting in Normandy. In the dock were seven Germans and fourteen Alsatians – one volunteer and thirteen conscripts. Whether for political reasons – Alsace had been German in 1944 but was part of France in 1953 – or for diplomatic reasons with the Cold War at its height, or because of a need to cover up the alleged Maquis atrocities, the sentences were not exemplary. The senior German accused was sentenced to death; four others were given forced labour of ten to twelve years; one was acquitted. The Alsatian volunteer was also sentenced to death; nine of the conscripts were given five to twelve years' hard labour; the other four received five to eight years' hard labour.

In the Limousin, the sentences were considered outrageously inadequate, yet in Alsace there was public indignation that the *malgré-nous* conscripts should be sentenced at all for obeying German orders, no matter what they had done. Since the accused had spent eight years in custody, the Alsatian conscripts were released immediately, as the judges had known would be the case when passing sentence. All the Germans, except the one sentenced to death, were liberated a few months later. The two death sentences were commuted, with both men released in 1959.

Pierre Seel survived Natzwiller and tried unsuccessfully to live down the stigma of being a 'notorious homsexual' by leading an outwardly normal married life. But his past caught up with him, he was rejected by his family and eventually 'came out' by writing his memoirs.

Heinz Stahlschmidt was given French nationality and lived in Bordeaux under the name Henri Salmide. He married his fiancée Henriette, but had to wait fifty years for the city to thank him. On 20 May 1994 Mayor Jacques Chaban-Delmas awarded him the Bordeaux medal. Six years later, his heroism was officially acknowledged by the nation when President Jacques Chirac invested him with the Légion d'honneur on 14 July 2000. Stahlschmidt/Salmide died during the writing of this book, in June 2006.

St-Amand: At first the testimony of Charles Krameisen was disbelieved, until the bodies began to emerge from the wells at Guerry. Accorded French citizenship in recognition of his suffering, Krameisen died in an insane asylum. Lécussan and other *miliciens* involved were shot in 1946.

Paul Touvier, head of the Lyons Milice, went undercover in 1944 after releasing a few prisoners and making deals with the Resistance, hoping to be left in peace to spend money he had amassed by extortion. Sheltered on religious premises and with false papers, he enjoyed contact with his family and was married in church, fathering two children by his second wife.

Condemned to death in his absence at Chambéry on 10 September 1946 for complicity in the murders of Hélène and Victor Basch and seven Jews machine-gunned at Rillieux, Touvier was arrested after several armed hold-ups in Paris the following year. In an attempt to save his own skin, he betrayed other members of his gang of former *collabos*. Sentenced to die by firing squad at Lyons, he 'escaped' en route and was sheltered by another succession of priests and religious houses, even living in his home town of Chambéry under an assumed name for some time.

After the 1967 Statute of Limitations annulled Touvier's sentences, he tried with help from Church dignitaries to regain his civil rights in order to inherit property and was pardoned by President Pompidou in 1971. An article in *L'Express* and legislation regarding crimes against humanity caused him to go underground once again in convents and monasteries where he was visited by his wife and children. The perseverance of gendarme Jean-Louis Recordon finally tracked Touvier down to the priory of St-François in Nice, where he was arrested on 24 May 1989 after the satirical weekly *Le Canard Enchaîné* made it impossible for the government not to arrest him. Thanks to an able defence by a Catholic barrister, the first case was withdrawn, but Touvier was tried and sentenced at the Yvelines Assizes Court in 1994 to life imprisonment. He died in Fresnes prison aged 81 and was honoured by a Requiem Mass, at which the eulogy praised the 'sensitive and delicate soul . . . whom God would pardon as earthly Justice had not'.[10]

Xavier Vallat was tried in 1947 for his conduct as General Commissioner of Jewish Questions and his part in drafting the Second Statute of the Jews. Unrepentant, he accused prosecutor Kriegel-Valrimont of being racially disqualified to appear in a French court. Sentenced to ten years' imprisonment, Vallat was released from prison with 'national indignity' two years later. He then became a passionate Zionist, seeing the existence of a Jewish state as the way to rid France of Jews permanently.

Otto Von Stülpnagel committed suicide while awaiting trial in Paris' Cherche-Midi prison on 6 February 1948.

P.G. Wodehouse was released before his sixtieth birthday and allowed to live in Berlin in return for making several indiscreet, but not treacherous, broadcasts over Nazi English-language radio. Sent back to France in September 1943 to avoid the Allied bombing of the German capital, he was briefly imprisoned after the Liberation, returned to his US home and was knighted in 1975, a few weeks before his death, aged 93 (see www.eclipse.co.uk/wodehouse).

NOTES AND SOURCES

INTRODUCTION

1. The Milice was a violent and extremely unpopular anti-terrorist police force set up in January 1943 to combat increasing Resistance activity. Recruits came mainly from the Service d'Ordre Légionnaire (q.v.).
2. P. Webster, *Pétain's Crime* (London, Pan, 2001), pp. 6–7.
3. P. Mignon, *De Castillon à Sachsenhausen* (Bordeaux, Publications Résistance Unie en Gironde, 1990).

CHAPTER 1

1. D. Barlone, *A French Officer's Diary* (Cambridge, Cambridge University Press, 1942), pp. 8–11.
2. T. Kernan, *France on Berlin Time* (New York and Philadelphia, Lippincott, 1941), pp. 223–9.
3. *Ibid.*, pp. 229–31.
4. C.D. Freeman and D. Cooper, *The Road to Bordeaux* (London, Readers' Union & Cresset Press, 1942), pp. 12, 13.
5. *Ibid.*
6. A. Hillgruber, *Hitlers Strategie: Politik und Kriegführung 1940–41* (Bonn, Bernard und Graefe, 1965), p. 38.
7. Figures quoted in E.R. May, *Strange Victory* (New York, Hill and Wang, 2002), p. 477.
8. *Ibid.*, p. 309.
9. *Ibid.*, p. 388.
10. *Ibid.*, p. 229.
11. *Ibid.*, p. 309.

CHAPTER 2

1. W. Thornton, *The Liberation of Paris* (London, Rupert Hart-Davis, 1963), pp. 91–2.
2. P. Burrin, *Living with Defeat* (London, Arnold, 1996), p. 8.
3. Paul Bourget, in *1940 La Défaite* (Paris, Tallandier, 1978), p. 285.
4. US War Department, February 1924. US casualties as amended by the Statistical Services Center, Office of the Secretary of Defense, 7 Nov. 1957, quoted in *Encyclopaedia Britannica* 2002 Deluxe CD-Rom edition.

5.   For greater detail, see D. Boyd, *The French Foreign Legion* (Thrupp, Sutton, 2005), pp. 249–58.
6.   Freeman and Cooper, *The Road to Bordeaux*, p. 90.
7.   *Ibid.*, pp. 112–13.
8.   May, *Strange Victory*, p. 450.
9.   Freeman and Cooper, *The Road to Bordeaux*, pp. 176–7.
10.   *Ibid.*, p. 189.
11.   H. Amouroux, *La Vie des Français sous l'Occupation* (Paris, Fayard, 1961), vol. 1, pp. 15–16.
12.   Kernan, *France on Berlin Time*, p. 177.
13.   E. Williams (ed.), *The Escapers* (London, Collins/Eyre and Spottiswoode, 1953), pp. 270–88.
14.   S. Berthon, *Allies at War* (New York, Carroll and Graf, 2001), p. 11.
15.   Henri Noguères, in *1940 La Défaite*, p. 555.
16.   The masculine form then included also French women.
17,   Gen E. Spears, quoted in *The Voice of War*, ed. J. Owen and G. Walters (London, Penguin, 2005), p. 56 (abridged by the author).

CHAPTER 3

1.   G.Q.G. No. 2004 – 3 FT, quoted in *1940 La Défaite*, p. 289.
2.   Henri Le Masson, *ibid.*, pp. 309–14.
3.   Admiral Auphan, Number 2 to Darlan, *ibid.*, p. 325.
4.   Kernan, *France on Berlin Time*, p. 260.
5.   *Ibid.*
6.   De Gaulle's address of 18 June 1940.
7.   H. Guillemin, *Parcours* (Paris, Seuil, 1989), p. 400.
8.   Personal communication to the author.
9.   H. Amouroux, in *1940 La Défaite*, p. 350.
10.   Duchess of St Albans, *The Road to Bordeaux* (London, W.H. Allen, 1976), pp. 143–6.
11.   Kernan, *France on Berlin Time*, p. 260.
12.   Abbreviations of *Stammlager* (POW camp for NCOs and men) and *Offizierslager* (POW camp for officers).
13.   Philippe Masson in *1940 La Défaite*, p. 304.
14.   German military intelligence organisation.
15.   Kernan, *France on Berlin Time*, p. 232.
16.   Barlone, *French Officer's Diary*, p. 89.

CHAPTER 4

1.   Quoted in Burrin, *Living with Defeat*, p. 47.
2.   Most of the 8,000,000 Occitan-speakers, 1,450,000 Bretons, 400,000 Corsicans, 200,000 Flemings, 200,000 Catalans and 150,000 Basques also spoke French. In a 1931 survey in Alsace, 700,000 had declared themselves German-speaking, 800,000 were bilingual and 200,000 spoke only French. See Burrin, *Living with Defeat*, p. 49.

3. Freeman and Cooper, *The Road to Bordeaux*, p. 315.

4. Madame Cahen d'Anvers, *Baboushka Remembers*, privately printed, 1972, pp. 186–94.

5. G. and J.-R. Ragache, *La Vie des Ecrivains et des Artistes sous l'Occupation* (Paris, Hachette, 1988), p. 32.

6. Renée De Monbrison, 'Mémoirs', unpublished manuscript.

7. *Populations abandonnées, confiez-vous au soldat allemand!*

CHAPTER 5

1. Spanish term for Franco as a military leader and head of state.

2. Established in 1933, the only legal political party in Franco's Spain.

3. '*Une grande bataille se prépare, j'y vais sans arrière-pensée et sans appréhension, car j'ai fait le sacrifice de ma vie, les souffrances physiques qui peuvent m'être imposées sont peu de chose en comparaison des tortures morales subies á cause de toi.*' Quoted by H. Amouroux, in *1940 La Défaite*, p. 482.

4. '*Quelques livres nous tiendront compagnie ainsi que quelques amis de choix, dont les anciens flirts, de part et d'autre, seront exclus.*' Ibid., p. 483.

5. '*Français, vous l'accomplirez et vous verrez, je vous le jure, une France neuve surgir de votre ferveur.*' Quoted by R. Aron, in *La Défaite*, p. 484.

6. D. Peschanski, *Collaboration and Resistance*, tr. L. Frankel (New York, Harry N. Abrams, 2000), p. 9.

CHAPTER 6

1. Quoted on www.spartacus.schoolnet.co.uk/2WWlaval.htm.

2. A. Nossiter, *France and the Nazis* (London, Methuen, 2001), p. 105.

3. P. Bourget, in *1940 La Défaite*, p. 280.

4. Boyd, *The French Foreign Legion*, p. 257–8.

5. Personal communication with the author.

6. F. Boulet, 'Histoire de Moissac', unpublished manuscript, St-Germain-en-Laye, 2005, p. 114.

7. P. Bourget, in *1940 La Défaite*, p. 326.

8. P. Masson, in *Ibid.*, pp. 461–70.

9. *Ibid.*

10. Article in *Le Figaro*, 15 July 1940.

11. A. Vulliez, in *1940 La Défaite*, p. 458.

CHAPTER 7

1. Facsimiles of Sir Ronald Campbell's memoranda to Pierre Laval dated 18 and 19 September 1931, reproduced in *The Unpublished Diary of Pierre Laval* (London, Falcon Press, 1948), pp. 187–98.

2. Laval, *Unpublished Diary*, p. 29.

3.   *1940 La Défaite*, p. 500.
4.   *Ibid.*, p. 502.
5.   *Ibid.*
6.   Burrin, *Living with Defeat*, p. 28.
7.   'C'était vraiment un marécage humain dans lequel on voyait à vue d'œil se dissoudre, se corroder, disparaître tout ce qu'on avait connu à certains hommes de courage et de droiture.' Quoted in *1940 La Défaite*, p. 492.
8.   *Ibid.*
9.   Laval, *Unpublished Diary*, p. 54.
10.   *1940 La Défaite*, pp. 494–5.

CHAPTER 8

1.   The slang for 'profiteer' was '*bof*,' standing for *beurre, oeufs, fromage* – the three staples from which money was most easily made.
2.   H.R. Kedward, *Resistance in Vichy France* (Oxford, Oxford University Press, 1978) p. 36.
3.   '*Vivre dans la défaite est mourir tous les jours.*'
4.   Amouroux, *La Vie*, vol. 1, pp. 384–7.
5.   H. Diamond, *Women and the Second World War in France* (London, Longman, 1999), p. 32.
6.   S. Berton, *Allies at War* (New York, Carroll and Graf, 2001), p. 46.
7.   D. Pryce-Jones, *Paris in the Third Reich* (London, Collins, 1981), p. 148.
8.   For further details see Pryce-Jones, *Paris in the Third Reich*, p. 150.
9.   *1940 La Défaite* p. 512.
10.   Pryce-Jones, *Paris in the Third Reich*, pp. 24–5.
11.   Le Boterf, *La Vie Parisienne sous l'Occupation* (Geneva, Famot, 1979), vol. 3, p. 7: '*Pour certains, le renom de Paris est tributaire de la beauté de quelques croupes joliment arondies.*'
12.   *1940 La Défaite*, p. 513.
13.   R. Bédarida, *Les Catholiques dans la Guerre 1935–1945* (Paris, Hachette, 1998), p. 45.
14.   Kernan, *France on Berlin Time*, p. 23.

CHAPTER 9

1.   Le Boterf, *La Vie Parisienne sous l'Occupation*, vol. 3, p. 241.
2.   Burrin, *Living with Defeat*, pp. 204–5.
3.   Pryce-Jones, *Paris in the Third Reich*, p. 255.
4.   Le Boterf, *La Vie Parisienne sous l'Occupation*, vol. 3, p. 122–3.
5.   *Ibid.*, vol. 1, pp. 95–6.
6.   *Ibid.*, p. 11.
7.   Ragache, p. 158.
8.   Pryce-Jones, *Paris in the Third Reich*, p. 92.
9.   Ragache, p. 147.
10.   L.H. Nicholas, *The Rape of Europa* (London, Macmillan, 1995), p. 157.

11. Lucien Steinberg, in *1940 La Défaite*, p. 549.
12. Burrin, *Living with Defeat*, p. 253.
13. Kernan, *France on Berlin Time*, pp 34–8.
14. Quoted in Burrin, *Living with Defeat*, p. 29.
15. Kernan, *France on Berlin Time*, pp. 28–9.
16. Pryce-Jones, *Paris in the Third Reich*, p. 64.
17. *Ibid.*, p. 50.
18. Kernan, *France on Berlin Time*, pp. 27–32.
19. *Ibid.*, pp. 27–32.
20. Pryce-Jones, *Paris in the Third Reich*, p. 164.

CHAPTER 10

1. Webster, *Pétain's Crime*, p. 88.
2. Burrin, *Living with Defeat*, p. 420.
3. *Ibid.*, p. 28.
4. Peschanski, *Collaboration and Resistance*, p. 39.
5. Amouroux, *La Vie*, vol. 1, pp. 85–6.
6. Interviewed in Pryce-Jones, *Paris in the Third Reich*, p. 250.
7. *Ibid.*, p. 94.
8. No single source is available. The figures given are in the writings of the historian Robert Aron and L'Institut National de la Statistique.
9. Burrin, *Living with Defeat*, pp. 264–7.
10. *Ibid.*, p. 273.
11. *Ibid.*, p. 373.
12. *Chronique de la France et des Français* (Paris, Editions Legrand, 1987), p. 1107.
13. Quoted in Burrin, *Living with Defeat*, p. 75.
14. Ragache, p. 64.
15. Kernan, *France on Berlin Time*, p. 26.
16. Laval, *Unpublished Diary*, pp. 86–7.

CHAPTER 11

1. Ragache, p. 108.
2. Chabrier's history is from the author's conversations with the Chabrier family and Colonel Rémy, *La Ligne de Démarcation* (Paris, LAP, 1966), pp. 153–62.
3. Nossiter, *France and the Nazis*, p. 89.
4. For Laporterie's full story, see J. Bacque, *Just Raoul* (Toronto, Stoddart, 1990).
5. Ragache, p. 120.
6. Referring to the colour headlamps had to be painted.
7. Burrin, *Living with Defeat*, p. 53.
8. Webster, *Pétain's Crime*, p. 124.
9. Arrested December 1941 but released in February 1942.
10. Le Boterf, *La Vie Parisienne sous l'Occupation*, vol. 1, p. 37.
11. Peschanski (ed.), *Collaboration and Resistance*, p. 98.
12. Pryce-Jones, *Paris in the Third Reich*, p. 63.

13. Unpublished manuscript on Prefect François Martin loaned to the author by Madame Gouzi: '*Puisse le Maréchal Pétain avoir une vie suffisamment longue pour nous soutenir alors de sa haute autorité et de son incomparable prestige. Nous sommes totalement dévoués à l'œuvre du Maréchal.*'

14. Quoted in a privately printed justification by his son of Prefect François Martin, loaned to the author by Madame Gouzi: '*Nous estimons que le mouvement de de Gaulle est une erreur. Nous sommes convaincus qu'on défend mieux son pays en y restant qu'en le quittant. Autour du Général de Gaulle sont rassemblés maints éléments indésirables. En résumé, le MLN n'a aucun lien avec le gaullisme et ne reçoit de Londres aucun ordre.*'

15. H. Michel, *The Shadow War* (London, André Deutsch, 1972), p. 123.

16. Originally the *deuxième bureau*, it became Service de Renseignements and eventually Le Bureau Central de Renseignements et d'Action.

17. All the Gaullist intelligence officers chose *noms de guerre* that were names of Paris Metro stations.

18. Colonel Passy, *Souvenirs: 2e Bureau London* (Paris, Editions Raoul Solar, 1947), pp. 70–1.

19. *Ibid.*, p. 173.

20. K. Doenitz, *Memoirs* (London, Cassell, 2000), p. 409.

21. Rémy, *La Ligne de Démarcation* (Paris, LAP, 1966), pp. 141–52.

CHAPTER 12

1. Burrin, *Living with Defeat*, p. 377.

2. Quoted by L. Chabrun *et al.*, *L'Express*, 10 October 2005.

3. H. Diamond, *Women and the Second World War in France*, p. 23.

4. G. Krivopissko (ed.), *La Vie à en mourir – Lettres de fusillés 1941* (Paris, Tallandier, 2003), pp. 43–6.

5. *Chronique de la France*, p. 1104.

6. Webster, *Pétain's Crime*, p. 141.

7. *Ibid.*, p. 143.

8. *Ibid.*, p. 140.

9. Undated photocopy of cutting.

10. R. Bédarida, *Les Catholiques dans la Guerre 1939–1945* (Paris, Hachette, 1998), p. 139.

11. Cahen-d'Anvers, *Baboushka Remembers*, pp. 210–12.

12. Pryce-Jones, *Paris in the Third Reich*, p. 117.

13. *La Revue des Deux Mondes*, 15 September 1940.

14. Peschanski (ed.), *Collaboration and Résistance*, p. 65.

15. P. Pétain, *Discours aux Français* (Paris, Albin Michel, 1989), p. 172.

16. Pryce-Jones, *Paris in the Third Reich*, pp. 236–9.

17. *Ibid.*, p. 124.

18. *Ibid.*, p. 117.

19. Boulet, 'Histoire de Moissac', p. 115.

20. *Ibid.*, p. 118.

CHAPTER 13

1. It is now 4 Place du Vieux Pont.
2. L. Schindler-Levine, *L'Impossible Au Revoir* (Paris, L'Harmattan, 1998), pp. 107–13.
3. Women's International Zionist Organisation.
4. The names have been changed to respect the children's privacy.
5. C. Lewertovski, *Morts ou Juifs* (Paris, Flamarrion, 2003), pp. 119–20.
6. For whatever reason, this one word was written in Hebrew, '*oneg*'; all the rest was in French.
7. Lewertovski, *Morts ou Juifs*, p. 121.
8. *Ibid.*, p. 130.
9. Quoted in Pryce-Jones, *Paris in the Third Reich*, p. 120.
10. A. McCutchan, *Marcel Moyse, Voice of the Flute* (Portland, OR, Amadeus, 1994), pp. 152–9.
11. Krivopissko (ed.), *La Vie à en mourir*, pp. 71–4.
12. *Ibid.*, pp. 79–81.
13. *Ibid.*, pp. 93–7 (abridged by the author, the original being written in the third person).
14. *Semaine religieuse du diocèse d'Arras*, 11 September 1941.
15. Krivopissko (ed.), *La Vie à en mourir*, pp. 99–103.
16. L. Paine, *Mathilde Carré, Double Agent* (London, Robert Hale, 1976), p. 168.
17. *Ibid.*, p. 85.
18. This was not done. Nor was a marked grave permitted.
19. Krivopissko (ed.), *La Vie à en mourir*, pp. 110–13.
20. L. Chabrun *et al.*, *L'Express*, 10 October 2005.
21. Personal interview with the author. Names changed.
22. G. Smadja, article in *L'Humanité*, 8 October 1996.
23. Burrin, *Living with Defeat*, pp. 245–9.
24. *Ibid.*, pp. 252–9.
25. Smadja, article of 8 October 1996.

CHAPTER 14

1. Quoted by L. Chabrun *et al.*, *L'Express*, 6 October 2005.
2. Peschanski (ed.), *Collaboration and Resistance*, p. 180.
3. C. Pinaud, *La Simple Vérité*, Paris, Julliard, 1960 (abridged by the author).
4. Quoted by J.-P. Guilloteau in *L'Express*, 31 May 2004.
5. *Ibid.*
6. *Ibid.*
7. *Comme toujours impassible / et courageux inutilement / je servirai de cible / aux douze fusils allemands.*
8. Krivopissko (ed.), *La Vie à en mourir*, pp. 124–5.
9. Schindler-Levine, *L'Impossible Au Revoir*, pp. 119–21.
10. Extract from letter preserved in the archives of CDJC in collection EIF.
11. Le Boterf, *La Vie Parisienne sous l'Occupation*, vol. 1, p. 65.
12. Quoted on www.spartacus.schoolnet.co.uk/2WWlaval.htm.

13. *Ibid.*
14. Amouroux, *La Vie*, vol. 1, pp. 158–61.
15. P. Claudel, *Journal* (Paris, Gallimard, 1969), vol. 2, pp. 400–1.
16. Amouroux, *La Vie*, vol. 2, pp. 134–5.

CHAPTER 15

1. S. Klarsfeld, 'La page la plus noire', p. 16, *Le Monde*, 14 March 1979.
2. Le Boterf, *La Vie Parisienne sous l'Occupation*, vol. 3, p. 187.
3. Pryce-Jones, *Paris in the Third Reich*, p. 140.
4. Article in *Le Monde*, 22 July 1997.
5. Webster, *Pétain's Crime*, p. 18.
6. *Ibid.*, p. 21.
7. Letter quoted in A. Michel, *Les Eclaireurs Israélites de France durant la Seconde Guerre Mondiale* (Editions EIF, 1984), p. 123.
8. Lewertovski, *Morts ou Juifs*, p. 170.

CHAPTER 16

1. Amouroux, *La Vie*, vol. 2, p. 29.
2. Burrin, *Living with Defeat*, p. 249.
3. Lewertovski, *Morts ou Juifs*, p. 175.
4. Letter from 'ancien maquisard E. Roux' in *L'Express* of 10 November 2005.
5. Quoted in Webster, *Pétain's Crime*, p. 182.
6. Pryce-Jones, *Paris in the Third Reich*, p. 178.
7. *Ibid.*, p. 55.
8. Diamond, p. 53.
9. *Ibid.*, p. 60.
10. L. Lazare, *La Résistance Juive en France* (Paris, Stock, 1987), p. 105.
11. Facsimile of letter at Centre Jean Moulin, Bordeaux.
12. For full details, see R. Marshall, *All the King's Men* (London, Collins, 1988).
13. Nossiter, *France and the Nazis*, pp. 158–9.

CHAPTER 17

1. Amouroux, *La Vie des français sous l'Occupation*, vol. 1, pp. 144–7. Released on probation, the prince joined the Maquis, was wounded and finished the war as a lieutenant in the Chasseurs Alpins.
2. *Ibid.*, vol. 1, pp. 155–6.
3. E. Paris, *Unhealed Wounds* (New York, Grove Press, 1985), pp. 93–7.
4. Krivopissko (ed.), *La Vie à en mourir*, pp. 223–4.
5. Letter of Simone Weill dated 4 February 1943, in *Lettres de Drancy*, ed. A. Sabbagh (Paris, Tallandier, 2002), pp. 297–9
6. L. Chabrun *et al.*, *L'Express*, 10 October 2005.
7. Diamond, p. 83.

8. There is a commemorative plaque in the firing range outside the camp.
9. Amouroux, *La Vie*, vol. 2, p. 39.
10. Quoted by L. Chabrun *et al.*, *L'Express*, 10 October 2005.
11. *Ibid.*
12. Obituary notice in *The Guardian*, 3 December 2005.
13. Krivopissko (ed.), *La Vie à en mourir*, p. 219.
14. Le Boterf, *La Vie Parisienne sous l'Occupation*, vol. 1, pp. 34, 36.
15. *Ibid.*, p. 67.
16. Le Boterf, *La Vie Parisienne sous l'Occupation*, vol. 1, p. 40.
17. L. Chabrun *et al.*, *L'Express*, 6 October 2005.

CHAPTER 18

1. The full story of Faytout's group is told by survivor P. Mignon in his book *De Castillon à Sachsenhausen*, published in Bordeaux by Publications Résistance Unie en Gironde, in 1990.
2. The story of the Bouchou family involvement in Faytout's group is from interviews with Cathérine Bouchou conducted by the author.
3. Mignon, *De Castillon à Sachsenhausen*.
4. Amouroux, *La Vie*, vol. 2, p. 58.
5. Martin manuscript.
6. A. Morris, *Collaboration and Resistance Reviewed* (New York/Oxford, Berg, 1992), p. 82.
7. Marshall, *All the King's Men*, p. 292.
8. *Ibid.*, p. 298.
9. *Ibid.*, p. 253.
10. M.R.D. Foot, *SOE in France* (London, HMSO, 1966), p. 302.
11. Facsimile, in Laval, *Unpublished Diary*, Appendix V.
12. Amouroux, *La Vie*, vol. 2, p. 43.
13. Webster, *Pétain's Crime*, pp. 232–5.
14. See www.lamaisondesevres.otg/cel/cel5.html.
15. English edition, *I, Pierre Seel, Deported Homosexual* (London, Basic Books, 1995).
16. *Ibid.*, pp. 42–3.
17. Documents at Natzwiller camp.
18. Krivopissko (ed.), *La Vie à en mourir*, pp. 226–30.
19. From interview with the author.
20. De Monbrison, *Memoirs*.
21. Paris, *Unhealed Wounds*, pp. 98–9.

CHAPTER 19

1. Letters 000094, 000096, 000097 and 000102 in the archives of Ste-Foy.
2. Interview with the author.
3. Quoted by L. Chabrun *et al.*, *L'Express*, 10 October 2005.
4. Interview in Pryce-Jones, *Paris in the Third Reich*, p. 215.

5. J. Duquesne, in *L'Express*, 14 June 2004, pp. 40–2.
6. Photostat of Gestapo file in the family archives at Château La Roque: '*Ein besonders gefährlicher Agent, mit allen Mitteln kaltzustellen. Wenn möglich lebend herzubringen. 1.000.000 Fcs. Belohnung wem derjenigen verhaftet oder ausliefert.*'
7. Amouroux, *La Vie*, vol. 2, pp. 53–5.
8. *Ibid.*, vol. 2, pp. 71–2.
9. For full details see www.farac.org, the website of FARAC (La Fédération des Amicales Régimentaires et des Anciens Combattants).
10. T. Todorov, *Une tragédie française* (Paris, Editions du Seuil, 2004), pp. 64–5.
11. Schindler-Levine, *L'Impossible Au Revoir*, pp. 148–53.
12. Quoted in Webster, *Pétain's Crime*, p. 210.
13. *Des libérateurs? La Libération! Par l'armée du crime.*
14. Krivopissko (ed.), *La Vie à en mourir*, pp. 287–9.
15. *Ibid.*, p. 294.
16. *Ibid.*, pp. 284–6.
17. *Ibid.*, pp. 283–4.
18. Thornton, *The Liberation of Paris*, p. 63.
19. Amouroux, *La Vie*, vol. 2, pp. 47–8.
20. Personal communication with the author.
21. Amouroux, *La Vie*, pp. 49–50.

CHAPTER 20

1. The events of 21 March are digested from interviews with Françoise and the manuscript accounts of Renée and Christian De Monbrison.
2. Monbrison manuscript accounts.
3. Marie-Rose's experiences condensed from personal interviews with the author.
4. Some sources give 640 or more killed.
5. Amouroux, *La Vie*, vol. 2, p. 233.
6. M. Abbadi, 'Actes du Colloque des Enfants cachés', unpublished manuscript, pp. 43–60.
7. Le Boterf, *La Vie Parisienne sous l'Occupation*, vol. 3, pp. 90–1.
8. O. Barton, *Mirrors of Destruction* (Oxford, Oxford University Press, 2000), p. 65.
9. Thornton, *The Liberation of Paris*, p. 109.

CHAPTER 21

1. Todorov, *Une tragédie française*, p. 30.
2. *Ibid.*, pp. 17–23.
3. J.-P. Azéma and F. Bédarida, *La France des Années Noirs* (Paris, Seuil, 1993), vol. 2, p. 396.
4. Todorov, *Une tragédie française*, p. 37.
5. *Ibid.*, p. 40.
6. Nossiter, *France and the Nazis*, p. 250.
7. Report of Adjutant-Chef Conchonnet, in *L'Express*, 6 October 2005.

8. *Arkheia* (magazine published in Montauban), No. 17–18 (2006), p. 58.
9. *Ibid.*, pp. 58–9 and A. Nossiter, *The Algeria Hotel* (London, Methuen, 2001), pp. 231–51.
10. Divisional orders signed by General Lammerding exhibited at the Centre de Mémoire, Oradour.
11. Letter to OKW complaining of these problems and signed by Lammerding exhibited at the Centre de Mémoire, Oradour.
12. Todorov, *Une tragédie française*, p. 78.
13. *Ibid.*, pp. 117–20.
14. *Ibid.*, p. 128.

CHAPTER 22

1. Thornton, *The Liberation of Paris*, p. 111.
2. Bédarida, *Les Catholiques dans la Guerre*, p. 113.
3. Boulet, 'Histoire de Moissac', p. 152.
4. *Ibid.*
5. Full report by A. Feytis, *Fusillée dans sa robe de mariée* in *Sud Ouest*, 30 September 2004, pp. 1–11.
6. Quoted by L. Chabrun *et al.*, *L'Express*, 10 October 2005.
7. *Ibid.*
8. Amouroux, *La Vie*, vol. 1, pp. 357–62.
9. See A. Kemp, *The Secret Hunters* (London, Coronet, 1988), pp. 776–8; and R. Kramer, *Flames in the Field* (London, Michael Joseph, 1995), pp. 115–27 and plates; see also documentation at Natzwiller.
10. Cahen d'Anvers, *Baboushka Remembers*, pp. 234–5.
11. Thornton, *The Liberation of Paris*, p. 127.
12. *Ibid.*, p. 117.
13. Amouroux, *La Vie*, vol. 2, pp. 82–4.
14. Thornton, *The Liberation of Paris*, p. 118.
15. Nicholas, *The Rape of Europa*, p. 292.
16. Pryce-Jones, *Paris in the Third Reich*, p. 187.
17. He was liberated there by the Russians in April 1945.
18. Laval, *Unpublished Diary*, facsimile copy in Appendix VI.
19. Thornton, *The Liberation of Paris*, pp. 132–3.
20. *Ibid.*, pp. 134–5.

CHAPTER 23

1. L. Chabrun *et al.*, *L'Express*, 10 October 2005.
2. Thornton, *The Liberation of Paris*, p. 146.
3. From the French for 'tank', which is *char d'assaut*.
4. Laval, *Unpublished Diary*, p. 175.
5. The original title was *Huis Clos*.
6. Personal communication with the author. Name of informant changed.
7. Personal communication with the author.

8.   Letter from police commissioner to his superior in Toulouse, dated 7 December 1944, quoted in Boulet, 'Histoire de Moissac', p. 155.
9.   *Ibid.* Police report dated 27 December 1944.
10. Interview with the author.
11. Nossiter, *France and the Nazis*, pp. 52–5, 70.
12. G. Penaud, *Histoire Secrète de la Résistance dans le Sudouest* (Bordeaux, Editions Sudouest, 1993), pp. 245–62.
13. Nossiter, *The Algeria Hotel*, pp. 217–18.

CHAPTER 24

1.   Thornton, *The Liberation of Paris*, p. 207.
2.   Amouroux, *La Vie*, vol. 1, pp. 362–7.
3.   Cahen-d'Anvers, *Baboushka Remembers*, pp. 243–4.
4.   Marie-Rose's story as told to the author.
5.   *Ibid.*
6.   F. Virgili, *La France Virile* (Paris, Payot, 2000), p. 88.
7.   *Ibid.*, p. 226.
8.   J.-P. Guilloteau, in *L'Express*, 31 May 2004.
9.   *Ibid.*
10. The cases of Mademoiselle Z, Anne S and Anita A are condensed from Guilloteau's article in *L'Express* of 31 May 2005.
11. D. Saubaber, *Pour l'amour d'un boche*, quoted by J.-P. Guilloteau in *L'Express*, 31 May 2004.
12. Virgili, *La France Virile*, p. 276.
13. *Ibid.*, pp. 23, 29.
14. See, at length, in Virgili, *La France Virile*.
15. Black market, 14.6%; denunciation, 6.5%; political/military 8%; foreign nationality, 2.1%; unknown 26.7%.
16. Morris, *Collaboration and Resistance Reviewed*, pp. 85–6.
17. Burrin, *Living with Defeat*, p. 207.
18. The figure seems questionable and no information is available as to how it was computed. See Burrin, *Living with Defeat*, p. 207.
19. See several articles in *Arkheia*, No. 17–18 (2006).

CHAPTER 25

1.   D. Lormier, *La Poche de la Rochelle* (Saintes, Les Chemins de la Mémoire, 2003), p. 29.
2.   Some sources say 20 October.
3.   Thornton, *The Liberation of Paris*, p. 122.
4.   D. Lormier, *La Poche de Royan* (Saintes, Les Chemins de la Mémoire, 2002), p. 21.
5.   Some sources give forty-six German dead.
6.   P. Lelaurain, *Le Musée de la Poche de Royan* (Le Gâ, Vauclin, 1996), p. 19.
7.   For more detail, see Lormier, *La Poche de Royan*.

CHAPTER 26

1. Amouroux, *La Vie*, vol. 1, pp. 134–9.
2. Pryce-Jones, *Paris in the Third Reich*, p. 206.
3. Interview with Mittre, in Pryce-Jones, *Paris in the Third Reich*, p. 217.
4. Obituary notice in *The Guardian*, 3 December 2005.
5. Quoted on www.spartacus.schoolnet.co.uk/2WW laval.htm.
6. Thornton, *The Liberation of Paris*, pp. 63–8.
7. Undated newspaper cutting loaned by Françoise De Monbrison.
8. Pryce-Jones, *Paris in the Third Reich*, p. 149.
9. Nossiter, *France and the Nazis*, pp. 272–3.
10. For further detail, see http://fr.wikipedia.org/wiki/Paul_Touvier.

FURTHER READING IN ENGLISH

Bacque, J., *Just Raoul*, Toronto, Stoddart, 1990

Berthon, S., *Allies at War*, New York, Caroll and Graf, 2001

Burrin, P., *Living with Defeat*, London, Arnold/Hodder, 1996

Kedward, H.R., *Resistance in Vichy France*, Oxford, Oxford University Press, 1978

Kramer, K., *Flames in the Field*, London, Michael Joseph, 1995

Marshall, R., *All the King's Men*, London, Collins, 1988

May, E.R., *Strange Victory*, New York, Hill and Wang, 2000

Nicholas, L.H., *The Rape of Europa*, London, Macmillan, 1994

Nossiter, A., *The Algeria Hotel*, London, Methuen, 2001

——, *France and the Nazis*, London, Methuen, 2001

Paris, E., *Unhealed Wounds*, New York, Grove Press, 1985

Paxton, R.O., *Vichy France: Old Guard and New Order 1940–44*, New York, Columbia University Press 2001

Pechanski, D. (ed.), *Collaboration and Resistance*, tr. L Frankel, New York, Harry N. Abrams, 2000

Pryce-Jones, D., *Paris in the Third Reich*, London, Collins, 1981

Seel, P., *I, Pierre Seel, Deported Homosexual*, London, BasicBooks, 1995

Webster, P., *Pétain's Crime*, London, Pan, 2001

West, N., *Secret War*, London, Hodder and Stoughton, 1992

INDEX

Abbadi, Moussa 193, 215–5
Abetz, Otto 68, 75, 82–3, 85–6, 88, 93, 111,
    124, 133, 150–3, 208, 233, 239, 240, 241,
    244–5, 267
Abetz, Suzanne, *née* De Bruycker 75, 85, 88, 111,
    141, 147
Abwehr 30, 134, 137, 169, 202
Académie Française 17, 42, 72
Achenbach, Ernst and wife 85, 88, 148, 201,
    267
Action Française 25, 118
Admiralty, British 51, 53
agriculture 92, 108, 126, 234
air raids 16, 27, 95, 108, 150, 183, 184, 187,
    261
Alexander, A.V. 24, 51
Allgemeine SS 117, 119, 145, 156, 186, 193,
    194, 195, 201, 202, 209, 239, 245, 250, 254
Allied invasion forces 238, 241, 242, 243, 244
Alsace 13, 31, 50, 77, 151, 181, 193, 208, 273
Anglo-German naval pact 24
animals 14, 47, 99, 104, 110, 111
anti-British sentiment 47, 57, 88
anti-German sentiment 38, 72, 87, 97, 184
anti-Nazi Germans 150
anti-Semitism xvii, xix, xx, 27, 28, 31, 32, 71,
    72, 73, 74, 81–4, 86–8,
    91, 92, 93, 96, 97, 98, 111,
    117–20, 123, 125, 132, 133,
    140, 149, 152–3, 157–9, 162, 167–9, 178,
    198, 214, 231, 234, 243, 244
Armbruster, Paul 114, 202
Armée de l'Armistice xx, 68, 175, 221–3
Armistice and Armistice Agreement xix, 19,
    28–31, 37, 49, 51, 67, 68, 103, 123, 149,
    150, 175, 237, 266
armoured warfare 2, 7, 8, 9, 11, 18, 20
Aryanisation 80, 93, 100
assassinations xviii, xx, 19, 63, 125, 134, 135,
    140, 189, 203, 206, 234, 235
assistance to escaped prisoners xxi
Astier de la Vigerie, Emmanuel 184
Aubrac, Lucie and Raymond 133, 198
Auch 72, 247–9
Auphan, Adm 24, 241–2
Auriol, Vincent 57

Auschwitz extermination camp xx, 149, 167,
    171, 179, 193, 196, 204, 213, 215, 244,
    245, 272
Aznavour, Charles 213

Baden-Powell, Sir Robert 37, 131, 203
Bankenaufsichtsamt 86, 96
banking 16, 34, 77, 86, 96, 112, 119
Bank of England 57, 86
Banque de France 14, 57, 77, 86
Barbie, Klaus 178, 188, 190, 198, 213, 242,
    244, 267
Barlone, Capt 2, 31
Basch, Victor and Ilona 204, 274
Bastianini, Giuseppe 182, 193
Battle of France 8–20, 152, 180
Baudouin, Paul 20, 47, 48, 49, 70, 97, 100, 267
Belgium 7, 9, 119
Bergson, Henri 72, 97
Bevan, John 171, 191–2
bicycles 73, 99, 103, 111, 120, 121, 197
black market 73, 80, 120, 137, 141, 149,
    169–70, 182–4, 192, 227
Blanchard, Daniel 221–3
Blitzkrieg 2, 8
Bloch, Marcel 'Dassault' 244
Blum, Leon 8, 60, 61, 147, 150, 182
Boemelburg, Sturmbannführer Karl 71, 190–2,
    267
Bonnard, Abel 111
Bonny, Pierre 191, 267, 270
books and publishing 76, 81, 85, 87–8, 93
Bordeaux, city 14, 16, 17, 19, 21, 23, 33, 34,
    43, 47, 49, 51, 76, 135, 154, 236, 251; port
    27, 251, 262
Bourges 221, 232
Bourse *see* Stock Exchange
Bousquet, René xx, 152, 157–8, 166, 180, 182,
    183, 203–4, 267–8
Bout de l'An, Francis and Simone 222–5,
    229–30, 26 8
Bradley, Omar 250
Braque, Georges 80, 84
Brasillach, Robert 87, 137
Breker, Arno 33, 75
Brest 23, 95, 262

Briand, Aristide 58
British Broadcasting Corporation *see* broadcasts
    and broadcasting
British diplomats 20, 27, 34, 57
British Expeditionary Force xvii, 7, 8, 13
broadcasts and broadcasting 20, 24, 25, 26, 31,
    98, 101, 108, 112, 118, 121, 135, 150, 151,
    177, 181, 184, 185, 191, 201, 215, 217,
    221, 222, 229
brothels *see* prostitution
Brünner, Alois 190–1, 195–6, 215, 240, 242,
    244, 245, 268
Buckmaster, Maurice 113, 171, 185, 192
Bullitt, William 11, 20, 80
Bureau Central de Renseignements et d'Action
    (BCRA) 113–4
Bureau Otto 71

Cabinet, French *see* Conseil des Ministres
Cabrero, Lazare 177, 268
Cahen d'Anvers, 'Baboushka' 34, 35, 38, 122–3,
    201, 238, 254
Campbell, Sir Ronald 20, 34
Camus, Albert 80, 93
Canaris, Wilhelm 30
Capitourlan crossing point 106, *106*, 115
cardinals: Baudrillart 17, 98, 123, 153; Gerlier
    92, 98, 153, 167, 168, 181, 234; Liénart
    121, 181; Lustiger 166; Suhard, 76, 168,
    181, 215, 234; Théas 166
carlingue 80, 191, 206
Carré, Mathilde 137–9
Castillon 103, 105, *106*
casualties, civilian xvii, 18, 95, 106–7, 150, 183,
    208, 215, 216, 224, 227–9, 236, 261–2,
    264–6
casualties, military 11, 12, 15, 16, 21, 103, 119,
    234, 265–6
Catholic Church xx, 5, 17, 44, 72, 92, 117, 121,
    123, 137, 168, 181, 234, 250
censorship 76, 79, 86, 87, 93, 103, 106
Chabrier, Georges 103–5
Chamber of Deputies xix, 33, 48, 74
Chamberlain, Sir Neville 3, 59
Chambon-sur-Lignon 156, 162, 181, 196
Chanel, Coco 73
Chantiers de Jeunesse 37, 38, 172, 176, 181,
    192, 196, 204
Chapou, 'Kléber' xx, 224
Charte du Travail 112
Châteaubriand 125, 135
Chevalier, Maurice 5, 81, 82, 179
children 9, 18, 38–9, 44, 123, 129–133, 141,
    142, 146, 150, 152, 154, 156–60, *160*, 162,
    166–8, 170, 172, 193, 196, 197–9, 202, 204,
    208, 211, 213, 223–4, 235, 240, 244–5
children of German fathers 146, 147, 180,
    256–8

Churchill, Winston 9, 14, 17, 24, 34, 51, 55, 91,
    172, 178, 217, 221, 262
Ciano, Galeazzo 82
Claudel, Paul 153
Clemenceau, Georges 4, 153
Clermont-Ferrand 36, 43, 47, 48, 54, 118, 121
clothing 5, 73, 109, 110, 121, 146, 149, 157,
    170, 216
Cocteau, Jean 5, 109, 158
Colette, Sidonie-Gabrielle 110, 153
Colette, Paul 126
collaboration xviii, xix, xx, 48, 87, 98, 150, 152,
    153, 166, 168, 196, 242, 248, 272
Colson, Gen 69
Comintern xviii, 113, 119, 221
Comités d'Organisation *see* state control of
    industry and commerce
Commissariat Générale aux Questions Juives 74,
    133, 152–3, 274
communications, disruption of 16, 50, 76, 93,
    253, 255
communism xvii, 13, 17, 81, 92, 151
Compagnons de France 69–70, 109, 112–3, 134,
    169, 193, 196, 206
Compagnons de la Chanson 109, 213
compulsory labour service *see* Service du Travail
    Obligatoire
concentration and internment camps xx, *155*,
    171 *also*: Bergen-Belsen 194, 215, 240;
    Buchenwald 139, 187, 237; Compiègne 140,
    152, 250; Dachau 190; Dora 187; Drancy
    120, 131, 140, 149, 159–60, 167, 171, 191,
    196, 201, 204, 213, 215, 240, 242, 244,
    250, 269, 272; Gurs 98, 129, 130;
    Mauthausen 99, 187; Natzwiller-Schirmeck
    181, 190, 193–4, 237, 242, 273;
    Neuengamme 187, 245; Neue Brem 187; Noé
    148, 166; Oranienburg 237; Pithiviers 130,
    159 ; Ravensbruck 139; Rivesaltes 130, 161,
    170; Septfonds 162, 249; St-Paul-d'Eyjeaux
    181; Vénissieux 167–8.
Condor Legion 42, 80
conscription and conscripts 36, 37, 42, 196,
    233
Conseil des Ministres (French Cabinet) 11, 12,
    19, 23, 43, 47, 48, 57, 59, 100, 203, 208
Conseil National de la Résistance 146
Constitution 60, 61, 62
Cooper, Douglas 13, 14–15, 33, 35, 51
Cooper, Duff 255
Corsica 51
courts martial 91, 205
crime 39, 40
Cruiziat, André 69
Crussol, Marquise de 4, 5
Cunningham, Adm 51, 56
curfews 40, 82, 116, 134, 135, 140, 212, 244
Czechoslovakia 4, 28

Daix, Pierre 99
Daladier, Edouard 3, 5, 27, 59, 60, 124, 147, 182
Danbé, Capt 53
Danneker, Theo 75, 120, 141, 146, 149, 157–8, 268
Darlan, Xavier-François 12, 17, 23, 24, 27, 29, 49, 51, 54, 55, 100, 110, 117, 118, 123, 148, 150–1, 178, 241
Darnand, Joseph 145, 180–1, 201, 203–5, 207, 222, 234, 241, 244, 268
Darquier de Pellepoix 132, 152, 203, 268–9
Das Reich, SS Division xx, 225–9, 269, 272
D-Day xx, xxi, 118, 192, 215, 216, 217
Déat, Marcel 88, 110, 117, 123, 126, 169, 201, 208, 244, 269
death sentences xix, 25, 38
De Beauvoir, Simone 36, 80, 106, 108, 158, 207
De Brinon, Fernand 73, 91, 100, 120, 153, 200, 244, 269
De Brinon, Jeanne-Louise 73, 153
De Châteaubriand, Alphonse 87–8, 269
De Courcel, Geoffroy 21, 24, 25
De Croy, Etienne 69
De Gaulle, Charles xviii, xix, 8, 11, 14, 21, 24–8, 36, 60, 62, 71, 76, 91, 110, 113, 114, 121, 145, 168, 171, 217, 221, 222, 233, 242, 243, 253–4, 262, 264
De La Bardonnie, Louis and family 25, 106, 114–5, 156, 202
De la Porte du Theil, Joseph 36–7, 172, 181, 196, 204
De Larminat, Edgard 262, 264, 266
De Lattre de Tassigny, Gen 61, 262
Delbos, Yvon 4
Delestraint, Charles 189, 190
Deloncle, Eugène 85, 117, 123, 126, 134, 169, 206
Delthil, Roger 6, 7, 9, 127, 156, 269
Demarcation Line 24, 54, 55, 93, 103, 104, 105, 106, 107, 108, 114, 115, 122, 154, 155, 175, 185
Demetrio, Helmut 186
De Miribel, Elizabeth 24
De Monbrison family 34, 35, 38, 121, 122, 122, 154–6, 196–7, 201, 211–13, 247, 255
demonstrations 99, 108, 123, 141, 158, 200
denunciations104, 105, 115, 130, 191, 195, 207, 209, 213, 215, 248
deportation xx, 120, 130, 149, 154, 157, 159–61, 166, 167, 170, 179, 200, 201, 204, 208, 234, 236, 242, 243
Depression, the 8, 42
Déricourt, Henri 191–2
De Rothschild, Anthony 35
De Rothschild, Edward 83
De Rothschild, Robert 34, 133
De Rothschild, Victor 254

De Saivre, Roger 175–7
desertion from German forces 200, 208
De St-Exupéry, Antoine 93
D'Estienne D'Orves, Louis 118
De Tournemire, Guillaume 112, 175, 196, 206
Deutsche Beschaffungsamt 71, 153
devaluation of the franc 202
Devau 5, 19, 31
Dewavrin, André see Passy
D'Harcourt, Pierre 138, 139
Dhavernas, Henry 69–70, 109
Diekman, Adolf 226–9
Dieppe raid 171
diplomatic recognition 63
disease 129, 183
division of France 29, 30, 31
divorce 5, 72, 117
Doenitz, Adm 114
Donati, Angelo 182, 193
Doriot, Jacques 88, 95, 123, 139, 146, 169, 189, 244, 269
Doumenc, Maj-Gen 23, 67
Doumergue, Gaston 42, 57
Drieu La Rochelle, Pierre-Eugène 75, 87, 137, 268
drugs 158
Duclos, Jacques 113
Dufay, Lt 52–3
Du Moulin de Labarthète, Henri 75, 101
Dunkirk, xix, 9, 17, 24, 47
Dupont, Marie-Rose xxi, 141–2, 180, 214–7, 249, 255–6, 259, 270

Eastern front 105, 147, 157, 241
Eclaireurs Israélites de France (EIF) 129–33, 148, 161, 197
education 50, 57, 63, 72, 97, 111, 123, 131–2, 150, 196, 199, 200
Eich, Hermann 87
Eichmann, Adolf 157, 180
Einsatzstab Reichsleiter Rosenberg 83
Eisenhower, Dwight 193, 221, 250, 262, 264
employers' associations 72
Entente Cordiale 58
entertainment and entertainers 5–6, 17, 73, 76, 79, 80, 81, 89, 100, 110, 118, 124, 134, 149, 150, 153, 157, 179, 193
escape routes and organisers 112, 135, 151, 162, 169, 177, 179, 181, 196
espionage 113–4
Etat Français 63
exchange rate 40
executions 38, 103, 119, 125, 134, 135, 137, 140, 147, 150, 152, 153, 179, 183, 189, 190, 191, 195, 203, 207, 208, 209, 213, 225–6, 230, 231, 235, 237, 238–40, 244, 254, 267, 268, 269, 270, 272, 273
evacuation and evacuees 6, 7, 9, 13, 18, 24

Fabien, 'Colonel' xvii, 125
false papers 107, 111, 132, 162, 168, 179, 197, 199, 201, 209, 212, 214, 256, 265
fashion 73, 109, 111, 121, 167, 216
Faynzylber, Victor 120
Faytout, Rodolphe 185–8, 270
Feldgendarmerie 40, 111, 140, 149, 183, 191, 212, 214, 225, 243
Fields, Gracie 6
fifth column 39, 85
Final Solution 157, 169–70, 180, 193
First World War xix, 7, 12, 14, 21, 28, 41, 58, 82, 98, 99, 103, 107, 244
Fleming, Ian 35
Foch, Ferdinand 28
Forbidden Zone 30
Forces Françaises de l'Intérieur (FFI) 203, 222–5, 229, 230, 234, 237, 243, 246–7, 249–51, 253, 255, 261–2, 266 – and Corps Franc Pommiès 234, 247, 249 see also Resistance
foreigners, restrictions on, 38, 95, 98, 153
Foreign Legion 50, 73, 180, 194, 238
Foreign Office, British 57
foreign volunteers in French forces 13, 50, 180, 194
francisque 74
Franco, Francisco 31, 42, 44, 50, 87, 98
Franco-German peace treaty, 67
Franco-Prussian War 7, 12, 14, 63
Freeman, Denis 5, 6, 13, 14–15, 33, 35, 36, 51
Freemasons 72, 88, 91, 114, 152
Free French forces 24, 71, 91, 145, 184, 241, 250, 252, 253, 261
Free Zone xx, 29, 30, 31, 36, 37, 68, 69, 77, 87, 103, 104, 105, 106, 107, 108, 114, 115, 130, 133, 143, 154, 155, 157, 166–7, 169–70
Freiser, Roland 124
Frenay, Henri 69, 113
French air force 8, 29, 30
French army (including colonial units) xvii, 2, 7, 8, 11, 12, 13, 15, 16, 17, 20, 23, 27, 29, 30, 36, 41, 42, 49, 98, 212, 239, 243
French navy 12, 17, 23, 24, 25, 27, 29, 35, 49, 51–6, 150–1, 178
French North Africa 11, 23, 27, 28, 29, 37, 42, 43, 51–2, 59, 60, 62, 63, 98, 112, 117, 145, 153, 161, 169, 172, 195, 197, 204, 212, 237
Front National 221–2
Fürtwangler, Wilhelm 76

Galtier-Boissière, Jean 93, 215
Gamelin, Maurice 7, 12, 147, 182
Gamzon, Robert 197
gazogène motors 112, 133, 166, 187, 193, 199, 213, 225
Geheime Feldpolizei 83, 138

Gendarmerie Nationale and individual gendarmes xx, 74, 105, 117, 132, 142, 145, 149, 152, 162, 166, 179, 182, 184, 197, 201, 205, 209, 225, 234, 235, 243
Gensoul, Marcel 51–6
German ordinances 40, 82, 117, 120, 121, 125, 137, 152
German-Soviet Non-Aggression Pact xviii, 7
Gestapo 31, 32, 71, 80, 95, 106, 140, 151, 153, 157, 178–80, 189, 193, 196, 207, 215, 221, 232, 239, 240, 241
Gieseking, Walter 77
Giraud, Andrée 196, 200, 211–12
Giraud, Henri 151–2
Glasberg, Alexandre 98, 167
Goebbels 42, 51, 83
Goering, Hermann 6, 7, 28, 73, 83–5, 93, 139
Goldfarb, Lucienne 207, 270
Gort, Lord John xvii, 2, 8, 9
Gouzi, Joseph and Paulette 13, 142
Grasset, Bernard 87
grey market 141, 170, 180
Groupes de Protection 100, 215, 245
Grumbach, Jacques 177, 268
Grynszpan, Herschel 87
Guderian, Heinz 9
Guibert, Gen 145
guillotine 126, 150, 195
Guingouin, Georges 99, 182, 250–1, 270
Guitry, Sacha 79, 81, 82, 89, 109, 111, 153, 179

Hague Conventions 77, 82, 83, 84, 124
Hardy, René 189–90
Harris, 'Bomber' 264
Heinrichson, Ernst 191
Heller, Gerhard 93, 99
Henriot, Philippe 180, 201, 203, 231, 233–4, 238
Herriot 60, 241
Heydrich, Reinhard 146, 148, 152
Himmler, Heinrich 31, 152, 178
Hirsch, Djigo 197–8
Hirt, Joseph 193, 195, 270
Hitler, Adolf xviii, xix, 2, 4, 6, 7, 9, 28, 29, 33, 42, 44, 48, 57, 59, 63, 81–5, 95, 98–100, 110, 113, 118, 123, 137, 148, 150, 171, 175, 192, 203, 215, 239, 244, 246, 261, 264
Hitler Youth 69, 70, 80
Holland, Capt 52–6
homosexuality 91, 194, 273
hostages 125, 134, 135, 137, 140, 182, 191, 204, 225, 230, 235, 237, 239, 254
Huntziger, Gen 28, 29

identity cards 80, 97, 105, 107, 111, 115, 116, 132, 154, 162, 180, 189, 190, 191, 197, 200, 238
IG Farben 143, 267
immigrants 92, 126, 143, 180

Infirmières Pilotes, Secouristes de l'Air *see* women pilots
inflation 93, 182
intelligence-gathering and sabotage networks: Alliance183, 196; Druids 196; Interallié resistance network 137–8; Musée de l'Homme 112, 145, 147; Prosper 171, 191; Scientist 171, 191; Valmy 110, 150
Internationale 6
Italian air force (Forza Aerea) 30
Italian occupation, 14, 29, *30*, 32, 149, *155*, 175, 182, 193, 195

Jacob, Max 17, 213
Jeanson, Henri 87
Jeu de Paume museum 83–4, 240
Jewish Consistory 133
Joanovici, Joseph 71, 267, 270
Joffre, Marshal 43
Joint American Distribution Committee 133
Jones, R.V. 196
Juin, Alphonse 153
Jünger, Ernst 73, 140, 157

Kämpfe, Helmut 228
Kapel, René 166
Keitel, Wilhelm 28, 82, 148
Kernan, Thomas 3, 86, 87, 96–7, 99
Kieffer, Josef 71
Knochen, Helmut 96, 134, 146, 182, 239, 270
Koenig, Marie-Pierre 229
Koestler, Arthur 49–50
Kramer, Joseph 194, *195*, 270
Krause, Albrecht 124
Kriegel-Valrimont, Maurice 221, 253, 274
Kriegsmarine xviii, 107, 114–5, 146, 181, 251
Kristalnacht 87
Kühnemann, Cdr 251, 252
Kunsberg, Baron 83
Kunstschutz 83

Lafont, Henri 191, 270
Lammerding, Heinz 229, 270, 273
Laporterie, Raoul 107–8
Laure, Gen 41, 100
Laval, José 58, 100, 101
Laval, Pierre xix, 19, 44, 45, 47–9, 57–64, 67–8, 74, 85, 91, 98, 100, 110, 117, 126, 148, 150–2, 157, 165, 169, 175, 177, 181, 189, 192, 196, 201, 205, 240, 241, 245–6, 270–1
League of Nations 59
Leahy, William 151, 172
Lebrun, Albert 11, 19, 47, 48, 49
Lecca 5, 19, 31
Leclerc, Philippe 241, 250, 252, 261–2
Lécussan, Joseph 204–5, 229–32, 273

Légion de Volontaires Français contre le Bolshevisme (LVF) xx, 123, 126, 139, 145, 146, 181, 233
Légion d'honneur 17, 54, 267, 273
Légion Française des Combattants 92, 137, 145
Légion des Combattants et Volontaires de la Revolution Nationale 145
Leguay, Jean 157–8, 204, 271
liaisons with German servicemen xxi, 141–2, 146–7, 180, 214–7, 248, 256–8
Liberation xix, xx, 71, 82, 111, 146, 151, 162, 203, 214, 221, 234, 236, 247–274
Lifar, Serge 80
looting 14, 77, 82–5, 97, 158, 240, 245
Lorraine 2, 31, 50, 77, 208, 226
Lospinoso, Guido 182, 193
Louvre museum 14, 84, 97
Luftwaffe, 7, 9, 16, 18, 27, 83, 107, 118, 149, 239, 253
Lyons 77, 92, 118, 167, 169, 178, 198, 204, 235, 242

Maginot Line 8, 12, 68
Maier, Sonderführer 86
malgré-nous, les 208, 273
Malraux, André 107
Mandel, Georges 4, 19, 27, 60, 182, 237–8
Maquis xviii, xx, 165, 168, 176, 182, 192–3, 200, 203, 209, 217, 221, 228, 233, 235, 236, 238–9, 243, 247, 252, 258, 272
Marceau, Marcel 169
Maréchal, nous voilà 44, 199, 252
Marseilles 69, 158, 180
Marseillaise, La 6, 44, 148, 153, 199, 246, 247
Martin, François 7, 127, 132, 142, 148, 166, 168, 189
mass arrests xx, 130, 158, 159, 163, 167, 180, 204
Mauriac, François xviii, 25, 38, 55, 87
Mayol de Lupé, Jean 123, 271
'medical experiments' in camps 193, 245
Mein Kampf 28, 61
Mendès-France, Pierre 27, 28, 118, 121, 201–2
Ménétrel, Bernard 50, 74–5, 120, 208, 245, 271
Mers el-Kebir 51–6, 59, 89, 95, 178
Metternich, Franz 83
Metro (Paris) xviii, 6, 82, 145, 153, 159, 243
Michelin company 47, 143
Mignon, Pierre xxi, 185, 187
Milice xx, 19, 119, 130, 137, 145, 175, 180, 189, 197, 201, 202, 203, 205, 206, 209, 215, 221–5, 229–32, 235, 238, 239, 241–3, 245, 248, 254, 268, 274
Militärbefehlshaber Frankreich 74, 82, 124
Mitterand, François xx
Moch, Jules 63
Moissac, 6, 7, 9, 50, 127, 130, 131, 141, 142, 161–2, 180, 196, 197–200, 209, 214, 216,

234, 238–9, 248–9, 255–6, 269; Maison de
　　Moissac, 7, 129–33, 148, 161–2, 191, 196,
　　200, 244
Moles, Louis 127, 141, 199, 216
Montand, Yves 214
Mont-de-Marsan airfield 107
Montgomery, Sir Bernard 233, 264
Mont Valérien 74, 119, 140, 147, 150, 207, 208
Moulin, Jean xviii, 20, 146, 188–90, 198
Mouvement Social Revolutionnaire (MSR) 85,
　　117, 134, 206
Munich Agreement 3, 5, 59
music and musicians see entertainment
Mussolini, Benito 14, 29, 32, 44, 48, 59, 81,
　　149, 215
mutiny 27, 41

Nake, Lt-Gen 251, 252
Napoleon Bonaparte, 33, 42, 69, 100
Napoleon, Prince 176–7
National Assembly xix, 48, 59, 61, 62, 63, 160,
　　241
Nazism and Nazi party 2, 50, 55, 67, 83, 85
neutral status of France after Armistice, 51
Nordling, Raoul 249–50
North, Sir Dudley 51, 53
NSKK Motorgruppe 181, 233
nurses 14

Oberg, Karl 124, 146, 152, 157, 169, 180, 183,
　　204, 239, 258, 271
occupation taxes, 32, 68, 101, 118
Occupied Zone xx, 29, 30, 31, 38, 75, 103, 106,
　　106, 107, 108, 117, 122, 154, 155, 157,
　　162, 170
Oberkommandantur der Wehrmacht (OKW) 8,
　　82, 148, 175
Operation: Anvil 243, 244; Barbarossa 60, 99,
　　104, 113, 119, 121; Catapult 51–6; Cockade
　　172, 191–2; Independence 262, 264; Lilac
　　175; Sealion 38, 83; Torch 172, 175
Oradour-sur-Glane 226–9, 251, 273
Oréal company 85, 206
Organisation Todt, 114, 165, 181
Orleans 16, 17, 216
Oxford Union xvii

Papon, Maurice xx, 107, 154, 271
Paris xx, 3, 5, 14, 16, 17, 20, 21, 33, 36, 49,
　　58, 63, 71, 74, 76, 79–87, 91–3, 96, 99,
　　109, 120, 124–5, 127, 140, 149, 152,
　　158–9, 163, 179, 182, 183, 189–92, 201,
　　213–15, 223–4, 233, 237–50, 253–4
Pariser Zeitung 80
Parodi, Alexandre 242, 250
Paroles aux Français 67, 72, 245
Parti Communiste Français (PCF) xviii, 58, 59, 72,
　　88, 99, 113, 119, 123–5, 137, 145, 169, 181,

182, 189, 195, 207, 209, 221, 223, 224,
　　242, 246, 247, 250, 251, 254, 264, 270
Parti Populaire Français (PPF) 95, 146, 158,
　　169–70, 183, 243
passeurs 107, 154, 169, 177, 179–80, 268
Passy, Col 114, 189
Patton, George 250, 252
Pétain, Eugénie, née Hardon, 43–4
Pétain, Marshal Philippe xix, 11, 12, 18–22, 25,
　　29, 31, 37, 40–5, 47–51, 57–63, 67–8, 70,
　　72, 74–6, 82, 87, 89, 91, 92, 95, 97–101,
　　103, 110, 113, 117, 119–21, 137, 139, 142,
　　145, 147, 148, 150–1, 153, 157, 166, 168,
　　172, 175, 177, 181, 201, 208, 215, 241,
　　245–6, 248, 254, 269, 271
Petitjean, Louis 159, 272
Petiot, Marcel 208, 271–2
Peugeot company 76, 143
phoney war 2, 14, 49, 87
Piaf, Edith 81, 107, 109, 214, 240
Picasso, Pablo 17, 36, 75, 80–1, 84, 85, 213
Pineau, Christian 145
pockets of resistance, German 258, 261–2, 263
Poland 2, 7, 28, 29, 59
Police aux Questions Juives 141, 153, 205
Police Nationale and individual policemen,
　　French xx, 100, 101, 110, 149, 152, 157–9,
　　162, 166, 168, 182, 183, 196, 200, 208,
　　242, 243, 246–7
Pommiès, André 175 see also FFI, Corps Franc
　　Pommiès
Popular Front government 8, 61, 62, 68
Portes, Comtesse de 4, 5, 19, 31, 60, 117
post-war planning 95
Pound, Sir Dudley 24, 51
power cuts xxi, 145, 243
POWs, British 17, 179
POWs, French 29, 32, 69, 70, 73, 101, 105,
　　112, 117, 140, 151, 152, 157, 165, 180,
　　214, 240, 258
press, newspapers and magazines 3, 15, 25, 33,
　　49, 58, 70–1, 86–88, 120, 137, 146, 166,
　　170, 181, 239, 240
prisons: Bordeaux, Fort du Hâ 187, Bourges,
　　Bordiot 231–2; Ile d'Yeu 271; Lyons, Montluc
　　178, 208, 212, 235, 244; Paris, Cherche-Midi
　　250; Paris, Fresnes 74, 75, 139, 189, 190,
　　239, 250, 270, 271, 272, 274; Paris,
　　La Santé 74, 87, 138, 237, 238; Toulouse
　　St Michel prison 211, 236, 237; Troyes 254
Prix Goncourt 140
propaganda 18, 33, 50, 51, 55, 86, 88, 92, 98,
　　112, 120, 149–50
Propaganda Abteilung 146, 258
Propaganda Staffel 86–8, 183
prostitution 73, 79, 117, 146, 255
Protestants 121, 122, 129, 148, 156, 162–3,
　　166, 168, 250

public records, 9,15, 16
Pucheu, Pierre 123, 126, 135, 141, 161, 272
Pujols 103, 105, *106*
purge, post-Liberation xx, 268

Quai d'Orsay 48, 85, 150, 161
Quakers 166

Rademacher, Helmut 79, 80, 246, 253
rafles see mass arrests
railways, national (SNCF) 39, 76, 91, 207, 209,
    237, 240, 242, 255
rape 39, 216
Rassemblement National Populaire 110, 117
rationing 6, 39, 68, 91, 93, 109, 110, 117,
    183–4
Rawa-Russka POW camp 151
Red Cross 18, 137, 140, 159, 213, 236–7, 240,
    253, 266
refugees 7, 9, 13, 16, 17, 27, 32, 33, 34, 38, 39,
    47, 50, 59, 60, 76, 105, 143, 155–6, 166,
    180, 182, 196, 226, 231
Régiments de Marche de la Légion Etrangère *see*
    foreign volunteers
Reichshauptsicherheit Amt (RHSA) 171
Relève see volunteers to work in Germany
Rémy, Col *106*, 114–6, 146
Renault company and factory 150, 201, 208
Renault, Gilbert *see* Rémy
Renault, Louis 143, 272
Renoir, Jean 89
Renseignements Généraux 148, 159, 169, 207,
    222, 272
reprisals xviii, 125, 137, 224, 231, 251
requisitioning 7, 17, 32, 38, 45, 49, 74, 75, 80,
    83, 86, 99, 109, 111, 126, 147, 168, 235,
    242
Reserved Zone *30*
Resistance xviii, xix, xx, 95, 113, 195, 217, 221,
    234, 242, 251; Armée Juive 179, 244; Armée
    Secrète 175, 222, 247; Comité d'Action
    Militaire (COMAC) 221; Combat 69, 188,
    203, 221, 223; Faytout 185–8, *188*, *189*;
    Francs–Tireurs et Partisans (FTP) 113, 188,
    200, 203, 221, 224, 228, 235, 249;
    Honneur et Police 71; Libération Nord 145;
    Libération Sud 188; Liberty 72; Mouvement
    de Libération Nationale 113, 202 :
    Mouvements Unis de la Résistance (MUR)
    188, 200 *see also* FFI
restaurants 80, 93, 95, 140, 146, 157–8, 178,
    179, 183–4
restrictions and shortages 6, 15, 16, 29, 39, 47,
    94, 110, 117, 123, 126, 137, 141, 145, 158,
    165, 170, 179, 183, 199, 235, 240, 241,
    243 *see also* rationing
Reynaud, Paul 4, 5, 9, 11, 14, 19, 21, 31, 42,
    43, 60, 117, 182, 237

Riom trial 118, 147, 150
Rodenstock, Odette 193, 215–6
Rommel, Erwin 36
Rol, 'Colonel' 242, 247, 250, 253
Roosevelt, Franklin 24, 118, 217
Röthke, Heinz 160, 171, 182, 272
Rothschild Hospital 191
Rouffanche, Marguerite 227
Royal Air Force xvii, xxi, 13, 21, 83, 85, 113,
    115, 117, 143, 150, 171, 183–6, 201, 206,
    208, 215, 216, 236, 261, 264
Royal Navy 25, 35, 51–6, 150
Royan 27, 262, *263*, 264–6, *265*
Royat 48
Royce, Ralph 264, 266
Rüdt Von Collenberg, Ursula 149–50

sabotage 28, 126, *127*, 166, 200, 208, 209,
    234, 237, 242
Sadrin, René 223, 225, 230
Salmide, Henri *see* Stahlschmidt
Sartre, Jean-Paul 72, 80, 108, 246
Sauckel, Fritz 157, 192, 207
Schaeffer, Carl 86, 96
Schindler, Laure 129, 148, 205–6
Schlesser, Lt Col 72, 175
Schueller, Eugène 85, 206
Scouting organisations excluding EIF 69, 70,
    148, 162
Seel, Pierre 194, 273
Senate, 19, 48, 62, 241, 244
Service de Police Anti-Communiste (SPAC) 123–4
Service d'Ordre Légionnaire (SOL) 145, 166, 180
Service du Travail Obligatoire (STO) xviii, 37,
    157, 165–6, 181, 182, 192, 196, 207–9,
    214, 216, 223, 258
Service Sanitaire Automobile *see* women
    ambulance drivers
Sicherheitsdienst (SD) 71, 74, 80, 134, 137, 151,
    191, 194, 206, 238, 239, 246
Signoret, Simone 88
Simon, Bouli and Shatta 129–33, 148, 161–2,
    180, 196–9, 205, 238
Sippenhaft 152, 152
Somerville, Adm 51–6
Sorbonne 99, 108, 124, 137
Spanish Civil War 6, 13, 49, 87
Spears, Sir Edward 21
Special Operations Executive (SOE) 113–4, 138,
    171, 185 also agents Borrel, Andrée 237;
    Cormeau, Yvonne 185–6; Leigh, Vera 237;
    Olschanezsky, Sonja 237; Rowden, Diana 237;
    Starr, George 185–6; Suttil, Francis 171,
    191–2
Speer, Albert 75, 157, 181
Speidel, Hans 83, 85, 137
Stadler, Sylvester 229
Stahlschmidt, Heinz 251, 273

St Albans, Duchess of 27
Stalin, Josef V. 44, 57, 88, 172, 264
St-Amand-Montrond 221–5, 229–232, 251, 273
state control of industry and commerce 89, 95, 96, 151
Statuts des Juifs 72, 96, 97, 119, 132
St-Cyr military academy 41
Ste-Foy-la-Grande 115, 199, 233, 244
Stock Exchange 96, 112
Strasbourg 124, 151, 193, 261
strategic bombing campaign xvii, 95, 115, 117, 150, 165, 201, 208, 215, 216, 233, 236, 242
strikes 119, 242
Szkolnikoff, Mandel 71, 73

Taurines, Jean 60, 62
Theis, Edouard 156, 162, 181
Third Republic xix, 5, 44, 48, 61, 62, 241
Thorez, Maurice 72, 113
Todt Organisation xvii, 114, 165, 181
torture xxi, xxii, 134, 137, 138, 140, 171, 178, 183, 186, 187, 190, 191, 194, 196, 205, 208, 215, 231
Toulon 24, 55, 178
Toulouse 16, 161, 197, 213, 216, 236, 238
Touvier, Paul 274
trade unions 72, 96, 112
Trenet, Charles 81, 100
trials, post-Liberation 186, 267–274
tricolore (French national flag) 40, 246, 247
Trocmé, André 156, 162–3, 181, 196
Troyes, 13, 254
Tulle xx, 16, 224–6, 228, 251, 272

Union Générale des Israélites de France (UGIF) 141, 158, 240
US government 14, 106, 140
US Federal Reserve Bank 57
USSR 17, 72, 91, 113, 121, 151

Valéry, Paul 42, 72
Valland, Rose 84, 240
Vallat, Xavier 49, 74, 133, 152, 252, 274
Van Gaver, René 221–4
Vatican xx, 268
Veil, Simone 178
Vélodrome d'Hiver 146, 158–159, 163, 169, 182, 201, 268
Verdun 21, 41, 42, 43, 103, 239

Versailles Treaty 58
Vichy regime and policies xix, 28, 29, 36, 62, 68, 69, 70, 72, 84, 87, 92, 109, 145, 149, 161, 166, 168, 175, 242
Vichy town 43, 48, 49, 57, 59, 60, 74, 101, 148, 151, 166, 224, 241, 243, 252
Vildé, Boris 112, 147–8
volunteers to work in Germany 38, 139, 157, 166
Von Choltitz, Dietrich 244, 246, 249–50, 253
Von Jesser, General 230, 251
Von Renthe-Fink, Cecil 208, 245
Von Ribbentrop, Joachim 85, 118, 150, 208, 244
Von Stülpnagel, Karl-Heinrich 148, 239
Von Stülpnagel, Gen Otto 74, 79, 117–8, 124, 134, 137, 148, 274
Von Vollard-Bockelberg, Gen 82
V-weapons 187, 196, 201, 238

Waffen-SS 43, 105, 124, 200, 203, 214, 238, 268 see also Das Reich
wages 119, 166, 170, 182, 183, 192
War Cabinet, British 52, 53
Warshavski, Louise 154–5, 211
weapons drops and caches 69, 175, 185–6, 188, 191, 195, 216, 223
Weber, Sonderführer 86–9
Wehrmacht xx, 5, 16, 17, 23, 31, 36, 38, 39, 50, 55, 60, 69, 74, 76, 77, 82, 85, 92, 97, 98, 104, 117, 124, 134, 140, 151, 154, 178, 196, 200, 221, 224, 233, 239, 242, 243, 250–3
Weygand, Maxime 11, 12, 13, 25, 28, 37, 49, 61, 70, 92, 172
Wheatley, Denis 171
Winterhilfe 16
Wodehoue, P.G. 36, 274
women agents 113–4, 237; ambulance drivers 16, 18; auxiliaries, German 106, 122, 124, 149; pilots 19
women, public humiliation of, xxi, 247–8, 255–9
women's rights 4, 61, 70, 147

yellow star 120, 133, 153–4, 158
YMCA 166

Zone annexed into the Reich 30
Zone attached to German military government of Belgium 30
Zyklon B gas 144